T0364606

TRANSFORMATION AND DEVELOPMENT

THE POLITICAL ECONOMY OF TRANSITION IN INDIA AND CHINA

edited by
Amiya Kumar Bagchi
Anthony P. D'Costa

OXFORD
UNIVERSITY PRESS

OXFORD

UNIVERSITY PRESS

Oxford University Press is a department of the University of Oxford.
It furthers the University's objective of excellence in research, scholarship,
and education by publishing worldwide. Oxford is a registered trademark of
Oxford University Press in the UK and in certain other countries

Published in India by
Oxford University Press
YMCA Library Building, 1 Jai Singh Road, New Delhi 110 001, India

ISBN-13: 978-0-19-808228-6
ISBN-10: 0-19-808228-2

Typeset in 10.5/12.5 Minion Pro
by Excellent Laser Typesetters, Pitampura, Delhi 110 034
Printed in India by G.H. Prints Pvt Ltd., New Delhi 110 020

Contents

Tables and Figures

TABLES

Preface and Acknowledgements

China and India have remained the two most populous countries of the world during the second millennium and beyond of the Common Era. They have been the home of one-third of humanity. The fates of those billions of human beings have naturally been of great interest to themselves. However, the lives of those beings were rendered almost invisible from the eighteenth to almost the second half of the twentieth century by the celebrations of the European miracle. The recent upsurge in measured growth rates of these two countries, apparently bucking the trend during the financial crisis that spread from the USA in 2007 to most of the developed countries and many of the developing countries as well, attracted renewed attention from politicians, the popular media and business press, and scholars. That attention was often embodied in peculiar metaphors, such as China as the dragon and India as the elephant. At the Institute of Development Studies Kolkata (IDSK) and Copenhagen Business School (CBS), where the two editors have worked, we believed in taking popular myths seriously, but examining the nature of the reality that the myths symbolize with rigorous scholarly attention. Believing that only the perspectives of a number of scholars can do some justice to the complexity of the phenomena through which the people of the two countries are travelling, the IDSK, in association with the Rabindranath Tagore Centre for Human Development Studies (a collaborative enterprise of the IDSK and the University of Calcutta), organized a two-day seminar in December 2009 on the interconnected themes of growth, innovation, and displacement in China and India.

We were lucky in being able to persuade some of the leading specialists on China, India, and the global economy and society in general to attend the seminar. The scholars who made presentations at the seminar included Sir James Mirrlees, the Nobel laureate in economics in 1996, Carl Riskin, Ho-Fung Hung, Anthony D'Costa, Robert Weil, Nirmal Kumar Chandra, Sunil Mani, Shailaja Fennell, Sunanda Sen, Parthasarathi Banerjee, R. Nagaraj, Bikramjit Sinha, Ashwani Saith, Ashwini Deshpande, Fung Kwan, Ishita Mukhopadhyay, and Ajit Banerjee. We are grateful to all of them for their participation in the seminar. We are also obliged to Prabuddhanath Roy, Debdas Banerjee, and Subimal Sen for chairing particular sessions of the seminar. There was a lively discussion among the presenters as well as other participants from which the eventual papers published in this volume benefited. The editors are grateful to all the contributors to this volume for their patience and readiness to reply to various queries, enabling us to prepare a coherent volume on this highly important and much canvassed subject.

The senior editor is very grateful to the Rabindranath Tagore Centre for Human Development Studies for funding the seminar and the Centre for Social Sciences and Humanities (CSSH), and its director, Bhaskar Chakrabarty, for the use of the auditorium of the CSSH. He is also grateful to the faculty and staff of the IDSK, and especially, Ramkrishna Chatterjee, for their untiring effort and cooperation in making the seminar a pleasant as well as a productive event.

The younger editor acknowledges the unstinting support he has received from the A.P. Møller-Mærsk Foundation, which has funded his Professorship in Indian Studies at the Asia Research Centre, Copenhagen Business School, and has given him the intellectual freedom to pursue the study of India in a deep and comparative way. He is grateful to his Centre colleagues for sharing their views of a changing China and to Janette Rawlings for her meticulous editorial assistance with the entire manuscript. Last but certainly not the least he is deeply appreciative of Amiya Bagchi for inviting him to undertake jointly a truly collaborative intellectual enterprise.

October 2011

AMIYA KUMAR BAGCHI
Kolkata

ANTHONY P. D'COSTA
Copenhagen

Abbreviations

ADB	Asian Development Bank
APL	Above Poverty Line
ATP	advanced technology products
BER	Business Environment Ranking
BPL	Below Poverty Line
CAS	Chinese Academy of Science
CASS	Chinese Academy of Social Sciences
CCP	Chinese Communist Party
CHIP	Chinese Household Income Project
CIP	Central Issue Price
CIT	Corporate Income Tax
CSA	country-specific advantages
CSRC	China Security Regulatory Commission
DD	double deflation
DE	domestic enterprise
DIR	detailed implementation regulation
DRC	domestic resource cost
EIU	Economist Intelligence Unit
EPO	European Patent Office
ERP	effective rate of protection
ETDZ	economic and technological development zone
FAO	Food and Agriculture Organization
FCI	Food Corporation of India
FDI	foreign direct investment

FEMA	Foreign Exchange Management Act
FIE	foreign invested enterprises
FSA	firm-specific advantage
GATT	General Agreement on Tariffs and Trade
GDP	gross domestic product
GERD	gross expenditure on R&D
GFCF	gross fixed capital formation
GRI	government research institute
HDI	Human Development Index
HNTE	high and new technology enterprise
HRST	Human Resource in Science and Technology
HT	high technology
HTDZ	high-tech industrial development zone
HYV	High Yielding Variety
IIS	India's industrialization strategy
IMF	International Monetary Fund
IPR	intellectual property rights
ISI	import substitution industrialization
IT	information technology
JPO	Japan Patent Office
JV	joint venture
LA	labour accumulation
LME	large and medium enterprises
LRS	Liberalised Remittance Scheme
LT	low technology
MFA	multi-fibre arrangement
MNC	multinational corporation
MPCE	monthly per capita expenditure
MSP	minimum support price
MT	medium technology
NCAER	National Council of Applied Economic Research
NREGA	National Rural Employment Guarantee Act
NREGS	National Rural Employment Guarantee Scheme
NSB	National Statistical Bureau
NSI	National System of Innovation
NSS	National Sample Survey
NSSO	National Sample Survey Organization
OBC	Other Backward Class

OECD	Organisation for Economic Co-operation and Development
OFDI	outward foreign direct investment
ONGC	Oil and Natural Gas Corporation
PDS	Public Distribution System
PLA	People's Liberation Army
PPP	purchasing power parity
PSA	primary socialist accumulation
QDII	Qualified Domestic Institutional Investor
QFII	Qualified Foreign Institutional Investors
R&D	research and development
RB	resource based
RCF	*Report on Currency and Finance*
RNF	rural non-farm
RPDS	Revamped Public Distribution System
RPW	Rural Public Works
S&T	science and technology
SAFE	State Administration of Foreign Exchange
SC	scheduled caste
SCI	space competitiveness index
SD	single deflation
SEZ	Special Economic Zone
SOB	state-owned bank
SOE	state-owned enterprise
SSI	Sectoral System of Innovation
ST	scheduled tribe
SWF	sovereign wealth fund
TFP	total factor productivity
TFPG	total factor productivity growth
TPDS	Targeted Public Distribution System
TVE	town and village enterprise
UNDP	United Nations Development Programme
UNIDO	United Nations Industrial Development Organization
USPTO	US Patent and Trademark Office
VCF	venture capital fund
WOS	wholly owned subsidiary
WTO	World Trade Organization

1

Transformation and Development
A Critical Introduction to India and China

ANTHONY P. D'COSTA AND AMIYA KUMAR BAGCHI

DEVELOPMENT AS CAPITALIST TRANSFORMATION

China and India, two of the most populous countries, still very agrarian, are also two of the largest economies in the world, which are contributing to a tectonic shift in the world economy. While this movement itself poses some interesting questions about the changing structure of the world economy and the concomitant realignment of East–West and North–South relations and regional balance in both economic and geopolitical terms, there is another set of questions that is germane to the broader issues of economic and social development. What are the economic, social, and technological sources of this realignment? Is this development a definitive turning point for the transformation of China and India? Are such high growth rates sustainable? What are the implicit and explicit tensions in this process of rapid and massive churning of the two economies? And where do the politically under-represented Chinese and Indian citizens stand in this major shake-up in the global capitalist economic order?

The objective of this volume is to capture some elements of these shifting dynamics in China and India through an interdisciplinary, historically sensitive, multilevel political economy analysis. The critical focus here is on the process of transformation of agrarian, essentially pre-industrial economies into industrialized ones. Given China's rapid growth and global presence, the discussion in the volume is tilted towards China. But any discussion of China brings up critical examination of India as well, and more importantly, Indian scholars looking at China are bound to reflexively bring with them insights that pertain to India. In this sense, it is a unique project since most of the contributors are India experts, based in India or located elsewhere, who are interested in the Chinese development experience. They have been complemented by a few China and comparative specialists based outside India.

In the discussion of transformation of two large economies two qualifications are in order. First, we recognize that the scale of the changes in both China and India is unprecedented. Quantitatively and qualitatively it involves nearly a third of humanity and hence cannot be subject to any simple reductionism that sweeps away diversity and regional variation. Of course, we are generally compelled to rely on the nation state as represented by central governments in the two countries as our unit of analysis, but we are sensitive to the idea that central governments oversee but do not subsume local, state, and provincial level governments or societies. We acknowledge that there is a wide variation in the process and impact of transformation on regions and on different social and economic groups. Both countries are internally heterogeneous—India even more than China—on a variety of dimensions and it would be erroneous to assume away regional differences. Hence, many of the contributors explicitly look at the changing relationship between the central and local governments and between different geographical regions in their treatment of the development process in China and India. Furthermore, internal decentralization has been as much a part of reforms as deregulation and liberalization in the two countries.

Second, while comparing China and India, we are aware of the enormous differences between the two countries not just in the magnitude of economic and social performance and initial conditions but in the governance structure of the economy as well. China's one-party state conveys a degree of centralization that is increasingly not reflected in its actual institutional arrangements, while India's democratic parliamentary system sometimes understates the centralized nature of national economic management. There appears to be considerable flexibility in China's institutional responses, be they in agricultural policy, industrial development, infrastructural investments, research and development (R&D) spending, or export drive, when compared to India. However, both countries in their different ways are undergoing capitalist transformation, rapid commoditization of old and new products and processes, proletarianization and wage labour formation, and primitive accumulation through land grabs even if questions are still being asked as to whether China is really capitalist.[1] In short, both countries are undergoing a process of 'compressed capitalism' (D'Costa 2011a). What is clear is that both China and India, with large populations and with substantial rural employment, are economically, industrially, and technologically transforming on a large scale. Hence, the sources and impact of this change remain subject to critical interpretation as do the expected outcomes of economic change for future social development.

This introductory chapter provides a political economy analysis to critically investigate the relatively recent transformation process of China and India, which could very well be stymied if the world economy does not expand or internal markets fail to grow due to increasing economic and social divides. In this chapter we lay out the broad canvas on which the individual chapters can be contextualized. We identify the key components of the transformation process along with the specific spheres undergoing change. For example, agricultural and industrial growth are two sources of economic and social transformation, while food supply chain management and patenting are specific areas of agriculture and technology that reflect microlevel dynamics in the overall transformation process. We also suggest that the ongoing transformation of India and China is a disruptive, displacing, and damaging process in a number of ways. Rural and urban land is being wrested from farmers, tribal communities and residents to make way for raw material extraction, industry, science and technology (S&T) parks, export zones, and real estate. Workers, and especially migrants from rural areas, are being made to bear the brunt of export competitiveness through low wages and harsh working conditions. And in the rush towards capitalist development, the environment has been given short shrift. Even if capitalist transformation is regarded as necessary to bring about a change in the horizon of expectations, the transformation process seems to enhance the already pronounced massive social divides. However, we refrain from making explicit policy recommendations. Our intent is to contribute to the larger debate about development and transformation and not provide pat solutions, though we believe the dialogue here indirectly indicates policy directions.

This chapter is divided into four sections. The next section presents the analytical framework by which we view the transformation process. Though centred on India, many of the issues are applicable to China as well. We present five key themes around which the transformation can be investigated. These are agriculture; savings and investment; industry, exports, and global finance; inequality; and S&T. When linked to the growth process, these themes reveal not only specific mechanisms of change but also contradictions that accompany growth. In the section following, chapter descriptions are presented. The final section concludes.

AN ANALYTICAL FRAMEWORK

To capture the transformation dynamics we focus on a few key areas. These are economic growth and its components such as agriculture, investment, industry and exports, global finance, inequality, and S&T. Naturally, for the two countries under examination, emphasis on these issues as well as the mechanisms behind the dynamics vary but not surprisingly, they are increasingly interconnected.

Agriculture and Economic Growth

One of the central arenas of economic transformation is the agricultural sector. How economic surplus is generated and transferred to the industrial sector is critical to widening and deepening capitalist markets. That China had state socialism and India a version of state capitalism are interesting points of departure, but the transformation *problématique* was the same: how to make agriculture productive, benefit rural residents, and contribute to the rest of the economy by increasing economic growth and income. One widely accepted view has been that of Arthur Lewis (1966) whose central concern was how to absorb 'surplus' labour in the countryside, found abundantly in both China and India. Exports of primary products was one way (Lewis was not an export pessimist), but given the fact that even industrial wages in the peripheral economies were low compared to the advanced capitalist countries, Lewis recommended industrialization as a way to absorb surplus labour. Rural–urban migration was a key transmission mechanism for increasing rural and urban wages, the latter through industrialization, which also drives up rural wages. A virtuous growth cycle was anticipated with increasing profits, reinvestment, and rising wages. Lewis astutely foresaw that increased profits earned by capital-ists would not necessarily be reinvested to lead to this virtuous cycle since capital flight has always plagued capital-poor countries (Cypher and Dietz 2004, p. 148). With globalization, the probability of such flight is high, especially if opportunities for investment at home are limited or the alternative of earning higher returns through financial instruments abroad is greater.

The Lewisian model took the development of the pioneering industrializing countries such as Britain as 'stylized facts' and trans-ferred them to the developing countries of the 1950s. However, the development of capitalism in Western Europe was predicated on the destruction of feudal political and social power. Anyone familiar with agrarian history in both India and China would appreciate the fact that if the dominance of (feudal) landlords is not broken in the countryside, there is no automatic process by which social change in the countryside would be guaranteed. Impoverished peasants without access to land and agricultural inputs would continue to contribute to the 'Lewisian' labour surplus. In India, most of the politicians assuming power in 1947 were not willing to face the fact that it was not possible to transform India into a dynamic capitalist economy let alone any kind of socialist society, without getting rid of landlord-ism, upper-caste domination, and varieties of patriarchy that denied women access to education and gainful work outside the confines of the household (Bagchi 2002a, 2002b). Planning started in an India in which landlords and upper-caste lineages exercised non-market power in most parts of the country, especially in those regions that had been under a zamindari or *taluqdari* tenure.[2] However, Independence was a major turning point for India (Nayyar 2006) and since then this non-market power has gradually eroded.

Almost as soon as India gained independence, there was a struc-tural break in the trend of per capita income. From the 1950s, Indian per capita income began to increase (Hatekar and Dongre 2005). The basic data on rates of growth from post-Independence to the formal institutionalization of the neo-liberal regime in 1991 is presented in Table 1.1.

Table 1.1   Decadal Rates of Growth per Annum of Agriculture,
Manufacturing, and the Secondary Sector, India, 1950–1 to
1989–90 (at 1948–9 prices)

Sector	1950–1 to 1959–60	1960–1 to 1969–70	1970–1 to 1979–80	1980–1 to 1989–90
Agriculture	2.9	1.3	1.9	3.1
Manufacturing	6.1	4.8	4.9	7.3
Secondary sector	6.1	5.4	4.7	6.9

Source: Sivasubramonian (2000, Table 9.3).

It is evident that acceleration occurred not only in the rates of growth of manufacturing but also of agriculture. While the growth rates remained low compared with those of East Asian high-performing economies, the reasons for the slow growth are very different from those advanced by the proponents of neo-liberalism. The leading cause was the continued weight of landlord power that constrained the choices and resources of peasants and rural artisans, whereas in several East Asian economies (and China) land reforms eliminated such power holders (for South Korea, see Hamilton [1986]). Another principal reason was the slow progress of literacy, because of both government apathy and the continued hold of the caste system, especially in regions where landlords continued to hijack policies in their favour.

One of the characteristics of Indian agriculture is uneven development due to rural social structures, asymmetric power, government indifference, and sheer scale of maldevelopment in the countryside. There have been periods when agricultural growth was good but there have been times when crisis beset the sector. For example, the change from an annual rate of growth of 0.34 per cent of agriculture before India's independence to 2.9 per cent after liberation was a big leap, as was the increase over the same period in the annual rate of growth of the secondary sector from 1.58 per cent to 6.1 per cent. But Table 1.1 also makes it obvious that Indian agriculture went through a bad patch in the 1960s: the years 1965–6 and 1966–7 witnessed near-famine conditions in several parts of India, and the country had to import 18 million tonnes of food grains during those years. The term lending by developmental banks at low rates of interest to industry had played its part in raising the rate of growth of industry, the main component of the secondary sector. After the nationalization of major banks in 1969, a similar role was played by public sector banks in facilitating the spread of high-yielding varieties (HYVs) of wheat and rice and bringing about the 'Green Revolution'.

There were two major policy planks supporting this strategy. First, under the branch-licensing policy, a bank was allowed to open a branch in a location that already had a branch (generally that location would be a metropolis or a large city) only if it agreed to open four additional branches in rural and semi-urban areas. Second, a mandate was given to the banks to segregate a certain proportion of its total credit to designated priority sectors such as agriculture, small-scale and cottage industries, and transport. They also obtained their credit at lower rates than the borrowers in non-priority sectors. It has been argued that the initiation of this policy had a significant impact on rural poverty, especially in the more backward regions, where banks, guided by the profit motive alone, would not have opened branches (Burgess and Pandey 2005, Basu and Mallick 2008). Consequently, the limited land reforms, the persistent grip of upper-caste landlords over peasants, and the selective adoption of modern agricultural practices have produced highly uneven agricultural development in India.

In China, the structural break was also quite definitive (Table 1.2). China's primary sector grew from 0.3 per cent during 1890–1952 to 3.3 per cent during 1952–78 and 4.5 per cent during 1978–2003. Industry performed even better, increasing from 1.7 per cent to 10.1 per cent to 9.8 per cent respectively. But what India missed out politically China introduced socially with its peasant revolution, namely, breaking the dominance of landlords through land reforms and collectivization of agriculture (Andreas 2010, p. 67). This, of course, has had far-reaching effects on Chinese transformation, despite some of the excesses of Maoist policies. Small-scale, peasant-based collectivized agriculture in China has had important impacts in China even after decollectivization under the Household Responsibility System as migrants from the countryside, despite restrictions on their mobility through the '*hokou*' system, were absorbed initially by the spread of small-scale private retail markets and by widespread labour-intensive export-based industrialization. Total output of all grains in China increased by 2.4 per cent a year over 1952–78 and by 1.7 per cent over 1978–2007 (Ash 2010, p. 49). State support for rural enterprises was crucial for the emergence of small rural businesses in the first decade of the reforms (Andreas 2010, p. 69).

Table 1.2   Growth of GDP by Sector, China 1890–2003 (constant prices)

	1890–1952	1952–78	1978–2003
Farming, fishery, and forestry	0.3	2.2	4.5
Industry	1.7	10.1	9.8
Construction	1.6	7.8	9.8
Transport and communication	0.9	6.0	10.8
Commerce and restaurants	0.8	3.3	9.9
Other services	1.1	4.3	5.6
GDP	·0.6	4.4	7.9
Per capita GDP	0.0	2.3	6.6

Source: Maddison (2007, p. 60).

Despite high rates of economic growth, neither country has been able to resolve the agrarian question, that is, how to make agriculture more productive, act as an engine of economic growth and development, and ensure the well-being of rural residents (for China, see Ash [2010]). This is especially true for India. Rural underemployment is a major challenge in both India and China, which to a great extent has constrained macroeconomic demand in a Keynesian sense, and in the context of contemporary high rates of economic growth, it has exacerbated the inequality hitherto not experienced at this level in either of these countries (see Chapter 7 by Banerjee *et al.*). This can be seen as the Achilles heel of the transformation experience of these two countries: translating economic growth into inclusive development.[3]

In response to growing inequality, the Government of India has begun addressing the rural–urban divide in a fast-changing economy by guaranteeing 100 days of employment every year for one member of every household in rural areas who volunteers to do unskilled manual work, aimed largely to build up rural infrastructure. Aside from the scale of the project, its budgetary implications, and the difficulty of implementation, only one other programme—the collectivization programme in China—matches the scale of the Indian effort (see Chapter 2 by Saith). Both programmes aimed to enhance the infrastructure in the countryside and thus lead to increasing productivity.

A related agricultural concern is ensuring food security in both countries. Recent price hikes amidst growing and changing patterns of consumption in both countries have introduced new kinds of uncertainty, made worse by weak supply chains, low productivity, emergent shortages of water, and toxicity of the land. Going beyond demand and supply, the issues today concern availability, accessibility, and affordability of food and food grains for low-income households (see Chapter 3 by Fennell).

Savings, Investment, and Growth

Returning to contemporary growth in India and China, it is obvious that growth rates, especially in China, have been fuelled by the investment rate. Even India, known for its 'Hindu rate of growth', perceptively moved up the growth path due to higher savings and investment from the 1950s to the 1980s. In a socialist economy, the state is the propeller of both savings and investment; most enterprises in such an economy are subject to soft budget constraints. In a market economy, however, private investment is the main driver of economic growth. There is no universally accepted theory of the determinants of private investment. John Maynard Keynes, the pioneer of the macroeconomics of a private enterprise economy, considered investment in fixed capital to be primarily determined by the state of long-term expectation and that expectation to be influenced by 'animal spirits', or one could say, the taste for risk-taking over a long time horizon.[4]

In India, the 'animal spirits' of capitalists were obviously lifted by India's independence, particularly after Nehru's government made it clear that there would be no headlong nationalization of private enterprises and that subsidized credit would be provided for investment in fixed capital. But the Indian capitalist class was very small in terms of the control of assets in the country. They simply did not have the resources to develop the basic capital goods needed for long-term development of the economy. The Mahalanobis strategy, partially embodied in the Second Five-Year Plan of India (1956–61), required the state to direct the major part of its resources to the development of so-called heavy industries and infrastructure projects, such as large-scale irrigation works that would benefit agriculture and thermal and hydroelectric plants that would provide subsidized electricity, primarily to industry and urban residents. State-sponsored production of such critical industrial inputs gelled with the aspirations of private capitalists who were happy to invest in consumer goods industries with low gestation periods and quick returns. But the implementation of the Mahalanobis strategy produced four kinds of tensions in a (soft) state that could discipline neither the capitalist nor the landlord class.

First, the development of a dynamic commodity economy was hampered by the use of non-market power by landlords, the lack of direct market access for poorer farmers, and Adivasis (indigenous or tribal populations) living in areas with poor rural infrastructure. This is partly indicated by the share of financial savings to total savings of the household sector. The share of financial savings was only 2.56 per cent of total household savings in 1951–2; it increased steeply to 42.78 per cent in 1961–2, decreased to 31.62 per cent in 1971–2, and then increased again to 48.90 per cent in 1981–2, and again to 60.00 per cent in 1991–2 (the figures are derived from Table 10 of Reserve Bank of India [RBI] 2010). In fact, the physical savings of the household sector and the gross capital formation of that sector are synonymous in the national accounting system adopted by India's Central Statistical Organisation (RBI 2010, Tables 10 and 13). Total domestic savings have been estimated (as a percentage share of gross domestic product [GDP]) to have increased from 8.04 per cent in 1951–2 to 11.24 per cent in 1961–2, 14.70 per cent in 1971–2, 18.08 per cent in 1981–2, and 21.55 per cent in 1991–2. This meant that up until the 1970s, the savings that could be financially mobilized by the state or the private sector remained much smaller than the total investment in a physical form.

Second, there was an inherent tension between investment needs and the revenue-raising policies of the government, the distribution of accrued incomes, and the resulting growth in demand for goods that had little potential for raising productivity (such as automobiles and other consumer durable goods for which no productive base had been built up in India) (Bagchi 1970). Consequently, both tapping potential savings and reducing the emergent excess capacity in capital and consumer goods were aborted (Bagchi 1970).

Third, there was a mismatch between the demand for goods with high income elasticity, generated by the growth of a higher-income class, to whom most of the incomes generated by accelerated government expenditure accrued, and the supply of commodities that were available from existing industries, including cottage and small-scale industries. Such a mismatch between supply and demand for commodities can be regarded as a disproportionality problem, but that mismatch was induced as much by the dissonance between capitalist expectations and government plans as by the inequality inherent in the social structure (Bagchi 1988).

Finally, the demand for imported consumer durables or their components and the squeeze on the supply of food grains soon led to a persistent balance of payments crisis. The slow growth of agriculture coupled with harvest failures in 1965–6 also led many analysts to regard agriculture as the principal constraint on India's growth during the first two decades after the beginning of central government planning. However, the constraint on the supply of food grains was loosened by the spread of the Green Revolution in India and sustained by public spending on rural infrastructure; the spread of nationalized bank branches in major states of India; and the supply of critical inputs such as fertilizers, water, and power at subsidized rates.

India's low savings rate contrasts sharply with China's steep increase in the rates of savings and investment from the 1950s, which then picks up sharply from the 1980s (see Figure 1.1).[5] One estimate places the Chinese total savings rate at 35.2 per cent in 1990, which rose to 53.2 per cent in 2008 (Ma and Yi 2010). Similar figures for India stood at 23 per cent and 33.6 per cent (Ma and Yi 2010, p. 5). However, China's total savings rate is very high, with households contributing the most, with 20 per cent (Wong 2008, p. 4), followed by the corporate sector and government (Figure 1.1). Interestingly, India's household savings are higher than China's but higher corporate savings in China means newer capital equipment due to depreciation (a source of savings). There is an obvious growth bias if domestic savings are mobilized and subsidized as capital for investment purposes, as in massive infrastructure spending. Furthermore, if reforms also mean competition in investment at both the central and provincial levels, there could be serious macroeconomic instability (Wong 2008). It also means higher growth rates and thus economic transformation.

In the current high-growth period in India, the argument that neo-liberal reforms would release the energy of the private sector, which had been depressed by the earlier license–permit–quota raj is only partly true.[6] Neither the savings rates nor the contribution of the private corporate sector displayed any new dynamism during the first decade of economic reforms. The ratio of savings of the private corporate sector to the country's GDP (in percentage terms)

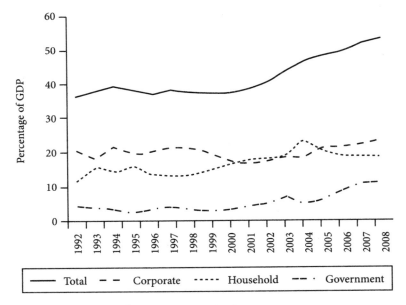

Figure 1.1   China's Savings Rates, 1992–2008

Source: Ma and Yi (2010, p. 10).

changed from 1.27 in 1951–2 to 1.73 in 1961–2, 1.55 in 1971–2, 1.50 in 1981–2, 3.10 in 1991–2 and 3.37 in 2001–2. Nor did the contribution of the private corporate sector display much dynamism during the first reform decade of the 1990s, as shown by the contribution of the private corporate sector to total capital formation. For example, private sector contribution to total capital formation in India was 25.8 per cent in 1981–2, 28.1 per cent in 1991–2, and 22.4 per cent in 2001–2. Likewise, neither the rate of savings nor the rate of overall economic growth displayed any dramatic upward movement during the period from 1991–2 to 2001–2. Total domestic savings as a percentage of GDP was 23.47 per cent in 2001–2, only a little higher than in 1991–2.

From 2003–4, a dramatic upward movement of the rates of private corporate savings, aggregate domestic savings, and conventional measures of economic growth began, with the rate of savings exceeding 30 per cent (see also in this connection, Jangili and Kumar 2011).[7] The rise in the private corporate sector savings rate definitely contributed to this. As a percentage of GDP, it rose to 6.6 in 2004–5, 7.5 in 2005–6, 8.0 in 2006–7, 8.7 in 2007–8, and 8.4 in 2008–9. The rate of domestic savings as a percentage of GDP rose to a peak of 36.9 per cent in 2007–8 but then slid to 32.2 per cent and 33.7 per cent in 2008–9 and 2009–10 respectively (Government of India 2011, Table 0.1).

Increasing gross savings rate, however, could not keep up with the investment rate. In recent years India's gross domestic capital forma-tion has hovered around 35–8 per cent, but gross domestic savings has failed to keep pace with it. India has run up increasingly large bal-ance of payments deficits in its current account from 2005–6 onward. The current account deficit grew from US$2.47 billion in 2005–6 to US$3.84 billion in 2009–10 (RBI 2010, Table 142). Of even greater concern, increases in income have been concentrated in the pockets of a small section of the population (at most 15 per cent) and their demand for consumer goods, following affluent-country standards, has also burgeoned (D'Costa 2005, Patnaik 2007). That demand has been sustained, not only by growth in incomes but also by growth in their creditworthiness from the point of view of financial institutions. But financial exclusion has gone hand in hand with the concentration of formal credit among an increasingly smaller section of the popula-tion (Bagchi 2007).

Growth and Inequality

In any discussion of economic transformation the issue of sharing the benefits of growth is unavoidable, especially in poor countries such as India and China, where mass misery is persistent and the absolute numbers are mind-boggling. The interesting question is what hap-pens to poverty and thus to income distribution under high growth. Of course well functioning markets are no guarantee of better income distribution. In fact, in capitalist markets the inherent logic is to produce uneven development due to different initial conditions and varying rates of growth among different sectors, industries, regions, classes, and so on, even as sustained growth rates imply a tendency toward income convergence. Yet it is common knowledge today that high growth in both China and India is producing a substantial degree of inequality, only partially captured by the Gini coefficient (for rural India and China see Bardhan 2010, p. 51, also Chapter 7 by Banerjee *et al.*).[8]

As Table 1.3 shows for India, all households above a threshold level of income are experiencing increases in income but it is amply clear that the higher income households are gaining far more. It is not difficult to interpret this although more rigorous studies might be warranted. Education, skills, social capital, and initial household endowments are likely to be important determinants in capturing a higher share of growth (D'Costa 2011b). The policy implication is to implement countervailing measures that would more than offset the tendencies toward inequality. Thus, if the rural–urban social divide is wide, as it is in both countries, income and jobs targeted at the rural sector, especially for the landless and small farmers, should be part of the policy response.

Table 1.3 Growing Prosperity in India (income in Rs/Year in 2001–2 prices) '000 of Households

	Income Class	1995–6	2001–2	Annual Growth (%)	2005–6[a]	2009–10[a]
Deprived	< 90,000	131,176	135,378	0.5	132,250	114,394
Aspiring	900,000–200,000	28,901	41,262	6.1	53,276	75,304
Seekers	200,000–500,000	3,881	9,034	15.1	13,813	22,268
Strivers	500,000–1,000,000	651	1,712	17.5	3,212	6,173
Near rich	1,00,000–2,000,000	189	546	19.4	1,122	2,373
Clear rich	2,00,000–5,000,000	63	201	21.3	454	1,037
Sheer rich	5,00,000–10,000,000	11	40	23.4	103	255
Super rich	>10,000,000	5	20	25.9	53	141
Total		164,876	188,192	2.2	204,283	221,945

Source: National Council of Applied Economic Research (NCAER) and Business Standard Ltd. (2004, pp. 1–2).
Note: [a] Projections.

Thus, transformation as conventionally understood is not being realized under the high-growth regimes of both China and India if distribution is an important societal goal. The transmission mechanisms of inegalitarian outcomes are not well established but they are integral to the growth process. Because there are different components of growth, the rate of change of the individual components is responsible for producing uneven outcomes. In the case of China it is evident that investment has been a driving force for growth, which is related to exports. Clearly, the emergent capitalist classes and their counterparts in the state benefit from this growth along with the rising middle classes in both countries. But maintaining a high rate of investment means compressing consumption in a macroeconomic sense or, in other words, accommodating a greater share of profits— clear evidence of China's *capitalist* transition.

In this macroeconomic dynamic, high growth is sustained by high rates of investment, which is structurally driven by an aggressive export thrust. Competitive exports demand either suppressing wage growth or appreciating currency, or both. Holding down wages is not possible under high growth (see Chapter 6 by Riskin) while currency manipulation draws the ire of trade partners and thus is not sustainable. However, to break out of this cycle is not just a policy conundrum, since growth is also lifting many poor people out of poverty and creating employment opportunities for urban, manufacturing-based activities in the coastal provinces. Wage suppression is possible due to massive inflows of rural migrants into the export-oriented manufacturing industries. Thus, it is also a political challenge to shift the bias away from profits to wages and private consumption (see Chapter 5 by Hung). The equality that was achieved through China's peasant revolution and subsequent agricultural policy from 1978 to the mid-1980s has been undone by massive investment-driven capitalist growth. In the countryside land has become alienable and there has been a race to grab agricultural land for industrial and real estate development. Equality in India has also worsened during the high-growth period, as reflected in the increasing Gini coefficient. But casual observations lead to the same conclusion: that millions of malnourished people under an agrarian crisis and never-ending informal sector growth share the same India with Indian billionaires making it to the Forbes Richest list, a growing number of millionaires and a middle class with increasing wealth.

One of the key features of capitalism is that in the competitive game, any instrument can be used to grab resources. The rise of the wealthiest family in India, Dhirubhai Ambani and his sons, through manipulation of the political system, takeover of public sector companies, and resources first explored by the state-owned Oil and Natural Gas Corporation (ONGC) has been extensively documented (McDonald 2010). But while the Ambanis may be the Everest of the rise of wealth and inequality, a whole Himalayan range has come up out of the plains of poverty in India, mostly by brazen grabbing of the nation's natural resources through political connections and manipulation of media. Recent scandals include the rise and fall of the information technology (IT)-related Satyam group in Andhra Pradesh, the accrual of wealth to the ex-chief minister of Maharashtra, Ashok Chavan; the enormous amount of land and wealth now owned by the family of Y.S. Reddy, the chief minister of Andhra Pradesh who died in a helicopter crash; and the Reddy brothers in the BJP-led ministry of Karnataka, who accumulated wealth through illegal mining activities.[9] Public resources have been grabbed by businessmen, politicians, and their cronies and supplicants, some with long criminal records, some of whom also happen to be members of state and central legislatures and ministries. The new age of finance capital turns out also to be an age of rampant primitive accumulation in India, with serious implications for technological progress and people's welfare that could otherwise be supported from the growth of the Indian economy.

When resources are used to produce for export, with a resultant surplus in the balance of payments, it can raise the local cost of manufactures and services, and can bias the economic structure in favour of non-traded goods and services, a phenomenon often labelled the 'Dutch disease'. The Indian case is different. Here the resources, except for illegal mining enterprises, have been used to develop real estate properties such as new housing estates, hotels, and infrastructure for special economic zones. The booming of finance capital, aided by tax concessions on long-term capital gains, favourable corporate tax rates and transactions in the stock market, as well as a double taxation agreement with Mauritius (with low tax rates and special concessions for housing development), have allowed the grabbers of resources to make their dubious gains fungible at low cost.[10] Rerouting illicit gains stashed abroad via Mauritius and the stock market has had the virtue of attracting investment for some productive projects. The near-convertibility of the Indian rupee has also led many wealth-holders to put their gains away in Switzerland and other countries that ask few questions about the provenance of the money.

If capitalist transformation in India has been driven by the private investment rate, the first theme of concentration of assets and income in a few hands accompanying transformation has accelerated due to four major factors. First, the privatization of public assets, often at an unreasonably low price, has increased the wealth of the rich, especially those who are major patrons of important politicians. Second, the government has virtually abolished long-term capital gains tax, so that high returns through a rise in real estate prices, increase in share prices, etc., accrue tax-free to the wealthy. Third, Mauritius has become a tax haven, which allows Indians to set up joint-venture companies with only 10 per cent corporate income tax. Some of this income finds its way into the stock market, real estate, and other assets contributing to inflationary pressures. Under an open economy, foreign investment further boosts capital gains in the stock market and this expansion acts as another magnet to attract foreign investment that bridges a large part of the gap in the current account deficit while appreciating the rupee, and thus increasing the prospect of a currency crisis. Once foreign investors begin to think that the exchange rate is unsustainable and begin to withdraw their funds from India in large quantities, and this becomes a contagious sentiment, the value of the rupee can nosedive, leading to a rapid erosion of foreign exchange reserves and a currency crisis for India. Fortunately, in the beginning of 2011, Indian exports were looking up, so that there is some hope that this will not happen in the near future. Fourth, in the context of the rich getting richer, at the other end, the denial of credit to increasing numbers of farmers and small entrepreneurs has led to distress sales and bankrupted many of them, leading to concentration of land and business assets.[11] This process also means that the mass of propertyless workers with little social insurance continues to grow, augmenting the natural growth of the labour force.

The second related theme of transformation is the concomitant increase in inequality. While the sources of inequality are many and there are both domestic and international transmission mechanisms, much of the inequality can be argued to be internally generated. Independent of the sources or means of transmission of inequality, it appears that, at least according to the Kuznets inverted U-curve hypothesis, inequality is likely to worsen as growth rates increase. But the implication of the hypothesis is that inequality ought to lessen over time. This is a contentious claim since on the one hand neither India nor China is willing to yield high growth rates for better income distribution and, on the other, a case could be made that in the absence of major countervailing distributive policies, high growth in itself is a cause of inequality. From a political economy perspective, inequality is argued to arise from the unequal distribution of the economic surplus between workers and capitalists. In theory, under certain 'socialist' forms of development, more of the share could be directed towards workers as wages and less to capitalists as profits. However, in an era of intense capitalist competition facilitated by new technologies, export competition, and a complex set of decentralized global production arrangements, policies increasingly favour profit-making over wages. The dismantling of social support systems in China and in India has also been responsible for income polarization (Andreas 2010, pp. 78–80 for China). Ironically, the belief that higher growth rates will percolate down to the masses gathers momentum with this growth fetishism, leading to even greater inequality. China perversely illustrates this dilemma where the share of domestic consumption has been sharply turned around in favour of profits (Chapter 5 by Hung and Chapter 6 by Riskin). In India the Gini coefficient, for all its drawbacks, seems to show a similar trend, and in both countries inter-regional and inter-sectoral inequality is on the rise (Chapter 7 by Banerjee *et al.*).

Industry, Exports, and Global Finance

It is evident that economic transformation via agriculture cannot be fully realized if the surplus rural labour released by investment-led productivity is not absorbed by some other expanding sector, namely industry. Lewis and many structuralists looked to industrialization as a direct extension of agricultural transformation, though some have placed industry as the forerunner of agriculture because of high income elasticity and larger multiplier effects. In fact, most ambitious developing countries have placed a great deal of emphasis on import substitution industrialization (ISI) as a leapfrogging strategy to narrow the economic and technological gaps between them and the West. Of course even within ISI there were many nuances: some went through the phased model of easy import substitution to exports (such as South Korea and Taiwan), while Brazil and Mexico much earlier moved on to the more complex phase of industrialization. India, often grouped with Latin American countries, pursued the even more difficult phase early, namely the promotion of the capital goods sector (the Mahalanobis model). China pursued a similar strategy in the early years of the People's Republic but diverged from everyone else through Mao's small 'backyard steel mill' approach and rudimentary export promotion in the 1970s. However, unlike India, China did pursue a rural development strategy, altered ownership structure through land reforms and contained the movement of migrants to cities, often at a cost to rural residents, through its *hokou* registration system (Mallee 2000). The 1978 reforms, and later the 1992 liberalization, contributed to China's absorptive capacity of rural labour through manufacturing exports.

The Indian industrialization experience was mixed: on the one hand India did create a substantial industrial foundation with its Second Five-Year Plan but characteristically, with its high capital–labour ratio, failed to generate large-scale employment or absorb rural migrants. A variety of institutional problems beset industrial transformation: excessive regulation, accounting trickery, speculation and blatant corruption, leading to mostly uncompetitive industries and technological inertia (D'Costa 2003). China's industries were also weak but for very different reasons. Agriculture received priority and with the Sino–Soviet split small-scale rather than big industry became the vehicle for transformation. However, the statist approaches to industrialization were discredited in both countries and international integration, as seen in the case of the smaller East Asian economies, was perceived to be part of the answer to industrial expansion. The reforms of 1978 in China and in the mid-1980s and 1991 in India gradually ushered in two different trajectories of development. China has surged ahead with its aggressive exports of labour-intensive manufactures, absorbing by some estimates over 100 million migrants, while India's industrial record is much weaker with industry growing slowly, if at all, and services taking a bigger share of GDP and an increasing share (around 25 per cent) of total exports (merchandise and services). This is a characteristic generally not witnessed in a country with high growth and low per capita income. With the support of the Chinese state, over time China has been able to diversify into higher value exports, likewise not commensurate with its level of development (Rodrik 2006).

Export-based industrialization, despite its positive association, is not without its challenges. Some of the East Asian countries exported their way out of poverty through state-led industrial transformation and rural reforms in an earlier phase of global capitalism when world demand was growing with few competitors and the United States offered captive markets to these Asian countries as part of its geopolitical strategy in the region (see Chapter 4 by Chandra). However, today global market conditions are different, with a far more volatile world economy. The key features today are greater international integration, rapid technological change, hyper-competition, and greater space for the role of the market. However, there is no agreement as to how the national economy can be favourably articulated with the global one under such changed circumstances, particularly when many of the adverse macroeconomic impulses seem to be generated exogenously. Of course, for smaller Asian countries export expansion was one such avenue of articulation but only under the large import capacity of the United States for low-wage goods. The individual volumes were small and non-threatening. The entente between the United States and China after Nixon's visit in 1972 was certainly a factor for China's successful strategy, which is similar to US multinational corporations (MNCs) refashioning East Asia to meet US market needs. However, for India, such a strategic partnership has been neither politically feasible at home nor commercially attractive.

China's export strategy has gradually evolved through experimentation but the sheer scale of exports has undermined US tolerance for high trade deficits, especially when the American job market remains jittery. While exports are seen as a way to keep industries competitive, earn foreign exchange revenues and gain economies of scale, excessive dependence on exports can have a deleterious effect on the stability of the economy. China is a case in point. After relegating the agricultural sector to emphasize exports in the mid-1980s (Khan and Riskin 2001, p. 4), followed by Deng Xiaoping's tour of the southern coastal provinces in 1992 exhorting exporters, China became deeply enmeshed with the world economy. While this in itself was not a problem, China's structural predicaments became intertwined with the growth mechanism. China has had to pursue a high level of exports because of overinvestment in the economy, which in turn has led to excess capacity and thus the pressure to maintain high export growth (Wong 2008, pp. 25–6). Though a high rate of investment is necessary for transformation, it is a double-edged sword since it can be inflationary, especially when leveraged to offset imbalances in the other components of aggregate demand (Yongding 2009), and the high rate of investment is reinforced by the need to maintain a high share of profits to induce investments. This means that wage consumption must be held in check.

Although export surplus has internally absorbed a substantial number of surplus Chinese rural labourers, it has not substantially raised their standard of living, corresponding to the high rates of investment and growth. Instead, it has resulted in widening the disparity of incomes and wealth. Externally, an export strategy has generated massive trade deficits in the United States and developing countries (see Chapter 4 by Chandra). China's export surplus has been used in lending to the United States to close the United States' twin deficits (Wang 2007). This deepening interdependency and export penetration is susceptible to trade friction and currency pressure, while holding large quantities of foreign exchange is likely to erode China's foreign assets due to devaluation (Chapter 8 by Sen). There also could be losses stemming from the appreciation of the Chinese yuan (RMB), a certainty if the United States is to rebalance its external account. In India's case, such export dependence is missing except in some sectors such as IT, which is not low wage. However, India, too, can suffer from global instability as witnessed by the recent employment and export impact of the financial crisis on the gems and jewellery and automotive industries, among others (D'Costa 2011c). There is of course no magic formula for the exact balance between domestic and foreign market shares. However, unlike China, India suffers from underinvestment, especially in agriculture and infrastructure, and from widening trade deficits and demand constraints resulting from severe maldistribution of income.

The redeeming feature of this perversity of export drive is the large absorption of rural labour by export-oriented manufacturing. However, as alluded to earlier, this is double-edged. China more than comfortably sits on a massive reserve of foreign exchange, generated from its huge export surplus. At the global systemic level, China's trade surplus more or less mirrors the United States' trade deficit and has been a source of major international tension. The export-driven model works well when wages are compressed, made possible by mass rural-to-urban migration and state-sanctioned political control of workers. But when combined with exchange rate manipulation to support China's export competitiveness, the model is politically strained, externally as well as internally. In fact, there is evidence to suggest that the export-driven model may indeed be socially and politically exhausted (Chapter 5 by Hung). In parallel fashion, public sector reforms entailing the restructuring of state-owned enterprises have led to mass layoffs, compressing wages further. The gradual withdrawal of the state from established economic activities is indicative of new economic spaces for the emerging Chinese bourgeoisie, which is often linked to the state, formally or informally (see D'Costa 2012). In India, privatization has been by stealth, that is, through the gradual attrition of employees, while private sector expansion has been facilitated by a nefarious nexus between business and politicians.

Aside from the interdependence of China and the United States, each with a very different political system and geopolitical ambitions, the question is whether China can continue to be a partner in such a delicate relationship, especially since its low-wage-based aggressive export drive and its US dollar-tied currency are already sources of irritation if not outright hostility. The current global financial crisis and the continued slide of the US economy are exacerbating the tensions associated with China's new-found financial prowess. At the same time, the virtuous set of interconnections between low-wage exports, employment, trade surplus, inflows of foreign direct investment (FDI), and rise in foreign exchange reserves is also a source of imbalances. As indicated, compression of wage rates and an export drive remain integral to the Chinese model. Structurally then, China is compelled to prop up US consumption by continuing to lend to the United States. This cycle could viciously unravel should the United States continue to suffer from a consumption slowdown. Another consequence of propping up the US economy, as alluded to earlier, is compression of China's domestic consumption. Furthermore, the investment drive results in inflation, at the expense of domestic consumption. Regionally, the southern coastal provinces are inextricably linked to this model. Thus, the rebalancing of the Chinese economy in favour of domestic development, away from the United States and exports, is daunting given that it would require the transfer of resources away from the dynamic coastal industrial belt towards the rural hinterland.

Technology and Transformation

The final theme covered in this volume is science, technology, and innovation. The intrinsic character of capitalist transformation has been generating surplus value by initially squeezing labour and later by technological change. Paradoxically, late industrializers, in their quest to narrow the gap with the West, have been compelled to use both, with mixed results. The newly industrializing countries of East Asia have moved away from a low-wage-driven growth model to one that is increasingly technology-based surplus generation. China and India are betwixt and between, still relying on raw labour-based accumulation as well as making selective advances in technology. Wage arbitrage continues to be in their favour even as they pursue innovations. A variety of strategies are being pursued: increasing spending on R&D, emphasizing higher education (particularly professional degrees in science and engineering), attracting MNCs in high-technology industries and outsourcing in R&D, and acquiring foreign firms to secure technologies (Parayil and D'Costa 2009, also Chapter 12 by Sinha).

One of the fundamental characteristics of contemporary developing countries, including China and India, is their follower status when it comes to modern technology. Innovation and technology partially explain increasing productivity and thus economic growth. Beyond a threshold level of development, technology and innovation play an even greater role in the economic prospects of a country. While the technological gaps in some areas have narrowed between China and India and the advanced capitalist countries, as in telecommunications and mature industries such as steel and automobiles, there are other areas where the gap either persists or is getting wider, for example, in high-technology capital goods, alternative energy sources, and aerospace. Hence, the transformation question looms large if these two high-growth countries are, for both institutional and financial reasons, unable to leverage technology.

There is more to technology-based transformation than meets the eye. First, it is unclear to what extent technology is contributing to growth, despite significant investments in R&D in China. As Krugman (1994) has argued, China's growth is of the 'extensive' kind (à la Reynolds 1985), a result of adding more units of inputs such as labour, capital, and raw materials and not due to 'intensive' growth based on efficiency in the use of inputs. While Krugman may be underplaying the qualitative shifts that have taken place in these economies, there is some merit to the argument where India and China are concerned (for India see D'Costa 2009).

Second, in spite of national technological efforts, a good part of innovative activity is led by foreign companies. For example, Gilboy (2004) and Hart-Landsberg and Burkett (2005) argue that China's development has been driven largely by foreigners, foreign technology, and low-wage manufactured exports. Of course foreignness is not the issue here, rather it is whether multinational production has spillover effects. In the case of the IT industry, China does not seem to benefit from MNCs because of their isolation in an industrial cluster (Wang 2006). The Indian IT industry is also isolated from the domestic market (D'Costa 2009). An examination of patent activity in India suggests that much of the innovative activity is undertaken by multinationals (Chapter 11 by Mani).

Third, at least for China, S&T policies have been used to regulate competition among provinces and thus for growth. This is a clever approach but the downside has been land grabs by local authorities to foster profitable economic activities and thus ensure fiscal flows to the provincial level from the central government and political mobility of provincial leaders within the party hierarchy. Transforming agricultural land for industry is not novel; the history of capitalism is replete with experiences. What is new is the scale and scope of the widespread displacement of economically vulnerable people by both the state and private business in India and China.

Both China and India are emphasizing their technology capability by attracting FDI as well as investing abroad. China is the world's largest recipient of FDI although 'round-tripping' may overestimate FDI (Chapter 9 by Nagaraj). Unlike China, India has not been a major recipient of FDI. However, both countries have ramped up their overseas acquisitions, with India's private sector displaying a greater commercial acumen than its Chinese counterpart. The maturity of capitalism in these two countries, and especially the financial sphere, is amply demonstrated by their investment patterns either in the real economy through the acquisitions of branded firms (such as Jaguar by the Tatas in India or IBM PC by Lenovo in China) and other large firms in mature industries such as steel, auto, oil and natural gas, or in financial assets (such as China's purchase of US Treasury bills). As of January 2011, China held US$1.2 trillion of US Treasury securities, representing 26 per cent of total foreign holdings (US Government, Department of the Treasury 2012).

China has made rapid progress in industrial technologies and is aggressively pursuing R&D for future development (Chapter 12 by Sinha). India, too, has made solid gains but its rate of investment in R&D and its institutional arrangements are not yet geared towards dynamic development (D'Costa 2009). Nevertheless, both countries recognize that S&T and the innovations that spring from them are critical to sustain economic growth. When combined with low wages, technological capability becomes a powerful instrument for international competitiveness. How China and India might evolve in the technology sphere, given that they are already active in some futuristic knowledge-intensive industries such as telecommunications, IT, and biotechnology, is critical to the overall transformation question.

One key dimension to national S&T development is their institutional arrangement (often dubbed the national innovation system [NIS]) (D'Costa and Parayil 2009). The concept of NIS is readily understood but hard to operationalize. In effect, NIS is about governance, which in turn is about sharing power. In a federated system power is distributed, and for S&T development much depends on how this power is shared between the central and local governments. China, despite its centralized one-party system, has gradually decentralized and extended autonomy to provincial governments. India on the other hand, despite its federated political structure, has not been able to govern its S&T institutions in a decentralized manner. Furthermore, in China S&T has been leveraged to bring about particular kinds of governance structures to encourage growth by inducing inter-provincial competition, a feat rarely matched by other developing countries (see Chapter 10 by Banerjee). Consequently, its R&D spending has shot up to unprecedented levels. However, as Wang (2006, pp. 389–90) shows, decentralization has also resulted in provincialism, undermining the formation of a national market, while, as we have alluded to, land transfers for S&T projects are rife with corruption at the provincial level and exploit the rural peasantry (see Gong 2006, Hsing 2006). The outcome of such spending is anybody's guess though we can anticipate some technological upgrading, a rise in patents, and even greater involvement of MNCs in China's innovation system. However, one thing we do know is that such massive spending is also likely to exacerbate growth-led imbalances from which China does not seem to be able to extricate itself.

CHAPTER DESCRIPTIONS

To capture the transformation process the following chapter descriptions indicate the vast and complex terrain of economic and social change currently underway in India and China. The chapters are roughly grouped under four key interrelated sources of transformation and transition: agricultural development and the accumulation process, models and paths of industrialization, global finance and sustainability of transformation, and S&T. These chapters are best seen as a package as they reveal layers of interconnections between and throw light on the similarities and diversity of experiences of India and China. In addition, most of the chapters, while acknowledging the tremendous progress these countries have made since their founding as sovereign states, illustrate the persistent tensions in the transformation process, social and economic imbalances, vulnerabilities, and deep-rooted challenges in engendering genuine inclusive transformation.

Ashwani Saith in Chapter 2 compares the massive phenomenon of 'labour accumulation' in rural China in the pre-reform era of high collectivism, with the huge recent Indian initiative to deliver a universal right to employment in the countryside through the National Rural Employment Guarantee Act (NREGA). While China's labour accumulation process, propelled by mass mobilization campaigns in rural China, was strategized, *ex ante* as a driver of overall collectivist rural transformation, the National Rural Employment Guarantee Scheme (NREGS) in rural India has been introduced recently, after decades of rural underdevelopment, essentially as an *ex post* secondary poverty-reduction device addressing the employment and livelihood deficits that even booming growth rates have been unable to correct. Saith demonstrates that Chinese collectivist labour accumulation far outperforms India's NREGA intervention in terms of scale, inherent self-financing capabilities, and productive asset creation as well as distributional outcomes. If the Chinese scheme generated long-term social investment, the Indian one, thus far, primarily dispenses short-term social consumption. While noting the futility of cherry-picking 'lessons' across path-dependent development trajectories, Saith concludes that without overcoming the institutional impasse in India through radical rural interventions and innovations, it will remain impossible to convert mass transfer payments into transformational investments that collectively begin to renew the productive potential of the countryside in an egalitarian fashion.

Challenges to agriculture are exacerbated by the institutional impediments to reforms in the food grain supply chain. To make sense of how agricultural public institutions are responding to national and local demands, Shailaja Fennell in Chapter 3 undertakes an analysis of the food grain supply chain. It is the institutional capacity to maintain the supply chain where each section of the chain performs its designated functions that makes for food security. India and China initially had different strategies with regard to the full supply chain. In the case of India, the reforms focused exclusively on the procurement section of the chain, while in China there was a greater concern with the production aspects of the chain. Fennell shows that for Indian agriculture there was a reduction in the linkages between production, procurement, and distribution, which was compounded by difficulties in reconciling the intended beneficiaries. As a result, the ability of the public sector to deliver needed food grain to the.poor was compromised. In contrast, high industrial growth in the reform period in China reduced poverty levels by half. It is evident that restructuring the role of agricultural institutions provides an important basis for ascertaining the ability of national agricultural systems to ensure both production and distribution.

In seeing transformation as a historical and path-dependent process, Nirmal Chandra in Chapter 4 summarizes the industrial development experience since 1950 in the two countries to show where they stand today. He argues that the initial import substitution model helped India establish a wide range of industries but overall growth and employment were circumscribed by the absence of a broad home market and accentuated by Western discrimination against the export of manufactures. The 1991 reforms in India abruptly liberalized imports, and yet most industries prospered due to their inherent strength. Chandra argues that India's GDP growth rate has recently accelerated because of a spurt in luxury consumption, fiscal deficits, and inflows of foreign capital. In contrast, China's industry expanded at a much faster pace than India's during the 1950–80 period but national income increased rather modestly. Deng's gamble with sweeping reforms, freer domestic markets, and an open door policy for foreign trade and capital greatly boosted incomes. Chandra indicates that the conditions for such growth included generous access to Western markets and technology in the wake of China's entente with the United States, which contributed to a stellar export-led growth outcome. However, one outcome of recent high growth rates in a neoliberal setting in both countries has been worsening socio-economic inequalities, raising questions about the long-run sustainability of this growth strategy. Both countries are locked into the present global system, and ironically, China's burgeoning exports are already deindustrializing many developing countries.

If China's transformation is inflicting harm on others, Ho-Fung Hung in Chapter 5 argues that it is also harming itself due to the contradictions unleashed by the export-driven model. For example, the exceptional competitiveness of China's export sector is rooted in an agrarian crisis. Induced by the urban-biased development policy of the government in the 1990s, a large rural surplus labour force has been created, which perpetuates the low manufacturing wage among rural migrant workers. While this 'unlimited supply of labour' fosters the cost advantages of China's export, China's agrarian crisis has been restraining the growth of its domestic consumption, forcing it to depend on the US market for its exports and deterring the reorientation of the Chinese economy into a more domestic-consumption–driven one. Hung argues that the latest global financial crisis has ended the debt-financed consumption spree in the United States, thereby precipitating the demise of such a developmental model. China's strong recovery in 2008–10 is based on massive investment spending (part of the stimulus package) that is financed by low-quality loans by state banks. Hence, the threat of financial calamity due to non-performing loans is unlikely to sustain the growth model. Therefore, China's transformation in the long run hinges on whether China can shift to a new model of development driven by domestic private consumption.

Carl Riskin in Chapter 6 shows that as the global downturn of 2008 hit China, three different sets of forces affected its economy. First, there was the attempt to rebalance the economic structure by reducing dependence on massive investment rates and exports, raising consumption demand relative to GDP, and thus reversing the inegalitarian nature of Chinese growth. Second, there was the financial crisis itself, and the move to counter it via massive expansion of investment and credit. Finally, there was the impending exhaustion of the large fund of surplus labour whose absorption into industry has been a prime enabler of China's rapid growth for three decades. Riskin argues that there was tension between the stimulus programme and the rebalancing objective, making the outcome uncertain, but that growing labour shortages and rising wages may make it easier for the centre to rebalance. As the Lewis model of unlimited labour is exhausted, development is expected to shift to the lower-cost interior. Rising wages and falling profits relative to GDP are likely to produce increasing rates of consumption and falling rates of investment, thus moderating growth rates and effectively beginning the rebalancing process along the lines China's central government has been advocating unsuccessfully for years.

It is evident that rebalancing the Chinese economy is a herculean task. In Chapter 7, Lopamudra Banerjee and a team of political economists—both Indian and Chinese—focus on the relationships among growth, reforms, and inequality. They undertake a comparative analysis of social, spatial, and temporal dimensions of economic inequality in China and India based on changes in the pattern and distribution of income and expenditure in the respective countries. Their investigation is motivated by the striking combination of accelerated economic growth and persistent social deprivation, peering into the nature of prosperity and inequality in these two countries over the last two decades. The authors seek to answer two important questions: first, what is the trend in inequality in India and China? And second, what additional information could be gathered by decomposing their aggregate trends in terms of (*a*) regional variations and (*b*) the urban–rural divide? In answering these questions, the authors compare income and consumption inequality in China with consumption inequality in India in the post-reform period over three (roughly comparable) points in time. They generate estimates of income/consumption and Gini coefficients for the two countries and decompose the Gini by rural–urban and region–state components. Based primarily on economic analysis, the chapter concludes that both countries need to devise special, comprehensive, and urgent measures sensitive to their different contexts to tackle these various dimensions of inequality—particularly the rapidly growing urban–rural divide—if they wish to maintain their drive towards greater economic prosperity without creating social upheaval.

The urgency of China's rebalancing cannot be overestimated, even if by growth and relative labour scarcity there could be a shift toward consumption, away from investment. As Sunanda Sen (Chapter 8) shows, the current global financial crisis has introduced considerable instability (and external imbalance) for China. With gradual capital account opening, China has drawn larger inflows of capital from abroad, both FDI and portfolio investment. Of late, a surge in these inflows has introduced problems for the monetary authorities in continuing with an autonomous monetary policy in China, especially with large additions to official reserves, the latter in a bid to avoid further appreciation of the country's currency. Like other developing countries, China today faces the 'impossible trilemma' of managing the exchange rate with near-complete capital mobility and an autonomous monetary policy. Facing problems in devising and sustaining this policy, China has been using expansionary fiscal policy to tackle the impact of shrinking export demand. Concerned about social divides, recently Chinese authorities have tried to boost real demand in the countryside and to revamp the domestic market. However, as Sen notes, the close integration of China with the world economy has not eliminated the concerns about the possible effects of the recent global downturn on China and, in parallel with the deindustrialization impact of China on the developing world, the second-round effects of a downturn in China for the rest of the world.

Notwithstanding the vulnerabilities associated with financial integration, China's financial strength is revealed through its increasing outward FDI. China's cumulative total outward FDI is two-and-a-half times that of India's. In Chapter 9, R. Nagaraj traces the patterns in the outflows to find out if such flows represent a new trend, the possible reasons for such a development, and the strengths of Indian and Chinese firms in coping with the challenges of international business. Nagaraj finds that Chinese capital mostly flows into its sovereign wealth funds operating from Hong Kong, which are invested in acquiring natural resources to support the domestic economy, are used by firms to access foreign technology, and to facilitate Chinese exports. In contrast, most of the outward investment from India is from large private firms and business houses and is used to acquire factories and firms in the developed economies, to access markets, and to acquire technologies to enhance domestic capabilities. A small fraction of the outflows representing Indian public sector enterprises has gone abroad to acquire natural resources, mostly oil. In manufacturing and services, in contrast to the developed economies, the outward flows from China and India are motivated by the need to acquire firm-specific advantages, while leveraging their country-specific advantages (mainly cheap labour). In facing the challenges of international business, state support and cheap finance underpin the strength of Chinese overseas investment, while the strength of the Indian investments to venture overseas seems to be founded on the domestic institutions, depth of the capital market, and the rule of law.

The influence of varying governance structures on outward FDI for the two countries is also evident in the case of S&T. In Chapter 10, Parthasarathi Banerjee demonstrates that China's economic and social transformation has been governed through support of S&T instruments. He argues that the preference for S&T instruments over other policies of governance is attributable to the power of S&T in shaping and directing growth. For example, S&T supported the governance of growth-seeking competition between regions of China. Close relations between political and economic governance with the growth and use of S&T as well as innovation signify the increasingly important role of S&T investment in the governance of regions of China. Funds needed for S&T and for innovation were provided through changes in fiscal powers, such as empowering local governments to undertake development projects involving land reuse. Investments in S&T, secured through fiscal changes and land conversion, transformed the asset ownership and economic power structures, and such powers generated inter-regional competition as the principal driver of economic growth. Banerjee argues that the key to governance in China remains in controlling and directing competition among regions. Consequently, economic transactions between the structures of power have cleverly manoeuvred alliances to control S&T resources and reinforce these powers.

China and India are definitely on a higher economic growth path, although the contribution of technology to economic growth is still not very clearly estimated. In Chapter 11, Sunil Mani provides some evidence to show that innovative activities in the industrial sector in both China and India have shown some significant increases during the post-reform process in the two countries. Knowledge content of both domestic output and exports is increasing in both countries.

A detailed comparative analysis suggests that the Chinese National System of Innovation (NSI) is dominated by the Sectoral System of innovation (SSI) of the electronics and telecommunications industries; for India it is dominated by the SSI of the pharmaceutical industry. In both countries, innovative activities are increasingly contributed by MNCs. In other words, both China and India have become important locations for innovative activities. However, a continued rise in innovative activity in the two countries is limited by the availability of finance and high-quality scientists and engineers. Fortunately, the two governments, according to Mani, are aware of this problem and are taking a number of steps to ease the supply of technically trained personnel. However, a rethinking of financial support schemes is still necessary to reduce distortions plaguing the innovation sphere and thus future opportunities for transformation.

Chapter 12 by Bikramjit Sinha continues with the theme of S&T to indicate how the Chinese state has been promoting the increasing industrialization of R&D. He argues that the state has been active even as the nation internationally integrates and allows the market to function more. The chapter shows that the share of the state as a source of R&D funds as well as a sector of R&D performance is much higher than portrayed, demonstrating that the state is playing a critical role in China's economic development by outsourcing R&D to enterprises through a variety of mechanisms. Using suitable direct and indirect tax incentive mechanisms and preferential insurance through the nationalized banks, the state is stimulating R&D. Furthermore, the state is guiding and supervising long-term R&D policies, implementing ambitious R&D programmes, identifying and designating R&D subjects, and providing the overall framework of an NIS. Sinha emphasizes that the industrialization of R&D in China is a conscious strategy to promote industrial development while retaining substantial regulatory power.

LOOKING AHEAD

So why do China and India keep growing despite such challenges and dislocation? India's growth can be attributed to four factors. The first is the continued growth of a young population with aspiration levels approximating those of the middle class in affluent countries. This stimulates demand for new housing, refrigerators, other white goods and cars, especially of the more expensive varieties. Second, IT services lead to direct and indirect growth of incomes and wealth. For example, the sector represents nearly a quarter of India's exports of goods and services, even though domestic employment generation is relatively marginal in the Indian context (D'Costa 2011a). Third, Indian labour in the unorganized sector continues to be among the cheapest in the world not only because population growth is not being matched by the growth in employment but also because of the headlong proletarianization of farmers and forest users who are losing their land and access to forest products and public land as pastures. Finally, as the global economy reels under the financial crisis, economies such as China and India remain attractive for investors[12] as the publicly-owned banking system is relatively well regulated. But this stability may have been bought at the cost of excluding the vast majority from the formal credit system (Bagchi 2005).

China's growth rests on similar factors with one important difference—its massive investment rates aimed at the export market. This has created a large Chinese middle class, but has been accompanied by a widening disparity. Furthermore, it is debatable which country has the worst record in environmental matters or the displacement of large numbers of people due to dams, highways, mining, and huge industrial projects. India may fare slightly better than China in this respect as in India there are active civic organizations that have been mobilized to oppose unilateral decisions on the transformation process.

China and India are also growing as changes in technology increasingly allow production to be decentralized from core economies. In this context China, and later India, were able to capture some of the economic benefits from the world economy. They are making a dent in the global industry and service sectors in part because non-critical technologies are increasingly subject to diffusion due to both local learning efforts and expansion of tertiary education. But as long as there is an unlimited supply of unskilled labour in the countryside and ongoing proletarianization in the agricultural sector, growth will be a combination of widespread low-wage and selective high-wage production. We can expect this uneven development to be a persistent feature of the two countries in the absence of tight coordination and major redistributive policies accompanying such capitalist transformation.

NOTES

1. Some see a renewed form of statism in China and a move away from rural entrepreneurialism since the Tiananmen Massacre (Huang 2008), although it would be simplistic to view statism as incompatible with capitalist economic systems.

2. In virtually all countries that have successfully industrialized, the state played a developmental role. But not all states could play this role effectively. For a more detailed discussion of the conditions for success, see Bagchi (2004) and D'Costa (1999).

3. The irony should not be lost since the making of capitalists through market reforms by the Chinese state structurally implies the intractability of the growing inequality problem that results from the very process of capitalist growth dynamics.

4. He pointed out that when that expectation is overly influenced by casino-like characteristics of the stock exchange, the job of channelling funds towards productive investment was likely to be badly done (Keynes 1936, Chapter 12).

5. There are measurement issues and Chinese savings data are often overestimated (Ma and Yi 2010). However, after adjustments, the recent numbers are not that far off from alternative measures.

6. License–permit–quota raj refers to the Indian bureaucracy that was charged with issuing licenses to businesses for production, for which permissions had to be sought, and whereby output was restricted by specific quotas.

7. This study confines itself to public limited companies. The growth of private limited companies has very probably contributed to the fast growth of corporate sector savings.

8. The measurement of inequality is based essentially on consumer expenditure. There are two problems with this. First, the expenditures of the top income earners cannot be captured by the usual survey methods. Second, it leaves out the inequality of wealth, which exercises an additional influence on the society and polity.

9. The brothers are G. Janarthana Reddy, G. Somashekara Reddy, and Karunakara Reddy.

10. China has its share of finance capital even though portfolio investment inflows have not been very high. The later reforms associated with an aggressive export drive from the southern coastal belt has let loose a reign of land grabbing for urban-industrial development. This has drawn a considerable amount of investment capital from the overseas Chinese, with Hong Kong and other locations acting as a conduit for round-tripping of investments to access preferential treatment in mainland China (Wang 2007, p. 31). The inter-provincial competition for FDI, aimed at exports, has often been at the cost of worker interests and the environment.

11. Karl Marx had discussed some of these processes, when analysing how capitalist ground-rent grows (see especially, Marx [1894/1971], Part VI).

12. Although it is not known what share of profits was obtained from India and China, GE of the United States made US$14.2 billion, of which two-thirds came from non-US locations (Kocieniewski 2011).

REFERENCES

Andreas, J. 2010. 'A Shanghai Model?', *New Left Review*, 65 (September–October): 63–85.

Ash, R. 2010. 'The Chinese Economy after 30 Years of Reform: Perspectives from the Agricultural Sector', *Copenhagen Journal of Asian Studies*, 28 (1): 36–62.

Bagchi, A.K. 1970. 'Long-Term Constraints on Industrial Growth in India 1951–1968', in E.A.G. Robinson and M. Kidron (eds), *Economic Development in South Asia*, pp. 170–92. London: Macmillan.

————. 1988. 'Problems of Effective Demand and Contradictions of Planning in India', in A.K. Bagchi (ed.), *Economy, Society and Polity*, pp. 227–66. Calcutta: Oxford University Press.

————. 2002a. 'Agrarian Transformation and Human Development: Instrumental and Constitutive Links', in V.K. Ramachandran and M. Swaminathan (eds), *Agrarian Studies: Essays on Agrarian Relations in Less-Developed Countries*, pp. 153–65. New Delhi: Tulika.

————. 2002b. 'Nationalism and Human Development', in S. Patel, J. Bagchi, and K. Raj (eds), *Thinking Social Science in India: Essays in Honour of Alice Thorner*, pp. 327–42. New Delhi: Sage Publications.

————. 2004. *The Developmental State in History and in the Twentieth Century*. Delhi: Regency Publications.

————. 2005. 'Rural Credit and Systemic Risk', in V.K. Ramachandran and M. Swaminathan (eds), *Financial Liberalization and Rural Credit in India*, pp. 39–49. New Delhi: Tulika.

————. 2007. 'Finance: Lessons for India', in A.K. Bagchi and G.A. Dymski (eds), *Capture and Exclude: Developing Economies and the Poor in Global Finance*, pp. 317–36. New Delhi: Tulika.

Bardhan, P. 2010. *Awakening Giants, Feet of Clay: Assessing the Economic Rise of China and India*. Princeton: Princeton University Press.

Basu, S. and S. Mallick. 2008. 'When Does Growth Trickle Down To the Poor? The Indian Case', *Cambridge Journal of Economics*, 32 (3): 461–78.

Burgess, R. and R. Pandey. 2005. 'Do Rural Banks Matter? Evidence from the Indian Social Banking Experiment', *American Economic Review*, 95 (3): 780–95.

Cypher, J. and J. Dietz. 2004. *The Process of Economic Development*. New York: Routledge.

D'Costa, A.P. (ed.). 1999. *The Global Restructuring of the Steel Industry: Innovations, Institutions and Industrial Change*. London: Routledge.

————. 2003. 'Capitalist Maturity and Corporate Responses to Liberalization: The Steel, Auto, and Software Sectors in India', in A. Mukherjee-Reed (ed.),

Corporate Capitalism in Contemporary South Asia: Conventional Wisdoms and South Asian Realities, pp. 106–33. Basingstoke: Palgrave Macmillan.

D'Costa, A.P. 2005. *The Long March to Capitalism: Embourgeoisment, Internationalization, and Industrial Transformation in India*. Basingstoke: Palgrave Macmillan.

—————. 2009. 'Extensive Growth and Innovation Challenges in Bangalore, India', in G. Parayil and A.P. D'Costa (eds), *The New Asian Innovation Dynamics: China and India in Perspective*, pp. 79–109. Basingstoke: Palgrave Macmillan.

—————. 2011a. 'Compressed Capitalism and Development: Primitive Accumulation, Capitalist Maturity, and Petty Commodity Production in India and China', European Development Research and Training Institute (Bonn) and Development Studies Association (UK) joint conference for Actually Existing Capitalisms International Workshop in Honour of Prof. Barbara Harriss-White, Europe-Asia Working Group, York University, York, UK, 19–22 September 2011.

—————. 2011b. 'Geography, Uneven Development and Distributive Justice: The Political Economy of IT Growth in India', *Cambridge Journal of Regions, Economy and Society*, 4 (2): 237–51.

—————. 2011c. 'Globalization, Crisis and Industrial Relations in the Indian Auto Industry', *International Journal of Automotive Technology and Policy*, 11 (2): 114–36.

—————. 2012. *Globalization and Economic Nationalism in Asia*. Oxford: Oxford University Press.

D'Costa, A.P. and G. Parayil. 2009. 'China, India, and the New Asian Innovation Dynamics: An Introduction', in G. Parayil and A.P. D'Costa (eds), *The New Asian Innovation Dynamics: China and India in Perspective*, pp. 1–26. Basingstoke: Palgrave Macmillan.

Gilboy, G.J. 2004. 'The Myth behind China's Miracle', *Foreign Affairs*, July/August, http://web.ebscohost.com.esc-web.lib.cbs.dk/ehost/pdfviewer/pdfviewer?vid =3&hid=15&sid=da22eb3c-0978-4df2-af9f-a2c2d37ad044%40sessionmgr14, accessed on 23 November 2009.

Gong, T. 2006. 'Corruption and Local Governance: The Double Identity of Chinese Local Governments in Market Reform', *The Pacific Review*, 19 (1): 85–102.

Government of India. 2011. *Economic Survey 2010–11*. Ministry of Finance, Government of India, New Delhi: Ministry of Finance, Government of India, indiabudget.nic.in/ub2010-11/ubmain.htm, accessed on 31 March 2011.

Hamilton, C. 1986. *Capitalist Industrialization in Korea*. Boulder, CO: Westview Press.

Hart-Landsberg, M. and P. Burkett. 2005. *China and Socialism: Market Reforms and Class Struggle*. New York: Monthly Review Press.

Hatekar, N. and A. Dongre. 2005. 'Structural Breaks in Indian Economic Growth: Revisiting the Debate With a Longer Perspective', *Economic and Political Weekly*, XL (14): 1432–5.

Hsing, Y. 2006. 'Brokering Power and Property in China's Townships', *The Pacific Review*, 19 (1): 103–24.

Huang, Y. 2008. *Capitalism with Chinese Characteristics: Entrepreneurship and the State*. Cambridge: Cambridge University Press.

Jangili, R. and S. Kumar. 2011. 'Determinants of Private Corporate Sector Savings: An Empirical Study', *Economic and Political Weekly*, XLVI (8): 49–55.

Keynes, J.M. 1936. *The General Theory of Employment, Interest and Money*. London: Macmillan.

Khan, A. and C. Riskin. 2001. *Inequality and Poverty in China in the Age of Globalization*. New York: Oxford University Press.

Kocieniewski, D. 2011. 'G.E.'s Strategies Let It Avoid Taxes Altogether'. *New York Times*, http://topics.nytimes.com/top/reference/timestopics/people/k/david_kocieniewski/index.html?inline=nyt-per, accessed 29 March 2011.

Krugman, P.K. 1994. 'The Myth of Asia's Miracle', *Foreign Affairs*, 73 (6): 62–78.

Lewis, W.A. 1966. *Development Planning*. Routledge library edition.

Ma, G. and W. Yi. 2010. 'China's High Saving Rate: Myth and Reality', Bank for International Settlements, Monetary and Economic Department, BIS Working Papers, No. 312.

Maddison, A. 2007. *Chinese Economic Performance in the Long Run, 960–2030 AD*. Paris: OECD (2nd Ed.).

Mallee, H. 2000. 'Migration, Houkou and Resistance in Reform China', in E.J. Perry and M. Selden (eds), *Chinese Society: Change, Conflict and Resistance*, pp. 83–101. London: Routledge.

McDonald, H. 2010. *Ambani & Sons: The Making of the World's Richest Brothers and Their Feud*. New Delhi: Roli Books.

Marx, K. 1894/1971. *Capital. The Process of Capitalist Production as a Whole*, Vol. III, edited from the German manuscript by Frederick Engels; translated into English. Moscow: Progress Publishers.

NCAER (National Council of Applied Economic Research) and Business Standard Ltd. 2004. 'The Great Indian Middle Class: Results from the NCAER Market Information Survey of Households'. New Delhi: NCAER.

Nayyar, D. 2006. 'India's Unfinished Journey: Transforming Growth into Development', *Modern Asian Studies*, 40 (3): 797–832.

Parayil, G. and A.P. D'Costa. (eds). 2009. *The New Asian Innovation Dynamics: China and India in Perspective*. Basingstoke: Palgrave Macmillan.

Patnaik, P. 2007. 'Budgetary Policy in the Context of Inflation', *Economic and Political Weekly*, XLII (14): 1260–2.

RBI (Reserve Bank of India). 2010. *Handbook of Statistics on the Indian Economy 2009–10*. Mumbai: Reserve Bank of India.

Reynolds, L.J. 1985. *Economic Growth in the Third World, 1850–1980*. New Haven, CT: Yale University Press.

Rodrik, D. 2006. 'What's So Special about China's Exports?' *China & World Economy*, 14 (5): 1–19.

Sivasubramonian, S. 2000. *The National Income of India in the Twentieth Century*. Oxford: Oxford University Press.

US Government, Department of the Treasury. 2012. 'Major Foreign Holders of Treasury Securities', http://www.treasury.gov/resource-center/data-chart-center/tic/Documents/mfh.txt, accessed 20 May 2012 .

Wang, J. 2006. 'China's Dualist Model on Technological Catching Up: A Comparative Perspective', *The Pacific Review*, 19 (3): 385–403.

Wang, X. 2007. 'China as a Net Creditor: An Indication of Strength or Weaknesses?' *China & World Economy*, 15 (6): 22–36.

Wong, J. 2008. 'China's Economy in 2007/2008: Coping with Problems of Runaway Growth', *China & World Economy*, 16 (2): 1–18.

Yongding, Y. 2009. 'China's Policy Responses to the Global Financial Crisis', Richard Snape Lecture, 25 November 2009, Australian Government Productivity Commission.

2

Guaranteeing Rural Employment—Tales from Two Countries

Right to Employment in Neoliberal India and Labour Accumulation in Collectivist China

Ashwani Saith

AN UNUSUAL COMPARISON

This chapter attempts an unusual comparison between two massive interventions designed to generate rural employment: the phenomenon of labour accumulation (LA) in rural China in the period of high collectivism preceding the reforms of 1978; and the huge Indian initiative to deliver a universal right to employment in the countryside since the enactment of the National Rural Employment Guarantee Act (NREGA) in 2005. It is motivated by dual objectives. On the Chinese side, it attempts a reappraisal, albeit partial, of the Chinese intervention both in its own right and time frame, and also in terms of its interface with the subsequent era of development: were the earlier years of monumental human effort just plain waste, or did they lay a foundational platform for rural and macroeconomic transformation? On the Indian side, the motivation is to provide a lateral perspective on the National Rural Employment Guarantee Scheme (NREGS)—often referred to as the largest single intervention for employment-driven poverty alleviation in the world. Might one identify some of its limitations, especially its unexploited developmental potential, by using the Chinese case as a comparator and independent frame of reference? Understandably, this idiosyncratic comparison attracts difficulties and demands caution, partly because NREGS is still in its formative stage and in part due to the nature of the empirical evidence for rural China during that turbulent period, complicated further by the heavy ideological overlays in later discourses and 'scientific' analyses of Chinese collectivism.

From a developmental perspective, both LA and NREGS simultaneously highlight the structural inability of the economy, especially agriculture, to productively absorb the entire rural labour force, while underscoring the vital potential role of rural infrastructure for successful rural development. A surplus supply of labour is absorbed in serving an unmet demand for infrastructure—clearly a win-win scenario, if handled well, and if the 'agency gap' can be satisfactorily bridged.

In this regard, both countries and systems demonstrate the acute dependence on the state—at local or higher levels—as the indispensable agent for large-scale infrastructural modernization in the countryside. If the Ricardian constraint to industrialization had to be broken, land reforms were essential, and the state would need to organize large-scale investment in rural infrastructure to escape the clutches of the law of diminishing returns. In India, no serious pro-peasant land reforms were enacted. With regard to large-scale infrastructure investment, the snag was that rural surplus labour would have to be paid wages up front for such work. This meant that the government would need to mobilize matching revenues—a task that proved to be insufficiently attractive for the government unwilling to tax its own paymasters.

It is against the background of this structural impasse that both the Chinese collectivist LA, and the later Indian NREGS initiatives need to be appreciated. Each illustrates a distinct approach to the simultaneous resolution of the surplus labour and scarce infrastructure equations. The Chinese way solves the conundrum through the power of collective institutions, which simultaneously guarantee full employment, and at the same time provide the mechanisms for self-financed creation of productive infrastructure on a massive scale. The Indian initiative is led by the state, with more limited employment guarantees functioning within the constraints set by having to pre-finance such popular programmes for the poor through unpopular resource mobilization from the elite. Not surprisingly, there is a striking comparison with respect to the divergent motivations and objectives driving the two interventions.

Mao argued that in a populous poor agrarian economy there was an opportunity to create rural land-related infrastructure through an investment of this peasant labour into accumulation projects, hence, LA.[1] Dramatically mobilized across China, LA formed one of twin engines of rural development; through its impact on agricultural productivity it provided both the demand- and supply-side impulses that catalyzed a dynamic growth process within the communes. The other engine was rural industrialization within the communes; this also used surplus labour from within the collective, and generated high financial surpluses, which went into four major uses: further diversification of the unit's non-farm portfolio of activities; significantly, into projects of agricultural development; into providing a social consumption floor to all the members of the unit; and into further strengthening the capacity of local government.

LA schemes were launched on a universal basis in all rural collective units. At the age of 16, every able-bodied member of the rural population effectively became a worker with a right to participation and remuneration within the collective. Thus, LA potentially engaged the entire rural workforce in its agenda. The nominal coverage was universal. The actual level of labour used in LA was determined by the scale of schemes adopted by the collectives, varying across units and regions, according to available possibilities and the opportunity cost of peasant labour. Coming out of an era of feudal and peasant agriculture, there was ample scope for productive collective investments in every rural collective. It was not a case, therefore, of a relatively limited scale of LA investment being spread and shared thinly by the entire rural workforce; it was more a case of a sustained drive for a maximal utilization of the vast reservoir of pre-existing rural surplus labour as was feasible to do within the local environment.

In contrast, in the Indian case, the prime motivation propelling NREGS since its inception has been poverty alleviation through assured employment on rural public works schemes. This immediately influences its scale, form, and content. But such a focus has been blurred by a de facto lack of clarity over the main objective of NREGS.

Thus, one document on the official NREGA website describes it as 'an important Central law [which] assures livelihood guarantee to the entire population above 18 years of age residing in rural areas of the country'; this is both inaccurate and an exaggeration. Then, an element of social inclusion has been added on through concessionary clauses in favour of scheduled caste (SC) and scheduled tribe (ST) communities. Further, in insurgency-affected areas, there is official exhortation for the bureaucracy to deliver employment without delay, giving the programme a dimension of a counter-insurgency intervention. And, on the fringes, there are calls for the programme to be extended to other activities, and to urban areas, in order to overcome some inherent exclusionary tendencies and to be more genuinely universal in its remit. This blurring of the edges notwithstanding, it would be fair to say that NREGS is fundamentally oriented towards the immediate provision of employment in the countryside.

NREGS is the single largest employment generation programme in the world. Launched in 2005 upon the enactment of the NREGA, its ambit was quickly widened from the initial 200 districts to cover all districts of the country. It offers 100 days of employment for any (combination) of adult members of every rural household on demand-driven basis. The Act specifies that the employment is for the creation of rural productive assets. The work rate is prescribed, and though thought to be unreasonably demanding, is often not really applied. Remuneration has to be at the official wage rate for agricultural labour set by the state governments, and there are clear directives about the distribution of job cards, of the announcement of works within set time periods, of the provision of adequate employment of legally mandated compensation in lieu thereof, and of the payment of wages within a limited time frame. Given the high leakages and poor works created through private contractors, there is an edict that no contractors are to be used and that the work is to be done through the panchayat; that the total outlay has to keep at least to a 60:40 ratio in favour of expenditure on wages; often, that no *pucca* structures are to be constructed. The projects are to be constructed on public lands. But, further provisions have been added for reserving a proportion of the total outlay for investments on the private holdings of members of the SCs or STs. Work sites have to meet prescribed requirements which include the provision of minimum facilities for workers as well as a crèche if the demand is present. There are provisions for all relevant information concerning budget utilization, details of works and employment to be available, and the recently enacted Right to Information Act has often been used as a lever by civil society and solidarity organizations to investigate the probity and performance of schemes, though this has often met resistance, sometimes with violence. Interestingly, this massive initiative was systematically opposed for an extended period by bureaucrats, economists, and politicians on financial grounds. However, this resistance mysteriously evanesced, and the same antagonists speedily reinvented themselves as prime protagonists for the scheme. This conversion is not difficult to understand given the demonstrated national vote-catching power of this huge employment scheme, this process being aided by campaigns by various civil society networks and movements.

The rapid rollout of this huge programme is impressive. Inevitably problems have emerged, ranging from the expected problems of governance and corruption, to poor design, tardy bureaucracy and delays, and the neglect of the mandate to generate assets. In addition, other problems of omission have also been identified, primarily in terms of the exclusion biases of the scheme.

Alongside these problems, there are also huge positive outcomes. On any scale of reckoning, NREGS is a massive intervention, and given its catalytic role in stimulating rural mobilization and organization around development rights, it has been referred to by some as having democratic revolutionary potential.

The following section contextualizes each intervention in its contemporary strategic scenario and time frame. Thereafter, the section 'The Right to Employment: Some Comparisons' provides a comparative review in terms in four chosen domains: scale, financing, asset creation, and distributional outcomes. The section 'NREGA: Which Way Ahead?' focuses on the options confronting NREGA at the present conjuncture, while the final section provides some bottom lines to the comparison.

STRATEGIC CONTEXT, TRAJECTORIES, POINTS OF INTERVENTION

To appreciate the relative significance and potential of the two employment-related interventions, it is essential to view each against the respective macro-strategic contexts, and to identify each with regard to the timing of the intervention in terms of the dynamics of overall rural and national economic transformation.

Broadly, there was a strong similarity between China and India around 1950 with regard to inherited legacies, initial conditions, structural constraints, and state development imperatives.[2] Despite the profound systemic and institutional differences between the two countries, at an abstract level there is also a remarkably strong similarity between the overall strategic approach adopted by the planners in both countries, though descending from the realms of abstraction to the fields of reality, there was a sharp divergence in outcomes as processed by the different institutional and political systems.

Mahalanobis and Mao both privileged public sector-led industrialization with the capital goods sector as the driver; both were relatively inward-looking as far as foreign trade was concerned; both acknowledged the limited capacity of such capital-intensive growth to generate sufficient employment; in response, both had special strategic interventions to mitigate the employment deficit through programmes of small-scale rural industrialization, and through land reforms.

However, given their systemic political and institutional difference, these strategic similarities in the abstract translate into sharply contrasting realities on the ground. The focus on the capital goods sector, and the pace of industrialization was hugely greater in China than in India; there were deep agrarian reforms towards rapid collectivization in China, but redistributive land reforms were a nonstarter in India. The rural development strategy also provided a sharp contrast: China's countryside was dynamized by the twin engines of LA in the rural industrialization drive that collectivized, mechanized, and modernized traditional non-farm enterprises, whereas in India, the strategy of rural industrialization was essentially protective and defensive leading inexorably to deindustrialization and the atrophy of most tradable forms of the traditional rural non-farm economy in the face of competition from the modern manufacturing sector. As far as agriculture was concerned, the central government's investments were of broadly similar relative orders of magnitude, but the key difference lay in the relative weak accumulation processes within agriculture in India, whereas intra-rural accumulation was powerful and sustained in China. A relevant contrast here is also between the inter-sector terms of trade policies: China used this as a device to siphon off significant tranches of the expanding rural surplus, whereas in India, the government provided significant subsidies to the richer peasants that represented one of its political constituencies. Agriculture was perhaps also—for an initial period—underemphasized in India on account of the false presumption that the economy faced a glut in agricultural markets, rather than a structural, long-term shortage. So while economic modernization and accompanying structural changes were dramatic and transformational in China, the Indian economy, especially in the countryside, displayed much slower, sometimes indiscernible change. The downstream consequence of this was that the Chinese rural population was universally and structurally linked to the ownership and production structures, and drew their entitlements from this relationship, whereas in India, a vast section of the rural population had only tenuous links to the productive sector and could only manage a below-the-poverty-line existence through selling labour power, or through declining rural crafts and services.

The NREGS programme is thus clearly a strategic policy add-on, designed to cover part of the gap in mass entitlements left uncovered by past and current industrialization and growth strategies.

Thus, while LA in rural China was strategized, *ex ante*, as a driver of rural accumulation and development as part of an overall collectivist rural transformation process, NREGS in rural India has been introduced *ex post facto*, after decades of rural underdevelopment, essentially as a poverty reduction device, where asset creation plays a discordant second fiddle to the prime slogan of employment generation per se.

THE RIGHT TO EMPLOYMENT: SOME COMPARISONS

The comparative reflections are limited to four sets of issues: first, the relative scale of the two programmes; second, the issue of the financial constraint; third, their relative development impact as proxied by rural infrastructure asset creation; and fourth, some distributional aspects.

Scale

Rawski's diverse evidence would support an approximate estimate of a total of 8.3 billion workdays of LA in rural China in 1975, when the campaigns were in full flow (Rawski 1979). This compares with an employment level of 2.16 billion days of employment countrywide for NREGS in 2008–9 (Tankha 2009).

For India, NREGS generated an average of about six to eight days per rural worker for 2008–9; for China, the average number of days worked on rural capital construction was estimated to have been between 26 to 34 days per rural worker in 1975 (Rawski 1979, Table 4.10, p. 115).

The Chinese effort in 1975 stands at four times the level of the present Indian one. Of course, on the Indian side, the overall scale of NREGS (in terms of days of employment per household) stood, in 2008–9, at about one-half of the targeted maximum level; so if NREGS were to generate the maximum of 100 days per household engaged, the Chinese scale of effort, measured in days of work, would be about twice that in India.

However, this indicator provides an overly favourable depiction of the Indian initiative for several reasons. First, the earthwork moved per day per worker was significantly more in the Chinese case—this on account of the better human condition of the worker; greater degree of commitment; priority given to strong able-bodied young workers; and much greater use of accompanying tools and equipment. Second, in terms of the quality, productivity, or longevity of the assets produced, all indications suggest that China far outstripped India. Third, in China in this period, there was a huge increase in rural labour absorbed in other agricultural and non-agricultural activities; there is no Indian equivalent of this.

Put together, these factors suggest that the scale of the Chinese initiative was a significant multiple of the Indian intervention, arising both from a higher number of days of employment generated, and a higher volume and quality of productive assets created by such employment.

Financing

Consider first the Chinese case. The systems of wage payments and financing farm capital construction, water conservancy, and other similar labour-intensive rural infrastructure projects varied over the different phases of China's institutional transformations. From the point of view of the comparison with NREGS, the contrast with the collectivist period, lasting from 1959 till 1978 is the most relevant, as it highlights the implications of the institutional distance between the Indian and the Chinese countryside.

The rise of the communes changed much of this. While peasant labour for projects above the level of the commune was still necessary and paid for, there was an increased emphasis on LA within the commune and *hsien*. For the latter, now workers were paid in terms of the work point system, the strengths and weaknesses of which are discussed elsewhere. What is significant is that collectivization of land ownership instantly meant that now peasants were investing their labour on their collectively owned land—this was treated as other high-quality labour and rewarded in terms of work points, the value of which was determined subsequently, depending on the economic performance of the collective unit, usually the production team, to which the workers belonged. Collective institutions provided the framework, in general, for the self-financing of LA in the countryside.

In contrast, the Indian scenario is ostensibly dominated by the perennial stranglehold of the fiscal constraint. The fragmented nature of the agrarian structure and the prevalence of private property undermine the attractiveness and viability of making large-scale infrastructure investments by farmers themselves. And state-led programmes inevitably have to rely on hired labour, mostly of landless workers who need to be paid wages, thus setting up the need for prior resource mobilization for financing the scheme. Each case in a wave of initiatives dating back to the 1970s has wrestled with, and usually submitted, to this bottleneck. That NREGS has broken through this barrier reflects the emergence of a political democratic dividend, where incumbent governments see electoral advantage in such universal employment generation programmes.

Assets

China: Building Assets for Long-term Development

In the Chinese case, the fundamental motivation driving LA was rural development and transformation, laying the base for long-term growth within the collective institutional framework. In turn, this growth would serve as an instrument of poverty reduction. Such employment was thus perceived and harnessed as a form of rural accumulation, with poverty reduction as a concomitant component. The language was not one of poverty reduction, but of constructing a socialist transformation. LA took many forms and took place at several levels: water conservancy projects, ranging from micro interventions on collective farms to gigantic national schemes; land reclamation and levelling; prevention of soil erosion; tree planting; roads and bridges; culverts, drainage and irrigation systems, again from small to vast in scale; restoration and improvement of surface water bodies, ranging from massive reservoirs to the creation and stocking of fish ponds; buildings of various community facilities including school buildings; digging of wells, installation of water pumps and tube wells; development of rural power plants for local electrification. This vast socialist modernization drive transformed the countryside in parts of China though the results were unavoidably uneven, bearing in mind the geo-natural and other structural diversity within rural China. Irrespective of arguments over the efficiency aspects of labour utilization, the impact on agricultural productivity was sustained and significant.

There are two other major dimensions of this phenomenon. First, through a secular increase in the share of the stable agricultural yield areas, the intervention acted as a macro-insurance device in a country characterized by volatile environmental conditions. Second, the rolling wave of LA activities set up extensive backward linkages with other rural productive sectors:

> [R]ural industry can provide the tools and construction materials needed for water-control and land-development projects which in turn stimulate local demand for pumps, fertilizer, threshers, electricity, and other industrial goods. Increased consumption of industrial products stimulates nonindustrial components of the farming cycle. Assured water supplies raise the returns to labor-intensive construction projects such as levelling of land, terracing and construction of feeder ditches; and rising consumption of chemical fertilizers improves not only the crop yield but also the yield and nutrient content of green manures and plant wastes that provide the raw material for organic fertilizers. The dynamic process of rural development stemming from the introduction of collective organization and industrial inputs has enabled China's farm economy to support a growing population at low but modestly rising living standards with no increase in cultivated acreage. (Rawski 1979, p. 114)

This synergy and dovetailing stimulated the other engine of rural accumulation, rural industrialization—the early phases of which were closely interdependent with LA (see Table 2.1).

Table 2.1   Industrial Inputs into the Rural Economy, China, 1957–78

Year	Rural Power Horsepower Consumption (billion kWhs)	Small-scale Cement Output (million tonnes)	Chemical Fertilizer Output (million tonnes)	Total[a] per Cultivated Hectare
1957	0.1	–	0.8	0.01
1962	1.6	1.6	2.8	0.07
1965	3.2	5.4	7.6	0.10
1975	14.4	27.7	28.8	0.54
1978	27.0	36.0[b]	48.0	0.87

Source: Extracted from Rawski (1979, Table 4–3, p. 80).
Notes: [a] Irrigation and drainage equipment plus tractors plus power tillers; [b] 1977.

Rawski emphasizes the role of the communes in this dynamic development process:

> [T]he communes that succeeded these early cooperatives have occupied a significant role in the process of labor absorption ... Water conservancy and greater attention to animal husbandry, horticulture, and forestry are aspects of agricultural intensification that owe their existence to rural collectivization. Local industry requires administration and organization of both production and distribution—and, for machinery, or maintenance and repair work as well. This industry is another component of China's rural development program that appears virtually inseparable from collectivization. (Rawski 1979, p. 142)

There have, inevitably, been a fair number of doubting Toms and Peters,[3] quick to spotlight failed white elephant projects (of which there were surely some) and widespread local experiments that failed, wasting the labour invested (of which there were surely many). 'Do these reports, which recall the excesses of the Great Leap Forward, merely reflect the inevitable weak points in a system whose decision-making units number in the millions? Or is it possible that a high incidence of defective management in agriculture has significantly retarded China's agricultural growth? A review of available evidence tends to support the first view' (Rawski 1979, p. 140). Such professional doubters of collective institutional arrangements need also to address the evidence on the remarkable transformation of the countryside, even after due allowance is made for the availability and reliability of statistics. The proof of the pudding remains as always in the eating.

Consider first a micro-level account which provides some texture of the local processes unleashed. In their account of Yangyi Commune, Crook and Crook (1979 [1966], pp. 93–4) report on local progress of LA works in the bad years:

> Throughout the county, from the summer of 1959 to that of 1960, 480 large and small water conservation and irrigation projects were carried out. In addition to the four Zhang channels, 9 reservoirs (including Yangyi's Long Sea) and over 900 ponds were dug, as well as 7546 storage tanks to trap rainwater. Many gulleys were dammed—at intervals, from top to bottom—to form giant, widening staircases, 1,930,000 'fish-scale pits' were made for fruit trees and general afforestation. The number of power pumps rose from 38 to 93, and in 45 places the old-style water-wheels were set up in series, one above the other, to raise water uphill from 30 to 60 metres. The result of all this activity was that the proportion of irrigated land in the county was increased by over 69 per cent and altogether 88 per cent of the erosion areas was estimated to have been brought under control.

Ideological doubters would wish to dismiss this as the proverbial single swallow. But, variations of this story were repeatedly recorded across the countryside; and they added up to a massive aggregate effect, as inferred by Rawski (1979):

> Each winter-spring season, tens of millions of people braved the biting wind and snow and worked on irrigation projects. They raised and reinforced 1,000 kilometers of dykes ... Several thousand rivers and tributaries were dredged ... freeing more than 6.6 million hectares of low-lying land from the threat of flooding and water logging. At the same time the inhabitants went in for water conservancy and other farm improvement projects, concentrating on fighting drought. Reservoirs and terraced fields were built and trees planted on the hilly areas ... to prevent soil erosion. Wells and ditches were dug on the plains and alkali leached from the soil, all of which involved a tremendous amount of work. By 1970, however, the three provinces were in the main self-sufficient in grain, while their record output in 1973 was 2.5 times that of ... 1949, and an increase of 16,500 million

kilograms over 1965. (Rawski, quoting official Chinese sources, 1979, p. 110)

India: Providing Employment for Short-term Poverty Alleviation

The Indian experience of NREGS follows a dramatically, and sadly, different trajectory. At this stage of the programme, it is plausibly arguable that NREGS is fundamentally about guaranteeing employment for short-term poverty alleviation without any serious credible attempt at prioritizing the construction of rural infrastructure. The latter is the functional device through which employment is generated, but the primary focus remains on the provision of employment rather than on the intermediate step of creating productive rural assets. The two aspects simply do not stand on an even footing and do not enjoy similar attention or priority.

It is legally prescribed that employment is to be generated through the process of the construction of productive assets. If indeed NREGS was following these directions scrupulously, there would be assets to show, and show off, at the end of every project line. There is a widespread acknowledgement, even amongst government circles, that the present ground reality is a far cry from this optimal state. There are several underlying contributory factors.

First, the maximum limit of 100 days of employment per household often interferes with the requirements of the creation of productive assets. There are reports of works stopping, of projects remaining unfinished, or not being taken up at all due to this stipulation.

Second, the prescribed minimum ratio of 60:40 for wage and non-wage expenditure of the project budget tends to rule out projects that involve constructing assets that need significant non-labour inputs, thereby ruling out very many long-term productive assets and limiting the choice to *kutcha* assets that are not designed or expected to survive a monsoon. There are indications that some state governments actually call for an even greater tilt in favour of wage expenditure, clearly prioritizing the objective of short-term poverty reduction over long-term investment and growth. For an increased focus on assets the government would either have to raise additional funds, or accept a reduced employment impact; neither option is particularly palatable.

Third, the formal exclusion of all contractors from the construction process effectively transfers the technical task of the design and construction of projects to the village panchayats, which are ill equipped to cope with the technical, logistical, and governance complexities of such projects. This requirement would also probably have a regressive impact, in that the weaker panchayats in the poorer areas would be the ones with relatively weaker capacity to step into the shoes of professional contractors.

Fourth, there appears to be lack of clarity about the status of the assets created, in terms of ownership and/or usufruct rights, or in terms of the responsibility for maintenance. Earthwork projects are notoriously difficult to keep alive anyway, as the extensive experience of the watershed development programmes demonstrates; when responsibilities are unassigned, unaccepted, or unenforceable, the longevity of the assets is seriously truncated.

Fifth, construction of productive assets on private property belonging to the members of SC/ST communities may not be sufficiently effective since it is unclear how much SCs/STs own and whether such assets will be profitable. Also, co-financing of these projects may trigger a debt trap for poor SC/ST households.

Sixth, scattered and environmentally compromised settlements and communities with low population densities are unlikely to be able to come together on a sufficient scale to create the kinds of assets that might be necessary for their rejuvenation.

Seventh, thus far, the greatest emphasis of governments as well as independent civil society solidarists is on governance gaps in the employment and wage-payment processes of NREGS. This is clearly necessary and entirely understandable, in view of the acknowledged creativity of a range of private actors and public 'servants' to continually find new ways to siphon off money intended for the beneficiaries of the NREGS. But the other side of this coin is the general lack of concern for the quality, sustainability, utilization, and impact—both in growth and distributional terms—of the assets created.

Eighth, there is a group of political economy factors that could go some way in explaining the stepchild treatment given to the asset creation function of NREGS. Assets do not vote, workers do. The government seems to have learnt the lesson that the way to a citizen's vote is through employment. Earlier roadblocks set up against NREGS by the czars of financial bureaucracy were quickly dismantled by converted politicians, and the scheme extended to all districts of the country on improved terms. The special provisions for NREGS investment on SC/ST private land, an exception to the rule, are open to plausible interpretation in the same political frame. Going through panchayats seems right, though the purchase of the poor on these bodies is questionable. There are extensive leakages reported, but the 'political economy' argument goes that these are function- ally necessary to underwrite the sustainability of the scheme—there has to be something in it for everyone. Perversely, roads that get washed away each monsoon would legitimize new road projects each year. Politicians would much prefer to be doling out employment funds—especially with frequent media opportunities—than worry- ing about monitoring asset quality deep in the countryside, a sure loser. All the while, various stakeholders insert their siphons into the NREGS value chain through well-oiled, finely crafted, institutionally embedded devices. One recent field study estimates that as much as 30–40 per cent was diverted in leakages through the PC (or percent- age system) through which bribes were collected and shared all the way up the chain to the block or higher levels.[4] There is also some talk of popular local capture, rather than just old-fashioned elite capture, of the scheme: 'in such a situation, the village leadership, along with the villagers and local functionaries, extract all it possi- bly can from the government, e.g., by over-reporting of work done and sharing out the benefits' (Tankha 2009, p. 23, citing Banerjee 2009). After all, panchayat leaders also need to get re-elected, not just parliament leaders.

Distribution

China: Collective Efforts for Collective Gains?

Peasants contributed high-productivity labour in rural non-farm activities, or hard manual labour into LA projects, but were paid in work points at an implicit wage rate that was linked to the average consumption level of the peasant households of the unit concerned. As a result, financial surpluses earned by the rural non-farm (RNF) units accumulated almost automatically and were recycled with their dynamic multipliers generating locally egalitarian growth. LA has been criticized, wrongly, by many as an example of corvée, or coerced, unpaid labour. This is patently incorrect, since the labour invest- ment of households in any one year on a productive project earned its returns once the project's benefits came on line after completion, and these benefits accrued to each and every member of the unit. While there were some white elephants, and while admittedly many unsound schemes might have wasted some effort, no serious scholar or observer of rural China of the period could fail to register the remarkable impact of such a massive bootstraps type of operation. It catalyzed the growth process and launched the rural development process. From the point of view of rural households, this was additional work for additional income, not just from the LA project, but also from the indirect returns that came from the rural industrialization that it enabled. Within this, mechanization was undertaken when it contributed to overall productivity, and labour displacement was not an issue, again, since the benefits were shared out. This process, which I call the mass-mobilization mode of transformation, was essentially fired by ideological zeal and commitment, though as mentioned, within the micro-level collectivist units there were well-thought out co-operative payment systems with a robust economic logic for that stage of development. The process was locally self-financing, and hence was both sustainable for an extended period and also capable of nationwide replication without the usually throttling precondition of pre-financing of such investments by the government. It was akin to the workings of the Lewis model of accumulation and growth working within the collectivist institutional framework of the people's commune.

Powerful as the collective wage payment system was, it was not free from internal tensions and contradictions typically involving the recognition, assignment, measurement, or valuation of labour and work, and the institutional mechanisms of local governance related to these; for example, between distribution according to work or need or between workers and non-workers; between strong and weak workers; between workers and peasants; between male and female workers; between the units within a commune; or between communes; between regions; or between sectors. At the local level, at the end of the day, these were mostly local contradictions within the people untarnished by corruption, exclusion, or exploitation, and as such capable of resolution through the dialectic of localized politics of the collective within the wider parameters of higher-level rule or norm-making. With hindsight, they bear little resemblance, if any, to the distributional, exclusionary, and exploitative attributes that characterize labour processes in contemporary China now, or in India then and now.

Another critique of collective labour utilization was that it distorted the structure of incentives thereby generating inefficiencies, both in the form of the undersupply as well as the oversupply of labour. Lin (1990) has emphasized the disincentive effect arising from the fact that peasants could not voluntarily exit from collective labour and farming arrangements. This locking-in would break the link between effort and reward, and thus create disincentives and also raise the likelihood of free-riding. A second type of disincentive effect is deemed to have arisen from the compression of the range of work points for a day's work. These usually varied between 7 and 10 and it is argued that better workers would be discouraged by the narrowness of the range. A third disincentive effect, it is argued, was due to the fact that the distribution of income within the commune was partly reckoned on the basis of needs, and only partly on work. The more politically advanced the commune, the higher would be the share of the distribution done on the basis of needs, the more egalitarian would be the outcome; and, it is argued, the greater would be the disincentive effect on the stronger households and workers.

On the other side, the fact that LA labour days were rewarded at the average wage (or consumption) level of the unit would encourage individual workers to offer themselves for LA work, resulting in an oversupply of labour at the level of the collective as a whole, driving down the marginal and average returns to labour inputs.

These two tendencies could come together and suggest that excessive labour was nominally offered to LA projects while at the same time workers would underwork on the schemes.

To this could be added another frequently made criticism: that the selection and parameters of LA projects were negatively influenced by the desire of local decision-makers to follow superior higher-level edicts on LA and by their wish to be seen to be politically in line. Taken together, these three effects would imply that LA over-absorbed labour; that such labour was inefficient; and that the programme was characterized by adverse project selection. There is a body of literature that has made one or more of these charges.

However, other readings of the experience are plausibly supported by available evidence, and offer specific responses to these criticisms. Indeed, the exit option for individual peasants was closed. This might have been attractive for some rich peasants, but the land reform and collectivization put paid to that. Given the ground realities, the critique then implies that such peasants would have shirked work and underperformed. This is partly an issue of supervision, and households with landed backgrounds were perhaps especially under close scrutiny, making such free-riding more difficult. Of course, these households could withhold labour up to a point, but this would lead directly to fewer work points earned resulting in a reduced household income; this would be tantamount to cutting one's nose to spite one's face. The second issue of a narrow spread of work points for a day's work is also complex. Even if it is assumed that all peasants were individual maximizers, a narrow spread could create some dampening of spirits for upper-end workers, but would simultaneously generate additional enthusiasm for a larger majority of weaker workers. It is also worth noting that work was often remunerated on piece rates. On the final issue of bad project selection, answers have to be found at the empirical level. While it is undoubtedly true that mistakes, some of them on a grand scale, were made, it is necessary to come to a balanced judgement about the totality over an extended time frame. The evidence on the pace and pattern of rural infrastructure development, and the simultaneous processes of accelerated agricultural intensification and rural industrialization confirm the flawed basis of this critique. It surely applied in part, but not to the phenomenon as a whole.

There remains the issue of whether such heavy inputs of labour were provided voluntarily, or extracted through a coercive framework. Views vary here reflecting the ideological predilection of the viewer. Certainly there are myriad accounts of the zeal and fervour of peasants and workers engaged in the process of social transformation and economic modernization, no doubt motivated by exhortations from a revolutionary leadership; see, for instance, the evocative eyewitness accounts of episodes of LA provided by Crook and Crook (1979 [1966], pp. 91–2).

Not many free-riders are to be found in most of these accounts, nor many prisoners with dilemmas. In underemphasizing, instead of underscoring, the motivation of political solidarity, the game-theoretic critiques of collectivist organizational forms have too often been barking up the wrong tree. Their fallacy is the assumption that though peasants had been part of the revolution and its transformation, their personal and world outlooks remained selfish and 'peasantist', and had not been transformed by the historic change of which they were prime movers. This curious construction could potentially apply to a section of the rural population that lost out in the revolution, but the assertion that this was true of the rural masses in general is untenable.

Even acknowledging the willingness and intensity of peasant effort, the question arises: What were the returns to such inputs? Was it all worth it? And, for whom?

It is arguable that while there was steadily more rice pudding, the peasants' share of it was meagre, and the price they had to pay for it in terms of hard work was very high. Between 1957 and 1975, Rawski (1979, pp. 128–9) estimates that while the total input of agricultural labour rose by 125 per cent, the national level of average agricultural productivity declined by 15–36 per cent, implying that the rate of decline of marginal labour productivity could only have been greater in significant parts of the country. Was the policy of 'manicuring the countryside' misguided? Was this worth it? Was it avoidable? Were there alternative paths? Resorting to counterfactuals is often the last resort of the ideologue aided by hindsight. Nevertheless, for such a critique, it would need to be demonstrated that there were alternative options for the productive absorption of such vast volumes of raw non-agriculturally skilled underemployed labour, and this is well nigh impossible to demonstrate. Besides, the double standard applied should not be underplayed: a peasant who keeps working on the farm regardless of the very low marginal rate of return to effort is lauded as a survival device displaying ingenuity and skill. But when a group of peasants display a similar behaviour pattern *collectively*, it seems to get labelled not as a demonstration of shared resilience but of collective inefficiency. This tendency spotlights the ideological element in the critique of collectivist strategies.

Even while recognizing the transformative contribution of LA to the construction of rural collectivist economy, it is necessary to ask what kind of deal it turned out to be, in the end, for the cohort of the peasantry and its descendent generations that provided the sheer raw labour. Puerile critiques of LA—and Chinese rural collectivism more generally—have tended to challenge voluntaristic interpretations of the zeal, commitment, and sacrifices of the peasantry in the midst of the era of red-hot revolutionary fervour. In doing so, they have relied on game-theoretic constructions based on the premise that the revolution had left peasant mentality untouched, and that the collective was an enforced arrangement of individual peasant households each seeking to maximize their respective benefits by subverting the game as much as they could. It is not overly difficult to refute this ideological thesis through empirical reference to the known realities of the rural transformation as widely documented by myriad observers.

A more cogent critique lies elsewhere and calls for a historical, not an axiomatic choice-theoretic, evaluative perspective. While accepting in full the huge sacrifices and contributions of the peasantry to collective rural development, and through that to the dramatic economic achievements at the national level, a query could be raised whether and to what extent these contributions were requited. What were the long-term benefits that might have accrued to the peasantry? Here, it might be argued with some justification that the peasantry could have been short-changed. There is a general consensus that low prices for agricultural produce were an instrumental device used by Chinese planners for transferring rural surplus into the non-agricultural sectors. In the context of Soviet industrialization, Chayanov had argued in favour of retaining the self-exploiting peasant mode on the grounds that it was the most efficient form of agricultural production, and had reconciled this with the macro-strategy by pointing to the possibility of using the terms of trade to transfer the surplus from the peasant into the modern, socialist, industrial sector. For him, primary socialist accumulation was entirely compatible with the retention of the peasant mode within the rural sector. Chinese collectivism, in one real sense, offers a similar configuration with the key difference that the self-exploiting peasantry is substituted by self-exploiting rural collectives. While the rural labour process was profoundly egalitarian and collectivist in nature, and the socialist rule of distribution was largely respected within the communes, there was one crucial loose variable: the money value of the work point. This depended overwhelmingly on the terms of trade set by the planners keen on accelerating primary socialist accumulation (PSA) and socialist large-scale industrialization. As a result, the valuation placed on rural labour was exceedingly low, which significantly eroded, or precluded, the capacity of the peasantry to share in the gains of development. The process gave the willingly toiling peasantry a post-dated cheque. Viewed with the benefit of hindsight, it appears that this cheque was never really honoured in full in the post-Reform period—as is suggested by the fate of the peasantry in the post-Reform period. Inter-sector and worker–peasant inequalities have widened dramatically, and the peasantry finds itself still labouring at the bottom of the pyramid. It is perhaps such readings of the history of the pre- and post-Reform periods that raise uncomfortable issues about the intrinsic, as against the instrumental, use of peasant collectivism in the strategy of national transformation. Would such disappointing outcomes have emerged if the old socialist path had persisted? Or can one ascribe this short-changing to the non-socialist values of the post-Reform period of transition to capitalism? Such counterfactuals can pose questions, but cannot answer them.

India: Are the Poor Subsidizing the Rich?

Virtually all discussions of the benefits arising from NREGS limit themselves to the construction phase of the project concerned. However, since each project is intended to create productive infra-structure, which should be expected to generate future flows of ben-efits, it is essential that any assessment of benefits also includes the operational phase of the project concerned.

Consider first the construction phase for NREGS. The scheme is universal for those above 18 years of age. As such the exclusions are voluntary, except for those that cannot engage in the hard manual labour demanded. The wages paid are supposed to be linked to the prevailing minimum wage rates, though there are exceptions, with some states trying to get by with lower offers. One adult or more of a household can claim up to a total of 100 person-days of employment at this rate. This payment can only cover a small part of the notional poverty line income for a household; this payment is also likely to overstate the net addition to the household's income since some of this new employment might be at the expense of other less-well remuner-ated work that is given up. Furthermore, it has been argued that much rural labour might well be caught in the poverty–nutrition trap, where the earnings of labour are too low to provide the nutrition necessary to maintain the capacity to work at the same level.[5] Yet, these factors notwithstanding, it is reasonable to expect that NREGS will make a significant impact on the incidence of rural poverty, especially in view of the universal scale of the scheme. However, there is great variability in the performance and governance quality of schemes across, and within, states. There are extensive reports of households not receiving their cards, of not getting employment within the stipulated time frame, of not getting subsequent legally mandated compensation for such delays, of not getting the 100 days of work, of not receiving the minimum wage, and of not receiving the wages in time.

This weakness becomes all the more evident when evaluating the *operational* phase of the project. A massive limitation here is that there appears to be little systematic emphasis on the construction of productive long-term assets. This implies that future streams of benefits generated by the schemes are likely to be relatively limited. An indirect approach can be used to confirm the potential significance of the operational phase, to demonstrate the very significant lost potential in NREGS, and to show that when productive assets are indeed created, the benefits generated by these would accrue disproportionately as windfalls not to the poor but to the relatively more prosperous rural households.

Data from an International Labour Organization (ILO)-funded programme in Bangladesh,[6] covering rural infrastructure creation, revealed that the poor households that formed the target group received about one-quarter of the overall benefits generated; three-fourths went to the non-target groups as windfalls! This was largely due to the skewed distribution of benefits accruing in the *operational* phase of the infrastructure. This is a shocking result, and raises uncomfortable issues in the context of NREGS in India, where also the focus is on the *beneficiaries* in the implementation phase while disregarding the pattern of incidence of the stream of direct benefits generated by the scheme in subsequent years.

The wage component from these schemes is not an adequate or equitable benefit for the poor: such as these are, they are sporadic, shifting, and not sustainable livelihood sources for even those households that can participate in them. But the total streams of benefits, including those to non-target groups, could be quite considerable, especially if the schemes are productive. The question is: how can the poor tap into this wider river, instead of being restricted to the fitful trickle-down flows that come their way? There is no automatic internal circuit that recycles the benefit streams into payments for past labour, and investments for future investments.

As it is, the dice is loaded against the poor working on such schemes. There is evidence to argue that the caloric value of the returns per day for performing hard manual labour on these schemes is much lower than, possibly as low as about one-half, the energy expended in earning these returns.[7]

Clearly new forms of institutional contracts are needed through which the working poor who create these public assets can also claim some version of ownership or lease rights which give them a rightful claim to the non-wage component of the value-added generated by the infrastructure. Such institutional arrangements have to be supplemented with direct and indirect financial instruments and devices that enable charges to be levied and recovered from the landowner or other groups which have thus far been receiving windfalls, either locally, or through more indirect higher level fiscal circuits. In turn, this requires a new kind of partnership between stakeholders. The existing arrangements lead to few productive investments, but suit everyone: the politician who gets publicity, the contractor who gets the money for low quality construction, the civil servant, the landowners who get something for nothing, and the poor, who at least get something out of it. That the quality and the longevity of the scheme do not bother any one of the stakeholders too seriously is then hardly a matter of surprise. Resources disappear into a black hole of expediency. But other ways are possible. In this regard, there is a stark contrast with the case of Chinese LA where the emphasis was on productive assets, and where the downstream benefits in the operational phase were shared by all households within the egalitarian distributional mechanisms of rural collectives.

NREGS thus contains complex distributional impulses: some of these, that is, the short-term impact in the construction phase, would be poverty alleviating; others, especially but not only in the operational phase, could well be distributionally regressive whether through local capture, or the regressive impact of inflationary tendencies generated by NREGS outlays unaccompanied by productivity increases in agriculture.

NREGA: WHICH WAY AHEAD?

Transfers or Transformation? Alternative Scenarios

Looking ahead, consider three alternative hypothetical configurations for the evolution of NREGS.

Low Growth, Pro-labour

The first is one where there is a high emphasis on employment genera-tion, with little, or ineffective, attention to the creation of sustainable productive assets. Here there are few windfalls for others outside the scheme since there are few local productive externalities. The inter-vention is low growth, but pro-poor distributionally.

High Growth, Pro-land

The second is one where there is a combined emphasis on employment generation as well as on the extensive creation of productive assets, which provide substantial windfalls to non-workers proportionately reflecting the asset ownership of the recipients of these windfalls. The intervention is high growth, but it is less pro-poor, and indeed most likely to be pro-rich, that is, distributionally disequalizing, though still poverty alleviating.

High Growth, Pro-labour

The third is a hypothetical institutional specification where the workers in the programme are also the owners of the assets, and/or claimants of a substantial share of the downstream value addition created by the productive assets generated by the labour of the workers. In this scenario, the intervention is high growth, and pro-poor distributionally.

NREGS seems at present to be languishing in the first scenario. The Bangladeshi Rural Public Works (RPW) project alluded to earlier provides a clear case of the second scenario. The Chinese people's commune is a powerful illustration of the third.

The relatively low prioritization thus far of asset creation in NREGS raises some wider issues about the official purposes and lost potential of the intervention. If assets are not to be a prime objective, the ques-tion arises why poor persons should be made to work to earn their incomes on useless schemes. Why not hand out cash grants, perhaps using the new smart card unique identifier system. Indeed, a lot of red tape, administrative costs, leakages, and wastages would be prevented, and a much higher proportion of the total outlay might get to their deserving destinations.

Three responses are necessary to this valuable, if rhetorical, question. First, some might argue even more cynically that the raison d'être for the massive scheme is precisely the façade of asset creation that allows huge leakages. Second, cash transfers, while injecting effective demand into the system, are unlikely to induce sufficient supply response from an agrarian sector constrained by poor infrastructure and a fragmented pattern of small holdings. The result of such 'primitive Keynesianism' is likely to be food price inflation, which would simply redistribute income from the employed and the unemployed to the newly employed. Third, if the resources mobilized were used up in cash transfer programmes, it would become well nigh impossible to raise further monies in a second round for infrastructural development.

Needless to say, each of these responses is contentious. The proponents of unconditional universal cash grants tend to argue that such cash injection would stimulate demand in the countryside, which in turn would induce supply-side responses in various sectors, education, health, as well as rural productive investment. This argument overlooks the critical role of rural infrastructure in enabling effective agricultural supply response, and also tends to ignore the likelihood and consequences of inflation. Nor is it plausible to assume that a little money in the pockets of the poor would induce the effective provision of adequate health and educational, water and sanitation, and housing and environmental services.

The only serious alternative is to focus on long-term asset creation that contributes to rural productivity. This would effectively shift the supply curve outwards and contain or postpone inflationary tendencies. However, if such growth is to be distributionally progressive, other institutional interventions are a precondition and mechanisms must be found to (in)vest sufficient property rights over new productive assets with the rural labour which creates them, thereby giving labour a right to a share in the non-wage components of the longer-term income flows generated downstream by these new infrastructural works.

Is there policy space for meaningful choice, or is each specification an outcome of a path-dependent process the constraints which limit the possibility of switching successfully from an inferior pathway or configuration to a superior one? At present, the NREGA movement is driven by political constituencies with solidaristic motivations, but implemented and managed by those who have perhaps the more limited political objective of being returned to power at the next elections. For this purpose, the maximand is the employment effect. This converges with the immediate concerns of the solidarity group, and as such, both stakeholders are reluctant, in the short term (but is there ever a long term?), to emphasize asset creation as an important objective. Indeed, a justification could well be, ironically, that the assets would primarily benefit the non-target groups, as we have shown earlier. So the only meaningful switch to generate is from the first to the third scenarios. This calls, perhaps, to crossing a bridge too far for either camp—though a movement in this direction should not be ruled out. A lot of hurdles—conceptual, logistical, administrative, and political—would need to be tackled to realize the third scenario.

Possibilities and Imperatives

There are a range of extensions and improvements that could be under consideration, if not quite on the anvil.

NREGS is a young programme, and as such retains flexibilities. There are five domains in which NREGS needs to change its ways, widen its ambit, and realign its objectives.

The first issue is governance reform. This can scarcely be achieved by fiat through the legal framework and more regulatory devices. Much depends on the degree of prior labour mobilization and organization and on the functioning and accountability of local-level democracy, though how this is to be achieved in the face of endemic local elite capture is not straightforward.

The second concerns gaps and potential improvements to ensure decent work conditions at project work sites. How should women's participation be dovetailed with childcare facilities: through facilities at work sites, or by strengthening the existing network of *anganwaris*? How should the norms of work be revised to take account of the bodily and health status of workers, especially women?

A third group of issues addresses the exclusionary tendencies of the scheme. Exclusion is inherent in any scheme where manual labour is the key ingredient. Should it be extended to less demanding forms of work in local services that could include less mobile or physically enabled persons to claim an equivalent entitlement to employment?

Indeed, should the scheme be extended spatially to urban areas? Clearly, accepting such inclusive expansion of the scope would also alter the identity of the programme from a rural employment guarantee scheme to a universal livelihood assurance programme, with all the myriad ramifications this would entail.

The fourth area of concern focuses on the crucial dimension of rural capital formation and seeks to maximize the transformative power of NREGS by ensuring that the employment generated also leads to the creation of sustainable productive infrastructure. This requires tweaking various counter-productive design stipulations and implementation guidelines of NREGS; the creation of a logistical and technical capacity for meeting the engineering requirements of such a massive intervention; but, above all, it requires a reaffirmation of the prioritization of the role of asset creation in the first place. At present, the scheme has lapsed through administrative and political expediency into an employment and income transfer programme. How this dimension is handled could have fundamental implications for the dynamic impact and wider transformative capacity of the programme as a whole.

Finally, it is necessary to assess the scope, design, implementation, and financing of NREGS within a dynamic macroeconomic framework. This spotlights important questions about the incremental employment impact of the schemes, and on the knock-on effects on other economic activities and sectors through labour market effects released by the scheme. More generally, there is a need to conceptualize and implement it as a full-scale, long-term macro intervention in the form of social investment, and not just a treadmill of perennial transfers in the form of social consumption. The focus needs to be on the wider transformative potentialities of this massive initiative, not just on its short-term poverty reduction role. There could be a historic opportunity here that needs to be grasped, not to be missed by default.

COMPARATIVE OUTCOMES: THE BOTTOM LINE

The two cases, each in their respective time and systemic frames, provide divergent objectives, processes, and outcomes. In revolutionary China, the LA campaign was a trigger and prime example of the mass mobilization mode of transformation; it was a massive intervention at an early stage of socialist transition and served as a prime driver of rural development; labour was converted into productive investment, and the benefits of this accrued to all through collective institutions. In sharp contrast, in capitalist India, NREGS has emerged as an *ex post* poop scooper for the employment and livelihood deficits that even high growth rates have been unable to correct; the initiative serves as a secondary compensatory device addressing some of the failures of Indian structure-cum-strategy. While ostensibly it is directed at the generation of productive assets, ground realities indicate that it has functioned thus far largely as a relief employment programme with limited dynamic impact, dynamic development potential, or any significant gains to the workers beyond the wages received. If the Chinese scheme generated long-term social investment, the Indian one dispenses short-term social consumption.

Years ago, Joan Robinson pointed out how the system of private property served as an acute constraint to effective rural development in the Indian countryside. The converse was demonstrated dramatically by the Chinese case.

Given deep path dependence, there are no direct lessons to cherry-pick from the Chinese experience and transplant into Indian reality. But there can be productive insights which spotlight key constraints. In this spirit, it could be fruitful to identify and investigate the viability of interventions and processes that could modify, overcome, or bypass the institutional barrier in the Indian countryside. In the distinct context of debates over systems convergence, Tinbergen offered the approach of functional socialism, where private property was stipulated to constitute a package of specific rights, and where specific problematic rights could be addressed through democratic constitutional means, thereby introducing malleability into the system of private property. Yet others have hypothesized possibilities of inducing institutional change through collective action within a spontaneous or evolutionary framework. At the present Indian conjuncture, some of these innovative possibilities need investigation and creative processing to validate their viability. Without success in the crucial institutional domain, it is likely to prove impossible to convert transfer payments into transformational investments that collectively begin to renew the productive potential of the countryside in an egalitarian fashion. The issue of property rights needs to be confronted frontally.

This invites a final reflection on the political dynamics and drivers of NREGS. The Indian political conjuncture could be viewed as a democratic moment, with the imperatives of electoral democratic politics providing the incentive to would-be political rulers to heed the needs of the people, more than two-thirds of whom live below the 'two-dollars-a-day' line. On the other side, the elite have a stranglehold on resources and finances. Large-scale, expensive, zero-sum games tend not to do too well in such a scenario. Sharing, spillovers, externalities, and dynamic indirect effects open up non-zero sum spaces that make seemingly financially burdensome interventions politically as well as economically attractive. Of course, the immediate non-zero possibilities can come via predation, through the leakages and corruption that are dished out on the regular gravy train. The alternative, more challenging, route involves converting zero-sum transfer programmes into non-zero sum productive transformative interventions by addressing the underlying structural and institutional constraints. This calls for political maturity working within wider and wiser social and temporal horizons. There are elements within the contemporary political configuration that seek and would settle for the instant gratifications of easy populism; but in the current class configuration of Indian society, there are also more mature constituencies that probably recognize the need to break the Ricardian impasse and to embrace radical rural institutional innovation, even if instrumentally, to ensure greater economic and political sustainability for the ongoing rapid growth process. Which way will it go? The bottom line of the comparison comes down to a tussle between belief and relief. Belief, in China, has been a marathon runner; relief, in India, keeps making false starts.

NOTES

1. For an insightful documentary account of the Chinese process of rural transformation in the era of high collectivism, see Selden (1979); for detailed analysis of the Chinese experience before and after the reforms, see Saith (1987, 1993, 1995, 2001, pp. 90–4), and Griffin and Saith (1981); for scholarly accounts of labour accumulation processes, see Vermeer (1977) and Nickum (1977, 1978) amongst others.

2. These are addressed in detail in Saith (2008) and Saith (2010).

3. See, for instance, the persistent and holistic critique of collective agriculture, including especially Chinese rural communes, by Nolan (1983, 1988), Watkins (n.d.), and Lin (1990, 1999) amongst others.

4. For a summary discussion, see Tankha (2009, pp. 19–20).

5. The critical comments of Nitish Kumar, chief minister of Bihar, have relevance in this regard: 'Workers are expected to remove 110 cubic feet of earth in a day. That is too much work. The guidelines have been fixed in Delhi; the States have had no say in determining the work norms. The authorities in Delhi blindly tell us to allot earthwork without understanding that this is not possible everywhere.'

6. The source of the information used is a study by Mahabub Hossain and Assaduzzaman, discussed in Saith (1992, Chapter 4).

7. For a summary discussion on this aspect, see ILO (2004, Chapter 14, pp. 371–2).

REFERENCES

Banerjee, A. 2009. 'A Job Half Done', *Hindustan Times*, 14 August.

Crook, I. and D. Crook. 1979 [1966]. *The First Years of Yangyi Commune*. London: Routledge and Kegan Paul.

Griffin, K. and A. Saith. 1981. *Growth and Equality in Rural China*. Singapore: Maruzen Asia.

ILO. 2004. *Economic Security for a Better World*. Report produced by the Socio-economic Security Programme. Geneva: ILO.

Lin, J.Y. 1990. 'Collectivization and China's Agricultural Crisis in 1959–1961', *Journal of Political Economy*, 98 (6): 1228–52.

———. 1999. 'China: Farming Institutions and Rural Development', in M. Meurs (ed.), *Many Shades of Red: State Policy and Collective Agriculture*, pp. 151–83. Lanham: Rowman and Littlewood.

Nickum, J.E. 1977. 'An Instance of Local Irrigation Management in China', *Economic and Political Weekly*, 12 (40, 1 October): 1714–16.

———. 1978. 'Labour Accumulation in China and Its Role Since the Cultural Revolution', *Cambridge Journal of Economics*, 2 (3, September): 273–86.

Nolan, Peter. 1983. 'De-Collectivisation of Agriculture in China, 1979–82: A Long-Term Perspective', *Economic and Political Weekly*, 18 (32, 6 August): 1395–1406.

———. 1988. *The Political Economy of Collective Farms: An Analysis of China's post-Mao Rural Reforms*. Cambridge: Polity Press.

Rawski, T.G. 1979. *Economic Growth and Employment in China*. Oxford: Oxford University Press for the World Bank.

Saith, A. 1987. 'Contrasting Experiences of Rural Industrialisation: Are the East Asian Success Transferable?' in Rizwanul Islam (ed.), *Rural Industrialisation and Employment in Asia*, pp. 241–304. New Delhi: ILO-ARTEP.

———. 1992. *The Rural Non-Farm Economy: Processes and Policies*. Geneva: ILO.

———. 'Chinese Rural Industrialization: Policy Perspectives and Emerging Problems', Working Paper, ARTEP-ILO, New Delhi.

Saith, A. 1995. 'From Collectives to Markets: Restructured Agriculture-Industry Linkages in Rural China: Some Micro-Level Evidence', *Journal of Peasant Studies*, 22 (2, January): 201–60.

——————. 2001. 'From Village Artisans to Industrial Clusters: Policy Agendas and Gaps in Indian Rural Industrialisation', *Journal of Agrarian Change*, 1 (1 January): 81–123.

——————. 2008. 'China and India: The Institutional Roots of Differential Performance', *Development and Change*, 39 (5, September): 723–58.

——————. 2010. 'India and China at Sixty: Convergence, Divergence, "Pervergence"', in I. Pande (ed.), *India, China: Neighbours, Strangers*, 48–67. New Delhi: Harper-Collins and India International Centre.

Selden, M. (ed.). 1979. *The People's Republic of China: A Documentary History of Revolutionary Change*. New York: Monthly Review Press.

Strong, A.L. 1964. *The Rise of the Chinese People's Communes—and Six Years After*. Peking: New World Press.

Tankha, A. 2009. 'NREGS and Rural Livelihood Promotion: Issues and Evidence', unpublished paper, 29 pages.

Vermeer, E.B. 1977. *Water Conservancy and Irrigation in China: Social, Economic and Agro-technical Aspects*. Leiden: Leiden University Press.

Watkins, T. n.d. 'The Control of the Huai River System in China', www.sjsu.edu/faculty/watkins/huairiver.htm (accessed 14 May 2012).

3

Government Policy and the Distribution of Grain

Revisiting the Reform of Agricultural Institutions in China and India

SHAILAJA FENNELL

The importance accorded to food grain security in China and India has changed over the last two decades as they continue to grow at 10 per cent a year and are emerging as global players. This growth rate has made them more confident in their economic ability and changed the state's perspective on its capacity to feed its population. In the early decades of national development, these two countries had serious concerns about their ability to ensure the food security of the nation. This initial concern is no longer apparent in national policy thinking as the rich and middle classes are now able to access food on national, even international markets, and the current relationship between procurement and distribution of grains is restricted to feeding the poor, often with a focus on the local access and affordability rather than on national levels of grain availability.[1]

This fundamental shift in national food grain policy has occurred within a context where international markets increasingly enter national food markets to meet the demand of the consumers in both high- and a growing number of middle-income countries, resulting in an increasing homogenization and commodification of food grains within national food grain systems (McMichael 2009). The increasing commercialization of national and sub-national agriculture that is now evident in developing countries has resulted in a reorganization of the agricultural system where there is now greater emphasis on supply conditions and how these can meet the growing demand for food grains in the international market.

In such a changed economic environment it is no longer adequate to calculate food availability in the national context from the total food grain levels in the country. It becomes important to gauge the capacity of public agricultural institutions to procure and distribute food grains and to be able to identify constraints that they face. It, therefore, behoves any current-day analysis to move beyond a review of food grain supply and distribution statistics and to undertake an examination of how current reform processes of agricultural institutions have affected procurement and distribution.

Expanding the analysis to include a study of the linkages in food supply through constituent agricultural supply chains permits a study of how agricultural production and distribution are affected by structural changes brought about by agricultural reforms. Food supply chains provide the pathways to move food grain from 'field to fork' and it is in the effectiveness of this delivery that institutional capacity can be identified. The ability to maintain the supply chain where each section of the chain performs its designated functions makes for adequate capacity and good logistics of an agricultural chain.

This chapter will begin with an examination of the changing contexts of food security in both countries and the implications for domestic reforms of agricultural institutions. A review will then be provided on how these reforms have impacted the ability of these countries to provide food grain availability to poorer sections of the population. This will be followed by the introduction of a supply chain methodology to map out how food grain procurement and distribution take place within the agricultural institutional framework in India and China. The existing supply chains in the agricultural sector will subsequently be reviewed to identify capacities and constraints in the supply chain. Finally, there will be a commentary on future implications of changes in the agricultural supply chain in both countries for food security and poverty reduction.

CHANGING CONTEXTS OF FOOD SECURITY

The world's two most populous countries, China and India, responsible for contributing a fourth and a fifth of the world's cereal production, have regarded food security as a major pillar of their national development plans since the late 1950s. The origins of food security can be traced to the growing concern about famines in both countries, linked to both increasing populations and stagnant food productivity levels. Hunger and malnutrition were widely prevalent in both countries in the previous century and consequently the ability to feed its people became the hallmark of an independent and powerful state. The importance of self-sufficiency in food grains has become a symbol of national independence for countries emerging from colonialism.[2]

India

The importance of having enough food to feed a rapidly growing population was a challenge that faced India from the outset of its national development. The discrepancy between food stocks availability and existing national demand increased on account of India's low levels of agricultural output through the 1950s. The gap widened in the second decade of independence, resulting in 16 per cent of the required food grain being imported in the mid-1960s (Acharya 2006).[3] The shortfall in food supply became a matter of national concern that India should not continue to be in a situation where it was forced to depend on foreign government aid to feed its population. The solution to this problem came in the form of the new technologies of high yielding varieties (HYVs) of rice and wheat that were to be the harbingers of plentiful food.

There was also a separate, standing, and pressing matter of improving the distribution of the existing food supplies across the country. The only institutional mechanism that was available for delivery of food in these early decades was that of emergency famine relief, introduced in the last years of the nineteenth century,[4] and supplemented by the fair-price shops that were introduced in 1942 as a measure to ration food supplies during World War II.[5] The need to provide for a more institutionalized system of food procurement and distribution was met by the promulgation of the Food Corporation Act (1964).

The Act set out the procedures for procurement of food grains with the central government having overall responsibility for the total procurement of food grains and allocation across states. It is the central government that determines the Central Issue Price (CIP) and the state government has the responsibility for the procurement price for the state procurement, the commodities it procures and distributes as well as the final price of issue. While both procurement and distribution are clearly identified in the sections of the Act, the primary concern in the mid-1960s with a falling output level in 1965 and 1966 was to increase food supply and the equity requirements subordinate to the concerns about supply constraints.[6] The Public Distribution System (PDS), was formally introduced in the mid-1960s as part of the policy objectives of the Act and with the primary objective of ensuring a functional distribution system for food grains so as to support the vulnerable sections of society (Suryanarayana 1995).

The procurement price rose between the 1970s and the 1980s and largely benefited the growing class of rich farmers who were able to harness the green revolution technologies to good effect.[7] The collection and storage of individual grain was the responsibility of the Food Corporation of India (FCI). It was the FCI that was responsible for (a) the PDS and food assistance programmes; (b) creating buffer stocks, and (c) open market operations.[8] While the procurement mechanism was successful in increasing the public procurement and holdings of food grains, this was not the case for the public distribution mechanism. The ability of the PDS to deliver food to households BPL, particularly in situations of drought and natural disasters that trigger hunger-related deaths, has been limited, even reduced in more recent decades.[9]

The lacklustre performance of the state distribution mechanism was addressed in the restructuring of the Ministry of Food and Civil Supplies into two departments in 1984. The Department of Food was separated from the Department of Civil Supplies and the latter was given charge of food distribution and the PDS. The inability of the existing PDS to reduce hunger, far less alleviate poverty, was seen to be a consequence of badly designed institutional policy, which did not necessarily have the ability or the capacity to help the poor (Subramanian 1993). Further reform followed, a decade later, to ensure greater focusing of the distribution mechanism under the Essential Supplies Programme and to provide a particular focus on disadvantaged areas under the title of the Revamped Public Distribution System (RPDS) in 1992. In 1997 the PDS was further reshaped to move it away from a national food channel to a specific focus on poverty alleviation.[10]

The introduction of the Targeted Public Distribution System (TPDS) was intended to focus the distribution of food to the BPL population. The identification of the poor in each Indian state was to be the starting point for ascertaining which families would be entitled to a certain quantity of food grains at specially subsidized prices.[11] The reforms that were brought into the public distribution mechanism to make the PDS more effective have continued to be bedevilled. In the case of the TPDS, the reform has not resulted in lower transaction costs or even improved the focus of the delivery as both Type I (excluding intended populations) and Type II (including unintended populations) errors seem to be large and threaten to undermine the institution (Swaminathan 2008).[12] The difficulty in identifying the poor has become the major focus rather than any improvement in the disbursement of food grains to the hungry. Additionally, there remains a mismatch in public institutions between the procurement system and the distribution process. This has led to a build-up of food grain stocks in public collection centres that are not regularly cleared out, resulting in major storage costs as well as deterioration in the quality of stored food grains.

China

The Communist Party of China came to power in 1949 after a protracted food shortage that resulted from two decades of civil war. This led to a very high priority being accorded to ensuring grain availability to the nation, and particularly to the socialist industrialization effort. There was a huge commitment to introducing a distribution network of food grains and reducing hunger from the outset of the establishment of the People's Republic of China (PRC), a feat that had never been achieved in the history of the country (Li 1982). In 1953, the Chinese government established the 'unified grain procurement and sale system' making the state grain agencies the single buyer and seller in the grain market. The procurement price (also known as the quota price) was at or a few per cent below cost price and remained at this level till the early 1970s.[13] The distribution system was controlled from the centre, and there was a process of redistribution by which grain stored in surplus provinces was real-located to deficit provinces that could be invoked by the State Council (Donnithorne 1966).

While procurement prices remained at, or below, cost prices during the Maoist period (1952–74) this was followed by a decade of agricultural reforms that ushered in higher procurement prices and a more liberalized grain market (Sicular 1988).[14] This first stage of agricultural reform replaced the previous state quota system of agricultural production by a system of household contracts.[15] While the production system was thereby separated from the state through the institution of household contracting, there was still the task of moving from a centralized and state-controlled food procurement and distribution system to a more decentralized and competitive food grain market. The State Council set up a separate department termed the State Grain Reserve Bureau to oversee this process of reform with the specific purpose of stabilizing grain purchase and increasing prices through the contractual system.[16] Additionally, between 1991 and 1993 there was a reduction followed by removal of subsidies and grain rations in urban areas.

Changing the institutional arrangements for grain procurement and marketing led to fluctuations in grain price, with a sudden spike in prices at the end of 1993 and provincial state bureaus were made responsible for dampening these prices through administrative interventions (Le 2007). This function was formalized into the provincial and mayoral 'grain bag' policies of 1995 that required the local administration to ensure food security through either direct procurement or purchase within the domestic grain market. Simply shifting responsibility for food security to sub-national and local state institutions did not work well (Cheng and Tsang 1994). In 1995 the State Council announced a new institutional set-up where there would be new players such as rural management organizations and private retailers in addition to a set of reorganized state grain distribution enterprises (Le 2007). This separation of functions between state agricultural institutions, local rural institutions, and private individuals was the first set of directives to reduce inefficient and illegal activities in the procurement and sale of grain.[17] The opening up of agricultural production and trade within the domestic economy created new opportunities for purchasing grain from farmers, as additional food production could be sold to the state agricultural institutions at a protected (floor) price.

There is a knock-on effect of a growing financial burden on the state institutions that might emerge on account of the inability to sell on this large food stock (Findlay and Chen 2000).

Changing Paradigm of Food Security

The primary concerns of national food security to ensure adequate food for a low income population and the need to feed the vulnerable of the early decades of independence have given way to more targeted agricultural reforms as a response to national difficulties in a continued expansion in food production and timely distribution of food to the poor.

While agricultural reforms have brought about a shift from general population coverage to a smaller and more targeted group of beneficiaries, there remain particular challenges of how to put in place a system that can successfully realize a move away from a national food procurement and distribution system to local systems that are able to ensure food availability and not impose huge costs on the public finances.

The reforms of agricultural institutions that was undertaken during the 1990s to create more responsive and flexible delivery of food grains has tended to be understood with regard to costs and size of operations in both countries. There has also been some concern about the low level of accuracy in the Indian case. While these matters are relevant for evaluating reforms, what is central to understanding the ability of an agricultural system to deliver is to map out the agricultural supply chain and read the impact of the reforms off this mapping.

SEQUENCING THE REFORM OF AGRICULTURAL INSTITUTIONS

While reforming agricultural institutions is important to ensure greater production and distribution, the ability of a nation to deliver food also depends on the strength and length of the agricultural supply chain. It is the institutional capacity to maintain the supply chain so that each section of the chain performs its designated functions that makes for an established capacity and good logistics of an agricultural chain. Improving the supply chain depends on fixing each of the operations of the supply chain as well as the linkages between each operation.[18]

Figure 3.1 presents the typical supply chain that operates in agriculture. Each section of the supply chain can be owned or managed by the state, private, or cooperative sector. There is no a priori reason why any section or a particular combination of several must belong to any one player. The total number and types of players as well as the size and capacity of institutions in the agricultural sector are a consequence of the type of agricultural policies followed in the past as well as the type of production system and agro-ecological environment within which production is being undertaken.

Inputs → Producer → Procurement → Storage → Distributor (wholesale and retail)

Figure 3.1 Supply Chain for Agricultural Institutions
Source: Author.

The process of reforming the Indian agricultural institutional system and the associated supply chain began in 1991 when the government made the decision to replace the procurement price with a minimum support price.[19] In addition to regulating the national price of grain with the existing buffer of grain, another key purpose of procurement of food grains was to ensure adequate food to those in danger of acute malnutrition and hunger.[20]

In India, the initial focus of the government reform in agriculture has been to introduce changes in procurement pricing policy. The objective of the reform was to separate the nature of government intervention in the market intended to shore up farmer incomes from that of the need to maximize food procurement. Second, there was a need to ensure that the accumulation of buffer stock was able to meet the annual fluctuations in agricultural production.[21] Third, there was a severe lack of storage facilities.[22] The failure within each component in the logistical supply chain for food grain deepens as we move from production to storage (see Figure 3.1), and each short-fall contributes a further hurdle to achieving a functional PDS. The irony of this situation is that India had nearly 500,000 Fair Price Shops by the 1990s, making it the largest distribution network in the world (FCI website, www.fciweb.nic.in) yet less than half of the food in the procurement system made its way to poor households (Saxena 2011).

The reform of Chinese agricultural institutions also began with similar concerns about the difficulties of ensuring that the price for procured grain did not send out the wrong signals in the grain market. With the move to the Household Responsibility System and the associated increase in quota and even higher above-quota prices, there was an increase in the national grain production.[23] The rising procurement prices that were experienced from the mid-1980s and through the 1990s resulted in growing buffer stocks and an associated escalation in the state financial burden due to the subsidization of the procurement price.

The response of the State Council was to abolish the quota price provision in 2001 as a remedy to the growing fiscal pressure of covering a growing agricultural subsidy. The consequence was that the bulk of food grain production was no longer required to be purchased by state agricultural institutions. These bodies were only required to retain purchase of the reserve procurement of top-quality grain (Le 2007).[24] The bulk of grain, particularly that of low-quality grain, was opened up to individuals and private companies in 2001 and grain surplus provinces were permitted to completely dismantle the state grain procurement operations. The reduction in state intervention in grain markets was not a simple withdrawal of state action but was undertaken alongside a restructuring of local state grain agencies. The greater responsibility accorded to the local grain institutions was accompanied by directives to link these local agencies, through vertical linkages, with market-oriented state institutions at the county and province levels.

The objective of the third stage of Chinese agricultural reforms was to ensure that the state agricultural institutions would be able to meet the needs of farmers in years when surplus grains pushed the market price below a minimum 'floor' that was to be determined by the provincial authorities. The distributional needs of the population were seen as largely relating to that of urban households, though rural households who were employed in rural non-agricultural activities were also taken into account (Le 2007). With the considerable growth rate maintained by the Chinese economy since the 1980s and the associated structural transformation for the subsequent two decades, the need for a PDS has disappeared as the levels of poverty have reduced.[25] What remains is a buffer system that serves the purpose of smoothing market fluctuations as well as taking care of any large-scale food insecurity (Zhou and Wan 2006).

The situation with regard to the Indian rural sector is hugely different. There are some 750 million people who depend largely on agriculture and the responsibility of ensuring both production and procurement lies with the state administration. The implementation of agricultural policy is the responsibility of the state bureaucracy and there has been varying success of rural development policy across Indian states and sectors. The effective decentralization of agricultural policies and the associated reform of agricultural institutions have been obstructed by difficulties in translating policies at the levels below that of district administration. The constitutional provision of the rural institution of the Panchayati Raj in 1992 was regarded as an important way forward to ensure food security and poverty alleviation.[26]

While the legal recognition of these local institutions was laudable, the lack of explicit linking of the *Gram Sabha* to the Panchayat and the district administration indicates a path with potential pitfalls.[27] There is evidence that the large variations in effectiveness of food security programmes under the PDS are closely related to the level of corruption in provision (Chakravarty and Dand 2005, Swaminathan 2008). This is particularly, true in the case where the local administration is responsible for identifying the households that are below the poverty line (Dreze 2003, Sainath 2002).

Another area where India differs quite radically from that in China is in the extent to which there has been a transformation of an agricultural population into urban industrial workers and rural industrial employees. In China, there has been a considerable reduction in the urban demand for food grain as well as in rural poverty, so that those who have designated residential addresses (registration) are now entitled to subsidized grain, irrespective of income (Zhou and Wan 2006). In contrast, the Indian government still finds itself presented with a very high food grain bill to support both urban and rural poor, approximating a quarter or more of its population.[28]

The sequencing of reforms in China and India present different patterns of improving operations in the supply chain. While China has focused on improving production and procurement in the agriculutural supply chain through improving its logistical ability and reducing the need for state agricultural institutions, India has tried to refashion the agricultural institutions involved in the distributional sector without adequate attention to production, procurement, and storage (Swaminathan 2010) and without taking due note of the fact that the PDS is not working as a targeted intervention. What is needed is a universal and rather widespread network, of PDS to ensure that the many millions who are below the poverty line can be prevented from starving (Sainath 2010).

The Chinese experience of reforms in the agricultural sector indicates that the interventions of the state can be reduced as the macroeconomic fundamentals of the economy are strengthening, however, where there remain huge holes in development policy, as is evident from India's growth experience, it is not realistic to imagine that reducing food security is a feasible option (Chandrasekhar 2010). There are also differences in the agricultural reforms in India and China with regard to the nature of state interventions, where the former has looked to reduce financial liability by restricting the distribution coverage and the latter has emphasized the need to replace the older central state institutions by local bodies that are linked through new forms of managerial control. Figures 3.2 and 3.3 show how the strengthening and weakening of the agricultural supply chain has affected the flow-through of food grains both with regard to logistics as well as effectiveness of delivery to specific groups.

The Indian insistence of increased targeting, which is in line with neoclassical thinking on economic policy, is misguided in a situation where identifying the poor is still beset with errors, of inclusion and exclusion. The large-scale presence of poverty, in both urban and rural India, makes it far more relevant to look to strengthening a universal provision rather than to further narrowing coverage (Sainath 2010). The Chinese case for restructuring agricultural institutions also shows

Producer ⇒ Procurement → Storage → Distributor

Figure 3.2   India's Supply Chain for Agricultural Institutions
Source: Author.

Producer → Procurement ⇒ Storage → Distributor

Figure 3.3   China's Amended Supply Chain for Agricultural Institutions
Source: Author.

the benefit of beginning with a universal coverage, for the move-ment from communal agriculture to local agricultural organizations in 2001, was the first shift from universal provision to selection of a specific local sub-population. The Indian case has been blighted by the awarding of the responsibility for defining BPL and the delivery of food grain under food distribution programmes to the state-district levels rather than the district-county level as was the case in twenty-first-century China.

TRAJECTORIES OF INSTITUTIONAL CHANGE

The changing relationship between the State and the provision of food to the poor through distributional mechanisms is an important deter-minant of the capacity of state institutions. It has been advocated by international agencies that the production and distribution functions of the state with regard to agriculture should be separated out.[29] The argument is that the production of food grains should be based on private sector decisions, driven primarily by farm decisions regarding crop cultivation and that distribution to the poor should be the only area of state intervention.

Reforms that make agriculture more market-oriented do not reduce the importance of sound and transparent public administration. Indeed, effective government at both the central and state level is a crucial component of reform.[30] The intervention by the Indian state in procurement through the minimum support price (MSP) is regarded as both costly and inefficient, as it is placing considerable demands on the national finances and it is still unable to support the marginal farmer (Chakravarty and Dand 2005). The TPDS has led to the large-scale exclusion of genuinely needy persons from the PDS, with its outreach to the poor still found to be wanting.[31] With the reduction in the coverage of distribution there is also no automatic surety that there will be a sustainable reduction in the cost of procurement. The consideration that the provision of MSP to the farmers would reduce costs is hasty as additional cost calculations for the transfer of cereals from surplus to deficit regions of the country, which forms the third linkage in the agricultural supply chain (see Figure 3.1), must be taken into account before any such conclusion can be drawn. The focus should be on the needed improvement in the procurement (upstream) and downstream activities of the agricultural logistical supply chain to ensure that there are no bottlenecks that further raise costs to the state finances.

The additional cost of cross-state transfers is particularly pertinent in a context where the growth and development of the PDS has been extremely uneven across India. In some states in the north-eastern region and the union territories, as well as states such as Andhra Pradesh, Kerala, and Tamil Nadu, the PDS has covered a wider section of the population and, therefore, has been more effective for the poor as well (Chandrasekhar 2010). While India's food stocks are expensive to obtain, and there has been debate in government circles about the possibility of reducing the MSP to reduce the fiscal burden on the state, there seems to be little concern about the waste that occurs within the state system. The most excessive form of squandering of government funds is evident in the manner in which the current procurement levels of 60 million tonnes of food grains are being managed. Only three-fourths of this grain is held in storage with adequate cover while the remaining 15 million tonnes lies relatively exposed to the elements and to pests. The shortfall in decent storage is a particular problem in the face of increased procurement uptake: the increase in the flow of procurement puts even greater pressure on the over-stretched storage facilities and this further impedes the logistical possibilities available within the existing agricultural supply chain. Despite several forms of government intervention and a number of marketing development programmes, the marketing system for farm products has continued to suffer from several weaknesses (Ghatak 2009).

The lack of balance between the expansion in procurement and the breakdown of the storage system makes it difficult, if not impossible, to ensure a regular flow of food grains for distribution (see Figure 3.2). In this situation, the implementation of a targeted PDS with an uneven delivery across states is problematic in relation to both logistics and supply effectiveness. The states where Above Poverty Line (APL) families were gaining access to food supplies are those with better logistics while in other states there was a considerable percentage of BPL families who were unable to use buffer stocks because of faulty logistical arrangements. The inverse relationship between effectiveness of supply in Indian states and the implications for poverty reduction raises serious concerns about India's food grain distributional ability.

The Tendulkar Committee also raised concerns in 2009 about the current estimates of BPL populations that were being declared by state governments, as well as the variation in numbers across states in relation to other sources of national data on poverty and hunger. The current estimates of the Committee have raised the BPL proportion across the country and meeting this challenge under the current system of operating the PDS seems unlikely. The biggest hurdle is that the current delivery mechanisms of the PDS appear to be less concerned with the availability of food grains to hungry populations and more caught up with the drawing down of food stocks and the future reduction in costs of procurement (Chandrasekhar 2010). This attitude is at distinct odds with the increase in BPL percentages, which would require a further increase in food grain stocks with immediate knock-on effects of quality storage. The direction required is clearly towards a universal food distribution model, and a sharp move away from the current version of TPDS.

The Chinese development model moved away from central financial control to a decentralized local state-funded system of development through the late 1980s to the early 1990s as part of the decision to minimize state administrative control and reduce the revenue collection of the state 'from maximising to minimising the state' (Bernstein and Lu 2003). In March 1998 the Chinese government launched an ambitious reform of the institutional structure of China's administrative system. The whole reform was scheduled to be implemented in three years starting at the central level in 1998 and then the provincial level in 1999, ending at the local level at the end of 2000 (Brødsgaard 2002). The gap between production and consumption has been rising since 2000 and the state agencies in many areas of agricultural marketing and processing no longer have monopoly positions for most aspects of both domestic and international trade. They are now required to cooperate with enterprises outside the state sector, particularly with private sector players.[32]

The financial burden does remain with the central government, which through the provincial administration has the responsibility of providing additional funds to local administration that are unable to meet the production costs of local farmers. This implies that while the state may no longer play a key role in the agricultural supply chain it does have a major role in financing the actual production section at the start of the agricultural supply chain.[33] The support provided by the central government has been through the abolition of agricultural tax on farmers, and while local governments have to ensure that the market for grain is strengthened, there is the availability of funds from the centre in case of hardship to individual farmers and villages (Liu *et al.* 2006).[34] The formalization of the restructuring of agricultural institutions was set out in Document Number 1 for 2006 which outlined a new rural development strategy. The publication of this document coincided with the first year of the 11th Five-Year Plan and the priorities set there were further developed in the plan and their implementation extended until 2010. The three important objectives of the plan: (*a*) ensure adequate supply of grains and other agricultural products, (*b*) steady increase of farmers' income, and (*c*) the harmonious development of rural society, point to an emphasis on the upstream activities in the agricultural supply chain and a keenness to withdraw from the downstream activities.

In the case of India, the debates around the type of PDS as well as the concerns around the cost of a public procurement system point to a focus on the front and back ends of the agricultural supply chain. There has been a relative neglect of the mid-chain components so that storage and the logistics of shifting of food grain has remained relatively unchanged while there has been a spate of activity, almost feverish at times; but the state of the Indian agricultural supply chain remains unhealthy. The Food Security Act introduced in 2009 has generated a considerable debate, culminating in demands for a fundamental restructuring of the final stage of the agricultural supply chain, where food security should be a universal right. This set of events provides a valuable opportunity for revisiting the various capacity constraints in each section of the chain and the evaluation of the cost implications of changing these constraints (Swaminathan 2010).

There is no reason that there should be an a priori preference for choosing a particular section of the agricultural value chain for intervention; rather what is needed is an evaluation of the most immediate areas that require further coupling or additional support. It would be to the advantage of both countries if they could learn from each other how improvement across the sectors of a supply chain can be undertaken. India, on the one hand, could gain from China's experience by learning to manage its buffer stock with more flexibility. Once the stock becomes excessive, different measures need to be exercised to dispose of the surplus, for example, exporting, as China did in 1998–2003, when it exported large quantities from its buffer stock, even though subsidy had to be provided (Zhou and Wan 2006). China, on the other hand, could benefit from a closer examination of India's PDS administration with a view to bringing transparency to its buffer stock management and reducing the high cost of maintaining China's buffer stock.

Furthermore, the implications of focusing on different parts of the supply chain also provide distinctive results. While India reduced the coverage of its agricultural distribution programme, China expanded the role of agricultural institutions. The immediate weakness that this introduced into the Indian agricultural supply chain was the difficult problem of identification of the poor. In the case of China, the reduction in the poor brought about by successful industrialization and rural diversification has meant that there is a considerable reduction in the poor so that there is little necessity in having to undertake an identification approach to ensure food security. Second, India has found that identification problems are not its only challenge for there is still considerable difficulty in getting food out of the storage blocks and into government distribution centres and into homes. In the case of China, the large level of grain stocks are being diverted to the creation of a processed foods sector or to enhance the production of meat and animal-based products, in an attempt to diversify the procurement stage of the agricultural food grain supply chain. The exercise of mapping out the supply chain and overlaying the reform of agricultural institutions onto this framework has permitted us to get a better sense of the strengths and weaknesses of agricultural distribution in both countries.

INSTITUTIONAL CAPACITY AND WEAKNESS IN FOOD DISTRIBUTION

The size and effectiveness of delivery food grains to the vulnerable and hungry is an important measure of institutional capacity. To be able to deduce how reliable a food distribution system is it becomes important to be able to get a sense of what represents institutional capacity (and weakness) in the food distribution chain. Such measures continue to be pertinent in both China and India, for even with powerful national growth experiences there are still deprived and vulnerable populations within these countries that are susceptible to hunger.

In China, the big difference is between urban and rural areas, with the expenditure undertaken by three farmers approximating that spent by a single city resident (Lu 2007). The Chinese state has devolved agricultural policy to the district level but this does not imply that there is no state intervention in the agricultural sector. The introduction of new players into the organization and distribution of agricultural produce, particularly to ensure the availability of food grain to the poor, has been put in place over the last decade. These reforms are focused on the market and strengthening the supply of produce using price as the central mechanism (Yang 2006). Distributional concerns are kept in the frame of the supply chain by retaining the tool of protective (floor) prices and local delivery mechanisms.

In the case of India, with nearly a third of the population still defined as poor under one or another definition of poverty and 45 per cent of its children identified as malnourished by international agencies, there is a considerably larger imperative to ensure that the reform of the public agricultural institutions does ensure that food grains are readily available and that they are of a quality that is fit for consumption.

While the agricultural supply chain has been used thus far to understand the possibilities and the limitations of ensuring food grain security for the poor in China and India there is also considerable value in using this mapping to examine future scenarios for national agricultural systems at the top end of economic activity.

In relation to the future prospects of the existing food stock available with public agricultural institutions, the existing supply chain in China indicates there is already approval for the state to deal only with top quality and standard quality grain. The emphasis is on purchase of the former to ensure that the agricultural supply chain is increasing the value of agricultural products obtained through the chain. The value of this proposition has already found favour among Indian business houses that are moving into the retailing of Indian food grains within the agricultural value chain (Figure 3.1). The shift from 'agriculture' to 'agribusiness' is the one theme that appears to link global to national trajectories of institutional change, yet this should not be regarded as a simple handover of state agricultural institutions to private production systems.[35]

The recommendation for uncoupling procurement and distribution should not be regarded as an automatic corollary that follows from the increased presence of market prices in the agricultural sector.

In the case of China, profitability through technological upgrading of the logistical processes in the grain procurement system has been introduced. In India, agricultural institutions have been too hasty in reforming grain policy and without due regard for the long-term interests of Indian agriculture (Expert Committee on Grain Policy, Government of India 2005).

To make the case that the use of supply chain analysis advocates the 'withdrawal of the state' from agriculture in a liberalizing trade environment does not follow through either. While there is a definite increase in the impact of international agricultural players, both corporate and institutional in both Chinese and Indian markets, it would be wrong to regard this as an imposition from without. There is now considerable interest within both countries to diversify their agricultural production systems. There are some concerns that this would expose the agricultural value chain in India to a set of players who would not have a set of institutional guidelines (Posani 2009). This cannot, however, be a justification for continuing with the current set of agricultural institutions for these have neither met the requirement for food security nor alleviated poverty (Swaminathan 2010).

In the Chinese case, the localization of agricultural distribution has led to large variations in the extent to which social services are provided in rural areas, with some districts having a far better track record than others (Lu 2007). In particular, after the abolition of the agricultural tax to reduce the costs borne by farmers in 2001, the central state has brought in fiscal transfers that will compensate districts for revenue shortfalls and to help the poorest in the villages. The extent to which these transfers are actually made to the poorest households shows considerable variation across districts (Oi 2008).

Understanding the supply chain of the agricultural sector, and the role that public institutions play within this chain, has shown that there is varying institutional capacity in each section of the chain in each country. The hasty dismantling of state institutions would not be conducive to bolster the capacity of the supply chain, to improve procurement and delivery as it is dependent on the ability of the state to bring in government regulations that would operate throughout the chain and not within a single section of the chain. There is no a priori reason that would be less difficult than reforming existing state institutions.

* * *

Governments have been major players in agriculture in the twentieth century in China and India, Their intent has tended to have a greater or lesser congruence with the following set of objectives: (*a*) to maximize the surety of output, and (*b*) to provide food for its citizens. The role of agricultural institutions has been to ensure the meeting of these objectives, often without looking across the entire breadth of the agricultural sector. The importance of examining the agricultural supply chain is that it permits the study of production, procurement, storage, and distribution aspects of agriculture.

In this regard, the overlay of current functions of agricultural institutions on existing agricultural supply chains indicates that the two countries initially had different strategies with regard to the full supply chain. In the case of India, the reforms focused exclusively on the procurement section of the chain, while in China there was a greater concern with the production aspects of the chain.

The implication of this different approach to reforms was that there was a reduction in the linkages between production, procurement and distribution in the case of Indian agriculture. This was compounded with difficulties in reconciling the intended beneficiaries, further reducing the ability of the public sector to deliver needed food grain to the poor. In the case of China, the growing power of industrial growth in the reform period was able to reduce poverty levels by half. The use of the largesse of industrial growth to provide transfers for the poorer sections of rural China was a far smaller and manageable task. However, there still remain challenges in relation to uneven coverage in different regions of the country. In particular, the importance of local-level institutions for ensuring delivery does not completely do away with the need for monitoring the effectiveness of delivery.

Additionally, the continuing financial demands of the PDS have resulted in demands for a replacement of state institutions by more market-based pricing rules. While these are helpful in reducing unnecessary costs on account of poor administrative action, it would be foolish and short-sighted to dismantle the state institutions in agriculture—while they remain within the food grain supply chain they are able to monitor from a position of proximity. If this is replaced by a need for an external regulator there will be a need for additional funds for this purpose.

Finally, further reform of the agricultural sector needs to be considered in relation to the major players in the national arena—public, corporate, and cooperative actors—who need to be brought in to gain a better sense of how they can each contribute to strengthening the national and sub-national supply chain to enhance both production and distribution in an increasingly global market for food grain.

NOTES

1. The Food and Agriculture Organization (FAO) currently links food insecurity to individual household poverty and vulnerability to hunger.

2. The ample availability of food was also important to provide a crucial precondition for industrial development, to ensure cheap and plentiful food to feed the growing urban population. This is the basis of industrialization as set out in the Lewis model, which was the primary blueprint for industrialization for developing countries in the 1950s and 1960s (Lewis 1954).

3. The ignominy of having to plead for food supplies from the United States under the food aid of Public Law 480 (PL 480) had an indelible impact on the nationalist feeling prevalent among India's ruling elite and the civil service. The period resulted in an active shift in agricultural policy to bring in a new technologically supported new method of agricultural production based on high yielding varieties (HYVs).

4. See Torry (1984).

5. See Zhou and Wan (2006).

6. Its key objectives were: (*a*) to ensure a minimum price for farmers and (*b*) to ensure food procurement for public distribution to ensure food security (Food Corporation of India [FCI] website).

7. The states that were the biggest beneficiaries from the public procurement programme were the three states of Punjab, Haryana, and Uttar Pradesh (Suryanarayana 1995).

8. See FCI website: http://fciweb.nic.in/

9. See Sainath (2002).

10. This shift was in line with national advice from the World Bank that targeting was a useful device for poverty alleviation.

11. The policy decision to distinguish between the APL and BPL groups in Indian states has been a contentious matter: firstly, because of considerable debate and difference between economists and policy-makers on where to draw the poverty line, and second, as the removal of assistance of those considered APL could work against their future entitlements (Chandrasekhar 2010).

12. The government's own evaluation report of TPDS indicated it is not even possible to calculate whether the delivery cost of TPDS is more or less than that of the universal PDS (Government of India 2005).

13. There were three types of purchasers permitted in the system: (*a*) the non-agricultural population (urban) who were issued with grain coupons, (*b*) the agricultural population who were engaged in non-grain production or did not produce grain in sufficient quantities, and (*c*) other grain users (food-processing units or food retailers such as restaurants) (Le 2007).

14. This was the beginning of the dual pricing policy, where food grains and non-food grains had differential pricing. For food grains, quota levels being paid at cost price, and above-quota levels price was set at 20 per cent above cost price. For non-food grains the period of 1982–8 saw a rapid opening up of the market, and a shift away from quotas.

15. The Chinese reforms, also known as the *Four Modernizations*, began in 1978 and the collective agriculture based on communes was replaced by the Household Responsibility System (*baogan daohu*).

16. The move from a state-controlled supply to a market-based system required new institutional mechanisms—one major investment was the setting up of a wholesale market in grain at Zhengzhou (Le 2007).

17. China experts in the US regarded this shift as a response to the excessive centralization of the Chinese state and welcomed the institutional reforms as a move to setting out legal rules for local cadres (Nee and Young 1992, Oi 1999). However, the shift should not be regarded as a simple process of decentralization as the experience of the early 1990s shows that by merely devolving power to the local sphere it is not necessary that rural households and financial institutions are made aware of their financial responsibility or legal liability (Fennell 2009).

18. In the field of agribusiness, feasibility analysis is undertaken of the consequences of reforms of agricultural institutions across the agricultural food chain, that is, from field to fork.

19. The simultaneous existence of a support price and procurement price resulted in conflicting signals as to whether national agricultural institutions were primarily concerned with shoring farmer incomes or maximizing food procurement.

20. This objective was met by the procurement of rice and wheat, with the bulk of the procurement coming from the surplus grain states of Punjab, Haryana, and western Uttar Pradesh, with the greatest beneficiaries being the larger farmers in these states.

21. The subsidy element present in the procurement of grain by the FCI has also come under scrutiny by international organizations such as the World Bank in the late 1990s (See Umali-Deininger and Deininger 2001).

22. The shortfall had been identified as far back as in 1970 when a Rural Godown scheme was established (Swaminathan 2010). Despite this early evaluation and attempts to build new storage facilities with an emphasis on the states of Punjab and Haryana where much of the grain is procured, there was no discernable improvement in storage structures.

23. The increase in grain production saw China emerge as a major agricultural presence of global markets by the end of the 1990s.

24. The second phase of economic reforms saw the growth of specialized households and town and village enterprises (TVEs) that created a new pillar of rural industrialization. As the rural population moved out of agriculture to other rural employment there was a considerable reduction in farmers and this resulted in a growing demand for food grains from the non-farming population and a rise in food grain prices in local economies.

25. Chinese poverty levels have halved over the last two decades.

26. These objectives are set out on the website of the Food Corporation of India.

27. The power of local elites can be a major detractor that prevents rural households from receiving their entitlements under government food security and poverty alleviation programmes. Bardhan and Mookherjee (1999) point out the political economy that makes local elites far more successful in rent-seeking activities than national institutions.

28. The inability of India to reduce poverty in a manner similar to that of China over the last two decades points to a future where it will take India another 40 years to reach the nutrition levels that China has achieved today (Dreze 2003).

29. The International Food Policy Research Institute and the World Bank have been advocating more market openness in agriculture. (See *World Development Report* 2008.)

30. The position of international advisors has been that it is enough if government provides safety nets while allowing the private sector to undertake the bulk of agricultural operations (Pinstrup-Anderson 2003).

31. Corruption has been identified as a major reason for the shift from universal to targeted PDS; the poor institutional delivery has been a longstanding bugbear. It is interesting that Tamil Nadu has a much better delivery mechanism (Vydiyanathan and Radhakrishnan 2010).

32. For a discussion of state marketing agencies in their early reform phase, see Sicular 1995.

33. In the EU, the subsidies in the input and production stages are a major form of support provided by the State.

34. While the contracting system in agriculture did give rise to a liberalization of land contracting for households (Waldron and Brown 2003), this did not occur in a context where the state exited the agricultural supply chain. What was underway was a restructing of the system rather than a dismantling—a form of crossing the river by groping for stones—policy that is a key framework of the Chinese reform process.

35. There has been a long history of state subsidies to the private sector. For instance, the Green Revolution technologies that were made available to farmers in the 1970s were supported by large-scale state investment in electricity and other infrastructure.

REFERENCES

Acharya, S.S. 2006. 'National Food Policies Impacting Food Security: The Experience of India', WIDER Research Paper 2006/70.

————. 2007. 'Agribusiness in India: Some Facts and Emerging Issues', *Agricultural Economics Research Review*, 20: 409–24.

Bardhan, P. and D. Mookherjee. 1999. 'Relative Capture of Local and National Governments: An Essay in the Political Economy of Decentralization'. Working Paper, Department of Economics, University of California, Berkeley.

Bernstein, T. and X. Lu. 2003. *Taxation without Representation in Contemporary Rural China*. New York: Cambridge University Press.

Brødsgaard, K. 2002. 'Institutional Reform and the Bianzhi System in China', *The China Quarterly*, 171: 361–86.

Chakravarty, S. and S. Dand. 2005. 'Food Insecurity in India: Causes and Dimensions', Occasional Paper, Indian Institute of Management, Ahmedabad.

Chan, K. and W. Buckingham. 2008. 'Is China Abolishing the Hukou System', *The China Quarterly*, 195: 582–606.

Chandrasekhar, C.P. 2010. 'Threat to a System', *Frontline*, 27 (17, 14–27 August), http://www.frontlineonnet.com/fl2717/stories/20100827271710900.htm (accessed 21 May 2012).

Cheng, Y. and S. Tsang. 1994. 'The Changing Grain Marketing System in China', *The China Quarterly*, 140: 1080–104.

Donnithorne, A. 1966. 'State Procurement and Agricultural Produce in China, *Europe-Asia Studies*', 18 (1): 38–56.

Dreze, J. 2003. 'Democracy and Right to Food', Third C. Chandrasekaran Memorial Lecture delivered at the International Institute for Population Sciences, Mumbai, 7 November.

Fennell, S. 2009. *Rules, Rubrics and Riches: The Interrelations between Legal Reform and International Development*. London: Routledge.

Findlay, C. and C. Chen. 2000. 'A Review of China's Grain Marketing System Reform', Australian Centre for International Agricultural Research (ACIAR), China Grain Marketing Policy Project Paper No. 6.

Ghatak, S. 2009. 'Agriculture and Development: A Rejoinder', http://www.esocialsciences.com/data/eSSResearchPapers/eSSWPArticle2009429121425.doc (accessed 5 March 2010).

Gobel, C. 2006. 'The Peasants' Rescue from the Cadre: An Institutional Analysis of China's Rural Tax and Fee Reform', Duisingburg Working Papers of East Asia, No. 69.

Government of India, Expert Committee on Grain Policy. 2005. *Performance Evaluation of Targeted Public Distribution System*, Performance Evaluation Organisation. New Delhi: Government of India.

Gulati, A., P. Sharma, and S. Kähkönen. 1996. 'The Food Corporation of India. Successes and Failures in Indian Food Grain Marketing', IRIS-India Working Paper No. 18.

Jones, S. 1995 'Food Market Reform: The Changing Role of the State', *Food Policy*, 20 (6): 551–60.

Le, Chen. 2007. *Grain Market Liberalization and Deregulation in China: The Mediating Role of Markets for Farmers in Jiangxi Province*, Ph.D. thesis, Wageningen University.

Lewis, W.A. 1954. 'Economic Development with Unlimited Supplies of Labour', *The Manchester School of Economic and Social Studies*, 22 (2): 139–91.

Li, L. 1982. 'Food, Famine and the Chinese State', *Journal of Asian Studies*, 41 (4): 687–707.

Liu, M., B. Song, and T. Rao. 2006. 'Perspective on Local Governance Reform in China', *China & the World Economy*, 14 (6): 16–31.

Lohmar, B., X. Diao, A. Somwaru, F. Tuan, and K. Chan. 2003. 'Softening the Impact of Adjustment to Reform: The China Experience'. Paper prepared for the Policy Reform and Adjustment Workshop, Witherdane Hall, Imperial College London, Wye Campus, 23–25 October.

Lu, X. 2007. 'The Changing in Agriculture, the Countryside and Farmers in China', Institute of Sociology, Chinese Academy of Social Sciences, mimeo.

McMichael, P. 2009. 'The World Food Crisis in Historical Perspective', *Monthly Review*, 61 (3, July–August): 32–47.

Nee, V. and F. Young. 1992. 'Peasant Entrepreneurs in China's Second Economy: An Institutional Analysis', *Economic Development and Cultural Change*, 39 (2): 293–310.

Oi, J. 1999. 'Two Decades of Rural Reform in China: An Overview and an Assessment', *The China Quarterly*, 159: 616–28.

—————. 2008. Development Strategies, Welfare Regime and Poverty Reduction, UNRISD background paper for UNRISD programme on Poverty Reduction and Policy Regimes.

Pinstrup-Anderson, P. 2003. 'Reshaping Indian Food and Agricultural Policy to Meet the Challenges and Opportunities of Globalization', EXIM Bank commencement lecture, 2002.

Posani, B. 2009. 'Crisis in the Countryside: Farmer Suicides and the Political Economy of Agrarian Distress in India', London School of Economics DESTIN Working Paper No. 95.

Sainath, P. 2002. *Everyone Loves a Good Drought: Stories From India's Poorest Districts*. New Delhi: Penguin.

—————. 2010. 'Food Security: Of APL, BPL, and IPL', Opinion Piece, *The Hindu*, 6 July.

Saxena, N.C. 2011. 'Hunger, Under-nutrition and Food Security in India', Chronic Poverty Research Centre, Indian Institute of Public Administration, Working Paper No. 44.

Sicular, T. 1995. 'Redefining State, Plan and Market: China's Reforms in Agricultural Commerce', *The China Quarterly*, 144: 1020–64.

—————. 1988. 'Agricultural Planning and Pricing in the Post-Mao Period', *The China Quarterly*, 116: 671–705.

Subramanian, S. 1993. Agricultural Trade Liberalisation in India, OECD.

Suryanarayana, M.H. 1995. 'PDS: Beyond Implicit Subsidy and Urban Bias–The Indian Experience', *Food Policy*, 20 (4): 259–78.

Swaminathan, M.S. 2008. 'Neo-Liberal Policy and Food Security in India: Impact of the Public Distribution System in India'. UNDESA Working Paper, October.

———. 2010. 'Pre-requisites of Sustainable Food Security', Opinion Piece, *The Hindu*, 20 July.

Torry, W.I. 1984. 'Social Science Research on Famine: A Critical Evaluation', *Human Ecology*, 12 (3): 227–52.

Umali-Deininger, D. and K.W. Deininger. 2001. 'Towards Greater Food Security for India's Poor: Balancing Government Intervention and Price Competition', *Agricultural Economics*, 21: 321–35.

Vydiyanathan, S. and R.K. Radhakrishnan. 2010. 'Behind the Success Story of Universal PDS in Tamil Nadu', *The Hindu*, 10 August.

Waldron, S. and C. Brown. 2003. 'State Sector Reform in China: Structural Considerations in Agriculture', Paper presented at the 15th Annual Conference of the Association of Chinese Studies, at Melbourne, Australia.

World Bank, 2008. *World Development Report. Agriculture for Development*, Washington D.C.: World Bank.

Yang, W. 2006. 'Reforms, Structural Adjustments, and Rural Income in China', *China Perspectives*, 63, http://chinaperspectives.revues.org/575#tocfrom1n1 (accessed 15 July 2012).

Zhou, Z.Y. and G. Wan. 2006. The Public Distribution Systems of Food grains and Implications for Food Security, WIDER Research Paper No. 2006/98.

4

Appraising Industrial Policies of India and China from Two Perspectives

Nationalist and Internationalist

Nɪʀᴍᴀʟ Kᴜᴍᴀʀ Cʜᴀɴᴅʀᴀ*

High gross domestic product (GDP) growth rates for over 30 years in China, and for a shorter stretch in India, combined with the fact that the two economies were relatively unscathed by the recent global crisis, have led the international media as well as academic circles to consider both as the miracle economies of this century.

One may first note some long-term trends. At constant international dollars, China's per capita GDP was 19 per cent of the US level in 2007, as against 3.5 per cent in 1978; the figures were respectively 9 per cent and 5.8 per cent for India (Penn World Table, Version 6.3 [PWT] 2009). In net output of manufacturing at constant international dollars, China's share rose from 0.92 per cent of the US level in 1970 to 1.63 per cent in 1980 and 13.8 per cent in 2006, while the figures for India were respectively 0.65 per cent, 0.68 per cent, and 2.02 per cent over the same years (UN database). China's percentage share in global

* I am indebted to Sudip Chaudhuri, Sushil Khanna, and Mritiunjoy Mohanty for useful discussions; to Amiya Bagchi, Rajani Desai, and Guilhem Fabre for interesting comments; and to Anthony D'Costa for combing through the chapter as an editor.

exports of manufactures shot up from 0.8 in 1980 to 13.5 in 2009, and that of India from 0.5 and 1.3 (WTO database).

Industrial policies in these countries are examined from two alternative perspectives. In the section 'India', I take a 'nationalist' position, emphasizing economic growth and national self-reliance. I begin with the Nehru–Mahalanobis strategy of self-reliant industrialization that was broadly followed from 1955 to 1984. From 1985 began a turn towards Washington-inspired liberalization culminating in the financial crisis of 1991. The changes since 1991 to date are then probed. The section 'China' is on China's economic reform of 1978 crafted by the Communist Party. China has now become the manufacturing hub of the world, and the largest exporter of high-technology manufactures. The section 'A Critique of Growth Experience in India and China' critiques the policies of the two countries from an 'internationalist' perspective of growth with equity, both within the country and across its borders.

INDIA

India before 1991

India's industrialization strategy (IIS) from 1956 to 1984 was outlined in the Mahalanobis plan frame that was endorsed by most Indian economists as well as leading Western scholars of a liberal or socialist persuasion. But the conservatives in the West were highly critical for several reasons: (*a*) IIS was biased towards heavy- and capital-goods industries that made too little use of overabundant surplus labour available in the country; (*b*) tariff walls across the board created high-cost industries that adversely affected domestic sales as well as exports; and (*c*) industrial investments required licensing by bureaucrats, and private entrepreneurs had to waste time and money to bribe officials, adding to the costs.

As a subcontinent, India fostered almost all industries. Thus Little (1960) found that 'the broad strategy of India's planned development is eminently sound'. A few years later he turned into a trenchant critic (Little *et al.* 1970). Mahalanobis (1953) had showed through simple algebra that a high proportion of investments going into heavy and capital-goods industries ensured the quickest way to attain the goal of industrial self-reliance, alleviating simultaneously the foreign exchange shortage. This target was achieved around 1980, as a bare 10 per cent of capital goods required by the country were imported, and aggregate savings nearly equalled investment.

But the main goal of approaching full employment in 10–15 years remained elusive, and the backlog of underemployment kept piling up (Shetty 1978, Chaudhuri 1997). Mahalanobis never expected that the heavy- and capital-goods industries would absorb much surplus labour. For employment creation, he had assumed, following Nehru's call for a 'socialistic' transformation of the country in 1954, that radical land reforms would give land to the tiller. With a significant rise in their income, the peasants' demand for foods and 'simple' manufactures would go up. If simultaneously, the government froze the capacities of large urban factories turning out goods that could be produced by labour-intensive urban or rural industries, employment could greatly expand over a short period with a multiplier effect (Mahalanobis 1955). Actually, the agenda of land reforms was aborted by the landlords, and the income of rural masses still remains depressed; two recent official reports have underlined this factor in the context of the Naxalite challenge (Planning Commission 2008, Ministry of Rural Development [MRD] 2009.) As for large urban factories competing with small units, the government measures were again half-hearted, thanks to opposition from big industrialists.

Although IIS incorporated export promotion schemes for manufactures, India's performance lagged well behind those of Asia's miracle economies like Japan, South Korea, or Taiwan. Following the logic of mathematical induction, can one argue that India could successfully emulate these countries by modifying drastically IIS?

From Washington's prestigious Institute of International Economics, Cline (1982) was sceptical about the mantra of export-led growth as a panacea. A decade later, Summers, who has held top positions in the World Bank, successive US Administrations, and Wall Street, wrote a piece jointly with Thomas (Summers and Thomas 1993), chiding the Bank for chanting the same mantra for *all* developing countries.

Why did a handful of countries actually succeed? In his Marshall Lecture at Cambridge on the Japanese miracle, Morishima (1982) underscored the fact that the United States of America was politically and militarily committed from the early 1950s to the economic prosperity of Japan as a bulwark against the USSR and China, and encouraged Japan to pursue a mercantilist trade and investment policy that ran against the immediate interests of US businesses. It does not contradict the claim of Johnson (1982) that Japan owed its success to the domestic policies inspired by Soviet planning, and that the United States of America as the hegemon should have approved of Japan's 'market-oriented planned economy'. Amsden (1989) rightly stressed Korea's policy on both import substitution and export promotion, but omitted altogether the US role as the Santa Claus. Once the USSR disappeared, Washington engineered, according to many, the financial crisis of 1997, while the media and numerous scholars in the United States scornfully referred to the Korean miracle as a gift from the United States of America.

Back in 1960, India was the world's second-largest exporter of cotton textiles with a share of 8.8 per cent of the total (Nayyar 1976, Table 4.3). From 1962, the Multi-Fibre Arrangement was enforced unilaterally against the General Agreement on Tariffs and Trade (GATT) rules, enabling rich countries to impose product-wise quotas on each exporter. As a friend of the USSR, India saw its quota nearly frozen for the benefit of the strategic allies of the United States of America in East Asia. In a quota-based trade regime the concept of comparative advantage loses all relevance. Furthermore, there is a spillover effect. Countries with high quotas in textiles earned a reputation in foreign markets and diversified into the export of other low-technology products. That may explain why India not only lost its share in world exports in textiles, but also failed to break into new areas.

Critics of IIS asserted that the effective rate of protection (ERP), that is, the extent of tariff protection required by a domestic industry to impede imports, was quite high and hence most of them were inefficient. (Bhagwati and Desai 1970, Bhagwati *et al.* 1975, World Bank 1990). The basic flaw in the argument was that the 'deemed' costs of domestic and imported inputs were artificially inflated, reducing the domestic value added as shown by a number of scholars (Nambiar 1983, Chandrasekhar 1992, Kathuria 1995, Chaudhuri 1997).[1]

An alternative to ERP is the domestic resource cost (DRC) that indicates the opportunity cost of saving a unit of foreign exchange. If the DRC of a product is higher (lower) than the import value at the current rate of exchange, the industry is regarded as inefficient (efficient). A series of studies from the 1970s indicate that by this yardstick India's industries have generally, with some important exceptions, been efficient. In particular, if one considers 'short-run'

DRC for firms that export only a small part of their output, Indian firms have been efficient almost without exception.[2]

Most telling are two in-depth studies on India's capital goods industries by the World Bank (1975 and 1984). For each study, large teams of engineers, accountants, and economists visited the plants and examined the balance sheets and other data. In textile machinery, the best Indian firms in 1975 had achieved global quality, and their prices were lower than abroad by 12–35 per cent. Somewhat similar was the finding for five major capital goods industries in the early 1980s. So far, both reports remain 'classified' by the Bank and mainstream writers in the West or in India still ignore them, though the 1984 report was summarized in the *Economic and Political Weekly* (Anonymous 1985).

Most writers also ignore another piece of evidence. The International Comparison Project of the World Bank and the UN compared the 'final purchaser' prices in 1975 of 76 manufactured products; Indian prices were more attractive, lower than in the United States of America with respect to 44 items, but were particularly high for 'luxury' goods like consumer durables with a high rate of indirect tax (Kravis *et al.* 1982).

In recent years, 'total factor productivity' (TFP) growth as a key indicator of macroeconomic efficiency has come to the fore in mainstream economics. In examining the East Asian miracle, World Bank (1993) put TFP growth rate at above 6 per cent for Korea (1966–85), as against 2 per cent for Japan (1960–79). But Krugman (1994) cited a study by Young (1994) to argue that Korean or Japanese growth was in some ways similar to Soviet or East European growth; value added in manufacturing rose fast for a long period, but TFP growth was negligible. Krugman was apparently vindicated by the Korean crisis that erupted soon after, though others questioned the statistical finding of Young. Sarel (1996) felt that most TFP estimates lacked robustness for a variety of reasons. Rodrik (1997) reiterated this point, added some weighty objections, theoretical and empirical, to the prevalent estimates, and concluded that the rate of accumulation is the best predictor of GDP growth. Strangely, Rodrik and Subramanian (2004) took a very different position on the Indian scene, discussed later.

Ahluwalia (1991) showed that TFP in Indian manufacturing declined annually by 0.4 per cent between 1959 and 1985, but there was a significant improvement in the 1980s. Goldar (1992) came to the opposite conclusion: TFP improved by 0.8 per cent p.a. from 1956 to 1984. Instead of the standard single deflation (SD) method deflating the time series of value added by the output price index, Balakrishnan and Pushpangadan (1994) used the double deflation (DD) method, deflating both inputs and outputs by their respective price indices for the years, 1970–88. In a period when raw materials prices shoot up, for example, after the oil shock of 1973, DD provides a better indicator of real growth and TFP. A more elaborate exercise along the same lines was that of Trivedi (2000) covering the years 1973 to 1997.

The findings of the two studies are presented in Table 4.1. Often 1980–1 is taken as the break point, but it was a 'bad' year well below the peak of 1978–9. I consider the latter as more appropriate, and in Part A of the table, two alternative sets of data are given. Now, the growth rates were higher in the 1970s than in the next decade with the new break point, and more so if the DD method is used. Trivedi's findings in Part B of the table confirms it. Further, compared to the previous period, growth accelerated during 1983–9, but fell steeply during 1989–96, using either TFP-S or TFP-D.

Table 4.1   **Annual Percentage Growth Rates in Value Added and Productivity in Indian Manufacturing, 1970–96**

Balakrishnan and Pushpangadan*

	VA-S	TFP-S	VA-D	TFP-D
1970/1–1978/9	5.4	0.6	10.0	4.0
1978/9–1988/9	5.2	0.2	6.0	−0.3
1970/1–1980/1	3.1	1.9	7.6	1.6
1980/1–1988/9	8.0	3.2	8.0	1.3

Trivedi**

	TFP-S	TFP-D
1973/4–1978/9	4.4	14.1
1978/9–1983/4	1.6	−0.4
1983/4–1989/90	2.2	4.5
1989/90–1996/7	1.6	2.4

Sources: Balakrishnan and Pushpangadan (1994), Trivedi (2000).
Notes: * VA and TFP denote respectively value added and total factor productivity, while the letters S and D stand for SD and DD methods respectively.
    ** Trivedi presented two time series of TFP-S, using slightly different methods; as the indices were highly correlated, I have taken a simple average. I did the same for the two series of TFP-D.

In an influential study, Rodrik and Subramanian (2004) observed that there was considerable progress in manufacturing during the IIS era, but asserted that the 'Hindu growth' phase ended in 1980, and per capita income growth doubled from 1.7 per cent in 1950–80 to 3.8 per cent in 1980–2000. They referred to many studies, including those in Table 4.1, and endorsed the view 'that manufacturing experienced a surge in productivity in the 1980s'. Clearly, they drew a wrong inference.

Thus none of the alleged drawbacks of IIS, namely neglect of the export potential, high costs of protected industries, and low TFP growth till 1980, stands up to a close scrutiny, putting a question mark over the narratives of Rodrik and Subramanian (2004) or of those echoing the Washington Consensus. The flawed diagnosis provided a rationale for the blitzkrieg of reforms after 1991.

India after 1991

In a prescient essay, Bliss (1989, p. 121) wondered whether developing countries with high levels of protection 'would benefit if a foreign power destroyed a part of the [inefficient] capital stock in a bombing raid. This is not a plausible assumption for most LDCs.' In fact, a surrogate bombing in the form of shock therapy was carried out on 2 January 1992 in post-Soviet Russia, devastating the whole economy.[3] An insider in the debate within the US administration in the late 1980s over the 'desirable' reform path for the USSR, Stiglitz (2000) revealed that along with several leading American economists like Arrow, he had suggested a path of gradual reforms that would enable the Soviet enterprises to adapt themselves to a market economy. But the US Treasury on grounds of realpolitik did not want a revival of socialism. The barely concealed objective was to prevent Soviet firms from posing a challenge to Western multinational corporations (MNCs). The Treasury view was echoed in the joint report of four multilateral institutions (International Monetary Fund [IMF] *et al.* 1991), prepared at the request of the then Soviet President Gorbachev, and was faithfully implemented by the successor President Yeltsin.

An advisory body appointed by the Indian prime minister, the National Manufacturing Competitiveness Council (NMCC 2008, p. 4) used the term 'big bang' to describe the impact of 1991 reforms on industry. Of course, India did not have a traumatic experience like

Russia. Yet there are parallels. A widely used textbook, by Joshi and Little (1996), strongly supported the reforms, since 'a good deal of Indian industry, after 40 years of almost total protection and limited domestic competition was in poor shape in 1991 to survive international competition with only very limited protection'. Curiously, they admitted that for capital goods there was for some years 'negative protection in some cases', and that 'everyone agrees that time for adjustment was needed—say seven years' (pp. 71–3). It is evident that the reformers expected that an abrupt liberalization of imports would cause a collapse of many Indian industries, especially in capital goods.

After a brief period of import compression, imports across the board began to surge. By 1994–5 import of capital goods jumped to US$8.5 billion, or 50 per cent more than in the pre-crisis year of 1990–1 (*Report on Currency and Finance* [*RCF*] 1994–5). Further, as noted by the NMCC and others, the import duties remained over the years virtually nil for capital goods required for 'mega projects' across the sectors; to add insult to injury, the domestic producers had to pay stiff indirect taxes without countervailing duties on competing imports. The extent of damage to domestic industry and employment was analysed by Nambiar *et al.* (1999). Indeed, the compound average annual growth rate of all manufacturing was higher in the 1980s (7.6 per cent) than in the post-reform years, 1990–2009 (6.2 per cent); much steeper was the fall in that of capital goods, from 11.3 per cent to 5.4 per cent over the same years. The shock therapy was quite effective for capital goods with the growth rate plunging to 3.8 per cent during 1990–2000, but it recovered to 7.3 per cent over the next nine years (Reserve Bank of India [RBI] 2010, Table 30). Apart from import liberalization, there were many other factors behind the deceleration in manufacturing growth.

As for export, the reformers confidently predicted acceleration in that of labour-intensive manufactures after 1991. Did it happen? United Nations Industrial Development Organization (UNIDO) classifies all commodities into: (*a*) resource based (RB), (*b*) low technology (LT), (*c*) medium technology (MT), and (*d*) high technology (HT); the number of SITC three-digit products in these groups are respectively 68, 44, 72, and 17 (UNIDO 2009, p. 127). From the UN Comtrade database, the percentage share of each group in India's total export was calculated for 1990 and 2008. What is most remarkable is the sharp rise of the RB group from 35 per cent in 1990 to 47 per cent in 2008. The earlier policy of restricting the export of minerals and preserving them for future use in domestic manufacturing was gradually lifted after 1991; this led to large-scale environmental degradation and displacement, especially of the tribal population, and generated sociopolitical tensions. Equally remarkable was the precipitous fall in the share of labour-intensive LT goods from 47 per cent to 28 per cent in those years. However, the share of more capital-intensive MT group went up from 13 per cent in 1990 to 20 per cent in 2008. At the other end, the share of the HT group was quite small and stagnant at 4–5 per cent.

Table 4.2 shows that though India's HT exports during 2000–9 rose impressively by a factor of 7, India remains a minor player with a share of less than 1 per cent of the total for six exporters.

Table 4.2   High-tech Export by Some Leading Countries, 2000–9 (US$ billion)

Countries	2000	2008	2009
China	40.3	270.2	239.1
USA	142.2	145.7	113.6
Japan	76.2	63.2	n.a.
EU-27	92.3	164.1	137.1
S. Korea	43.2	68.3	59.4
India	1.4	6.7	10.0

Source: UN Comtrade.

A highly significant high-tech area where the 1991 reforms literally destroyed the incipient domestic industry is telecom manufacturing. The C-DOT, a government-funded research and development (R&D) unit, made remarkable progress in designing, developing, and commercializing a range of digital automatic exchanges within five years of its creation in 1984; the total outlay was just Rs 1,000 million, or a tiny fraction of the R&D costs incurred by MNCs. Further, the fixed cost per installed landline using C-DOT equipment was just one-third of that for imported equipment (Meemansi 1994). After 1991, the government marginalized C-DOT, encouraged private players, domestic or foreign, and permitted duty-free import of equipment. Apparently, the new policy was a great success: The subscriber-base, fixed line and mobile, expanded exponentially from 5.0 to 650 million during 1991–2010, and the revenue of service providers reached US$35 billion. But for telecom equipment with a domestic sale of around US$30 billion, local production (mainly, peripherals like telephone sets) accounted for less than one-fifth. It is ironical that India's major suppliers are Chinese SOEs that were entirely dependent on MNCs up to the mid-1990s. Since software plays a crucial role in manufacturing telecom equipment, and India is still well ahead of China in software development, the C-DOT and similar entities could, with appropriate state support, offer a stiff challenge.

The only major Indian industry that emerged after 1991 and captured global admiration is the export-oriented software industry. Its growth was fuelled by the information technology (IT) revolution in the USA, the presence of a large body of Indian expatriates occupying key managerial posts in that country, and the abundance of highly skilled workers in India earning a fraction of their American counterpart. The Indian government provided various tax incentives in tune with international practice; similar concessions were available to Indian exporters even before 1991.

Indian reformers, prompted by Washington, deliberately abjured an 'industrial policy'. Their overriding objective was to 'lock' India into the global financial system by moving as fast as feasible towards a free cross-border flow of capital. Thus shortly after 1991, control on current account transactions was removed, and unlimited inflow of foreign portfolio capital with virtual exemption from all domestic taxes was solicited. More slowly, big Indian firms were encouraged to raise equity and debt funds in international capital markets, and Indians can now invest abroad using domestic resources. This more or less free mobility of capital is of immense benefit for the large firms and rich individuals; however, whether India as a poor country could gain from such flows has been questioned by many mainstream economists.

For a net inflow of capital, the current account has to be in deficit. The import surplus ballooned from US$6 billion in 2000–1 to US$119 billion in 2008–9, or about 10 per cent of the GDP. The surge in India's software exports and sizeable private transfers covered a large part of the trade deficit. There was still an almost persistent deficit in the current account. From 1990–1 to 2008–9, the cumulative current account deficit amounted to US$91.3 billion while the surplus on capital account was as high as US$337.9 billion, and foreign exchange reserves increased by US$248.9 billion. The corresponding figures (in

US$ billion) for 2000–1 to 2008–9 were 47.6, 260.8, and 215.9 respectively (RBI 2009, Table 142). The huge capital inflows entailing high costs, did not invigorate the productive sectors of the economy, but were locked in low-yield foreign exchange reserves. The consequent annual drain from the country amounted to 4–5 per cent of the 2007 GDP (Chandra 2008).

CHINA

Compulsions behind the Reform

Economic reform in China was the result of a tectonic political shift in 1978 under Deng Xiaoping from 'iron rice bowl' to 'let some get rich first, others will benefit later' as the guiding principle of state policy. The gradual spread of market relations in lieu of very detailed central planning was almost a logical corollary, affecting both agriculture and industry. There was also a compulsion behind the reform that has not received adequate attention.

In absolute terms, China has enormous reserves of natural resources as compared to most other countries, but these are not so abundant per head of the population. After three decades of fairly rapid growth in manufacturing, energy consumption may have approached the sustainable limits by 1978. In that year the ratio of energy consumption (in units of 10,000 tonnes of standard coal equivalent for different types of energy) to the GDP (in units of 100 million yuan at constant 1970 prices) stood at 16.99. Thanks to 'socialist modernization', in 2007 the ratio fell to less than a third at 4.99 (Statistical Yearbook of China [SYC] 2008). However, in 2003, China's energy intensity (in oil equivalents per international dollar of GDP) was higher than the world average by 10 per cent, and also exceeded that of USA, India, Mexico, Brazil, and others (World Resources Institute 2009). Moreover, the country is still heavily dependent on imports and has been acquiring foreign sources of energy and minerals at a feverish pace. Without a change in track around 1978, China's growth would have been stymied.

The bulk of modern industries in China were built in the 1950s with Soviet technology and equipment. When Soviet experts withdrew in the wake of the Sino-Soviet rift, the Chinese bravely faced the challenge, but took many years to complete the unfinished plants.[4] The Soviets had acquired Western technologies in the 1930s to set up most big industries (Sutton 1971, R.W. Davies 1996, pp. 490–9) and replicated these over time. During World War II, significant technical advances were made in the USA to which the Soviets had no access owing to the US embargo during the Cold War. The Soviet economists in the 1950s began to complain about excessive material costs in their industries. Liberman's reform proposal (1962) on pricing of inputs and outputs, and on replacing profits rather than gross output as the 'success indicator' for a firm, was designed to correct these as well as other systemic deficiencies, without diluting state control over the economy. But the Soviet leaders apprehended that the reform would slow down economic growth and rejected it (Lewin 1974). Rather, they opted in the 1970s for massive loans from Western banks to purchase some plants from the West for modernizing Soviet industries; they hoped to repay the loans through exports of such products. But the US-backed embargo on such exports upset the Soviet calculation, and the country was saddled with a huge debt burden.

The Chinese drew two lessons. Relying primarily on indigenous efforts, China could hardly modernize its industries fast enough to avoid a resource crunch. As the import bill for modernization was going to be huge, China could escape a debt trap only if exports rose in step.

An opening was created during President Nixon's Beijing visit in 1972 to meet Mao Zedong. Both agreed that the USSR was the main danger for world peace. In the years, 1972–5, China's exports to the West rose rapidly. A de facto Sino-US strategic alliance was struck, and was cemented during Deng's visit to the USA in 1979. China obtained exceptionally high quotas for textile exports to the USA under the Multi-Fibre Arrangement (MFA). However, China's state-owned enterprises (SOEs) were unlikely to satisfy the requirements of US consumers. On the other hand, capitalists from the Chinese diaspora in Hong Kong, Macao, and so on, were already well-entrenched in Western markets, faced rising labour costs, and were keen (with US blessing) to relocate production in China. To accommodate them, China had to change its foreign direct investment (FDI) rules. Further, the planning system with centralized allocation of inputs and of price-fixing, had to be radically changed to give priority to exports. Indeed, the number of centrally planned products was reduced gradually, allowing a greater leeway for market forces—under the state's overall control.

In short, China embraced market socialism with an 'open door' to FDI out of domestic compulsion. Today's left-wing critics in China have not questioned the need for the market forces or for FDI, but attacked the systemic tendency aggravating multi-layered inequalities; they believe that the trend can still be reversed to salvage socialism (Open Letter 2004, Lee and Selden 2008).

Industrial Policy after 1978

China proceeded carefully with reforms without a clear blueprint, and retained a number of policies from the Maoist era, while discarding others. The state-party maintained its iron grip over the polity. The economic goal of catching up with the advanced capitalist countries remained and the state exercised as much control as it thought necessary over all economic transactions, domestic or foreign. FDIs and technology imports played a critical role in this process. Market forces were encouraged in ever-widening spheres, not as an end in itself, but as a tool of state policy. This basic feature of 'socialism with Chinese characteristics' contradicts the essence of neo-liberalism as formulated by Hayek or Milton Friedman, although some of Deng's key ideas were indistinguishable from those of the latter.

Despite an enormous appetite for foreign capital, over the years China's domestic savings generally financed domestic investment and the external account was rarely in the red. Being self-reliant on these two fundamentals, the state decided on the kind of foreign capital to be encouraged or barred. To promote exports and rapid modernization of domestic industries, FDI in export-oriented sectors was mollycoddled with income tax breaks and liberal imports of capital goods or intermediates. But many restrictions, though changing over time, were imposed on FDI seeking to exploit the domestic market. Further, in each case to this day, the foreign investor must sign a prior contract with the state, specifying the foreign contribution (in the form of technology, capital goods, and cash), and the contract period (usually 30 years, but renewable) beyond which the investor would have no claim over the residual assets.

Till the late 1990s, the foreign investor was obliged to form a joint venture (JV) with a Chinese SOE; the latter would have the majority stake and appoint the chairman. The foreign partner had to disclose full details of the technology and capital goods supplied, so that the

Chinese could assimilate the know-how and know-why of the technology.[5] Further, foreign exchange outflows (import of capital goods and raw materials, dividends, and so on) had to be balanced by exports either from the JV itself or from a 'third party' to be identified by the foreign investors (Chandra 1999).

The constraints mattered little for investors from the Chinese diaspora in Hong Kong, Macao, and elsewhere in Southeast Asia, as they set up low-technology, labour-intensive units for 'processing exports'. The overwhelming bulk of FDI into China till the late 1990s came from these sources.

Foreign investors (till the late 1990s) seeking to exploit China's domestic market were irked by the restrictions mentioned earlier. Yet they came in droves to have a slice of the enormous market. Owing to the disclosure requirement, they rarely inducted the latest technologies. Still, they profited from China's protected markets. Critics of the official policy lamented that the country lost precious foreign exchange, while the pace of modernization was slow. The same argument has been made with respect to other developing countries, and needs closer scrutiny.

Had China insisted on obtaining state-of-the-art technologies in the early 1980s, few MNCs would be interested, even if they became the sole owners with full control over the ventures. For, the market for such expensive products was quite small owing to the low income of the Chinese. Indeed, India's Foreign Exchange and Regulation Act, 1973, put a 40 per cent cap on foreign equity, but relaxed it to 50 per cent or more, if a firm utilized 'sophisticated' technology not available in the country. At the end of the 1970s, only two or three out of hundreds of foreign firms fulfilled the requirement (Chandra 1994).

Conversely, could China in the early 1980s successfully absorb the latest technologies in different sectors? As noted earlier, the USSR in the 1970s had imported such technologies from the West in several industries. But these plants were like islands with no linkages to the rest of the economy, and could not be replicated by Soviet engineers (Gomulka *et al.* 1984). It should have been true *a fortiori* for China in the 1980s. On the other hand, the somewhat dated technologies of the JVs were fully assimilated by the Chinese personnel who set up new production facilities on their own with much lower imports than before. Moreover, through further development work, the Chinese kept production cost pegged at a low level. Technology diffusion spawned a large number of new domestic firms and intense competition among them as well as the JVs exerted a downward pressure on market prices, resulting in a rapid expansion in domestic sale and exports of low-cost manufactured goods.

Foreign invested enterprises (FIEs) do now play a leading role in China's exports. In Figures 4.1 and 4.2 the values of their export and net export and the share of FIEs in China's manufacturing exports are shown. On the FIE share, I have no data prior to 1991 when it was just 22 per cent; it improved gradually to 50 per cent in 2000, soared to a peak of 62 per cent in 2004, but came down to 58 per cent in 2008. On the other hand, their net foreign exchange earning was in the red till 1997, and became positive, though quite small, up to 2004.

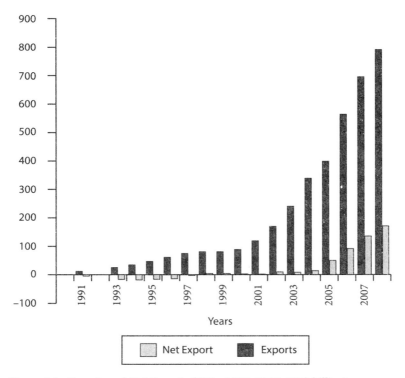

Figure 4.1 Exports and Net Export of FIEs, 1991–2008 (US$ billion)

Source: SYC, various years.

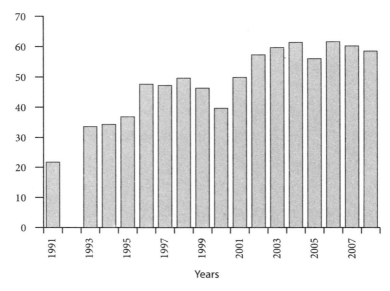

Figure 4.2 Share of FIEs in Manufacturing Exports, 1991–2008 (per cent)
Source: SYC, various years.

Subsequently, the positive balance jumped from U$50 billion in 2005 to a massive US$171 billion in 2008. Still, their trade balance as a proportion of exports was just 22 per cent in 2008. The surge in FIE export from the late 1990s is related to China's quest for high-tech industries with the help of foreign capital and technology, and I shall discuss it shortly.

Another common perception is that the FIEs are mainly engaged in 'processing trade' in which local value added is small. Indeed, of FIE export in 1996, as much as 86 per cent consisted of processing export, according to the customs data; the percentage came down to 81 in 2000, and 73 in 2008 (UNCTAD 1996 and Invest in China, Investment Promotion, Agency of Ministry of Commerce, Beijing).

Data on processing export by all firms, including FIEs, are given in Figures 4.3 and 4.4. Such exports gathered momentum from the mid-1980s, and consistently exceeded one-half of China's manufacturing export from 1989, reaching a peak of nearly two-thirds in 1996. The share began to drop slowly thereafter, reaching barely 50 per cent in 2008. Net export was negative till 1988, and positive but small up to

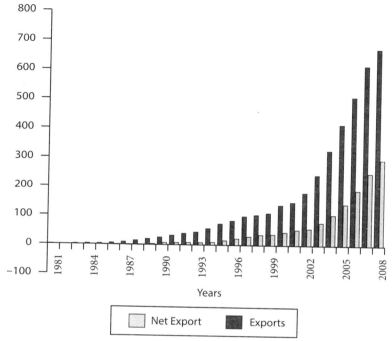

Figure 4.3 Processing Trade: Exports and Net Export, 1981–2008 (US$ billion)
Source: SYC, various years.

1995. Over the years there was a significant improvement, and the ratio of net to total export rose to 44 per cent in 2008. The percentage is quite high compared to that for overall manufacturing exports from many countries, for example, South Korea. Viewing China's processing export as a kind of *entrepôt* trade is outdated.

At this stage, one must put in a caveat. Observers have long noted that a part of FDI is not 'foreign', but represents 'round-trip' investments by Chinese SOE affiliates in offshore locations, notably Hong Kong. How important has it been? A widely quoted scholar, Huang (2003, p. 38) referred to an unsubstantiated 1992 World Bank report as well as others to suggest that the percentage of such investment in total inflow in the early 2000s was 25 or less, and hence round-trip FDI was not very significant. On the other hand, in an OECD paper Sung (1996) looked closely at China's outward FDI policy from the early 1950s, and explored the reasons why the

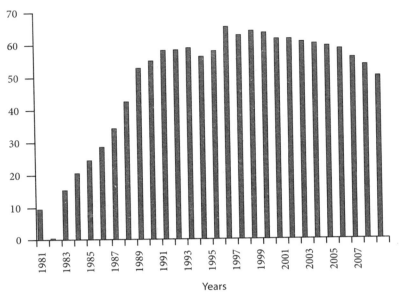

Figure 4.4 **Share of Processing Export in Total Manufacturing Exports, 1981–2008 (per cent)**

Source: SYC, various years.

state encouraged the SOEs affiliates in Hong Kong. They would gain, for instance, access to information on overseas market conditions, act as listening posts to gather data on technology, management, and so on. Sung provided data on how individual SOE affiliates expanded over the years, but gave no figure on the overall magnitudes of outward FDI. He concluded that in the mid-1990s, the stock of outward FDI should have been a significant proportion of the stock of inward FDI.

A detailed study for the Asian Development Bank (ADB) by Geng Xiao (2004) put the percentage of round-trip to total FDI inflow at anywhere between 26 and 56 in the early 2000s. Next, China's Central Bank reported that one-half of FDI into China in 2004–5 was owing to round-trips by domestic firms through Hong Kong and the Caribbean offshore centres to avail of tax-breaks (*Hindu Business Line*, 10 August 2005). In 2007, offshore locations like the Virgin Islands, Cayman Islands, and Samoan Islands became major sources of FDI, accounting for 28 per cent of the total of US$72 billion (SYC 2009); apparently, these were instances of round-tripping. Further, the current definition of 'FIE' includes any firm with a foreign equity of at least 10 per cent (Kennedy 2007). Hence a significant, though unknown, proportion of FIE exports and imports was on account of enterprises directly or indirectly controlled by the SOEs or other Chinese firms.

Returning to the question of the relative importance in export of domestic firms and FIEs (including the round-trip cases), I have compiled in Table 4.3 figures for some years. One finds that: (*a*) up to 2000 the domestic firms were the main exporters, but in 2008 the FIEs went far ahead, (*b*) in processing trade, the FIEs had a clear lead over domestic firms all through, and (*c*) conversely, in ordinary trade the local firms consistently outperformed the FIEs, even in 2008. However, it would be hazardous to extrapolate into the future from the trend between 2000 and 2008.

Table 4.3   The Contribution of FIEs and Domestic Firms to China's Processing Export and Ordinary Export, 1995–2008 (US$ billion)

	Processing	Ordinary
1995		
FIEs	40.3	6.6
Domestic firms	33.4	47.0
2000		
FIEs	71.8	16.8
Domestic firms	65.9	69.2
2008		
FIEs	492.8	297.7
Domestic firms	182.3	380.0

Source: SYC, various years.

High-tech Industries

From the late 1990s China adopted a variety of well-coordinated measures to promote HT industries and their export. In 2002, Beijing radically revised the existing legislation in order to promote smoother and faster movement of technology and know-how into China by shifting the emphasis toward approval rather than tight control. As Table 4.2 shows, China's exports rose almost six-fold to US$279 billion during 2000–8, the last pre-crisis year, while that of the US or Japan remained stagnant or fell, and that of the EU-27 expanded by 80 per cent. This is corroborated by a US National Science Foundation study cited by an EU (2009) report, each using a somewhat different scheme of classification for 'HT'. The latter study found that 'the labour-skill structure of imports from China increasingly mirrored that of intra-EU trade'. On the other hand, China recorded impressive gains in virtually all those industry groups that witnessed falling unit-values. Although China was successfully upgrading technology in export sectors to provide a 'competitive challenge' for the EU, much of it took place outside the 'genuinely' Chinese enterprises. Excluding export from the FIE, China was still specializing in labour-intensive goods, the EU report concluded.

A joint study by scholars from China's National Development and Reform Commission and the US International Trade Commission (Ferrantino *et al.* 2008) prepared two sets of estimates, based respectively on China's definition of HT, and that of the US Census Bureau on 'advanced technology products (ATP)'; the absolute levels are different, but both show a similar trend over time. The combined export of China and Hong Kong (often used as an *entrepôt* by Chinese firms) of ATP to the United States rose from US$5.5 billion in 1996 to US$73.5 billion in 2006. While the United States had a small surplus of US$2.3 billion in 1996, the deficits were very large at US$49.3 billion in 2006, and US$65.0 billion in 2008 (US Bureau of Census website). The Americans are worried by the rising imbalance in their ATP trade with China and Hong Kong. Since 'wholly foreign owned' firms accounted for the overwhelming bulk (over 95 per cent in many product lines) of China's exports, American firms obviously set up labour-intensive manufacturing subsidiaries there to remain globally competitive. Moreover, these firms are also creating very large R&D centres in China (and India). In the not-too-distant future, the employment prospects for America's highly skilled labour force that has ensured since 1950 the nation's global supremacy, may be jeopardized.

Mainstream Western economists had welcomed cheap imports of textiles, and so on, from developing countries in the hope that the West would specialize in high-value goods. Quite a few of them, including Nobel Laureate Samuelson (2004) and Gomory and Baumol (2004), are now having second thoughts about the benefit of free trade. Should

America lose its leadership in ATP, it might be irreversible under free trade conditions. Krugman's (1987 and 1993) new trade theory shows why, for an advanced industrial country, a selective protectionist trade policy may be beneficial. The response to Samuelson by Bhagwati *et al.* (2004) missed the point as they focused on arm's-length transactions typified by 'business process outsourcing' by a Western firm to a contractor in a low-wage country.

Radical critics of China's FDI policy contend that the country is highly dependent on exports channelled through the MNCs, subjecting China to the volatility of global markets; besides, these exports have a low domestic content, much of it in the form of subsistence wage (or less) for migrant labour from rural areas (Hart-Landsberg 2008). This pattern of trade brings little benefit to China as it reproduces the traditional hierarchy of the colonial era in the international division of labour.

Table 4.4 shows China's trade performance in electronic goods, but the coverage may be incomplete. China improved her percentage share of the world market dramatically from 4.5 to 24.5 over the eight years, while its net import of US$959 million in 2000 turned into a massive export surplus of over US$150 billion in 2008. Of the three sub-groups, China in 2008 became the world's leading exporter in EDP and office equipment as well as in telecom equipment, and the

Table 4.4   China's Share in World Export and Its Trade Balance in Electronic Goods, 2000 and 2008

Product Group	2000	2008
1. All electronic goods (4.3)		
Share in world export (%)	4.5	24.5
Net trade balance $ million	−929	150,724
1a. EDP & office equipment (4.3.1)		
Share in world export (%)	5	32.2
Net trade balance $ million	7,780	130,313
1b. Telecom equipment (4.3.2)		
Share in world export (%)	6.8	27.1
Net trade balance $ million	7,095	124,963
1c. ICs & electron. component (4.3.3)		
Share in world export (%)	1.7	10.5
Net trade balance $ million	−15,804	−104,552

Source: WTO website.

Note: The figures in parentheses refer to the code for each product group.

corresponding trade balance was a staggering US$254 billion. But in intermediates, namely ICs and electronic components, despite a six-fold rise in China's share of world exports, its net imports were quite large at US$105 billion. These figures give some credence to the view that China is primarily assembling imported kits for exports, mostly through the FIEs.

To probe further into the issue, one may look at Table 4.5 on the shares in 2008 of different types of enterprises in China's exports. For all commodities, the highest contribution came from the FIE, followed by domestic private firms, the SOE group (including collectively owned firms), and, finally, other foreign firms. The proportions are somewhat different for electronic goods; the FIEs play a dominant role in export and net export, leaving others way behind. By clubbing together FIEs and other foreign firms, many analysts consider China's export success as a by-product of her ability to attract foreign capital, and recommend other developing countries to tread the same path.

Table 4.5   **Contribution of Different Types of Enterprises in China's Exports and Net Export, 2008**

Commodities	Export ($ million)	Share (%) in Export	Net Export ($ million)	Net Export/ Export (%)
All commodities	1,428,869	100.0	297,401	20.8
SOE[a]	311,908	21.8	−70,303	−22.5
FIE	545,477	38.2	115,999	21.3
Other foreign firms[b]	245,355	17.2	54,602	22.3
Private[c]	325,845	22.8	200,909	61.7
Electronics[d]	542,140	100.0	160,728	29.6
SOE[a]	67,118	12.4	10,944	16.3
FIE	324,162	59.8	103,339	31.9
Other foreign firms[b]	100,531	18.5	28,171	28.0
Private[c]	50,298	9.3	18,508	36.8

Source: China's customs statistics as compiled in US–China Economic Security Review Commission, Hearing 24 March 2009, www.uscc.gov.

Notes: [a] SOEs and collectively owned enterprises.

[b] Includes Sino-foreign joint contractual ventures and Sino-foreign equity joint ventures.

[c] Includes private enterprises and private firms.

[d] Includes communication equipment, consumer electronics, electronic components, equipment manufacturing, industrial electronics, and semiconductors.

Against this I have two reservations. First, as noted already, since the threshold of foreign equity is only 10 per cent, many FIEs may be SOE-controlled. Second, 'other foreign firms', comprising of two kinds of joint ventures with local firms, have a large share of export, and one cannot label these either as domestic or as foreign. Nevertheless, there is no doubt that a very large part of China's export of electronic and other goods is of a 'processing' type by Western MNCs.

The figures do not reveal the potential of China's domestic firms. For analogy, one may recall that Korea's Samsung and LG began assembling electronic components as subcontractors of US majors, but became eventually global leaders. Let me now quote from the testimony by Scalise (2005), then president of the US Semiconductor Industry Association, before a US Congressional Committee. In semiconductor technology, China chose

> the low end of the foundry business as the entry vehicle into the global ... industry. [The] foundries are advancing rapidly to becoming world-class in leading-edge process technology. In addition, the Chinese Government proactively supports an entire local ecosystem including fabless design houses, integrated device manufacturers (IDMs), contract manufacturers (EMS) and designers (ODMs), test and packaging houses, venture capital and start-up firms.

Why do MNCs opt for China?

> Chinese government policies, and not lower labour costs, are the major contributor to 10 year, a $1 billion cost differential, between building and operating a semiconductor plant in China compared to the U.S. About 70% of the cost difference is due to tax benefits, 20% due to capital grants, and only 10% due to lower labour costs. Operating costs such as lower utility costs or cheaper logistics are also slightly lower overseas.

'Haier, the leading Chinese consumer electronics firm ... started as an OEM manufacturer for several Japanese electronics firms, evolved into TV and DVD design, and are now marketing as a branded entity in the U.S. and Europe. They have become [by 2005] the world's fifth largest supplier of consumer electronics equipment from a cold start in 1984.' Another excellent example is Flextronics, little known outside the industry circles. Over the years it 'has evolved from a pure U.S.-based contract manufacturer in the 1980s to a global force in the design and manufacture of cell phones and other high value consumer devices. [It has] over 2000 ... engineers ... in China, designing products for companies such as Motorola, Sony, Ericsson, and Siemens.'

If China offers incentives to MNCs not available elsewhere, a wide spectrum of SOEs, especially some 159 SOEs under the State-owned Assets Supervision and Administration Commission (SASAC) that are monitored on a daily basis by Beijing, and characterized by the German magazine, *Der Spigel* (2007), as Red China Inc., are nurtured like plants in a hothouse to become global players. In terms of value added, the SASAC group does not contribute much to the GDP, but its profits amount to 3–4 per cent of the GDP, thanks to a range of fiscal bounties. Further, these firms account for the bulk of China's R&D that has increased exponentially in the last decade (Kuijs 2006, Naughton 2007).

Encouraging both the MNCs and the SOEs appears to be contradictory, but as the 11th Five-Year Plan for Use of Foreign Investment explained, China will

> Encourage foreign enterprises—especially large-scale multinationals—to transfer the processing and manufacturing processes with higher technology levels and higher added value and research and development organisations to China, ... to develop a technology spillover effect, and strengthen the independent innovation ability of Chinese enterprises ... [T]he overall strategic objective of use of foreign investment in China is to ... change the emphasis in use of foreign investment from making up the shortage of capital and foreign exchange to introducing advanced technologies. (Introduction 2009)

In addition, China promotes its own technical standards to tip the scale in favour of its own SOEs; the best example is that of 3G technology for mobile telephony that helped Huwawei and ZTC to penetrate the equipment market in the EU and India, among others. Last but not least, government procurement policy consistently favours domestic firms and brand names so that the huge budgetary funds for R&D outlays and even larger bank credits at low rates of interest are channelled into the SOEs.

Against radical critics like Hart-Landsberg, my arguments can be summed up as follows: (*a*) Some of the SOEs have emerged as world-class players, setting the norms for global industry. (*b*) In view of the advantages of locating business in China, John Chambers, the CEO of Cisco Systems (US), a front-ranking IT firm, was reported saying in 2003: 'China will become the IT center of the world. What we're trying to do is to outline an entire strategy of becoming a Chinese company' (quoted from Jones 2008). Washington was alarmed. (c) After the 1997 Asian financial crisis, China has been investing in infrastructure at a feverish pace through the budget as well as directed credit from the commercial banks. The contracts are typically awarded to the SOEs. The latter often collaborate with MNCs that agree to part with technical know-how and know-why. As a result, the SOEs began to win an increasing number of big contracts to develop infrastructure at home and abroad. I may cite just one. In 2004 an SOE obtained the Japanese bullet train technology from Kawasaki for $1.6 billion, including the cost of 60 train sets. The first trains ran in 2007. The Chinese improved upon the original design parameters so that in 2010 only 15 per cent of the value of train sets came from import. The market in China is worth US$100 billion, and rising rapidly (Dickie 2010). China is also bidding for a project in Los Angeles.

Ceteris paribus, China's industrial policy has been eminently successful from a narrow nationalist perspective. But the social benefits of enormous investments (close to 50 per cent of GDP) in modernizing industry, in grandiose public works or in esoteric HT areas, have not been investigated, taking into account financial costs and the colossal environmental damage.

A CRITIQUE OF THE GROWTH EXPERIENCE IN INDIA AND CHINA

While the growth rates of India and China have 'mesmerized' the international community, there are two major flaws of a systemic nature. In both countries there has been an astonishing rise in inequality. In foreign trade and investments these countries have derived enormous benefits from their integration with the neoliberal international economic order.

Inequality

Estimates of the Gini coefficient of income distribution for India do not exist as household surveys exclude savings. The Gini coefficient from China's official surveys of household income has of late crossed the generally accepted 'danger' level of 0.40 to reach 0.47. Actually, it is worse. 'Grey income', not captured in the surveys, amounted in

2008 to US$1.4 trillion, or about 30 per cent of China's GDP, and 80 per cent of the total belonged to the top 20 per cent of households, according to a study sponsored by Credit Suisse (Forsythe 2010).

More revealing are the global estimates made annually since 1996 by Capegimini (www.capgemini.com) of the wealth of the super-rich, each with assets of US$1.0 million or more. In China their number in 2009 was 415,000, while their combined wealth amounted to 26 per cent of the GDP; the corresponding figures were 127,000 and 28 per cent for India. Further, the number and wealth of the group have been increasing at a much faster pace than the GDP in these countries over the last 15 years.

At the other end, only one-fifth of the population In India had an income exceeding the unacceptably low official poverty level by 50 per cent in 2004 (NCEUS 2007). Hunger and malnutrition are still widely prevalent. The Human Development Index (HDI) of the United Nation Development Programme (UNDP) gave a lowly rank of 119 to India, and 89 to China, out of a total of 169 countries in 2009 (*Human Development Report* 2010).

In China the overwhelming majority of the population now enjoys a far higher level of real income than in 1980, and the incidence of poverty is much smaller than in India. Yet for 65–70 per cent of the population, mainly farmers and migrant workers, earnings (currently US$1,000, as against a per capita GDP of US$3,800) have either stagnated or risen very slowly for two decades (*People's Daily*, 31 October 2005, Fan Gang 2010). Indeed, the share of household consumption in the GDP fell sharply from 48 per cent to about 33 per cent (the lowest ever in the world) during 1997–2007 (TDR 2010, Chart 2.10).

A leading establishment economist, Yu Yongding (*China Daily*, 23 December 2010) began by quoting Premier Wen Jiabao: 'China's growth is '*unstable, unbalanced, uncoordinated and ultimately unsustainable*' [emphasis added]. There was massive overinvestment on 'luxurious condominiums, magnificent government office buildings and soaring skyscrapers ... Some local governments are literally digging holes and then filling them in to ratchet up the GDP ... [In the meanwhile] China has become one of the world's most polluted countries'. The author characterized the present system as one of 'collusion between government officials and businesspeople', that is, 'capitalism of the rich and powerful'. Further, 'breaking this unholy alliance will be the big test for China's leadership in 2011 and beyond'.

Thus, for all the recent rhetoric of 'harmonious development' in China and 'inclusive growth' in India, the actual trends are in the opposite direction. Not surprisingly, it has spread to the sphere of international economic relations.

Foreign Trade

China is now the world's largest exporter with a share of 9.6 per cent in 2009, ahead of Germany (9.0 per cent) and the US (8.5 per cent), with India (1.3 per cent) lagging far behind. What is the pattern of China's trade with other developing countries?

In textiles and clothing, China's global share increased from 14.7 per cent in 2000 to 20.8 per cent in 2004; after quotas under MFA were abolished, it shot up to 31.7 per cent in 2009. Over the same decade Africa's share barely rose from 3.7 per cent to 3.9 per cent, and that of Latin America and the Caribbean countries shrank from 1.4 per cent to 1.0 per cent. South Asian countries saw a marginal rise in their share from 6.6 per cent to 7.3 per cent (WTO database). A telling case is that of Central America that had the same share (12.0 per cent) as China of the US imports of garments in 2001; despite the creation of the Central American Free Trade Association, the region's share of the US market plunged to 8.7 per cent as China's soared to 38 per cent in 2008 (Gallagher 2010).

Next, consider the trade between China and India, respectively ranked first and second in manufacturing competitiveness, ahead of Korea, USA, and Brazil, in a recent study by Deloitte and the US Commission on Competitiveness (*The Times of India*, 3 December 2010). Bilateral China–India trade rocketed from US$2.3 billion in 2000 to US$40.0 billion in 2009, while China's surplus jumped from US$0.8 billion to US$19.3 billion over the same years. In 2009 India had a surplus of US$2.8 billion in primary goods, while China had a surplus of US$4.0 billion in labour-intensive manufactures, including US$1.5 billion in textiles and clothing, and $18.1 billion in medium- and high-tech manufactures (UNcomtrade database).

China's two-way trade with Africa leapt from US$6 billion in 1997 to US$107 billion in 2008. China's imports consist predominantly (around 90 per cent) of oil and other primary commodities, while manufactures dominate the exports (Harsch 2007, Wang and Bio-Tchné 2008). Similarly, Latin America's imports, predominantly of manufactures, from China stood at US$44 billion in 2009, indicating a ten-fold rise since 2000; but in exports primary goods constituted over 80 per cent of the total. The share reached 90 per cent in Brazil's exports to China. By contrast, manufactures constituted 38 per cent of Brazil's aggregate exports. (Bárcena and Rosales 2010, Barbosa and Mendes 2006).

China's emergence has benefited other developing countries in several ways. It is estimated that in the last two decades, a rise by 1 per cent in China's export had a positive 0.5 per cent impact on the growth of the rest of the world (Arora and Vamvakidis 2010). Moreover, the monopoly stranglehold of Western MNC firms has been breached in many areas. Prices of primary goods have risen sharply. For a wide range of manufactures from low- to high-tech goods the prices have come down. These claims are valid on the *ceteris paribus* premise, namely that the present architecture of global trade and investment flows is *given.*

A recent German study posed the question: China and Latin America—A partnership of equals or the one-sided securing of access to raw materials? Latin American countries with a large manufacturing base face 'threats' from China in a wide range of their exports (GDI 2010, Gallagher 2010). Africa faces the same predicament with factories in textiles and other consumer goods closing down (Hanson 2008).

Thus China's recent trade pattern vis-à-vis Africa, Latin America, and India is a mirror image of that in the colonial era when the periphery was de-industrialized by the metropolitan powers. Thanks to its opaque system of taxation, subsidies, government procurement policy, directed credit from banks, and so on, China has taken full advantage of the loopholes under the WTO rules to push exports and block imports simultaneously.

Global Capital Market

China's huge trade surpluses enabled it to build up astronomical foreign exchange reserves. There is a strong presumption that the reserves have been deployed in a non-transparent manner to acquire foreign assets other than treasury bonds of rich countries. The stock of Chinese outbound FDI, according to a recent estimate, shot up from US$28 billion in 2000 to US$246 billion in 2009 (K. Davies 2010).

In recent years China and the USA were 'the real engine[s] of the world economy', contributing over one-half of the world's GDP growth from 2002 to 2008. There was a 'symbiotic relationship between the two giants'; China's BOP surplus and America's deficit complemented each other, and the term, Chimerica, was coined to describe the world order (Ferguson 2008, Fabre 2009). Even earlier, *The Economist* (30 July 2005) wrote on 'How China runs the world economy'.

More than two years after the crisis of 2008, the spectre of prolonged depression haunts the rich countries, despite sizeable bail-out and stimulus packages. China had a more effective stimulus package, propping up its GDP growth, trade surplus, outbound FDI, and foreign exchange reserve. India, too, weathered the storm thanks to portfolio capital inflows, but remains as vulnerable as before. Thus both countries are locked, for different reasons, into the neo-liberal world economic order.

Since the system is detrimental to the long-term interests of an overwhelming majority of mankind, including those in China and India, one must replace it by one that is fair and equitable for all concerned, and ensures national sovereignty of all developing countries in determining their foreign trade and investments policies. From this perspective the expanding trade and investment relations of China and India with other developing countries is a matter of serious concern.

NOTES

1. Bhagwati *et al.* (1975) found that the unweighted averages were 97 per cent for 61 industries in 1963–5, and 84 per cent for 30 industries in 1970, while World Bank (1990), after examining 500 products 1987–9, put the average ERP at 46 per cent. In these exercises, the 'deemed' cost of a domestic input is equated to that of a similar import plus the nominal import tariff, even if the actual domestic input was lower; for an item with quantitative restrictions on import, the cost was put at that of import *plus* the black market premium, even if import covered a part of the domestic requirement. Since the black market premium assumes that the rupee was overvalued, the product prices should also have been raised correspondingly. Thus Kathuria (1995) put ERP at just 4 per cent for the World Bank set of products. Using a price-based method, and after eliminating the 'noise' created by higher domestic taxes and raw material costs in India, Nambiar (1983) found that for 170 traded goods the ERP was above 40 per cent in 1961 and 1968, but became negative at −17 per cent in 1973. For the capital goods sector, Chandrasekhar (1992) observed that the ERP was favourable for Indian products.

2. For DRC, the domestic value added is enhanced by the amount of indirect taxes paid on inputs that are usually much higher in India than abroad. World value added is the difference between world product price and the value of imported inputs needed to produce the good in the country, both calculated in dollars. The ICICI (1977 and 1985), then a leading development bank, made two studies for 1974–5 and 1980–1, based on samples of around 50 borrower companies that furnished data; some corrections were made to compute 'adjusted' DRC (see Chandra 1986). The DRC declined over the benchmark years, especially for capital goods industries. Short-run DRC that considers only the actual variable costs was found to be significantly below the official exchange rate across the board for the entire sample. The BICP, an official agency that replaced the Tariff Commission, estimated DRC for many industries in the 1980s; these are summarized by Kelkar and Kumar (1990). Broadly, the industries were found to be competitive, especially in engineering and capital goods required for aluminium processing or power generation, though it was not true for many petroleum-based industries.

3. Per capita real GDP at international dollars nosedived from US$13,680 in 1991 to a trough of US$7,104 in 1998, and then recovered somewhat; in 2007 it was still US$13,401 (PWT 2009). A leading Russian scholar, Khanin (2006) found that even under President Putin, the structural weaknesses of the economy persisted, and industrial output was a pale shadow of its glory days up to 1990.

4. Based on archival materials, publications and interviews with relevant persons both in Russia and China, Shen (2002) provides a rare insight into the story of Soviet technical assistance to China from 1949 to 1960 that was perhaps unparalleled in human history. Soviet experts numbering about 20,000 were dispatched to China to help build the 'modern' sectors of the economy, including its planning and management, higher education and the armed forces. The guidelines were set at Mao's meeting with Stalin in 1949. Over the years, the Chinese wanted more experts than what the Soviets offered, as China had a paucity of qualified personnel. There were also criticisms in both countries about the role of Soviet experts. In July 1959 Khrushchev offered to withdraw them, but at China's request the programme continued though the number of Soviet experts gradually came down, and only a handful remained after 1960 in the wake of the Great Schism. Apart from the Soviet experts in China, a very large number (the exact figure is not available) of Chinese students entered Soviet universities, and trainees were attached to Soviet industries. Given the scale of China's industrialization in the 1950s, skill shortage was still quite acute in 1960, and this may have prolonged the country's agony after the Great Schism. This may explain why China under Deng required foreign technology suppliers to disclose details of imported technologies.

5. See Note 3.

REFERENCES

Ahluwalia, I.J. 1991. *Productivity and Growth in Indian Manufacturing*. New Delhi: Oxford University Press.

Amsden, A.H. 1989. *Asia's Next Giant: South Korea and Late Industrialization.* New York: Oxford University Press.

Anonymous, 1985. 'Economic Efficiency of the Machinery Sector in India: Findings of a World Bank Study', *Economic and Political Weekly*, 12 October, 20 (41): 1724–25.

Arora, V.A. Vamvakidis. 2010. *China's Economic Growth: International Spillovers.* July, International Monetary Fund, WP/10/165.

Balakrishnan, P. and K. Pushpangadan. 1994. 'Total Factor-Productivity Growth in Manufacturing Industry: A Fresh Look', *Economic and Political Weekly*, 30 July, 29 (31): 2028–35.

Barbosa, A.F.. and R.C. Mendes. 2006. *Economic Relations between Brazil and China: A Difficult Partnership.* FES Briefing Paper. Sao Paulo: Friederich Ebert Stiftung, January 2006.

Bárcena A. and O. Rosales. 2010. *The People's Republic of China and Latin America and the Caribbean: Towards a Strategic Relationship*, Santiagi: Economic Commission for Latin America and the Caribbean, May.

Bhagwati, J.N. and P. Desai. 1970. *India: Planning for Industrialisation.* Paris: OECD.

Bhagwati, J.N., T.N. Srinivasan, and V. Panchamukhi. 1975. 'Static Allocational and Efficiency Impact on Growth', in J.N. Bhagwati and T.N. Srinivasan (eds), *Foreign Trade Regimes and Economic Development: India.* New York: National Bureau of Economic Research.

Bhagwati, J., A. Panagariya, and T.N. Srinivasan. 2004. 'The Muddles over Outsourcing', *The Journal of Economic Perspectives*, 18 (4): 93–114.

Bliss, C. 1989. 'Trade and Development', in H. Chenery and T. N. Srinivasan (eds), *Handbook of Development Economics*, Vol. II. pp. 1188–1240. Amsterdam: North Holland.

Chandra, N.K. 1994. 'Planning and Foreign Investment in Indian Manufacturing', in T. J. Byres (ed.), *The State and Development Planning in India*, pp. 477–527. New Delhi: Oxford University Press.

—————. 1999. 'FDI and Domestic Economy: Neoliberalism in China', *Economic and Political Weekly*, 34 (45): 3195–212.

—————. 2008. 'India's Foreign Exchange Reserves: A Shield of Comfort or an Albatross?', *Economic and Political Weekly*, 43 (14): 39–51.

—————. 2009. 'China and India: Convergence in Economic Growth and Social Tensions?', *Economic and Political Weekly*, 44 (4): 41–53.

Chandrasekhar, C.P. 1992. 'Investment Behaviour, Economies of Scale and Efficiency in an Import-Substituting Regime: A Study of Two Industries', in A. Ghosh, K.K. Subrahmanian, M. Eapen, and H. Drabu (eds), *Indian Industrialisation: Structure and Policy Issues*, pp. 80–107. New Delhi: Oxford University Press.

Chandrasekhar, C.P. and J. Ghosh. 2008. 'India's Hitech Lag', *Macroscan*, 8 September, www.macroscan.com/fet/sep08/fet08092008Hitech.htm.

Chaudhuri, S. 1997. 'Debates on Industrialisation', in T.J. Byres (ed.), *The Indian Economy: Major Debates Since Independence*, pp. 249–94. New Delhi: Oxford University Press.

Cline, W.R. 1982. 'Can the East Asian Model of Development be Generalised?', *World Development*, 10 (2): 81–91.

Davies, K. 2010. *China Has Become a Major Force in Outward Foreign Direct Investment, with $246 Billion of Funds Invested as of 2009*, Vale Columbia Centre on Sustainable International Investment, New York, 19 October.

Davies, R.W. 1996. *The Industrialisation of Soviet Russia Vol. 4; Crisis and Progress in the Soviet Economy, 1931–1933*. London: Macmillan Press.

Der Spiegel. 2007. 'Red China, Inc: Does Communism Work after All?', Spiegel Online, 27 February, www.spiegel.de.

Dickie, M. 2010. 'Japanese Inc. Shoots Itself in the Foot on the Bullet Train', *Financial Times*, 9 July.

EU. 2009. *European Competitiveness Report 2009*. Brussels: Commission of the European Communities.

Fabre, G. 2009. 'The Twilight of "Chimerica"? China and the Collapse of the American Model', *Economic and Political Weekly*, 27 June, 44 (26–7): 299–307.

Fan Gang. 2010. 'China's War on Inequality', 29 October, *Project Syndicate*

Ferguson, N. 2008. 'Geopolitical Consequences of the Credit Crunch', 30 September, www.Niallferguson.org

Ferrantino, M., R. Koopman, Z. Wang and F. Yinug. 2008. 'Classification of Trade in Advanced Technology Products and Its Statistical Reconciliation: The Case of China and the United States', Brookings-Tsinghua Centre for Public Policy, Working Paper no. WP200709006EN, www.brookings.edu/papers/2008/spring_china_btc.aspx (accessed 28 May 2011).

Forsythe, M. 2010. 'China's Rich Have $1.1 Trillion in Hidden Income, Study Finds', *Bloomberg News*, 12 August.

Gallagher, K.P. 2010. 'Latin America Must See China as a Trade Threat, as Well as a Partner', 11 November, http://blogs.ft.com/beyond-brics/.

GDI. 2010. 'China and Latin America—A Partnership of Equals or the One-sided Securing of Access to Raw Materials?'. Bonn: German Development Institute, 6 October.

Geng Xiao. 2004. *Round-tripping Foreign Direct Investment in People's Republic of China: Scale, Causes and Implication*. Discussion Paper No. 7. Manila: Asian Development Bank Institute.

Goldar, B. 1992. 'Productivity and Factor Use Efficiency in Indian Industry', in A. Ghosh, K.K. Subrahmanian, M. Eapen and H.A. Drabu (eds), *Indian Industrialisation: Structure and Policy Issues*, pp. 13–32. New Delhi: Oxford University Press.

Gomory, R.E. and W.J. Baumol. 2004. 'Globalisation: Prospects, Promise and Problems', *Journal of Policy Modelling*, 26 (4): 425–38.

Gomulka, S., A. Nove, and G.D. Holliday. 1984. *East-West Technology Transfer*, OECD, Paris.

Hanson, S. 2008. 'China, Africa, and Oil', 6 June, http://www.cfr.org/publication/9557/china_africa_and_oil.html.

Harsch, E. 2007. 'Big Leap in China-Africa Ties: Beijing Offers Continent More Aid, Trade and Business', *Africa Renewal, January*, http://www.un.org/ecosocdev/.

Hart-Landsberg, M. 2008. *The Realities of China Today*, http://groups.google.com, posted 12 November.

Huang, Y. 2003. *Selling China: Foreign Direct Investment in the Reform Era.* Cambridge: Cambridge University Press.

ICICI. 1977. *Export Performance of Companies: ICICI Portfolio*, Bombay: Industrial Investment and Credit Corporation of India.

————. 1985. *Export Performance of ICICI-Financed Companies (1978–79 to 1980–81)*, Bombay: Industrial Investment and Credit Corporation of India.

International Monetary Fund, World Bank, Organization for Economic Cooperative and Development and European Bank for Reconstruction and Development. 1991. *The Economy of the USSR: Summary and Recommendations*, Washington DC.: International Monetary Fund.

Johnson, C. 1982. *MITI and the Japanese Miracle: The Growth of Industrial Policy*, Stanford, C.A.: Stanford University Press.

Jones, W. 2008. 'Statement' in *Research and Development, Technological Advances in Key Industries, and Changing Trade Flows with Chin: Hearings before the U.S.-China Economic and Security Review Commission*, 16 July, Washington.

Joshi, V. and I.M.D. Little. 1996. *India's Economic Reforms 1991–2001.* New Delhi: Oxford University Press.

Kathuria, S. 1995. 'Competitiveness of Indian Industry', in D. Mookherjee (ed.), *Indian Industry: Policies and Performance*, pp. 148–90. New Delhi: Oxford University Press.

Kelkar, V.L. and R. Kumar. 1990. 'Industrial Growth in the Eighties: Emerging Policy Issues', *Economic and Political Weekly*, 25 (4): 209–22.

Kennedy, S. 2007. 'Testimony', *The Extent of the Government's Control of China's Economy: Hearings before the U.S.–China Economic and Security Review Commission*, 24 March, Washington DC.

Khanin, G. 2006. 'Economic Growth and the Mobilisation Model', in M. Ellman (ed.), *Russia's Oil and Natural Gas: Bonanza or Curse?*, pp. 151–72. London: Anthem Press.

Kravis, I.B., A. Heston, and R. Summers. 1982. *World Product and Income: International Comparison of Real Gross Product.* World Bank and John Hopkins University Press.

Krugman, P.R. 1987. 'The Narrow Moving Band, the Dutch Disease, and the Competitive Consequences of Mrs. Thatcher: Notes on Trade in the Presence of Dynamic Scale Economies', *Journal of Development Economics*, 27 (1–2): 41–55.

————. 1993. 'The Narrow and Broad Arguments for Free Trade', *The American Economic Review*, 83 (2): 362–6.

————. 1994. 'The Myth of Asia's Miracle', *Foreign Affairs*, 73 (6): 62–78.

Kuijs, L. 2006. *How Will China's Saving-Investment Balance Evolve?*, Policy Research Working Paper 3958. Washington DC.: World Bank.

Lee, C.K. and M. Selden. 2008. 'Inequality and Its Enemies in Revolutionary and Reform China', *Economic and Political Weekly*, 27 December, 43 (52): 27–36.

Lewin, M. 1974. *Political Undercurrents in Soviet Economic Debates: From Bukharin to Modern Reformers*. Princeton: Princeton University Press.

Li, H. 2009. 'China's FDI: Net Inflow and the Deterioration of the Terms of Trade: Paradox and Explanation', www.fas.nus.edu.sg.

Liberman, E. 1962. 'Plan, Profit, Premium', *Pravda* (in Russian), 9 September.

Little, I.M.D. 1960. 'The Strategy of Indian Industrial Development', *National Institute Economic Review*, 9 (May) 20–4.

Little, I.M.D., T. Scitovsky, and M. Scott. 1970. *Industry and Trade in Some Developing Countries: A Comparative Study*. Paris: OECD.

Maddison, A. 2007. *Historical Statistics of the World Economy: 1-2003 A.D.*, March, www.ggdc.net/maddison/Historical.../horizontal-file_03-2007.xls.

Mahalanobis, P.C. 1985 [1953]. 'Some Observations on the Process of Growth in National Income', *Sankhya*, in P.K. Bose and M. Mukherjee (eds), *P.C. Mahalanobis: Papers on Planning*. Calcutta: Statistical Publishing Society.

——. 1985 [1955]. 'Recommendations for the formulation of the second five year plan', in P.K. Bose and M. Mukherjee (eds), *P.C. Mahalanobis: Papers on Planning*. Calcutta: Statistical Publishing Society.

Meemansi, G.B. 1994. *The C-DOT Story*. New Delhi: Kedar Publications.

Ministry of Rural Development (MRD). 2009. *Committee on State Agrarian Relations and Unfinished Task of Land Reforms, Vol. 1, Draft Report*, Ministry of Rural Development, New Delhi.

Morishima, M. 1982. *Why Has Japan 'Succeeded'? Western Technology and the Japanese Ethos*. Cambridge: Cambridge University Press.

Nambiar, R.G. 1983. 'Protection to Domestic Industry: Fact and Theory', *Economic and Political Weekly*, 18 (1–2): 27–8, 30–2.

Nambiar, R.G., B.L. Mungekar, and G.A. Tadas. 1999. 'Is Import Liberalisation Hurting Domestic Industry and Employment?' *Economic and Political Weekly*, 34 (7): 417–24.

Naughton, B. 2007. 'Testimony', *The Extent of the Government's Control of China's Economy: Hearings before the U.S.-China Economic and Security Review Commission*, March 24, Washington DC.

Nayyar, D. 1976. *India's Exports and Export Policies in the 1960s*. Cambridge: Cambridge University Press.

NCEUS. 2007. *Report on Conditions of Work and Promotion of Livelihoods in the Unorganised Sector*, April, New Delhi: National Commission on Enterprises in the Unorganised Sector.

NMCC. 2008. *Measures for Ensuring Sustained Growth of the Manufacturing Sector*, National Manufacturing Competitiveness Council, Government of India, September.

Open Letter. 2004. 'A letter to General Secretary Hu [Jintao] from a group of veteran CCP members, veteran cadres, veteran military personnel and intellectuals', *Links*, Issue no. 27, http://links.org.au/node/17.

Planning Commission. 2008. *Development and Challenge In Extremist Affected Areas: Report of an Expert Group*. New Delhi.

PWT. 2009. *Penn World Table, Version 6.3*. Philadelphia: Centre for International Comparisons of Production, Income and Prices at the University of Pennsylvania.

RBI. 2009. *Handbook of Statistics on Indian Economy*. Mumbai: Reserve Bank of India.

RCF. *Report on Currency and Finance*, various years. Mumbai: Reserve Bank of India.

Rodrik, D. 1997. *TFPG Controversies, Institutions and Economic Performance in East Asia*. NBER Working Paper No. 5914. Cambridge, M.A.: National Bureau of Economic Research.

Rodrik, D. and A. Subramanian. 2004. '"*Hindu Growth*" to Productivity Surge: The Mystery of the Indian Growth Transition'. NBER Working Paper No. 10376. Cambridge, MA: National Bureau of Economic Research.

Samuelson, P.A. 2004. 'Where Ricardo and Mill Rebut and Confirm Arguments of Mainstream Economists Supporting Globalisation', *Journal of Economic Perspectives*, 18 (3): 135–46.

Sarel, M. 1996. *Growth in East Asia: What We Can and What We Cannot Infer From It*, IMF Economic Issues, No. 1, September. Washington DC.: International Monetary Fund.

Scalise, G. 2005. 'Testimony of George Scalise, President, Semiconductor Industry Association, 21 April, 2005, http://www.uscc.gov/hearings/2005hearings/hr05_04_21_22.htm.

Shen, Zhihua. 2002. 'A Historical Examination of the Issue of Soviet Experts in China: Basic Situation and Policy Changes', *Russian History/Histoire Russe*, 20 (2–4, Summer–Fall–Winter).

Shetty, S.L. 1978. 'Structural Retrogression in the Indian Economy Since the Mid-Sixties', *Economic and Political Weekly*, 13 (6–7): 185–244.

Statistical Yearbook of China (SYC), various years. www.stats.gov.cn/english/. Beijing: China Statistics Press.

Stiglitz, J. 2000. 'The Insider: What I Learned at the World Economic Crisis', *The New Republic*, 17 April.

Summers, L.H. and V. Thomas. 1993. 'Recent Lessons of Development', *The World Bank Research Observer*, 8 (2): 239–54.

Sung, Y-W 1996. *Chinese Outward Investment in Hong Kong: Trends, Prospects and Policy Implications*, Technical Papers No. 113. Paris: OECD Development Centre.

Sutton, A.C. 1971. *Western Technology and Soviet Economic Development, 1930 to 1945*, Stanford: Stanford University Press.

Trivedi, P. 2000. *Productivity in Major Manufacturing Industries in India: 1973–74 to 1997–98*, Reserve Bank of India, DRG Studies Series No. 20, 26 August.

UNCTAD 1996. *World Investment Report: Investment, Trade and International Policy Agreements*. Geneva: UNCTAD.

UNDP. 2010. *Human Development Report 2010*. New York: UNDP.

UNIDO. 2009. *Industrial Development Report 2009*. Vienna: United Nations Industrial Development Organisation.

U.S.-China Economic and Security Review Commission. 2009. 'Chair and Vice-Chair's Introduction', *Policy and Its Impact on U.S. Companies, Workers and the American Economy: Hearings before the U.S.-China Economic and Security Review Commission*, 24 March, Washington.

UN Database, http://unstats.un.org/unsd/default.htm (accessed 28 May 2011).

Wang, J-Y and A. Bio-Tchané. 2008. 'Africa's Burgeoning Ties with China', *Finance & Development*, IMF, March, www.inf.org/external/pubs/ft/fandd/2008/03/wang.htm.

World Bank. 1975. *India: Survey of the Textile Machinery Industry*, Report No. 976-IN, Washington, DC: World Bank, http://documents.worldbank.org/curated/en/1975/12/1559974/india-survey-textile-machinery-industry (accessed 23 August 2012), http://www.imf.org/external/pubs/ft/fandd/2008/03/wang.htm (accessed 23 August 2012).

————. 1984. *India: Non-electrical Machinery Manufacturing—A Subsector Study*, Report No. 5095-IN.

————. 1990. *India: Strategy for Trade Reform*, Report No. 8998-IN, in 3 volumes.

————. 1993. *The East Asian Miracle: Economic Growth and Public Policy*, New York: Oxford University Press.

World Resources Institute, www.earthtrends.mri.org (accessed 30 September 2009).

WTO Database, http://stat.wto.org/StatisticalProgram/WSDBStatProgramHome.aspx?Language=E (accessed 28 May 2011).

Young, A. 1994. *The Tyranny of Numbers: Confronting the Statistical Realities of the East Asian Growth Experience*, NBER Working Paper No. 4680. Cambridge, MA: National Bureau of Economic Research.

5

China in the Global Crisis

*Death Knell of the East Asian
Developmental Model?*

HO-FUNG HUNG

Ever since Western core countries in the global capitalist systems encountered a prolonged economic downturn precipitated by over-production, rising labour cost, and declining profitability in the 1970s, the East Asian developmental experiences—those of Japan, South Korea, Taiwan, Hong Kong, Singapore, and most recently China—have been lauded as representing a more efficient, low-cost, and profitable model of capitalist development. Though the literature tends to characterize the East Asian model by the central role of the developmental states in facilitating economic growth, the diversity of state–economy relations in fact defies this generalization. The government of Hong Kong, for example, has been reluctant in intervening in the economy throughout its take-off years, while economic governance in China has been far more decentralized than the developmental state in Japan, South Korea, and Taiwan (Hung 2008). What binds these East Asian economies together and accounts for their rapid growth, at the most fundamental level, is their export-oriented industrialization, which was made possible by the geopolitical constellations of East Asia, as well as East Asia's historical legacy of industrious manufacturing since the early modern times (see Arrighi, *et al.* 2003). This mode of industrialization fosters globally competitive manufacturing sectors in their economies, and the subsequent vast accumulation of foreign exchange reserves, which insulate them against indebtedness and macroeconomic instability that had haunted many other developing countries.

The global financial catastrophe that culminated in the US in the fall of 2008 and the spring of 2009 brought about the collapse of the export market for most East Asian economies and the prospect of the collapse of either the US Treasury bonds market or the US dollar, in which these exporters have been investing massively. That is a wake-up call for the vulnerability of the East Asian model of development. Later in 2009, it became apparent that the thrust of state-directed, debt-financed investment under the mega stimulus programme that China rolled out in late 2008 did successfully foster a strong recovery in China and helped prop up other East Asian economies. But the growth generated by the stimulus is not likely to be sustainable. Chinese economists as well as government policy advisers have been worrying that China would falter again once the stimulus effect fades and non-performing loans surge, as it is certain that US consumers will not come back any time soon to pick up the slack (Yu 2009, Roach 2009). The global crisis, which is far from resolved, shows the urgency for these East Asian economies to reorient their growth from an export-dependent to a more domestic-consumption–driven pattern.

In this chapter, I trace the historical and social origins of the deepening dependence of China and its East Asian predecessors on the consumption market in the Global North as the source of their export-led growth, as well as their dependence on US financial vehicles as the store of value for their savings. With these two dependences I show that China and its Asian neighbours have few choices other than continuing to help sustain US global economic dominance amid the global crisis by extending more credits to the US in the short run, despite all the talk within and without Asia about China's intention and capacity to destroy the reserve currency status of the dollar and construct a new global financial order centred in Asia. Towards the end of the chapter, I discuss what options China has in the long and medium run to lead East Asia out of its market and financial dependency on the US, and to facilitate the formation of a more autonomous economic order in Asia.

COLD WAR AND THE RISE OF EAST ASIAN EXPORTERS

The story of the rapid economic ascendancy of Japan and the Four Tigers as dynamic exporters of manufactured goods to the Global North in the post-war era is well known and need not be repeated here. What is often neglected in the discussion is that their ascendancy would have been impossible without the context of Cold War geopolitics (Hung 2009d, Arrighi 1996). During the Cold War period, what was being fought in East Asia was actually a hot war, as Communist China's support of rural guerrillas in Southeast Asia and its involvement in the Korean War and the Vietnam War led the region into a permanent state of emergency. Washington, therefore, regarded the region as the most vulnerable link in the containment of communism, considering its key Asian allies, that is, Japan and the Four Tigers, too important to be allowed to fail. This consideration accounts for Washington's generous offering of financial and military aid to these East Asian governments, providing them with abundant financial resources to jump-start and direct industrial growth. Washington also kept US and European markets wide open to East Asian manufactured exports. It constituted another advantage that other developing regions did not enjoy. Without this openness in the Western market for their manufactures, it is simply unimaginable how these Asian exporters could have any chance of success.

Viewed in this light, the rapid economic growth of Japan and the Tigers was consciously engineered by the US as part of its effort to create subordinate and prosperous bulwarks against communism in the Asia-Pacific. These East Asian economies never meant to challenge US geopolitical and geoeconomic interests. Instead, they were subservient partners that helped the US realize its geopolitical design in the region.

Organized under a Japan-centric and multilayered subcontracting production network, different Asian exporters occupied different segments of the value chain, and each of them specialized in exporting goods at a particular level of profitability and technological sophistication to the Global North. While Japan specialized in the most high-value-added items, the Four Tigers specialized in middle-range products, and the emerging Tigers in Southeast Asia specialized in low-cost, labour-intensive ones. This famous flying-geese formation of Asian exporters constituted a network of reliable suppliers of all sorts of consumer products to the Global North (Arrighi 1994, Cummings 1987).

Staring in the 1980s, when US fiscal and current account deficits were mounting as a result of neo-liberal tax cuts and escalating military expenditure at the final stage of the Cold War and beyond, the Asian exporters, instead of breaking away from the orbit of US hegemony, tightened their ties to the US by financing US's skyrocketing twin deficits. East Asia's export-oriented industrialization had been coupled with a low domestic consumption rate of the economies. The subsequent trade surplus and high savings rate enabled these Asian exporters to accumulate substantial financial power in the form of large foreign exchange reserves. Regarding US Treasury securities as the safest investment in global finance, most East Asian exporters voluntarily parked their hoarded cash in US Treasury bonds, turning themselves into the largest creditors to the US. Their financing of the US current account deficit in turn fuelled the escalation of US's appetite for Asian exports, and the resulting increase in trade surpluses in Asian economies led to yet more purchases of US Treasury bonds. These constituted two mutually reinforcing processes of increasing Asian exports to the US and increasing Asian holding of US debt that continuously deepened the market and financial dependence of East Asia on the US. Asia's massive investment in low-yield US Treasury bonds is tantamount to a tribute payment through which Asia's savings were transferred into Americans' consumption power, prolonging the US's fragile prosperity when its hegemony unravelled.

Beginning in the 1980s and accelerating in the 1990s, China's market reform turned it into a late-coming Asian exporter. The rise of export-oriented industrialization in China led many to foresee that China would be a unique Asian exporter capable of breaking away from Asia's double dependencies on the US, because of China's geopolitical autonomy from the US and its exceptional demographic and economic size in comparison to other Asian economies (Arrighi 2007). But as the discussion below illustrates, China so far has not overcome the servitude of providing cheap credit and low-cost export to the US as practised by earlier Asian exporters. Worse, the extremity of China's export-led and private-consumption-repressing growth model has made China's market and financial dependence on the US even greater than that of earlier East Asian Tigers. This model in turn creates a strong vested interest within Chinese politics that is adamant in perpetuating the bias towards the export sector and counterbalancing any efforts to rebalance China's economy.

CHINA AS AN EXTREME ASIAN TIGER

Given the ascent of China in the global economy over the last three decades, the debate about the sources of China's success and the unique characteristics of the 'Chinese model' of development has been gaining momentum in recent years. But if we compare the most important aspects of China's macro-political economy with its East Asian neighbours at a comparable stage of development, we can see that the Chinese model of development is largely an extreme replication of earlier East Asian models, which were grounded on export-oriented industrialization, low consumption, and high savings (Hung 2008, 2009b). The Chinese economy's export dependence, as measured by the total value of exports as a percentage of gross domestic product (GDP), has been mounting continuously, rising from 21 per cent in 1991 to 40 per cent in 2006, while the average of Japan, Taiwan, and Korea never exceeded 20 per cent. On the other hand, the weight of Chinese private consumption as a percentage of GDP has been declining, dropping from 50 per cent in 1991 to 38 per cent in 2006, while the figures for Japan and the Four Dragons always have stayed above 50 per cent since their take-off (Hung 2009a, Figure 1.2).

As in the case of earlier Asian Tigers, the US constituted the single most important market for China's export, only to be surpassed by the EU as a whole recently. The rapid expansion of China's export-oriented industries has already made China the biggest exporter to the US among all Asian exporters. In 2005, China's total export value to the US reached $163 billion, in comparison to $136 for Japan and $141 billion for all Four Tigers combined (IMF Direction of Trade Statistics). The drastic expansion of China's export engine not only accounted for its stellar economic growth, but also turned China into the biggest holder of foreign exchange reserves, surpassing Japan in recent years.

So far, China has been investing most of its foreign currency reserves in US Treasury bonds like other East Asian exporters (Table 5.1). On the eve of the current global financial crisis, China had emerged as the largest exporter to the US, and at the same time served as the largest creditor that financed the US's current account deficit, sustaining its capacity for absorbing Asian exports. While China's low-cost exports helped lower US's inflation, its massive purchase of US Treasury bonds helped lower their yields and therefore interest rates across the US economy. In other words, China has come on top as the most significant saviour of US economic vitality through its low-cost manufactured exports and low-interest credits in recent years.

Table 5.1   East Asian Holdings of US Treasury Securities (US$ billion, as of March)

Country	2000	2005	2008	2010
China	71.4	223.7	490.6	895.2
Japan	307.6	681.6	597.4	784.9
Four Tigers	142.7	205.5	175.3	361.3
Total foreign holdings	1,085.0	1,952.2	2,505.8	3,884.6

Source: US Treasury.

AGRARIAN ORIGINS OF CHINA'S RISE

China's capability in instituting an extreme, and so far highly successful, version of the East Asian export-led growth model hinges on both the global conjuncture and China's internal political economy in the last three decades. First, China's labour-intensive take-off was coincidental with the onset of unprecedented expansion of global free trade since the 1980s, when core capitalist countries started to alleviate the crisis of falling profit rates in the industrial sector through manufacturing outsourcing (Brenner 2002, D'Costa 1999, Harvey 1990). Without the outsourcing of manufacturing from the Global North and its mounting appetite for low-cost manufactured imports, China would have found it impossible to export its way to prosperity. More importantly, China's exceptional export competitiveness is largely grounded on the prolonged stagnation of its manufacturing wage level in comparison with other Asian exporters at comparable stage of development (Figure 5.1).

China's development under the condition of unlimited supply of labour is not a natural phenomenon, given China's population

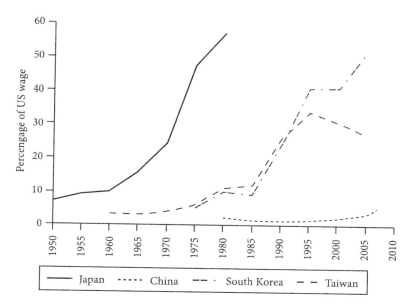

Figure 5.1   East Asian Manufacturing Wage as a Percentage of US Wage

Source: US Bureau of Labor Statistics, Foreign Labor Statistics for Japan and Asian Tigers; *China Statistical Yearbook for China*.

structure. China's high rate of growth is a consequence of the government's rural–agricultural policies—such as: (*a*) privatization of township and village collective enterprises that led to their decline as mass employment generators in the countryside, and (*b*) the grain market liberalization and cancellation of government procurement that fomented a long-term drop in grain prices. These policies intentionally or unintentionally impoverished the countryside and generated a continuous exodus of rural population over the last 20 years. In the same period investment by the Chinese government was largely concentrated in coastal cities and towns to boost foreign direct investment (FDI) and the export sectors, while rural and agricultural investment lagged behind. State-owned banks also focused their effort on financing urban-industrial development, while rural and agricultural financing was in tatters.

The relation between these policies and low wage levels can be illustrated by contrasting China's rural development with that of

Japan, South Korea, and Taiwan, which also had large rural populations and agrarian sectors at the beginning of their economic take-off. In post-war Japan, the ruling Liberal Democratic Party had actively directed resources to the countryside through rural infrastructure spending, agricultural development financing, farm subsidies, and tariffs on foreign produce. In South Korea, the Park regime launched the New Village Movement (*Saemaul Undong*) in the early 1970s, diverting significant fiscal resources to upgrade rural infrastructure, finance agricultural mechanization, and set up rural educational institutions and co-operatives. This initiative was a remarkable success. It increased rural household income from 67 per cent of urban income in 1970 to 95 per cent in 1974, virtually obliterating the rural–urban income gap. In Taiwan, the KMT government pursued similar policies in the 1960s and 1970s, alongside conscious efforts to promote rural industrialization. The resulting decentralized structure of Taiwanese industry allowed farmers to work seasonally in nearby factories without abandoning farming altogether or migrating to big cities. This helped retain a considerable share of labour resources in the village, fostering a more balanced rural–urban growth; throughout the 1960s and 1970s, per capita rural income was always above 60 per cent of the urban level. Under such policies, it is not surprising that the surplus of rural labour rapidly dried up and manufacturing wages soared in these countries (Ho 1979, Lie 1991, Mulgan 2000).

The emergence of this urban bias in China's development is at least partially caused by the dominance of a powerful urban–industrial elite—including private or state enterprises aimed at the global market and their allies in the local governments—from southern coastal regions in the phase of China's integration with the global economy. This elite, which germinated after China's initial opening up, accumulated financial resources and political influence with the export boom, and became increasingly adept at shaping central government policy in their favour (Gallagher 2002, Kaplan 2006, Shih 2008, pp. 139–88, Zweig 2002). Their growing leverage in the policy making process of the central government secured the priority given to enhancing China's export competitiveness and China's attractiveness to foreign investors at the cost of rural–agricultural development. Their increasing influence is illustrated in Table 5.2, which shows that the Politburo of the Chinese Communist Party (CCP)—the pinnacle of power in China's party-state—has been dominated by elites with a coastal urban background vis-à-vis elites with ties to the rural–agricultural sector since the 1990s.

Table 5.2   Composition of Politburo Standing Committee of the Chinese Communist Party

	Members with agricultural background (%)[a]	Members with coastal background (%)[b]
13th Congress (1987)	27.8	22.2
15th Congress (1997)	8.3	45.8
17th Congress (2007)	16.0	40.0

Source: Author's compilation from official biography of members of Politburo Standing Committee.

Notes: [a]Refers to members with at least one year experience in agriculture-related post before entering the Politburo.

[b]Refers to members with at least one year experience in governing coastal provinces or cities before entering the Politburo.

The urban revolts in 1989 stemming from hyper-inflation and deteriorating living standard in the cities only made the party-state more determined in ensuring economic prosperity of big cities at the expense of the countryside in the 1990s and beyond (Yang and Cai 2000).

The result of this self-reinforcing urban bias is the relative economic stagnation in the countryside and the concomitant fiscal stringency in rural local governments. From the 1990s onward, the deterioration of agricultural income, rural governance, and the demise of collective rural industries in the form of township and village enterprises, which used to be vibrant employment generators in the early stage of market reform in the 1980s, urged most young labourers in the countryside to leave for the city, creating a vicious cycle that precipitated a rural social crisis (Huang 2002, Wen 2005, Yu 2003, Zhang 2005).

China's rural–agricultural sector was not only neglected, but also exploited in support of urban–industrial growth. A recent study estimates the direction and size of the transfer of financial resources between the rural–agricultural sector and urban-industrial sector in China in 1978–2000 (Huang et al. 2006). Taking into account the transfer through the fiscal system (via taxation and government spending), financial system (via savings deposits and loans), and other means (such as grain marketing and remittance of urban migrants), it finds that there was a sustained and ever-growing net transfer of resources from the rural–agricultural sector to the urban–industrial one, except for the years when the urban economy experienced temporary downturn such as in the aftermath of the Asian Financial Crisis of 1997–8 (see also Bezemer 2008, Huang and Peng 2007, Knith *et al.* 2006, Lu and Zhao 2006, Xia 2006).

In sum, the urban-biased development pattern that impoverished the countryside and forced villagers to leave their land is the origin of the prolonged unlimited supply of rural labour, as well as the subsequent overall urban wage stagnation, in China's export-led economic miracle. It in turn accounts for China's global financial power rooted in China's rising trade surplus. On the other hand, the low manufacturing wage and rural living standards brought about by this same strategy of development have been restraining the expansion of China's domestic consumer market and deepening China's dependence on the Global North's consumption demand, the growth of which increasingly relies on the North's massive borrowing from China and other Asian exporters. Before turning to discuss the peril of this development pattern in greater detail, I outline in the next section how earlier East Asian exporters are increasingly integrated with China's export engine through the regionalization of an industrial production network in the last 15 years, a production network that turned East Asia into a Sino-centric regional workshop with the US as the most important consumer of its products. I also discuss how the regionalization is turning the vulnerabilities of the Chinese economy into the vulnerabilities of the East Asian region at large.

NEW EAST ASIAN REGIONALISM

When China just started to establish itself as the most competitive Asian exporter of products at various levels of technological sophistication in the 1990s, earlier Asian exporters including Japan and the original Four Tigers, together with a group of emerging exporters in Southeast Asia such as Malaysia and Thailand, were put under intense pressure to adjust. Export competitiveness of China lured a lot of export manufacturing to relocate from other Asian economies to China. Some have even argued that the erosion of manufacturing profitability under the competition from China was one of the underlying causes of the Asian financial crisis of 1997–8 (Krause 1998).

Amidst the turmoil that the rise of China's manufacturing power brought to the existing export-oriented industrial order in the region, China's neighbours painstakingly restructured their export engines to minimize head-on competition with China and to profit from its rise. In the old export-oriented industrial order in East Asia, each economy exported specific groups of finished consumer products. The rise of China fomented a new, Sino-centric export-oriented industrial order under which most Asian economies increased the weight of their export of high-value-added components and parts (for example, Korea and Taiwan) and capital goods (for example, Japan) to China, where these capital goods and parts were used to assemble the finished products to be exported to the Global North (Ando 2006, Baldwin 2006, Haddad 2007, see also Setser 2009). Under this structure, China emerged as the most important destination for other Asian exporters. Japan's export to China as a percentage of total exports increased from 7.1 in 1985 to 13.5 in 2005 (with a concomitant drop of export to the US from 37.6 to 22.9). Both South Korea's and Taiwan's export to China jumped from 0 in 1985 (during the Cold War) to 22 in 2005 (with a simultaneous drop of exports to the US from 36 to 15 for Korea and from 18 to 15 for Taiwan) (IMF Direction of Trade Statistics).

Under this Sino-centric production network, as seen in Figure 5.2, and East Asia's increasing dependence on China for export growth, the limit and vulnerability of the Chinese development model—given by its overdependence on consumption demand in the Global North and the slow growth of its domestic market relative to the expansion of the economy at large—is inevitably translated into the limit and vulnerability of other Asian economies. The rebalancing of China's development, therefore, is important not only for the sustainability of China's economic growth, but also for the collective future of East Asia as an integrated economic bloc.

THE POLITICAL OBSTACLES TO REBALANCING CHINA'S ECONOMY

China's developmental model, which is based on hyper-growth in its export to the Global North at the expense of the growth of its domestic consumption, makes the Chinese economy, together with its Asian partners, vulnerable to any major contraction of consumption demand in the Global North. The compulsion of Chinese and other

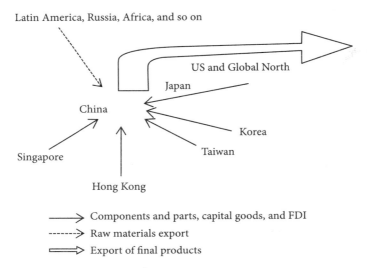

Figure 5.2   The Sino-centric and Export-oriented Network of Production in East Asia, c. 1990–Present

Source: Author.

Asian governments to employ their foreign reserves to purchase US debt is not just a result of the presumably stable and safe return of the US Treasury bonds, but is also due to a conscious effort among Asian central banks to finance the US's escalating current account deficit and hence to secure the continuous increase in US demand for their own exports.

Thus the growth of China's export engine and the growth of its financial power in the form of the accumulation of US debts are both linked to the consumption spree in the US. Most observers realize that the current account deficit of the US can not expand indefinitely. It will eventually end up in a fall in the value of dollars or a collapse in the Treasury bonds market and hike in interest rates in the US economy, terminating the US consumption spree. This will not only be a death blow to China's export engine, but will also decimate China's global financial power through a drastic devaluation of its pre-existing investment in Treasury bonds. The current US economic crisis, which has already badly affected China's exports by setting off a free fall of the export growth rate from 20 per cent in 2007 to -11 per cent in 2009 (World Bank 2010, p. 10), as well as the imminent collapse of the dollar and Treasury bonds, seems to be the worst nightmare coming true.

Before the current financial crisis struck, the Chinese government was experimenting with different ways to diversify and increase the return of its foreign reserve investment. It had tried investing in foreign equities and financing state-owned companies' acquisition of transnational corporations, but nearly all attempts ended up in embarrassing failures, such as Lenovo's acquisition of IBM PC and the acquisition of major stakes in Blackstone, a private equity fund, by China's sovereign wealth fund (Hung 2009a, pp. 17–18). These failures are more a result of the constraint posed by the exceptional size of China's foreign reserves than a result of bad investment decisions per se. Given the size of China's foreign reserves, it is difficult for China to move in and out of certain financial assets freely without disrupting the global market for those assets. And no other market except the US debt market has liquidity deep enough to absorb China's gigantic reserves. Paul Krugman was not exaggerating when he claimed that China had been caught in a 'dollar trap', in which it had few choices other than to keep purchasing US debts and other dollar assets to help perpetuate the hegemonic role of the dollar (Krugman 2009).

Besides making the Chinese economy vulnerable to the vicissitudes of the global economy, China's export-oriented developmental model also curtails China's consumption power. As discussed earlier, China's export competitiveness has been built upon a long-term wage stagnation, which in turn was precipitated by an agrarian crisis under an urban-biased policy regime. The thriving export sector turned most of their profits into enterprise savings rather than allowing them to raise living standards and consumption power of their employees. These enterprise savings constituted a large proportion of the aggregate national savings (National Development and Reform Council of China 2005). As Figure 5.3 shows, the fall of total wages as a share of GDP was in tandem with the fall of private consumption as a share of GDP over the 1990s and beyond. These two falling trends are in contrast with the mounting share of corporate profits in GDP.

Private consumption has been growing in absolute terms, but this growth has been much slower than the growth of investment (Hung 2009a, Figure 8).

As an impetus to rebalance China's development, which was duly characterized by Premier Wen Jiabao in 2007 as 'unstable, unbalanced,

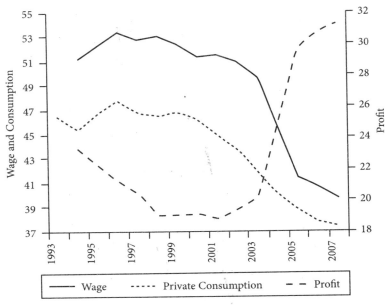

Figure 5.3   Compensation, Profit, and Private Consumption as a Percentage of GDP in China

Source: China Statistical Yearbook.

uncoordinated, and unsustainable', the central government has tried since about 2005 to fuel a take-off of China's domestic consumption by boosting the disposable income of the peasants and urban workers, even at the expense of China's export competitiveness. The first wave of such initiatives includes the abolition of agricultural taxes, increase in government procurement prices of agricultural products, and an increase in rural infrastructure investment. Though this redirection of attention to raising rural living standards was no more than a small step in the right direction, its effect was instantaneous. The slightly improved economic conditions in the rural–agricultural sector slowed the flow of rural–urban migration, and a sudden labour shortage and wage hike in the coastal export-processing zones ensued, inducing many economists to declare that the 'Lewis turning point', that is, the point at which rural surplus labour was exhausted, had finally arrived in the Chinese economy (Cai and Du 2009). This sudden tightening of the labour market is reflected in the steep increase in Chinese manufacturing wage as share of US manufacturing wage after 2005 (see Figure 5.1).

Just as the prolonged 'unlimited supply of labour' in China was more a consequence of urban-biased policy than a natural precondition of Chinese development, the coming of the 'Lewis turning point' is in fact an outcome of government's attempt to reverse the urban bias instead of a natural process driven by the market's invisible hands. Concomitant to the rising peasant income and industrial wage was an unprecedented growth in retail sales on the eve of the current global crisis, even when the figure is controlled for inflation (Hung 2009a, Figure 9). But when the government took the first step away from excessive export dependence and toward a domestic-consumption-driven growth, vested interests in the coastal export sector complained aloud about the grim prospects that the new policy initiatives brought to them. They asked for compensation policy to safeguard their competitiveness, and attempted to sabotage further initiatives of the central government to elevate the living standards of the working classes. Government initiatives include the implementation of the New Labour Contract Law, which elevates workers' remuneration and makes firing labourers more difficult. They also include the managed appreciation of the yuan after 2005.

When the global financial crisis struck and China's export engine stalled, China's central government immediately (in November 2008) rolled out a mega fiscal stimulus package amounting to US\$570 billion (including both government spending and targeted loans from state-owned banks) to revive growth. Many initially celebrated this massive stimulus as a precious opportunity to accelerate the rebalancing of the Chinese economy into a more domestic-consumption-driven mode, and expected that the stimulus would be constituted mainly by social spending, such as financing of medical insurance and social security accounts, that could further raise the disposable income and hence purchasing power of the working classes.

To the disappointment of many advocates of structural rebalancing of the Chinese economy, the stimulus package in fact carried no more than 20 per cent of social spending, while the major fraction of the spending went into investment in capital assets such as highway construction and expansion of sectors already plagued by overcapacity such as steel and cement.[1] Since the stimulus package will not bring much benefit to social welfare institutions and small and medium labour-intensive enterprises, it will not be able to generate much increase in disposable income and employment. Worse, seemingly horrified by the sudden collapse of the export sector, the central government retreated from the rebalancing efforts and restarted a number of export promotion measures, such as cutbacks in value-added taxes and halting of yuan appreciation. Vested interests in the export sector even made use of the crisis to call for a suspension of the New Labour Contract Law for the sake of the survival of export manufacturers.[2]

The massive fiscal stimulus, despite its impressive size, would do little to rebalance the Chinese economy via promoting domestic consumption and hence reducing China's export dependence.[3] Though a larger part of the stimulus fund has been directed to the Western provinces and helped redress the development gap between coastal and inland areas, the mostly capital-intensive, urban-oriented growth under the stimulus, such as increasing production capacity in the steel industry and construction of the world's longest high speed rail system, has aggravated rural–urban polarization. It has put a brake on the narrowing rural–urban gap and rising rural areas' relative living standard under the government's rebalancing effort since 2005, which helped fuel a modest domestic consumption growth, as discussed earlier (Hung 2009a, Table 3).

What the massive spending actually is doing is keeping the economy roaring with a state-led investment spurt in the short run while waiting for the export market to turn around. By the summer of 2009, the fiscal stimulus had successfully stalled the free fall of the Chinese economy and fostered a modest rebound. But at the same time, nearly 90 per cent of GDP growth in the first seven months of 2009 was solely driven by fixed asset investments fuelled by loan explosion and government spending under the stimulus program.[4] Most of these investments are of low quality and repetitive, with dubious profitability (Pettis 2009). If the turnaround of the export market does not come in time, the fiscal deficit, non-performing loans, and exacerbation of overcapacity created by the stimulus will generate a deeper downturn in the medium run. In the words of a top Chinese economist, this mega stimulus programme is like 'drinking poison to quench the thirst'.[5]

If the export-oriented establishment is influential enough to continue its domination of China's response to the global crisis, it is likely that China could waste the crisis and fail to shift to a more balanced growth model that relies more on domestic private consumption and can turn China into a genuinely autonomous economic powerhouse.

SWITCHING TO CONSUMPTION-DRIVEN GROWTH

Over the course of the last two decades, China has emerged as the final assembler and exporter in the East Asian network of production. China also attained the status as the largest creditor to the US and the largest holder of foreign reserves, and manifested the potential of becoming the market of the world on top of being the workshop of the world, given its large economic and demographic size. With all these endowments and leverages, China is well poised to become a large market for its own industrial establishment and manufacturer in other emerging economies, capable of carving out a new regional and global economic order by facilitating Asia and the Global South to move out of its market and financial dependence on the Global North in general and the US in particular (Hung 2009c, 2009d).

China's potential to lead, however, is far from being actualized. So far, China's pursuit of the strategy of lending to the US to facilitate its purchase of Chinese exports only deepened the dependence of China, as well as the suppliers of its raw materials, components, and capital goods, on US consumers as the source of final demand and the US bond market as the store of their national wealth. Furthermore, because of China's export-driven industrialization, other countries became dependent on China for raw materials, components, and capital goods. The consequent economic dependence of China and Asia on the Global North makes them vulnerable to any turbulence of the global economy like the current crisis.

China's long-term export competitiveness is grounded on the developmental approach that bankrupts the countryside and prolongs the unlimited supply of low-cost migrant labour to coastal export industries. The resulting, ever-enlarging trade surplus of China inflates China's global financial power in the form of increasing holdings of US debt. But the long-term suppression of wages contributes to the far-below-potential growth of domestic consumption demand in China, hence restraining the growth of China's consumption power.

The current global financial crisis, which decimated consumer demand in the Global North and increased the likelihood of the collapse of the US bond market or the dollar, is a belated wake-up call about the urgency of shifting the course of Chinese development from an export-oriented to a domestic-market-oriented one. But at the same time, the vested interests that have taken root over several decades of export-led growth make this shift a daunting task.

China's central government is well aware that further accumulation of global financial power is counterproductive as it would increase the risk of the assets that China already holds or induce China to move to ever riskier assets. The government is also well aware of the need to reduce the country's export dependence and stimulate the growth of domestic demand by increasing the disposable incomes of the lower classes. Such redirection of priority from promoting export and global financial power to promoting domestic consumption has to involve the shift of resources and policy favours away from the coastal urban to rural inland areas, where protracted social marginalization and under-consumption entails ample room for consumption growth. Officials and entrepreneurs from the coastal provinces, who have become a powerful group capable of shaping the formation and implementation of central government policies, are so far adamant in resisting such redirection.

To foster a domestic-consumption-driven pattern of growth with less urban bias, China perhaps could learn from the experience of India, the rapid development of which in the recent decade has been grounded more on the expansion of domestic private consumption than on exports and investment. The robust growth in private consumption relative to the overall growth of the economy in India is attributable in part to relatively lower (though increasing) rural-urban inequality, which in turn is related to the improving agriculture's terms of trade with manufacturing since the 1980s, in contrast to agriculture's declining terms of trade with manufacturing in China (Bardhan 2010, pp. 46, 99–101, Das 2006, Fan *et al.* 2005, Huang and Khanna 2003). In the aftermath of the recent wave of global financial crisis of 2008, *The Economist* lauded that 'the strength of rural demand [in India] is one reason why India escaped from the crisis so lightly' (Cox 2009). As I have outlined earlier, the main obstacle to China's transition to a consumption-driven growth pattern is the entrenchment of coastal urban-industrial vested interests in the political systems. Further studies need to be done to examine whether India's more egalitarian, consumer-driven growth is a function of its particular political system grounded in liberty and democracy.

NOTES

1. 'Siwanyi neiwai' (inside and outside of the four thousand billion), *Caijing*, 16 March 2009.

2. See 'jiuye xingshi yanjun laodong hetong fa chujing ganga' (Severe unemployment jeopardize labor contract law), *Caijing*, 4 January 2009.

3. 'Zhongguo GDP zengzhang jin 90% you touzi ladong' (Nearly 90 per cent of China's GDP growth was driven by investment), *Caijing*, 16 July 2009.

4. 'Zhongguo GDP zengzhang jin 90% you touzi ladong' (Nearly 90 per cent of China's GDP growth was driven by investment), *Caijing*, 16 July 2009.

5. The comment is from Xu Xiaonian at the China Europe International Business School in Shanghai. See 'China Stimulus Plan Comes Under Attack at "Summer Davos"', *China Post*, 13 September 2009.

REFERENCES

Ando, M. 2006. 'Fragmentation and Vertical Intra-industry Trade in East Asia', *The North American Journal of Economics and Finance*, 17 (3): 257–81.

Arrighi, G. 1994. *The Long Twentieth Century: Money, Power, and the Origins of Our Times*. London: Verso.

————. 1996. 'The Rise of East Asia: World-Systemic and Regional Aspects', *International Journal of Sociology and Social Policy*, 16 (7–8): 6–44.

Arrighi, G., T. Hamashita, and M. Selden. 2003. *Resurgence of East Asia: 500, 150, 50 Years Perspectives*. New York and London: Routledge.

————. 2007. *Adam Smith in Beijing: Lineages of the Twenty-first Century*. London and New York: Verso.

Baldwin, R. 2006. 'Managing the Noodle Bowl: The Fragility of East Asian Regionalism', Discussion Paper No. 5561, Center for Economic Policy Research, London.

Bardhan, P. 2010. *Awakening Giants: Assessing the Economic Rise of China and India*. Princeton, NJ: Princeton University Press.

Bezemer, D. 2008. 'Agriculture, Development, and Urban Bias', *World Development*, 36 (8): 1342–64.

Brenner, R. 2002. *The Boom and the Bubble. The US in the World Economy*. London and New York: Verso.

Cai, F., and Y. Du (eds). 2009. *The China Population and Labor Yearbook, Vol. 1: The Approaching Lewis Turning Point and its Policy Implications*. Leiden: Brill.

Cox, S. 2009. 'An Imperfect Storm'. *The World in 2010*, London: The Economist.

Cummings, B. 1987. 'The Origins and Development of the Northeast Asia Political Economy: Industrial Sectors, Product Cycles, and Political Consequences', in F.C. Deyo (ed.), *The Political Economy of the New Asian Industrialism*, pp. 44–83. Ithaca, NY: Cornell University Press.

D'Costa, A.P. 1999. *The Global Restructuring of the Steel Industry: Innovations, Institutions, and Industrial Change*. New York and London: Routledge.

Das, G. 2006. 'The India Model', *Foreign Affairs*, July/August 85 (4), http://www.foreignaffairs.com/articles/61728/gurcharan-das/the-india-model (accessed 20 July 2012).

Fan S., C. Chan-Kang, and A. Mukherjee. 2005. 'Rural and Urban Dynamics and Poverty: Evidence from China and India', Food Consumption and Nutrition Division Working Paper, International Food and Policy Research Institute, Washington DC.

Gallagher, M.E. 2002. 'Reform and Openness: Why China's Economic Reforms Have Delayed Democracy', *World Politics*, 54 (3): 338–72.

Haddad, M. 2007. 'Trade Integration in East Asia: The Role of China and Production Networks', World Bank Policy Research Working Paper No. 4160, Washington DC.

Harvey, D. 1990. *The Conditions of Postmodernity: An Inquiry into Cultural Change.* Cambridge: Blackwell.

Ho, S.P.S. 1979. 'Industrialization and Rural Development: Evidence from Taiwan', *Economic Development and Cultural Change*, 28 (1): 77–96.

Huang, P. and P. Yusheng. 2007. '*Sanda lishixing bianqiande jiaohui yu zhongguo xiao guimo nongye de qianjing*' (The conjuncture of three historical trends and the prospect of small-scale farming in China) *Zhongguo shehui kexue*. No. 4.

Huang, J., S. Rozelle, and H. Wang. 2006. 'Fostering or Stripping Rural China: Modernizing Agriculture and Rural to Urban Capital Flows', *The Developing Economies*, 44 (1): 1–26.

Huang, P. 2002. '*bupingheng fazhan geju xia de nongcun kunjing*' (Rural Impasses Under the Structure of Uneven Development), Chinese University of Hong Kong University Service Center, www.usc.cuhk.edu.hk?PaperCollection/Details.aspx?id=1786 (accessed 20 Junly 2012).

Huang Y. and T. Khanna. 2003. 'Can India Overtake China?' *Foreign Policy*, July–August, http://www.foreignpolicy.com/articles/2003/07/01/can_india_overtake_china (accessed 20 July 2012).

Hung, Ho-Fung. 2008. 'Rise of China and the Global Overaccumulation Crisis', *Review of International Political Economy*, 15 (2): 149–79.

————. 2009a. 'America's Head Servant? PRC's Dilemma in the Global Crisis', *New Left Review*, November/December.

————. 2009b. 'Asian Tigers in Extremis: Sources and Limits of China's Global Financial Power', paper presented at the conference on 'Regional Powers, New Developmental States, and Global Governance', Watson Institute of International Studies, Brown University, 13–14 March.

————. 2009c. 'East Asian Developmental Model and the Dilemma of China's Global Financial Power', paper presented at the conference on 'BRICs and the New World Order', Observer Research Foundation and Ministry of External Affairs, the Indian Government, New Delhi, India, 13–14 May.

————. (ed.). 2009d. *China and the Transformation of Global Capitalism.* Baltimore: Johns Hopkins University Press.

Kaplan, S.B. 2006. 'The Political Obstacles to Greater Exchange Rate Flexibility in China', *World Development*, 34 (7): 1182–1200.

Knight, J., S. Li, and L. Song. 2006. 'The Rural-Urban Divide and the Evolution of Political Economy in China', in J. Boyce, S. Cullenberg, P. Pattanaik, and R. Pollin (eds), *Human Development in the Era of Globalisation. Essays in Honor of Keith B. Griffin*, pp. 44–63. Northampton, MA: Edward Elgar.

Krause, L.B. 1998. *The Economics and Politics of the Asian Financial Crisis of 1997–98*. New York: Council on Foreign Relations.

Lie, J. 1991. 'The State, Industrialization and Agricultural Sufficiency: The Case of South Korea', *Development Policy Review*, 9 (1): 37–51.

Lu, M. and C. Zhao. 2006. 'Urbanization, Urban biased Policies, and Urban-Rural Inequality in China, 1987–2001', *The Chinese Economy*, 39 (3): 42–63.

Mulgan, A.G. 2000. *The Politics of Agriculture in Japan*. New York and London: Routledge.

National Development and Reform Council of China. 2005. *Zhongguo jumin shouru fenpei niandu baogao* (Annual report of Chinese resident's income distribution).

Pettis, M. 2009. 'More Public Worrying about the Chinese Stimulus', blog entry at China Financial Markets, 24 July 2009, mpettis.com/2009/07/more-public-worrying-about-the-chinese-stimulus/ (accessed 19 May 2012).

Roach, S. 2009. 'Kidding Ourselves about an Asian Recovery', *Time*, 9 June.

Setser, B. 2009. 'This Really Doesn't Look Good', Blog entry at Council on Foreign Relations, 11 January 2009 http://blogs.cfr.org/setser/2009/01/11/this-really-doesnt-look-good/ (accessed 19 May 2012).

Shih, V. 2008. *Factions and Finance in China: Elite Control and Inflation*. New York: Cambridge University Press.

Tao, D.Y. and C. Fang 2000. 'The Political Economy of China's Rural-Urban Divide', Stanford: Center for Research on Economic Development and Policy Research Working Paper No. 62, 2000.

Wen, T. 2005. *Sannong wenti yu shiji fansi* ('Rural China's centenary reflection'). Beijing: Sanlian Shudian.

World Bank. 2010. 'China Quarterly Update', March 2010. Beijing: World Bank Beijing Office.

Xia, Y. 2006. 'gongyehua yu chengshi hua: chengben tanfen yu shouyi fenpei' (Industrialization and urbanization: division of cost and distribution of benefits) *Jianghai xuekan*, 5: 84–9.

Yu, J. 2003. 'nongcun hei'e shili yu jicheng zhengquan tuihua: Xiangnan diaocha' (Mafia in the village and regression of local governments: a survey of Southern Hunan), *Zhanlue yu guanli*, 5.

Yu, Y. 2009. 'China's Stimulus Shows the Problem of Success', *Financial Times*, 25 August.

Zhang, Y. 2005. 'litu shidai de nongcun jiating: mingong chao ruhe jiegou xiangtu zhongguo' (Rural family in the age of migration: how the tide of peasant labour outmigration is deconstructing rural China), Chinese University of Hong Kong University Service Center, http://www/usc.cuhk.edu.hk/PaperCollection/Details.aspx?id=4638 (accessed 20 Junly 2012).

Zweig, D. 2002. *Internationalizing China: Domestic Interests and Global Linkages*. Ithaca, NY: Cornell University Press.

6

Harmony, Crisis, and the Fading of the Lewis Model in China

CARL RISKIN

'Historians will look back on the 2000s,' states a recent World Bank Report, 'as the decade when China shifted gear from its earlier focus on economic development to its new balanced approach to development and emphasis on a harmonious society' (Wagstaff *et al.* 2009, p. 201). It is a bold author who predicts how history will treat the present. The 2000s are now over but it is far from clear whether China indeed shifted to a new development paradigm. That question is the subject of this chapter.

Hallmarks of China's economic development since the period of reform and transition to a market economy began are very rapid growth rates, reduced poverty but widening inequality, and serious deterioration in environmental quality. Despite generally improved living standards, China's growth model is commonly regarded as unbalanced, including by the Chinese leadership, which fears the potential it creates for social and political instability. The government has pledged—so far unsuccessfully—to alter the model. Just as their efforts to do so were ramping up, however, the global crisis hit China in the form of a sharp downturn in exports, which reinforced the simultaneous downward pressure of widespread over-capacity in the domestic economy. Economic crisis, posing a more immediate threat to social stability than growing inequality and environmental decline, tempted China's leaders to abandon serious rebalancing goals, at least temporarily, and fall back on tried and true methods of restoring jobs, thus strengthening the model they sought to replace. There was a struggle for the 'soul' of China's giant stimulus package and it evolved over time into a somewhat more progressive programme than it originally appeared to be. With growth restored, widespread labour shortages began to appear in early 2010 along the developed eastern seaboard, prompting big increases in wages paid to migrant workers. After 30 years of extraordinarily rapid economic growth, based in large part on the absorption of China's 'unlimited' supply of labour, it appears that China may finally be moving beyond the world of the Lewis model. If so, the central government's past and present efforts to rebalance the economy by investing in health, education, and infrastructure development in the less developed interior may make the transition easier by facilitating changes already pushed along by market forces.

CHINA'S UNBALANCED GROWTH MODEL

China's growth path has been epitomized by Deng Xiaoping's famous injunction to 'let some people get rich first', although the last word may prove irrelevant. United Nations Development Programme's (UNDP) *Human Development Report* 2006 listed only 30 countries out of 177 with income inequality greater than China's. The 2007/2008 HDR gives the most recently calculated Gini coefficients for China and nine of its Asian neighbours, as shown in Figure 6.1, to which one for Bangladesh has been added (from Khan 2009). Of these, China's is the largest. Although it seemed for a while in the late 1990s and early 2000s that income inequality might be moderating (Khan and Riskin 2005), recent information suggests that it has continued to increase. The World Bank's poverty assessment report for China (World Bank 2009a) concludes, inter alia, that income inequality has risen significantly, the responsiveness of poverty to economic growth has decreased, and the burden of health and education expenditures for the poor has grown.

In addition to normative concerns about inequality, there are some very practical ones. China's ruling party and government have expressed open concern about the potential threat to political and

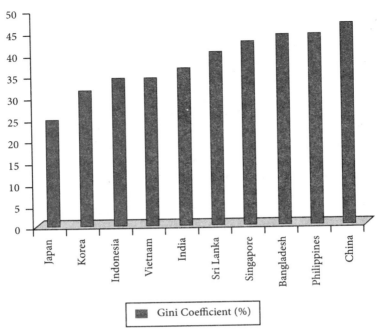

Figure 6.1   Gini Coefficients of Income Distribution for Selected Asian Countries, 1990s and Early 2000s

Source: UNDP (2007).

social stability posed by growing economic inequality. Official Chinese statistics indicate that the number of 'mass incidents' (the official term for collective protests of various kinds) in China grew by 10 times, from 8,700 to 87,000 over the 12 years from 1993 until 2005, when the government stopped releasing statistics on them.[1] An unofficial estimate for 2010 of such incidents was 180,000,[2] suggesting that the trend is still upward.

The issues provoking such protests are manifold, including confiscations of peasant land holdings by local governments, layoffs, arbitrary fees, and exactions imposed on people, chemical pollution of villagers' water and land, compulsory relocations due to dam or other construction, and so on. Whereas economic and political inequality may not overtly cause such protests, the proximate causes are surely rooted in the growing disparity of resources and power between social groups and classes. Fear of the potential growth of such instability provides at least the backdrop, if not the principal motive, for the Hu Jintao–Wen Jiabao administration's adoption of a programme to transform China's development strategy into one that is more balanced, less disequalizing, and more pro-rural and pro-poor than the one China had been following since the mid-1980s. Much has been written about Wen's projection of a 'Harmonious Society' and of a 're-balanced economy' as goals for China's development strategy.

Despite the historically unprecedented scale of poverty decline, for which China deserves credit, the fact remains that much poverty remains. Based upon the World Bank's corrected US$1.25 a day (in purchasing power parity dollars) international poverty standard, there were still some 254 million poor people in China in 2005, the second-highest national number of poor after India, and the poverty standard itself remains very low (World Bank 2009a). The problem of poverty is thus far from having been solved in China. Rising inequality has constrained the impact of economic growth on poverty reduction. China would have done an even better job of eliminating poverty had its economic growth been less inegalitarian (see Wan 2007). As the *Financial Times* put it (29 November 2009), 'In China's current development model, household income is taxed, to support corporate profits.' Thus, functional income inequality is closely bound to rising inequality of personal income.[3]

The current model has been in place since the 1990s. It produces growth from extremely high rates of fixed investment and upon rising exports. These characteristics are associated not only with widening income inequality but also with an inability to address effectively other major concerns, such as the need to protect an increasingly stressed natural environment. China's rate of fixed investment in gross domestic product (GDP), already at world historical highs from 1993 until 2002, rose further to unprecedented levels, surpassing 40 per cent from 2003 through 2007. In 2008, gross capital formation came to almost 44 per cent of GDP. China's *net* exports (exports minus imports) increased from near zero in the late 1980s and early 1990s to 8 per cent of GDP in 2007. Thus, growth leading up to the global downturn of 2008 relied upon large global trade imbalances and extremely high investment rates. Conversely, at only 35 per cent of GDP in 2007 and 2008, the rate of household consumption was extraordinarily low for any country and especially one of China's still meager income per capita (US consumption has ranged between 62 per cent and 70 per cent of GDP).

High investment rates require effective means of channelling financial resources to industry. The most direct way to do so is for companies simply to retain their profits, and retained earnings are indeed the major source of finance for investment in China. The rapid growth of corporate profits has thus helped to fuel the investment boom. Keister and Liu (2001) show that, even in the 1990s, surveyed firms turned overwhelmingly to retained earnings for financing. After that, however, industrial profits took off, rising faster than either industrial value added or GDP, as shown in Table 6.1. This is what made possible the extraordinary investment rates of 2003–7. Between 1998 and 2007, profits of large industrial enterprises rose from 1.7 per cent to almost 11 per cent of GDP, an increase that more than matched the rise in investment from 36 per cent to 42 per cent of GDP over the same period (National Bureau of Statistics of China 2008).

Table 6.1   Growth of Industrial Profits of Large Enterprises, 1998–2007

	1998	2007
Industrial profits as per cent of value added by industry (%)	7.5	23.0
Industrial profits as per cent of GDP (%)	1.7	10.8

Sources: UNDP (2008), Khan (2009).

Booming corporate profits, as well as increasing government saving, have dramatically pushed up national saving. China's national savings rate actually reached 52 per cent of GDP in 2006 and even higher in 2007 (see Figure 6.2). Because the government acted to slow an over-heated economy by moderating domestic investment, the increase in investment lagged behind that in saving in 2007, and the current account surplus grew to almost 11 per cent of GDP (Dadush 2009).

The Chinese model is thus one of hyper-investment enabled by the very high fraction of GDP corralled by the corporate sector, itself, as well as by the preferential access to bank credit of large capital-intensive industries. It is a growth model in which further accumulation and exports are the main objectives. Machines are made to produce more machines and more exports. As the *Financial*

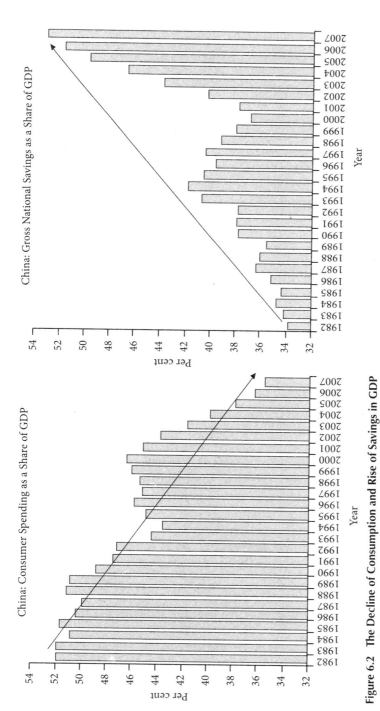

Figure 6.2   The Decline of Consumption and Rise of Savings in GDP

Source: Ritholtz.com at http://www.ritholtz.com/blog/wp-content/uploads/2009/05/china-savings-vs-spending-rate.png, which credits Merrill Lynch, 'U.S. Economics, January 2009' as its source.

Times (29 November 2009) put it, 'investment cures this year's excess capacity by increasing next year's.' In this respect, the hyper-growth of the early 2000s resembles the growth of the collective era, in which growth was its own objective and which many later decried as being economic development without 'fruit' (see Riskin 1987, pp. 261–8), such as improved food consumption, housing, or other advances in material living standards. In the present case there are certainly fruits, but these go overwhelmingly to persons connected closely with the state, the large-scale industrial (and increasingly, services) sector and with exports.[4] The political economy of such a situation generates feedback that further contributes to inequality by concentrating power in a few favoured sectors and regions.

China thus presents the extraordinary phenomenon of a still quite low income country with a large poor population, but which consumes only 35 per cent of its GDP (Figure 6.2). Small and medium enterprises, which could create jobs and income, are stymied by lack of access to capital. Large capital-intensive enterprises, fed by artificially cheap credit, generate profits but few jobs and little wage income. China's elasticity of formal employment with respect to GDP is extremely low. A crude calculation of the gross GDP elasticity of employment for the period 1995 to 2008 yields a value of 0.03. That is, a 1 per cent increase in GDP is associated with a .03 per cent increase in employment.[5] This of course includes agriculture, where employment is declining. If we perform the same calculation for value added of the secondary (manufacturing and construction) and tertiary sectors separately, the output elasticity of employment works out to 0.13 in both cases, still very low.[6] Yet the generation of employment is a sine qua non for maintaining social stability, which is the leadership's most fundamental objective. Under such circumstances, only hyper-growth of the sort China has experienced in recent years can create adequate new employment, albeit at the cost of greater inequality and environmental destruction.

National saving is very high both because of the large share of income going to profits, and because the personal savings rate is high—around 39 per cent of household income in 2008 (Wiemer 2009). Most Chinese lack an effective safety net, and are dependent upon their own savings to pay for education, medical emergencies, and old age. Moreover, an undervalued currency raises consumer prices and discourages consumption. China thus seems to be bound into a growth model that under-consumes, over-saves, magnifies economic inequality and chews up the environment, but through all of this generates such fast growth that the lid has remained on the large reservoir of social and economic grievances. This description does not take account of the *international* imbalances on which China's growth model has depended, especially the large bilateral imbalance in Sino–US trade.

High investment rates are of course a prerequisite of rapid growth and, within reason, a necessary part of successful development. However, rates have been so high that they have generated very large external costs, an objection that recalls the debates of more than 40 years ago about the optimum choice of techniques in developing countries.[7] As Amartya Sen (1960) pointed out early on, the arguments that favoured maximizing capital intensity (for example, Galenson and Leibenstein 1955, Dobb 1960) did so on the assumption that the higher the income share of profits, the higher the investment rate and the faster was growth and (potential) future consumption, whatever the cost in foregone present consumption. Sen's own technical choice criterion allowed the opportunity cost in foregone present consumption to be taken into account in choosing a growth rate. In today's world, moreover, costs may be reckoned more broadly to include also repercussions for the political economy of excessive income inequality as well as the external cost of environmental destruction.

It is obvious from the above discussion, and from much additional evidence, that China's increasing inequality, whether regional or urban-rural, has not grown ineluctably out of economic reform and growth, itself, but has been at least partly a result of specific economic strategies and policies. This in turn implies that the disequalizing character of China's growth could be ameliorated by adopting changed strategies and policies.

THE EFFORT TO REBALANCE

China's leaders have famously promised to 'rebalance' the country's economic growth model in a number of ways, including making growth more pro-poor, pro-rural, protective of the natural environment, and more dependent upon domestic demand, especially consumption, and less correspondingly dependent upon exports and extraordinarily high investment rates. Sen's solution of subjecting choice to a social welfare function that recognizes all costs and benefits is analogous to what the 'Harmonious Society' and 'rebalancing' proposals have sought to do. Premier Wen Jiabao accordingly spoke in favour of slower growth in March 2004, calling for a moderate 7 per cent rate which would permit greater control over the nature of growth.[8] However, the growth rate instead accelerated, reaching over 12 per cent before the downturn came in 2008.

The new policy posture became manifest in the late 1990s, and was officially embedded in China's planning when the current administration of Hu Yaobang and Wen Jiabao came to power in 2003. From the early 2000s, the national leadership has moved forcefully on virtually all aspects of its rebalancing agenda, with substantial increases in coverage of major social insurance programmes (Naughton 2008). Rural fees were abolished in 2003 and the agricultural tax eliminated in 2006. Basic education was made free and health insurance expanded for urban residents and extended to the countryside, so that it now covers 90 per cent of the population (Wong 2010). An expanded social security system is being created, including pensions for 130 million rural migrant workers. The China Development Research Foundation, a government think tank, states that the country must invest RMB5.74 trillion by 2020 in building an all-round social welfare system. In fact, central government transfers to local governments in support of these programmes have grown from RMB435 billion in 2002 to RMB2.4 trillion in 2009 (Wong 2010).

As a result, the reach of these programmes increased significantly. By 2008, the number of workers covered by a basic pension grew by 23 per cent to 219 million; those receiving basic health insurance grew by 80 per cent to 317 million; workers compensation increased its coverage by 78 per cent to 138 million; and coverage of unemployment insurance increased by 10 per cent to 124 million. These statistics should be taken with some reserve: 'coverage' does not necessarily imply adequacy or consistency and these programmes remain works in progress. However, the scale of expenditure increase attests to the seriousness of purpose of the central government.

Despite these accomplishments, the fraction of GDP spent by all levels of government on social insurance and safety net programmes rose only slightly between 2002 and 2007 (Lardy 2008). Moreover, the basic growth model not only did not change, its worst features intensified in the years leading up to the global crisis: household consumption fell as a proportion of GDP, investment and net exports rose further. Thus, even before considering the competing demands for attention of global recession, China's growth model was proving highly resistant to change. This is because the incentives facing decision-makers favour rapid and unqualified growth, and because a dysfunctional public finance system makes it very difficult for the central government to implement its non-growth objectives.

Regarding incentives, the national personnel system put in place in the 1980s for government officials at all levels includes sets of success indicators that provide the basis for assessing official performance. The predominant components of these indicators are those that are directly tied to economic growth, such as GDP growth and tax collections. Evaluation results determine cadres' prospects for upward mobility and, more immediately, their year-end bonuses. As in the US financial sector, a cadre's bonus can double his/her annual income. Added to this very immediate and direct incentive is the more general motive for rapid local growth, namely, to increase the amount of resources available to local leaders to pay for public services and provide patronage. It is thus hardly surprising that local public officials are generally blind to any criteria but the most rapid possible growth (Naughton 2008, Whiting 2004).

Given this structural bias toward growth above all, the central government lacks the fiscal instruments to overcome it and promote alternative objectives at the local level. Yet, that is where over 90 per cent of social spending takes place. Local government expenditure assignments are not matched by their revenue sources, while the revenue system itself is highly inegalitarian. The centre cannot efficiently implement its priorities at the local level, and 'the government is hobbled—through the whole administrative set-up—by agents whose revenue-hunger dominates decision-making' (Wong 2008, see also Wong 2007, World Bank 2002).

Thus, to the degree that China was accomplishing various objectives of the 'harmonious society', this was being done by a kind of *force majeure* on the part of the central government, using its own growing fiscal resources to override the normal channels of social spending to fund directly the new education and social insurance initiatives. At the local level, where most social spending is done, there was no indication of similar commitment, and this raises the question of how sustainable the centre's initiative is.

THE DOWNTURN OF 2008 AND THE STIMULUS

The global crisis posed a challenge to the more balanced and equitable approach to development that China's leaders had been promoting. First, it threatened to retard China's growth sharply, and, as a general matter, redistributive initiatives are easier to accomplish when they can be done marginally out of a large growth premium, without the need for absolute losers. Thus, despite the fact that the progressive moves of the 2002–7 period came at a time of extraordinarily fast growth rates, reaching well above 10 per cent,[9] yet total expenditures on health, education, social security, and unemployment by all levels of government hardly increased at all as a share of GDP. Indeed, government expenditures as a whole grew by over 15 per cent per year during this period, which exceeded the growth rate of GDP. Therefore, the social expenditures listed above must actually have fallen as a proportion of total government spending. In that sense, one can say that the spending increases were not really redistributive at all. They were financed by an essentially constant proportional share of a very large growth premium. If economic slowdown shrinks that growth premium, then any continuing expansion of social spending becomes more of a zero-sum game, coming at the expense of other kinds of spending, and resistance is bound to increase. It is hard for progressive change to survive in a lower growth environment.

Second, when the crisis hit China, the government's primary agenda changed radically. According to the Chinese Academy of Social Sciences (CASS), some 41 million workers lost their jobs as a result of the downturn, an indication of the magnitude and urgency of the problem. The US$586 billion stimulus package that China adopted in late 2008 was in fact a vigorous one—larger relative to GDP than that of the US, and more stimulatory in nature. Moreover, the extraordinary surge in bank credit in early 2009 further magnified the impact of the stimulus. But, China's mode of economic growth is highly inefficient at job creation in the core sectors of the industrial economy, as we have seen. Absent a change in that mode, it would take large increases in GDP to restore jobs lost in that sector.

Several components of the stimulus were potentially balancing and inequality-reducing: for example, investment in public housing focusing on urban low-rent units and renovation of rural housing; investment in rural infrastructure, such as water supply, conservation, irrigation, roads, and the power grid; increased spending for health and education, including improved local clinics and renovation of schools in the interior; increased spending on public transport systems (11 Chinese cities already have underground rapid transit systems, and many more are under construction); increases in the extremely meagre payment standards for China's urban anti-poverty programme, the 'Minimum Living Allowance' scheme;[10] increased grain procurement prices for farmers and farm subsidies. Subsidies for rural purchases of home appliances, farm machinery and vehicles have stimulated rural consumption and steep cuts in sales taxes on energy efficient cars boosted sales.

Yet, at the March 2009 National People's Congress (NPC), familiar large-scale industries dominated the list of industrial beneficiaries of the stimulus package: steel, auto, machinery, ship building, textiles, electronics, and petrochemicals. This brought a rebuke from Cai Fang, a distinguished demographer and economist and a member of the NPC standing committee, who complained that 'The central government's incentives seem more attentive to big companies than small ones, which are the mainstay of employment' and who warned against the danger of a 'jobless recovery.'[11] Indeed, the surge in investment spending at first ran far ahead of any increase in consumption. By the end of 2008, excess capacity in China's steel industry was already approximately equal to Europe's entire output, yet 58 million tonnes of new capacity were under construction. Capacity utilization rates were very low in aluminium, wind power, cement and chemicals, among others, yet 'vast additional capacity is on the way' (FT.com, 29 November 2009).

Similarly, environmental protection, a key objective of the Harmonious Society and rebalancing plans, although a recipient of substantial funds in the stimulus, got shoved aside in the fervour to approve stimulus projects: 'In the rush to invest US$585 billion in stimulus spending and revive flagging industrial production, China has at least temporarily backpedaled on some environmental restraints....'[12]

In an economy whose core industrial sector is so resistant to job creation, it takes very high investment rates—the antithesis of 'rebalancing'—to have an impact on employment. And if restoring employment is the most important short-run objective, then perhaps rebalancing would have to wait. Employment levels in China in fact did recover from the middle of 2009 as a result of the extraordinary expansion of bank lending and heavy public investment. Recovery was not 'jobless', as Cai Fang feared. The researchers at the CASS reported that, of the 41 million Chinese workers who lost their jobs as a result of the crisis, some 18 million had regained employment as of early September 2009,[13] and by February 2010 there were actually widespread reports of labour shortages in the coastal export zones.

China's previous major stimulus package, the one adopted in the late 1990s to combat the impact of the Asian crisis, did have a regionally equalizing effect, as much of it was aimed at less developed areas of the centre and west. The redistributive impact of the earlier programme was picked up by the 2002 China Household Income Project (see Khan and Riskin 2005), which found improved intra-rural distribution due largely to the increase in off-farm employment in poorer provinces that was probably due to the huge increase in interior infrastructural spending (Riskin 2007). What about the 2008–9 stimulus?

As amended by the National People's Congress in March 2009, China's stimulus programme contained some RMB 3 trillion, excluding spending on earthquake reconstruction. In its inevitable reliance on investment to shore up demand and create jobs, the stimulus certainly contradicted the shift in demand composition toward consumption that is a major objective of rebalancing. Capital formation shot up from 42 per cent of GDP in 2007 to almost 48 per cent of GDP in 2009 and even higher in 2010, whereas final consumption fell from 50 per cent of GDP in 2007 to 48 per cent in 2009 and lower in 2010. However, not only the amount but also the type of spending, and of investment in particular, are also relevant to rebalancing. The categories of expenditure, as broken down by Barry Naughton, are shown in Table 6.2. As Naughton (2009) observes, the composition of spending changed, at least in the first two rounds of spending, from the original emphasis on transport and power infrastructure to a greater emphasis on affordable housing, rural village infrastructure and health and education, all categories with a more direct impact on living standards. In the February 2009 round, these three categories comprised almost 60 per cent of total spending. Moreover, infrastructure spending was focused on the less developed interior provinces, as during the Asian Crisis. In the first half of 2009, fixed asset investment grew by 42 per cent in the Western provinces, compared with 24 per cent in the east. Output growth in 12 western provinces outpaced that in 11 eastern ones by 8 per cent to 7 per cent (FT.com, 13 September 2009). Thus, in respect of type and location of expenditures, the stimulus evolved into something that was more compatible with the rebalancing objective than it seemed at first.

Table 6.2   Expenditure Composition of Stimulus Package

Sector	Per cent of total spending in plan	First round of spending (RMB 100 billion), Dec 2008	Second round of spending (RMB 130 billion), Feb 2009
Transport and power infrastructure (roads, railroads, airports, power grid)	50	25	21
Rural village infrastructure	12	34	24
Environmental investment; natural areas	7	12	8
Affordable housing	13	10	22
Technological innovation & structural adjustment	12	6	12
Health & education	5	13	13

Source: Naughton (2009).

Table 6.3 presents basic information on per capita income of seven provinces, three of them relatively well off and four quite poor. The data come from annual surveys of rural and urban household income carried out by China's National Bureau of Statistics. In Table 6.3, the

Table 6.3   Rural and Urban Income of Selected Provinces, 2007 (yuan)

Province	Per capita net income of rural households	Per capita disposable income of urban households
Shanghai	10,145	23,663
Zhejiang	8,265	20,574
Jiangsu	6,561	16,378
Sichuan	3,547	11,098
Shaanxi	2,645	10,678
Guizhou	2,374	10,763
Gansu	2,329	10,012

Source: China Data Center Online (University of Michigan), http://141.211.142.26/.

list of provinces is sorted by income. Note that the correlation between the urban and rural rankings is perfect, and that the range between high and low income provinces is much greater for rural income than for urban income.

Figure 6.3 shows formal sector employment quarterly over the period from March 2007 to September 2009 for three high-income provinces (Shanghai, Zhejiang, and Jiangsu) and four poor ones (Sichuan, Gansu, Shaanxi, and Guizhou). The all-important migrant

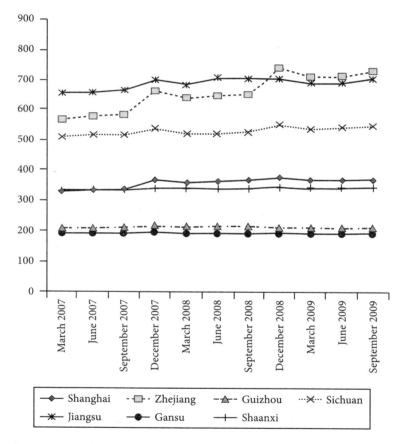

Figure 6.3   Employment of Workers and Staff during Crisis, Selected Rich and Poor Provinces (10,000 persons), Quarterly, 3/2007 to 9/2009

Source: All China Data Centre, China Data Online.

labour force, which is much more vulnerable to economic fluctuations, is excluded from these data. There is a perceptible difference between the short formal employment histories of the rich and poor provinces, respectively. The three well-off provinces (and especially Zhejiang) experience rising trends over the period as a whole, although mostly before the crisis hits in August 2008. Employment in Zhejiang and Shanghai continues to rise in the fourth quarter, as exports plummet and GDP growth slows, then falls off a bit and stabilizes. Jiangsu's employment is flat from the middle of 2008.

The three poorest provinces (Guizhou, Gansu, and Shaanxi) experience no rising trend at all. By the same token, their employment does not fall once the crisis hits. They are evidently shielded by their interior locations and backward economies from the global storms. Finally, Sichuan appears to be an intermediate case, with a slight rising trend before the onset of crisis and then a slight reduction followed by stability, as in the case of the richer provinces. These data are representative of the growing regional imbalance occasioned by globalization in China, the great dynamism of the developed coastal provinces but also their greater vulnerability to global forces. One can speculate about the impact of including the migrant labour force[14] in the analysis. Migrants who lost their jobs would have returned to their native villages in places like the three economically backward provinces in Figure 6.3 and so would not be picked up by employment data there. However, because there is little doubt that the greatest burden of rising unemployment has fallen on migrant workers, the graph of total employment in the richer provinces, including migrants, would display much greater fluctuation than in Figure 6.3, which largely excludes migrants.

It has long been evident that China's labour market is segmented. Full status urban residents do not generally build skyscrapers, wash their windows or fill export processing factories. Their enterprises' capital costs are artificially low and their technologies excessively capital-intensive, creating few new jobs. Export industries and urban construction, on the other hand, are filled with migrant workers, their production more labour-intensive, and employment grows along with output. These sectors, then, are exceptions to the employment averse nature of recent industrial growth discussed above. There, labour-intensive techniques have predominated precisely to take advantage of China's formerly large pool of surplus workers. And for that reason, after some 30 years of very rapid growth based upon tapping this pool, it finally shows signs of exhaustion.

REBALANCING AND THE END OF THE LEWIS MODEL

By March 2010, with exports recovering, labour shortages and consequent rising wages were reported for much of the export-oriented southeast coastal region where migrant labour is predominant. China was returning to the growing tightness of the labour market that had been experienced just before the 2008 downturn and that had already begun to push wages up in the export zones. There are grounds to suspect that reported labour shortages are not merely frictional. First, as we have seen, a large part of stimulus spending was aimed at interior, less developed regions, as was the case during the Asian Crisis of the late 1990s. The jobs this has created in the interior, along with improved conditions for farmers as the government moved to cut taxes and raise purchasing prices for agricultural goods, as well as construction booms in inland cities such as Chongqing and Wuhan, have all combined to raise the opportunity cost of migrating to eastern export enclaves far from home (*Wall Street Journal*, wsj.com, 22 February 2010).[15] The same Cai Fang who criticized the stimulus at the National People's Congress in 2009, said in March 2010, 'It's certain that the migrant worker shortage is here to stay in China.' Cai reported that wages for China's 150 million or so migrant workers increased 19 per cent in 2008 and 16 per cent in 2009, despite the downturn; companies were shifting production to the interior to take advantage of lower labour costs; and local governments would have to shift from being 'pro-capital' to 'pro-labour', by raising minimum wages and easing living conditions for migrants and their families in their new urban homes.[16]

Strong recovery of exports in 2010, after their collapse a year earlier, left net exports contributing 2.4 per cent of GDP, but China's trade appeared to be more balanced in 2011. As long as China remains burdened with a large pool of surplus labour and expanding exports appears to be a means of employing it, China will be tempted to rely on export promotion to create jobs, although aborted recoveries throughout Europe and North America challenge the efficacy of this model. Moreover, the shrinkage of the surplus labour pool and consequent increases in labour costs in the export zones also threatens the addiction to exports. As the Lewis model of unlimited labour is left behind, development will shift to the lower cost interior. Rising wages and falling profits relative to GDP will produce increasing rates of consumption and falling rates of investment, and growth will moderate—that is, China's economy will begin to rebalance along the lines its central government has been advocating for years. At that point, the 'developmental state' functions of the central government (Bagchi 2004)—its vigorous expansion of spending to improve and extend rural education and health care (World Bank 2009b), build up transport and energy infrastructure in the underdeveloped interior, and even initiate a rural pension system—will facilitate the market-driven change by making interior regions more attractive than before to investors escaping from high coastal labour and real estate costs.

NOTES

1. O'Brien (2008), p. 412 cited in Perry (2008).

2. Sun Liping (2011). This was reported in Bloomberg News, 6 March 2011.

3. Functional distribution of income refers to its distribution among wages and salaries, profits, interest, and rents.

4. Nevertheless, China's high-income group is numerous enough to surpass the US in car sales in 2009 as well as of refrigerators and desktop computers. See Keith Bradsher, 'Cutting Back? Not in China,' *The New York Times*, 10 December 2009.

5. Hu (2004) estimates the GDP elasticity of employment growth from 1996 to 2001 at 0.17.

6. A discussion of the problems of China's labour and employment statistics can be found in B-net's 'Manufacturing Employment in China,' at http://findarticles. com/p/articles/mi_m1153/is_7_128/ai_n15927825/?tag=content;col1.

7. See Sen (1960), Dobb (1960), and Galenson and Leibenstein (1955). A good review of this literature can be found in Stewart (1972).

8. See http://www.leleux.be/leleux/JLCHome.nsf/files/10-06-THU/$file/10-06-THU.pdf.

9. In the second quarter of 2007, China's annual rate of growth of GDP reached 14 per cent. See Lardy (2009).

10. The payment standards are discussed in Gao and Riskin (2008).

11. See China Daily Online at http://www.chinadaily.com.cn/bizchina/2009npc/2009-03/09/content_7553041.htm.

12. 18 April 2009. *The New York Times* reported that environmental impact assessments were being cut back from 60 days to as little as five.

13. This was the analysis of the Chinese Academy of Social Sciences' *China Population and Labor Yearbook*, 2009, as reported by *China Labour Net*, at http://www.worldlabour.org/eng/node/253. The Yearbook's editor is Cai Fang.

14. There have been various estimates of the size of China's migrant work-force. The National Bureau of Statistics put the number at 130 million at the end of 2006. See http://en.chinagate.cn/features/rural_poverty/2008-02/22/content_16965925.htm. This compares with a formal labour force ('staff and workers,' in Chinese parlance) of about 112 million and total national employment of about 764 million at the end of 2006. See National Bureau of Statistics of China 2008, Tables 4.2 and 4.8.

15. Enrolment in colleges and universities has also been growing very rapidly, quadrupling from 5.6 million in 2000 to 21.5 million in 2009. Although only a minor influence on the supply of migrant labour, this has probably somewhat tightened the labour supply offered by full status urban residents.

16. See 'China wages to rise as labor shortages grow,' Reuters, at http://www.reuters.com/article/idUSTRE62I14B20100319 (accessed 25 March 2010).

REFERENCES

All China Data Center, China Data Online. China Yearly Provincial Macro-economy Statistics, Table on Employment, Staff and Workers, http://141.211.142.26/ (accessed 30 May 2012).

Bagchi, A.K. 2004. *The Developmental State in History and in the Twentieth Century*. New Delhi: Regency.

Dadush, U. 2009. 'Bilateral U.S.-China Imbalances Not the Issue', *International Economic Bulletin Viewpoint*, November 2009, http://m.ceip.org/2009/11/19/bilateral-u.s.-china-imbalances-not-issue/8odk&lang=en (accessed 17 May 2012).

Dobb, M. 1960. *An Essay on Economic Growth and Planning*. London: Routledge.

Galenson, W. and H. Leibenstein. 1955. 'Investment Criteria, Productivity and Economic Development', *Quarterly Journal of Economics*, 69 (3): 343–70.

Gao, Q. and C. Riskin. 2008. 'Generosity and Participation: Variations in China's Urban Minimum Living Standard Assistance Policy', Paper prepared for meeting of China Task Force of Columbia University Initiative for Policy Dialog and Brooks World Poverty Institute, University of Manchester Manchester, UK.

Hu, A. 2004. 'Economic Growth and Employment Growth in China (1978–2001)', *Asian Economic Papers* 3 (2): 166–76.

Keister, L.A. and J. Liu. 2001. 'The Transformation Continues: The Status of Chinese State-Owned Enterprises at the Start of the Millennium.' *NBR Analysis*, 12 (3): 5–31.

Khan, A.R. 2009. 'Growth, Inequality and Poverty in Our Times: A Personal Reflection', Employment, Growth and Poverty Reduction in Developing Countries: A Conference in Honor of Professor Azizur Khan, Political Economy Research Center, University of Massachusetts, Amherst.

Khan, A.R. and C. Riskin. 2005. 'China's Household Income and Its Distribution, 1995 and 2002', *China Quarterly*, 182 (June): 356–84.

Lardy, N.R. 2008. 'Sustaining Economic Growth in China', in C. Fred Bergsten, Nicholas R. Lardy and Derek J. Mitchell (eds), *China's Rise: Challenges and Opportunities*, Peterson Institute for International Economics, Washington D.C.

—————. 2009. 'China and the Global Crisis', Presentation, http://www.iie.com/publications/papers/lardy0309.pdf (accessed 25 March 2010).

National Bureau of Statistics of China. 2008. *Zhongguo tongji zhaiyao* ('Statistical Abstract of China') *2008*. Beijing: China Statistics Press.

Naughton, B. 2008. 'Chinese Economic Growth: From Quantity to Quality', Conference on Three Decades of Reform and Opening: Where Is China Headed? Pardee Center for the Study of the Longer Range Future, Boston University.

—————. 2009. 'Understanding the Chinese Stimulus Package', *China Leadership Monitor* (8 May 28), http://media.hoover.org/sites/default/files/documents/CLM28BN.pdf (accessed 17 May 2012).

O'Brien, K.J. (ed.). 2008. *Popular Protest in China*. Cambridge: Harvard University Press.

Perry, E.J. 2008. 'Popular Protest in China: Playing by the Rules', Conference on Three Decades of Reform and Opening: Where Is China Going?, Pardee Center for the Study of the Longer Range Future, Boston University.

Riskin, C. 1987. *China's Political Economy: The Quest for Development since 1949*. Oxford and New York: Oxford University Press.

—————. 2007. 'Has China Reached the Top of the Kuznets Curve?' in V. Shue and C. Wong (eds), *Paying for Progress in China*, pp. 29–45. London and New York: Routledge.

Sen, A. 1960. *Choice of Techniques: An Aspect of the Theory of Planned Economic Development*. Oxford: B. Blackwell.

Stewart, F. 1972. 'Choice of Technique in Developing Countries', *The Journal of Development Studies*, 9 (1): 99–121.

Sun, Liping. 2011. '*Shehui shixu shi dangxiade yanjun tiaozhan*' (Social disorder is currently a severe challenge), *Jingji Guanchawang* (Economic Observer), 28 February 2011, at www.eeo.com.cn/Politics/by_region/2011/02/28/194539.shtml (accessed 8 March 2011).

UNDP (United Nations Development Programme). 2007. *Human Development Report* 2007/2008. New York: Palgrave.

Wagstaff, A., M. Lindelow, S. Wang, and S. Zhang. 2009. *Reforming China's Rural Health System*. Washington, D.C.: The World Bank.

Wan, G. 2007. 'Understanding Regional Poverty and Inequality Trends in China: Methodological Issues and Empirical Findings', *Review of Income and Wealth*, 53 (1): 25–34.

Whiting, S.H. 2004. 'The Cadre Evaluation System at the Grass Roots: The Paradox of Party Rule', in B. Naughton and D. Yang (eds), *Holding China Together: Diversity and National Integration in the Post-Deng Era*, pp. 101–19. New York: Cambridge University Press.

Whyte, M.K. 2009. *Myth of the Social Volcano: Perceptions of Inequality and Distributive Injustice in Contemporary China*. Stanford, CA: Stanford University Press.

Wiemer, C. 2009. 'The Big Savers: Households and Government', *China Economic Quarterly*, 13 (4): 20–5.

Wong, C. 2007. 'Can the Retreat from Equality be Reversed? An Assessment of Redistributive Fiscal Policies from Deng Xiaoping to Wen Jiabao', in V. Shue and C. Wong (eds), *Paying for Progress in China*, pp. 12–28. London and New York: Routledge.

——. 2008. 'Rebuilding Government for the 21st Century: Can China Incrementally Reform the Public Sector?' Unpublished paper, Oxford University.

——. 2010. 'Fiscal Reform: Paying for the Harmonious Society', *China Economic Quarterly*, 14 (2): 22–7.

World Bank. 2002. *China: National Development and Sub-National Finance*. Washington, D.C.: The World Bank.

——. 2009a. *From Poor Areas to Poor People: China's Evolving Poverty Reduction Agenda: An Assessment of Poverty and Inequality in China*. Washington. D.C.: The World Bank.

——. 2009b. *Reforming China's Rural Health System*. Washington, D.C.: The World Bank.

7

Growth, Reforms, and Inequality
Comparing India and China

LOPAMUDRA BANERJEE, ASHWINI DESHPANDE, YAN MING,
SANJAY RUPARELIA, VAMSICHARAN VAKULABHARANAM, AND
WEI ZHONG*

> The most exciting countries for me today are India and China. We differ,
> of course, in our political and economic structures, yet the problems
> we face are essentially the same. The future will show which country
> and which structure of government yields greater results in every way.
>
> —Jawaharlal Nehru, 1954[1]

Since the 1950s, many observers have sought to understand the
strategies, trajectories, and consequences of development in India
and China. The rationale was relatively clear. On the one hand, both

* The authors were fellows of the India China Institute (ICI), New School,
New York, during 2008–10. This collaborative work is a part of the fellowship
programme entitled 'Prosperity and Inequality', sponsored by the ICI during
this period. We would like to thank conference participants at the Institute for
Chinese Studies conference in New Delhi, Institute for Development Studies conference in Kolkata, India China Institute conference in New York (March 2010)
and the Annual Conference on Development and Change in Johannesburg (April
2010) for useful comments and suggestions. However, we alone are responsible
for all remaining errors and omissions.

countries were large, populous, and ancient civilizations that had become modern nation-states, seeking to transform their rural agrarian societies into modern industrialized economies. On the other hand, their respective paths towards modernity exhibited striking differences. India's pursuit of a mixed planned economy under the auspices of constitutional democracy after Independence in 1947 contrasted sharply with China's vision of a radically egalitarian society ruled by an authoritarian political regime after the communist revolution in 1949. Nehru's question carried, and carries, immense historical significance.

Yet their respective paths over the last three decades, particularly since the advent of liberal economic reform,[2] have exhibited important common attributes. Both countries have recently experienced historically unprecedented growth rates, averaging around 6 per cent over 1980–2005 for India and 10 per cent post-1978 for China, increasing their share of world income from less than one-tenth in 1950 to approximately 20 per cent today (Bardhan 2010, p. 1). Despite these high rates of economic growth and steady decline in aggregate poverty figures, however, large economic differentials mar both countries' records. According to the most recent estimates by the World Bank, 42 per cent of Indians were living on less than US$1.25 per day in 2005 (in terms of purchasing power parity [PPP]), which means that the number of persons in poverty rose from 421 million in 1981 to 456 million in 2005 (Chen and Ravallion 2008b). China's record is much better. Yet 16 per cent of the population still lives on less than US$1.25 per day (PPP) in 2005, 130 million more than previously thought (Chen and Ravallion 2008a). Put bluntly, the number of individuals living in poverty in both countries remains a staggering figure.

This striking combination of accelerated economic growth and persistent social deprivation motivates our investigation into the nature of prosperity and inequality in India and China over the last two decades. In particular, this chapter undertakes a comparative analysis of economic inequality based on changes in the pattern and distribution of income and expenditure as captured by the Gini coefficient.[3] Comparative analyses of growth rates between the two countries have received generous attention in popular media and academic discourse. Systematic comparative analyses of the social, spatial, and temporal dimensions of economic inequality have been relatively few in number, however. Thus, this chapter seeks to answer two important questions. First, what is the trend in inequality in India and China? Second, what additional information can we gather by decomposing their aggregate trends in terms of: (*a*) regional variations, and (*b*) the urban–rural divide?

STUDIES ON INEQUALITY

India

By international standards, post-independent India had fairly low rates of economic inequality. Since the process of liberal economic reform began in the mid-1980s, scholars have tracked the impact of these larger macroeconomic changes on the incidence of inequality and poverty. The existing literature on estimates of Indian inequality is a varied terrain: individual studies reach different conclusions regarding the trends in inequality as well as its level in various domains. Bhalla (2003) finds that inequality in general declined between 1993–4 and 1999–2000. According to his estimates, rural inequality declined in 15 out of 16 major states in India, and urban inequality declined in 8 out of 17 states. Singh *et al.* (2003) find no strong evidence of greater inequality at an all-India level in the 1990s. Other studies focus on the sharp rural–urban differences as well as the regional variation in the Indian experience. A study by the Government of India, the *National Human Development Report* (GOI 2001), examining the evidence from the 38th, 50th, and 55th rounds of the National Sample Survey (NSS), corresponding to 1983, 1993–4 and 1999–2000, found that 7 out of 32 states experienced increased rural inequality, while 15 out of 32 states suffered greater urban inequality, over the 1990s. Moreover, urban inequality was higher than rural in most states. Jha (2004) reaches a slightly different conclusion. According to his estimates, the rural Gini coefficient increased from 26.33 to 28.50 between 1993 and 2000, but the urban Gini remained virtually unchanged over the same period, from 34.50 to 34.25. Finally, Sen and Himanshu (2005) calculate the adjusted Gini estimates for the 50th and 55th rounds (for states as well as for India as a whole) and find that the rural Gini increased from 25.80 to 26.30, while the urban increased to a greater extent, from 31.90 to 34.80.[4] Using alternative data (income tax reports), Banerjee and Piketty (2005) concur with this general picture of rising economic inequality. In the 1990s, they contend, the real incomes of the top

1 per cent of income earners in India increased by 50 per cent. Indeed, within this group, the richest 1 per cent increased their real incomes more than threefold over the 1990s.

Comparing regional inequality in India and China is not a straightforward exercise. For one thing, conventional regional groupings in India (North, South, East, West, and Northeast) do not exactly match those routinely used in China (Eastern, Central, and Western, or Coastal versus Inland). Both these groupings conceal substantial internal variation, with possibly greater within-group heterogeneity in India compared to China. Second, the sources of regional inequality in both countries are deeply embedded in their distinct initial conditions and respective historical trajectories. In other words, they are not simply a product of liberal economic reforms since the 1980s. Nevertheless a significant empirical question remains: has the process of economic liberalization in either country exacerbated or dampened their previous levels of regional inequality?

Existing studies of regional inequality in India—where the 'region' may be classified either as a state or Union Territory (UT) or larger geographical area comprising several states and UTs (North, South, East, West, and Northeast)—provide some evidence of growing disparities. Singh *et al.* (2003) found absolute divergence in inter-state per capita consumption expenditure. Jha (2004) found little evidence for inter-state convergence and found that the rank order of states had not changed over the reform period. Ahluwalia (2002) largely concurs. Deaton and Dreze (2002) observe three dimensions of rising economic inequality. First, there is strong evidence of 'divergence' in per capita consumption across states. Second, they find a significant increase in rural-urban inequalities at the all-India level, and in most individual states. Third, their decomposition exercise shows that the rising inequality within states, particularly in the urban sector, has moderated the effects of growth on poverty reduction. The authors argue that the evidence of rising inequality since 1993–4 is a new development for the Indian economy: until this time, the all-India Gini coefficients of monthly per capita expenditure (MPCE) in rural and urban areas were fairly stable. They also suggest that the rate of increase of economic inequality in the 1990s is 'far from negligible' (Deaton and Dreze 2002, p. 3740). Looking at China's experience of sustained rise in inequality for over 20 years, the authors fear that this might not be a short-term temporary phenomenon for India—there might be further accentuation of economic disparities in India in the near future. In short, Bhalla (2003) notwithstanding, most of the existing literature suggests that economic disparities—sectoral, inter-state, and regional—increased through the 1990s. However, the precise level of economic inequality, relative weight of urban–rural disparities in the larger all-India picture in these sectors remains contested.

China

Discussions of economic inequality in China differ from those in India due to its revolutionary past. The Chinese Communist Party (CCP) made concerted efforts after coming to power to create a classless society on the foundations of a deeply unequal social order. Its capacity to do so, particularly in urban areas and across the provinces, was striking for a vast poor country in comparative historic perspective. But it was not comprehensive. In particular, urban–rural inequality grew from the late 1950s until the late 1970s. One the one hand, relatively low levels of state investment in agriculture and the underpricing of farm products exacerbated the sectoral terms of trade (Riskin 1989, pp. 223–56). On the other, increasing female participation in the labour force and stricter birth control in urban areas raised household incomes and reduced the dependency ratio, respectively (Naughton 2007, pp. 132–3). Hence the characterization of pre-1978 China as 'egalitarian' but 'dualistic' (Naughton 2007, p. 217).

The post-1978 reforms have reversed these general earlier achievements, however, stimulating concerns about social opportunity, political stability, and the sustainability of economic growth. Lee and Selden (2008) compare inequality before and after 1978. In the former phase, inequality was not founded on property ownership or market outcomes, but instead defined by the Party through the *chengfen* (class) categories, inverted from the pre-revolutionary period (for example, landlords were designated as class enemies and hence comprised the lowest echelons of the collective order). Thus rural areas were characterized by relatively high levels of income equality. However, its inhabitants had limited social protection in terms of education and health care, provided by the collectives (communes), inferior to their provision in urban areas by the state. In both urban and rural areas, the deepest divide is not within the ranks of workers but between workers and party cadres, mediated by a graded pay scale based on the Soviet model. In an early study, Kmietowicz and Ding (1993) analyse changes in the distribution of household income in rural Jiangsu between 1980 and 1986. Their analysis shows that average household income per head increased considerably after the 1978 reforms, but inequality increased too. Gustafsson and Li (2000), while exploring the gender disparities in urban wages in China, discuss how the Chinese reform process has had a clear regional dimension. Since the reforms started in the eastern regions, growth has been much faster there than in the inland provinces, as is well known. Lee and Seldon (2008) extensively discuss Chinese inequality not only in terms of numbers but also in terms of the conceptual frameworks used to analyse contemporary inequality. They argue that the number of empirical studies on Chinese inequality have grown as fast as the inequality itself. Specifically, they find the stratification paradigm, which most studies use, unsatisfactory for several reasons. First, it lacks a deeper causal understanding of the social structure that generates inequality. Second, it fails to shed light on the moral meaning and political significance of inequality in the Chinese context, which has seen a transformation from a revolutionary to a market-driven economy.

Khan and Riskin (2005) analyse changes in income distribution and absolute poverty between 1988 and 1995. They find a sharp increase in inequality between coastal and inland provinces and between urban and rural areas. Fan, *Kanbur, and Zhang* (2010) study the latest developments in regional inequality in China (which continues to be persistent since its growth post-1978). They suggest that the global financial crisis has compelled the Chinese government to put in place a stimulus package largely geared towards improving the inland economy, by building long overdue infrastructure and establishing a social safety net, in previously neglected rural and inland regions. They believe that the current crisis might prove to be a turning point in rebalancing China's regional disparities.

India–China Comparisons

While there are plenty of single-country studies that examine economic inequality in India and China, comparative studies are relatively few. Borooah *et al.* (2005) use micro-data to compare income inequality and poverty in the two countries. They find that in the mid-1990s income inequality in rural China and rural India was relatively similar. Their results show that differences in mean income across regions are much larger in China than in India and account for a much larger proportion of income inequality in rural China. They also find that economic status in India is more influenced by the educational level of household head than in China, where illiteracy is far lower than in India, due to its revolutionary past. However, there are some factors common to both countries that impact poverty and inequality significantly, such as land ownership and minority status (for more, see Bardhan [2010]).

Chaudhuri and Ravallion (2006) argue that fast growth in India and China has resulted in high rates of urbanization and growing demand for skills, both of which have contributed to rising inequalities within these countries. They make a distinction between 'good' and 'bad' inequalities and argue that while both countries have seen both kinds of inequalities, there is a danger that 'bad' inequalities (those that prevent individuals from connecting to markets and from accumulating physical and human capital) might undermine the sustainability of the growth process.

Bardhan (2010) systematically compares India and China across a range of dimensions, including growth, poverty, and inequality. He finds evidence to suggest that various domestic factors, rather than global economic integration, explain poverty reduction in both countries to a greater degree (ibid., pp. 92–3). He also finds that poverty reduction is lower in India vis-à-vis China, not only because aggregate economic growth has been lower and more recent, but also because the poverty elasticity of economic growth is greater in China due to greater prior equalities regarding land and education (ibid., p. 95). He underscores the need for rigorous causal analysis to tease out the inter-relationships between growth, liberalization, globalization, inequality and poverty.

STATISTICAL ANALYSIS: TRENDS IN INEQUALITY IN INDIA AND CHINA SINCE THE LATE 1980s

Consumption Inequality in India

The National Sample Survey Organization (NSSO) of India collects data on monthly consumption expenditure of households through large-scale quinquennial surveys and thin annual surveys. MPCE is calculated as the monthly household expenditure divided by household size. To maintain comparability with China, where our data points are 1988, 1995, and 2002, we use three quinquennial NSSO surveys from three years: 1987–8, 1993–4, 2004–5. To convert nominal to real values, we use Consumer Price Indices (agricultural labour) and Consumer Price Indices (industrial workers) to deflate, respectively, the nominal rural and urban figures. For India, we conduct a regional analysis based on the following grouping of states (Table 7.1).

All-India Inequality Trends

The overall inequality trends (measured in terms of Gini) in India based on MPCE show a distinct rising trend during the period under consideration (see Table 7.2). After remaining stable between 1987–8 and 1993–4, the level of inequality rose from 0.33 to 0.36, between 1993–4 and 2004–5.

The trend in rural inequality differs from the overall trend. It decreased mildly between 1988 and 1994, from 0.30 to 0.29, but returned to its earlier level in the later period (1994–2005). In contrast, the rise in rural inequality in China was much greater over a shorter time period (0.29 to 0.38). The increase in urban inequality in India is consonant with the overall inequality trend, although its level in 2004–5 was higher than the all-India level. It declined slightly between 1988 and 1994, from 0.35 to 0.34, but thereafter rose substantially to 0.38 between 1994 and 2005. For China, the corresponding figures are 0.30 to 0.33 between 1995 and 2002.

The trends in real MPCE growth are clear. While the overall MPCE annual growth is approximately 0.97 per cent, urban consumption grew at 1.21 per cent, whereas rural consumption grew at 0.65 per cent. This suggests a rising urban–rural gap, which the decomposition analysis below confirms, given that the proportion of the population in urban areas is low by international standards and has changed very little over the last two decades (28 per cent in the 2001 census compared to 23 per cent in the 1981 census).

In terms of decile shares, the bottom eight deciles saw a decline in their share of total consumption, whereas the top decile gained more than 3 per cent over this entire period (see Table 7.3). The next decile has gained, but marginally. The fifth, sixth, and seventh deciles have seen the largest decline in their shares of MPCE, suggesting increasing

Table 7.1 Regions of India

North	South	East	West	Northeast
States: Uttar Pradesh, Madhya Pradesh, Haryana, Himachal Pradesh, Jammu and Kashmir, Chhattisgarh (2004–5), and Uttaranchal (2004–5).[a] UTs:[b] Chandigarh, New Delhi.	States: Andhra Pradesh, Karnataka, Kerala, and Tamil Nadu. UTs: Pondicherry, Lakshadweep, and Andaman and Nicobar Islands.	States: Bihar, Jharkhand (2004–5), Orissa, and West Bengal.	States: Maharashtra, Gujarat, Rajasthan, and Goa. UTs: Dadra Haveli and Daman and Diu.	States: Arunachal Pradesh, Assam, Manipur, Mizoram, Meghalaya, Nagaland, Tripura, and Sikkim.

Source: Authors' own classification of the Indian states and union territories into North, East, West, South, and Northeast regions.

Notes: [a] The states of Chhattisgarh, Jharkhand, and Uttaranchal became separate states after the 1993–4 quinquennial survey.
[b] UT stands for Union Territory.

Table 7.2 Inequality in India

State	1987–8			1993–4			2004–5			Total Gini Change (1987–8 to 2004–5)
	Rural Gini	Urban Gini	Total Gini	Rural Gini	Urban Gini	Total Gini	Rural Gini	Urban Gini	Total Gini	
										Gini (Consumption)
Andhra Pradesh	0.31	0.36	0.33	0.29	0.32	0.31	0.29	0.38	0.35	0.02
Assam	0.23	0.31	0.25	0.18	0.29	0.22	0.20	0.32	0.24	–0.01
Bihar	0.26	0.31	0.27	0.22	0.31	0.25	0.21	0.33	0.24	–0.03
Gujarat	0.26	0.28	0.28	0.24	0.29	0.28	0.27	0.31	0.33	0.05
Haryana	0.29	0.29	0.29	0.31	0.28	0.31	0.34	0.37	0.36	0.07
Himachal Pradesh	0.27	0.29	0.28	0.28	0.46	0.32	0.31	0.32	0.33	0.05
Jammu & Kashmir	0.30	0.28	0.30	0.24	0.29	0.27	0.25	0.25	0.26	–0.04
Karnataka	0.30	0.34	0.33	0.27	0.32	0.31	0.27	0.37	0.36	0.03
Kerala	0.32	0.37	0.33	0.30	0.34	0.32	0.38	0.41	0.39	0.06
Madhya Pradesh	0.29	0.33	0.32	0.28	0.33	0.32	0.27	0.40	0.35	0.03
Maharashtra	0.31	0.35	0.36	0.31	0.36	0.38	0.31	0.38	0.39	0.03
Manipur	0.18	0.17	0.18	0.15	0.16	0.16	0.16	0.18	0.17	–0.01
Meghalaya	0.27	0.31	0.31	0.28	0.25	0.29	0.16	0.26	0.21	–0.10
Nagaland	missing	0.16	0.16	0.16	0.20	0.18	0.23	0.24	0.26	0.10
Orissa	0.27	0.31	0.29	0.25	0.31	0.28	0.29	0.35	0.32	0.03
Punjab	0.30	0.29	0.30	0.28	0.28	0.29	0.29	0.40	0.35	0.05

Rajasthan	0.32	0.35	0.33	0.27	0.29	0.28	0.25	0.37	0.30	−0.03
Sikkim	0.23	0.29	0.28	0.21	0.25	0.23	0.27	0.26	0.29	0.01
Tamil Nadu	0.33	0.36	0.36	0.31	0.35	0.34	0.32	0.36	0.38	0.02
Tripura	0.25	0.28	0.26	0.24	0.28	0.26	0.22	0.34	0.28	0.02
Uttar Pradesh	0.29	0.34	0.31	0.28	0.33	0.30	0.29	0.37	0.33	0.02
West Bengal	0.26	0.35	0.31	0.25	0.34	0.31	0.27	0.38	0.35	0.04
A & N Islands	0.27	0.31	0.30	0.25	0.40	0.34	0.34	0.38	0.38	0.08
Arunachal Pradesh	0.33	0.32	0.33	0.31	0.28	0.32	0.28	0.25	0.28	−0.05
Chandigarh	0.30	0.35	0.36	0.24	0.47	0.47	0.25	0.36	0.37	0.01
Dadra & Nagar Haveli	0.30	missing	0.30	0.26	0.32	0.28	0.35	0.30	0.39	0.09
Delhi	0.25	0.40	0.39	0.27	0.41	0.40	0.28	0.34	0.34	−0.05
Goa	0.25	0.33	0.31	0.31	0.28	0.30	0.32	0.42	0.37	0.06
Lakshadweep	0.33	0.26	0.30	0.25	0.30	0.28	0.31	0.39	0.36	0.06
Mizoram	0.18	0.20	0.21	0.17	0.18	0.20	0.20	0.25	0.25	0.04
Pondicherry	0.40	0.31	0.35	0.29	0.30	0.30	0.35	0.32	0.34	−0.01
Daman & Diu				0.25	0.21	0.24	0.26	0.25	0.26	NA
Chhattisgarh							0.30	0.44	0.37	NA
Jharkhand							0.23	0.36	0.31	NA
Uttaranchal							0.29	0.33	0.31	NA
Total	0.30	0.35	0.33	0.29	0.34	0.33	0.30	0.38	0.36	0.03

Source: Authors' computations based on National Sample Survey Consumer Expenditure Data (Ministry of Statistics, Government of India) for the years, 1987–8, 1993–4, and 2004–5.

Table 7.3   Decile Shares in India

Deciles Number	1987–8				1993–4				2004–5				Difference in Shares (1988–2005)
	Decile	% of Median	Share	Cumulative Share	Decile	% of Median	Share	Cumulative Share	Decile	% of Median	Share	Cumulative Share	
1	79.24	56.64	3.65	3.65	146.55	56.67	3.73	3.73	285.80	56.32	3.49	3.49	−0.16
2	95.93	68.57	4.96	8.61	176.18	68.13	4.99	8.72	341.67	67.32	4.61	8.10	−0.35
3	109.73	78.44	5.79	14.40	202.50	78.31	5.82	14.54	393.58	77.55	5.38	13.48	−0.41
4	123.87	88.54	6.58	20.98	228.90	88.52	6.63	21.17	447.00	88.08	6.16	19.63	−0.43
5	139.90	100.00	7.42	28.40	258.59	100.00	7.48	28.65	507.50	100.00	6.95	26.59	−0.46
6	159.30	113.87	8.41	36.81	293.35	113.44	8.47	37.12	581.25	114.53	7.94	34.53	−0.46
7	185.14	132.34	9.67	46.47	339.25	131.19	9.69	46.81	684.80	134.94	9.20	43.73	−0.46
8	224.49	160.47	11.46	57.93	409.89	158.51	11.43	58.24	848.45	167.18	11.10	54.83	−0.36
9	301.71	215.66	14.51	72.44	549.85	212.63	14.45	72.68	1193.63	235.20	14.54	69.37	0.02
10	27.56	100.00	27.32	100.00	30.63	100.00	3.08						

Source: Authors' computations based on National Sample Survey Consumer Expenditure data (Ministry of Statistics, Government of India) for the years 1987–8, 1993–4, and 2004–5.

polarization (see D'Costa 2005 for further analysis). For China, the picture is similar. The *National Human Development Report* (UN 2008:, p. 42) reports that the top 20 per cent have been increasing their share of national income or consumption, whereas the share of the bottom eight deciles has been declining.

Inequality Trends at the State Level

These national trends become far more uneven at the state level. The outliers comprise two groups. States that have witnessed relatively greater economic inequality include Kerala, West Bengal, Gujarat, Haryana, Himachal Pradesh, Goa, Uttar Pradesh, and Mizoram. Among UTs, Dadra and Nagar Haveli, Lakshadweep, and Andaman and Nicobar Islands have witnessed higher than national trends in inequality. Conversely, states such as Arunachal Pradesh, Delhi, Jammu and Kashmir, and Bihar have seen fairly significant declines in inequality. Given the considerable state-level heterogeneity within each group in terms of their distinct levels of development, patterns of growth, policy records and state–society relations, it is hard to infer a general causal trend from the data itself. In short, the underlying mechanisms may differ across these states and UTs. Nonetheless, the fact that previously more egalitarian states such as West Bengal and Kerala have witnessed growing economic inequality suggests that liberalization has had an adverse impact upon the latter.

Inequality Trends at the Regional Level

Regionally, as Table 7.4 demonstrates, economic inequality has risen the most in the East and South (by 4 percentage points). The growth in inequality in the North and West reflects the national trend (by 3 percentage points). Finally, the Northeast has witnessed a mild decline (–0.1). In terms of the levels of inequality, the North and South have the highest Gini levels (0.38 and 0.37 respectively), followed by the West (0.36) in 2004–5. All three regions exceed the national average. In contrast, the East (0.33) and Northeast (0.25) are relatively more equal.

Significantly, urban inequality is greater in every region in India than rural inequality. Moreover, the level of urban inequality is roughly the same across regions except for the Northeast, where it

Table 7.4 Inequality by Region, India, 1987–8 to 2004–5

Region	1987–8			1993–4			2004–5			Total Gini Change
	Rural	Urban	Total	Rural	Urban	Total	Rural	Urban	Total	
North	0.31	0.36	0.34	0.30	0.36	0.34	0.32	0.39	0.37	0.03
East	0.26	0.34	0.29	0.25	0.33	0.29	0.26	0.38	0.33	0.04
West	0.30	0.34	0.33	0.28	0.33	0.33	0.28	0.36	0.36	0.03
South	0.32	0.36	0.34	0.30	0.34	0.33	0.34	0.38	0.38	0.04
Northeast	0.24	0.29	0.26	0.21	0.28	0.24	0.21	0.31	0.25	–0.01
Total	0.30	0.35	0.33	0.29	0.34	0.33	0.30	0.38	0.36	0.03

Source: Authors' computations based on National Sample Survey Consumer Expenditure data (Ministry of Statistics, Government of India) for the years 1987–8, 1993–4, and 2004–5.

is substantially lower, at 0.31 (see Table 7.4). Rural inequality is lowest in the East and Northeast. This picture is similar to China when inequality is measured in terms of consumption. However, when measured by income levels, rural inequality is greater than urban inequality in China. This is because in contrast to India, local urban residents with urban *hokou* are highly protected by local government, receiving food and housing subsidies until 1995 (Naughton 2007, pp. 219–20). Moreover, given that living costs are relatively high, rural migrants are not able to settle down in urban areas unless they get a well-paid job, which would be quite rare. Finally, because of the sampling methodology, migrant workers are not included in urban surveys in China. Although land is distributed relatively evenly, the importance of agricultural income, relative to non-agricultural income, has decreased in rural areas. In the urban sample, only the non-agricultural sector is included in the survey, whereas in the rural sample, both agricultural and non-agricultural sectors are counted, which results in a picture of higher rural inequality as compared to urban inequality.

In terms of real MPCE, the southern and western regions in India are growing faster than the country as a whole. Significantly, the South is leading the pack in terms of both urban and rural real MPCE growth. Indeed, rural MPCE values are growing very slowly in every region of India, except for the South. Growth in urban real MPCE has outstripped its rural counterpart in every region except for the North and Northeast.

Some of the trends in our figures for India find support in the broader political economy literature, while others raise puzzling questions. First, the growth in income/consumption inequality since the late 1980s seems to have undone the greater social equality achieved in Kerala (more comprehensive equality) and West Bengal (more income based) in previous decades. The compulsion to liberalize, with upper-class beneficiaries of reform, may explain this turnaround. Our results indicate that the annual rate of growth of MPCE in Kerala has been 2.47 per cent and in West Bengal 1.20 per cent, both greater than the national average, but the Gini coefficients in both the states have risen as well. Second, is it the case that limited economic reform and middling economic growth account for declines in inequality in Arunachal Pradesh, Jammu and Kashmir, and Bihar, and in the Northeast? This is a correlation that lacks obvious causal mechanisms.

Third, it is noteworthy that the South has the highest Gini levels, has witnessed the greatest increase in economic inequality, and has the highest rate of growth of real MPCE. It suggests that the pattern of growth and reform in the South post-1991 has undermined earlier decades of social levelling, which highlights the need to minimize the inherently unequalizing consequences of capitalist development, demanding the implementation of more progressive social policies and greater public action to broaden human capabilities and counteract diverging life-chances (see Dreze and Sen 2002, Nayyar 2008).

Decomposing Economic Inequality in India

In this section, we seek to decompose the overall inequality figures into their constituent parts in order to understand the relative contributions of the different components (Table 7.5).

Table 7.5   Decomposing the Indian Gini by Sector, State, and Region

Decomposition of inequality in India	1987–8 Proportion	1993–4 Proportion	2004–5 Proportion
Sector[a]			
Within	89.54	86.25	80.15
Between	10.46	13.75	19.85
Gini	0.33	0.33	0.36
State			
Within	91.71	89.46	85.96
Between	8.29	10.54	14.04
Gini	0.33	0.33	0.36
Region[b]			
Within	98.44	97.29	96.12
Between	1.56	2.71	3.88
Gini	0.33	0.33	0.36

Source: Authors' computations based on National Sample Survey Consumer Expenditure data (Ministry of Statistics, Government of India) for the years, 1987–8, 1993–4, and 2004–5.
Notes: [a] Sector: Rural versus Urban
[b] Regions: North, East, West, South, Northeast

The results point to the following trends. First, looking at urban–rural disparities in 1987–8, the between-group (that is, sectoral)

component accounted for 10.46 per cent of overall inequality. In 1993–4, it constituted 13.75 per cent. By 2004–5, however, the between-group component covered almost 20 per cent of the total. This is a rapid and significant change. This period coincides with the following broad trend in the Indian economy. Starting in the early 1990s, rural consumption/incomes stagnated significantly while urban consumption/incomes rose rapidly. As a result, the rural–urban gap has grown, which explains the rising between-group component in sectoral terms. Second, the between-state inequality component explained 8.29 per cent of overall inequality in 1987–8, whereas it accounted for about 10.54 per cent in 1993–4, and 14.04 per cent by 2004–5. This is also a case of rising inter-state disparities in post-reform India (see Rudolph and Rudolph 2001). Third, the between-region component accounted for only about 1.56 per cent of overall inequality in 1987–8, 2.71 per cent in 1993–4, and 3.88 per cent in 2004–5. While there is a rising trend in this component, its relative size is fairly small in comparison to the between-sector and between-state dimensions. This suggests that regional groupings in India hide substantial heterogeneity in terms of their constituent states, which enjoy massively greater powers vis-à-vis zonal councils in India's federal parliamentary system.

Income Inequality in China

The Data

The following tables have been calculated using the Chinese Household Income Project (CHIP) survey for different years (Tables 7.6 and 7.7).[5] Chinese data are available for both consumption and income. Tables 7.6 and 7.7 show the rate of growth in both variables. It should be noted that the levels are reported not in RMB but in PPP US dollars. The latter methodology is not perfect for comparing income levels. However, it is better than using RMB comparisons with rupee values directly, or by changing to US dollar by its nominal exchange rate.

China Inequality Trends

We have already made references to the comparative picture between India and China for the rate of growth of consumption. Table 7.5 reiterates well-known features of the Chinese economy—a high rate

Table 7.6   Income and Consumption Each Year in China (in 2005 PPP US$)

	Nationwide	Rural	Urban
Income			
1988	803.9	582.4	1,427.6
1995	1,047.9	684.1	1,932.9
2002	1,732.0	1,042.5	2,804.3
Annual Growth Rate (1988–95)	3.9	2.3	4.4
Annual Growth Rate (1995–2002)	7.4	6.2	5.5
Consumption			
1988			
1995	668.1	415.9	1,281.3
2002	1,094.0	609.0	1,847.0
Annual Growth Rate (1995–2002)	7.3	5.6	5.4

Source: Authors' computations based on China Household Income Project (CHIP) surveys from 1988, 1995, and 2002.

of growth for income and consumption, with rates of growth being higher after the mid-1990s vis-à-vis the early years of reform.

As Table 7.7 indicates, urban areas[6] show better indicators of material standard of living as compared to the rural areas, although the gap in consumption is higher than for income. Table 7.8, however, presents a puzzle. Based on income, urban inequality in China is lower than its rural component (in contrast to India). Based on consumption, however, it is the reverse, with urban equality greater

Table 7.7   Urban–Rural Divide in China

Year	Income	Consumption
1988[a]	2.38	
1995	2.70	3.10
2002	2.76	3.12

Source: Authors' computations based on China Household Income Project (CHIP) surveys from 1988, 1995, and 2002.
Note: The figures reported for urban–rural divide equals urban per capita income/consumption divided by its rural counterpart in terms of current value.

[a] Not all items of consumption were included in the 1988 survey, thus we do not have estimates for consumption for that year.

Table 7.8   Gini Coefficients[a] by Year for China (based on current value)

Year	Nationwide	Rural	Urban
Income			
1988	0.369	0.319	0.233
1995	0.453	0.388	0.332
2002	0.450	0.375	0.350
Consumption			
1988			
1995	0.424	0.299	0.303
2002	0.465	0.376	0.331

Source: Authors' computations based on China Household Income Project (CHIP) surveys from 1988, 1995, and 2002.

Note: [a] Urban areas are defined as per the *hokou* registration system. Thus, urban households would be those that have an urban *hokou*. China's urban area consists of cities and towns. China uses two criteria to define urban, one is the size of inhabitants in a given area and the other is percentage of the non-agricultural population in the given area. Both these criteria are used, but have changed several times since 1949. The most recent change defines a town as a place with 10 per cent or more non-agricultural population. A town, as an economic centre in the area, with 60,000 or more people and at least 200 million yuan GDP, can be changed to a city (1986). Definitions of what is meant by urban populations have also changed several times. There were years when both agricultural and non-agricultural populations were counted as urban as long as they were in the administrative territory of the town or city. There were also times when agricultural population within the territory of city or town was excluded from urban population. But since 1982, whether the agricultural population was counted as urban would depend on the administrative 'level' of the city. The administratively higher-level cities would encompass both non-agricultural and agricultural populations while the lower level cities only non-agricultural population. So the Chinese urban population figure is inconsistent both in terms of time and across the country. No doubt, the *hokou* and drastic population movement have made it even more complicated.

than its rural counterpart just as in India. In 1995, urban inequality was slightly higher than rural, but in 2002, urban inequality was lower than rural, mirroring the pattern based on income.

The UN HDR (2007, p. 52) figures substantiate the gravity of the urban–rural gap. They suggest that the urban–rural gaps in income and development are rooted, in part, in the gaps in the provision of public services. In 2007, the ratio of urban to rural per capita incomes was 3.33 to 1, but they cite research that demonstrates that if the distribution in the access to basic public goods like health care and education are taken into account, then the ratio reaches 5.6 to 1.

Decomposing Economic Inequality in China

As Tables 7.7 and 7.8 indicate, within-group inequality in rural and urban China is rising, whether based on consumption or income. In contrast, between-group inequality, although significantly larger than in India, is declining. This seems paradoxical at first sight, but can be explained. What the tables show is the change in the contribution of the urban–rural gap to total Gini. Basically, the total Gini is increasing faster than the urban–rural gap. To understand this better, consider another hypothetical opposite scenario. Suppose the gap between urban and rural areas had decreased and the overall Gini had decreased even faster—even then the contribution of the 'between-group' effect would have been smaller. Hence, this is a result of some rural areas being reclassified as urban, thus lowering the contribution of the rural–urban inequality to overall inequality.

However, looking at the decomposition between the three regions, the between-group component is much smaller, albeit also rising. Taken together, these two tables suggest that urban–rural disparities are far more acute than inter-regional inequalities in China today (Tables 7.9 and 7.10). This overall finding suggests that the decisively pro-urban strategy of growth pursued in China since the late 1990s—compounded by increasing foreign investment along coastal regions, persistent restrictions imposed by the *hokou* system and the relative decline of agricultural prices in China following its accession to the World Trade Organization (WTO) in 2001—has reversed the declining sectoral gap witnessed in the 1980s after the decollectivization of agriculture (Naughton 2007, pp. 133–4, 218, Bardhan 2010, p. 93).

Table 7.9   Gini Coefficient Decomposed by Urban and Rural China

	1988	1995	2002
Income			
Within	55.7	56.3	57.5
Between	44.3	43.8	42.5
Consumption			
Within		44.8	50.9
Between		55.2	49.1

Source: Authors' computations based on China Household Income Project (CHIP) surveys from 1988, 1995, and 2002.

Table 7.10 Gini Coefficient Decomposed by Three Regions for China

	1988	1995	2002
Income			
Within	89.6	88.8	88.6
Between	10.4	11.2	11.4
Consumption			
Within		94.5	92.2
Between		5.6	7.8

Source: Authors' computations based on China Household Income Project (CHIP) surveys from 1988, 1995, and 2002.

COMPARING AND ASSESSING INEQUALITY IN CHINA AND INDIA

The increasing disparity between the urban and rural sectors, and rising urban inequality, are the most important aspects of uneven economic growth in India over the last 20 years. For India, our findings confirm myriad studies that have focused on the issue of agrarian distress as well as the phenomenon of rapid urbanization with all its discontents. Some of our data show a significant measure of growing inter-state inequality too, corroborating the divergence story that some other analysts have found. Finally, our analysis reveals a significant intertwining of the growth of MPCE and increasing economic inequality. By and large, states, regions, and sectors that are growing more rapidly have also witnessed greater inequality. Put briefly, growth and inequality have become intertwined in the Indian story of development over the last 20 years. This is clearly a break from the past, wherein growth and inequality seemed to have different causal determinants, except in the case of the Green Revolution in those regions where it was implemented (see Nayyar 2008). This makes the recent Indian experience interesting to study, but somewhat alarming. Rising overall prosperity has caused increasing economic inequality in terms of the distribution of income.

Regarding China, our analysis confirms the findings of several other studies. It underscores the dramatic historical transformation of China since the early 1980s from a relatively poor but equal country in comparative historical terms to a strikingly dynamic yet increasingly divided society in the early twenty-first century.

Indeed, the unprecedented economic prosperity of China over the last three decades has simultaneously unleashed powerful new social asymmetries.

Two of the authors of the present chapter have attempted in another exercise (Vakulabha•anam and Jinjun 2010) to discuss the income/consumption inequality picture in the two countries via the apparatus of class structure. For India, they find that the bulk of the rise in inequality can be accounted for by a rise in inequality between classes, whereas for China, the bulk of the rise in inequality is accounted for by a rise in within-class inequality. For India, they find the urban professionals at the top and marginal farmers and agricultural workers at the bottom, revealing a tendency towards greater stratification. The largest increase in intra-group inequality is seen for non-agricultural workers. This could be because of an increasing number of agricultural workers and farmers/tenants moving towards non-agricultural occupations. For China, the authors of the study suggest that a process of rapid urbanization and consequently rural–urban migration—driven by distress in the countryside, as in India—can explain the rise in intra-urban inequality (whose contribution to overall inequality increased over the period). Thus, for both countries, social elites, especially service professionals, seem to have been the big gainers from the liberalization of the economies. In India, the big losers seem to be small and marginal farmers, agricultural workers and urban unskilled workers. In China, the biggest losers are the farmers, the unemployed and informal sector workers.

These conclusions are supported by other studies of post-reform China. Gustafsson and Li (2000) point to widening skill differentials across sectors as well as within sectors as an important factor in explaining earnings gaps. They argue that the wage-setting process in the post-reform era relies more on productivity differences: skill differentials matter much more now than in the pre-reform period with the onset of the services revolution. This is an important factor even within state-owned enterprises (SOEs) as they have much greater freedom to decide on wages. The simulation exercise undertaken by Bussolo et al. (2008) forecasts a rise in the skill premium in both India and China by 2030 that will widen wage gaps, possibly leading to an increase in inequality, unless there are countervailing factors such as a lowering of rural–urban wage gaps, a lowering of gender differentials and changing returns to other worker characteristics. Only very drastic socio-economic changes could enable such reversals, however. Thus, their prediction of increasing inequalities seems more likely to materialize. Naughton (2007, p. 219) adds that clientelistic political networks are another important factor in determining economic opportunities in the urban sector. Lee and Selden (2008) discuss a specific state institution that has shaped inequality in China—the *hokou*—which erects a wall between the urban and rural areas and makes non-sanctioned transactions between rural and urban areas difficult. They also discuss how the reform of the Hukou system has resulted in a vast migrant population, highlighting the mix of old and new (post-reform) patterns of inequality. They suggest that in the post-reform period, inequalities based on property and shaped by domestic and global capital have increased. Transformations in citizenship rights have become more complex— social benefits have been drastically curtailed for all, whereas certain civil rights, including right to possess property, geographical mobility, and recourse to legal justice, have all increased. The growth of TVEs, rural entrepreneurship, regional patterns of differentiation within rural China and the privatization of SOEs—all of these changes have simultaneously produced the urban poor and the new rich while transforming the character of the cadre elite.

Many have commented on the large domestic markets of India and China. The middle classes of both countries comprise the bulk of the internal market. There have been recent comparative exercises (see, for instance, papers in Jaffrelot and van der Veer 2008). Zhou (2008) evaluates China's 2004 National Bureau of Statistics definition of the middle class: annual income ranging from 60,000 to 500,000 yuan per household. He points out two problems. First, the middle class is translated as *zhongchan jieji*, that is, middle property class, which overemphasizes the propertied. Second, he highlights the tendency to conflate the middle class with the notion of a middle class society. Given these shortcomings, Niu Wenyuan, the leader of a research team for sustainable development strategy studies at CASS, proposes five standards of middle class society. These include: (*a*) rate of urbanization over 70 per cent, (*b*) white-collar work force as large as, if not larger, than a blue-collar one, (*c*) an Engel coefficient lower than 0.3 on average, (*d*) maintenance of the Gini coefficient between 0.25 and 0.30, and (*e*) an average term of over 12 years of education for an individual. Juxtaposing these attributes with other characteristics of the economy, Zhou (2008) argues that the Chinese middle class has taken shape and is rapidly growing, but China is still not a middle class society. He suggests that the earlier pyramid structure is now gradually giving way to an onion-shaped one, with a slightly expanded middle part and an even larger base.

* * *

This chapter has provided detailed inequality estimates for India and China, and decomposed these measures along several dimensions. In doing so, we have presented a precise analysis of the spatial and temporal dimensions and trends of income-based inequality in both countries. Suffice to say, our analysis is a limited first step in this direction and raises as many questions as it answers. But we believe that a better understanding of the causes and consequences of the story of prosperity and inequality in India and China must first take account of its general trend, discrete patterns, and multidimensional nature. Indeed, we believe our results have important policy implications for India and China: both countries need to devise special, comprehensive, and urgent measures sensitive to their different contexts in order to tackle these various dimensions of inequality—particularly the rapidly growing urban–rural divide—if they wish to maintain their drive towards greater economic prosperity without creating social upheaval.

NOTES

1. See Frankel (1978, p. 120), cited in Ghosh (2002).

2. India achieved independence from Britain in 1947. The Chinese Revolution was in 1949. Most scholars date the start of liberalization in China in 1978 and in India in the mid-1980s. That said, some initial reforms began in the latter in the late 1970s (see D'Costa 2005).

3. This chapter is a part of a larger collaborative research agenda that seeks to explain comparative patterns of inequality in India and China. A second paper, titled 'Wealth Inequality: Analysis of India and China', examines the pattern and distribution of wealth in both countries using the same data generated for this chapter from the perspective of social justice. In the future, we hope to extend our project by analysing other dimensions of inequality, such as education and health, as well as the distribution of power and status and the nature and organization of social structure and political representation in both countries.

4. Users of NSS data are aware of the well-known problems of comparability between the 55th round and earlier rounds, and the need to adjust the 55th round estimates to ensure compatibility. There are at least three adjustment methods

suggested by experts to ensure comparability. Sen and Himanshu (2005) represent one of these methods.

5. The CHIPS sample sizes range between 8,000 and 11,000 households in rural China and between 7,000 and 9,000 households in urban areas. The surveys are implemented by the National Statistical Bureau (NSB) survey team and, thus, are a subset of the regular NSB survey. The questionnaire is designed separately by the project team researchers, however.

6. For the purpose of this chapter, rural residents' income in 1995 had to be recalculated for the following reason. The data set has a variable called 'average monthly wage for non-agricultural workers' (AMW, for short). Multiplying AMW in this dataset by 12 to calculate yearly wages yielded an income that was much higher than the NSB's estimate. Thus, we calculated a new variable that indicated the non-agricultural work time of those who work in non-agricultural areas and used this new indicator to calculate the yearly earnings based on AMW. As a result of this recalculation, the rural residents' income becomes lower as does the Gini coefficient, but the rural–urban divide becomes higher. Hence the nationwide Gini is not affected as much.

REFERENCES

Banerjee, A.V. and T. Piketty. 2005. 'Top Indian Incomes, 1922–2000', *World Bank Economic Review*, 19 (1): 1–20.

Bardhan, P. 2010. *Awakening Giants, Feet of Clay: Assessing the Economic Rise of China and India*. Princeton: Princeton University Press.

Borooah, V., B. Gustafsson, and S. Li. 2005. 'China and India: Income Inequality and Poverty North and South of the Himalayas', presented at an International conference on 'Liberalization Experiences in Asia: a Comparative Appraisal', jointly organized by Centre de Sciences Humaines (CSH) in Delhi, the Indian Statistical Institute, Kolkata and the Indian Council of Social Science Research ICSSR, Delhi.

Bhalla, S.S. 2003. 'Recounting the Poor: Poverty in India. 1983–99', *Economic and Political Weekly*, 38 (4): 338–49.

Bussolo, M., R.E. De Hoyos, D. Medvedev, and D. van der Mensbrugghe. 2008. Global Growth and Distribution: Are India and China Reshaping the World?, Helsinki: UNU-WIDER Discussion Paper 29.

Chaudhuri, S. and M. Ravallion. 2006. 'Partially Awakened Giants: Uneven Growth in India and China', in L.A. Winters and S. Yusuf (eds), *Dancing with Giants: China, India and the Global Economy*, pp. 175–210. Washington, D.C: World Bank.

Chen, S. and M. Ravallion. 2008a. 'China is Poorer than We Thought, but No Less Successful in the Fight against Poverty', Policy Research Working Paper 4621, Washington, D.C.: The World Bank.

———. 2008b. 'The Developing World Is Poorer than We Thought, but No Less Successful in the Fight against Poverty', Policy Research Working Paper 4703, Washington, D.C.: The World Bank.

D'Costa, A.P. 2005. *The Long March to Capitalism: Embourgeoisment, Internationalization and Industrial Transformation in India*. London: Palgrave Macmillan.

Deaton, A. and J. Dreze. 2002. 'Poverty and Inequality in India: A Re-examination', *Economic and Political Weekly*, 37 (36): 3729–48.

Dreze, J. and A. Sen. 2002. *India: Development and Participation*. New Delhi: Oxford University Press.

Fan, S., R. Kanbur, and X. Zhang. 2010. 'China's Regional Disparities: Experience and Policy', Department of Applied Economics and Management Working Paper, Cornell University, WP 2010-03, January.

Government of India. 2010. 'National Human Development Report'. New Delhi: Planning Commission.

Gustafsson, B. and S. Li. 2000. 'Economic Transformation and the Gender Earnings Gap in Urban China', *Journal of Population Economics*, 13 (2): 305–29.

Jaffrelot, C. and P. van der Veer (eds). 2008. *Patterns of Middle Class Consumption in India and China*. New Delhi: Sage Publications.

Jha, R. 2004. 'Reducing Poverty and Inequality in India: Has Liberalization Helped?, in G.A. Cornea (ed.), *Inequality, Growth and Poverty in an Era of Liberalization and Globalization*, pp. 297–327. UNU-WIDER Studies in Development Economics, New York: Oxford University Press.

Khan, A.R. and C. Riskin. 2005. 'China's Household Income and Its Distribution, 1995 and 2002', *The China Quarterly*, 182 (June): 356–84.

Knietomicz, Z.W. and H. Ding. 1993. 'Statistical Analysis of Income Distribution in the Jiangsu Province of China', *The Statistician*, 42: 107–21.

Lee, C.K. and M. Selden. 2008. 'Inequality and Its Enemies in Revolutionary and Reform China', *Economic and Political Weekly*, 43 (52): 27–36.

Naughton, B. 2007. *The Chinese Economy: Transitions and Growth*. Cambridge, MA: The MIT Press.

Nayyar, D. 2008. *Liberalization and Development: Collected Essays*. Oxford: Oxford University Press.

Rudolph, L.I. and S.H. Rudolph. 2001. 'Iconisation of Chandrababu: Sharing Sovereignty in India's Federal Market Economy', *Economic and Political Weekly*, 36 (18): 1541–52.

Sen, A. and I. Himanshu. 2005. 'Poverty and Inequality in India: Getting Closer to the Truth', in Angus Deaton and Valerie Kozel (eds), *Data and Dogma: The Great Indian Poverty Debate*, pp. 306–70. New Delhi: Macmillan.

United Nations Development Programme. 2008. *Access for All: Basic Public Services for 1.3 Billion People*. China Human Development Report. Beijing: UNDP, China.

Vakulabharanam, Vamsicharan, Wei Zhong and Xue Jinjun. 2010. Does Class Count? Class Structure and Worsening Inequality in China and India. *mimeo*.

Zhou, X. 2008. 'Chinese Middle Class: Reality or Illusion?' in Christophe Jaffrelot and Peter van der Veer (eds), *Patterns of Middle Class Consumption in India and China*, pp. 110–26. New Delhi: Sage Publications.

8

China in the Global Economy

Encountering the Systemic Risks

Sunanda Sen

China is uniquely positioned among growing countries in the developing region for at least *four* reasons: These include: (*a*) its large volume of exports and trade surplus, the latter at around 10 per cent of its gross domestic product (GDP), huge official reserves at US$2.58 trillion by end of February 2010 (with US$2.28 trillion invested in securities, much of it in US Treasury bonds) (IMF 2010); (*b*) the growing trade as well as investment links with Asia (especially with Hong Kong, the self-governing territory of the People's Republic of China); (*c*) for being a major importer, especially of intermediate goods from the neighbouring countries in Asia; and (*d*) China's success in achieving reasonable stability in the financial sector since the beginning of reforms in 1978 and more recently during the current global financial crisis. The crisis, however, has given way to signs of potential instability, especially since the onset of the global crisis in the autumn of 2008. This has been with efforts on the part of the monetary authorities to cope with free capital flows while maintaining national autonomy in monetary policy and management of exchange rates, a situation described in the literature as an 'impossible trilemma' (Glick and Hutchison 2008).

The close integration of China with the world economy over the last two decades has raised concerns from different quarters which relate both to: (*a*) the possible effects of the recent global downturn on China and (*b*) the second round effects of a downturn in China for the rest of world. If affected adversely by the crisis, the Chinese downturn will directly impact those nations that are its major trading partners. A majority of these supply-chain countries are in developing Asia. We would like to examine both issues (*a*) and (*b*) above in this chapter, that is, the impact of a global downturn on China and the impact of China's slowdown on the rest of the world economy.

As had been held by one school in 2008, China was and might have been heavily affected by the global crisis. As argued, 'China is supported by a three-legged stool, but two legs (exports, real property) are now broken.' The last of these include government spending. 'So what is left is government spending ... but can increased government spending make up for the other legs of the stool?' (Ng 2008).

A similar position offered in 2009 ran as follows: 'China's real exposure to the global financial crisis is huge and has many dimensions ... (which include) ... international trade ... as well as foreign direct investment.' Moreover, China's foreign reserves, at about US$2.58 trillion in 2010, with more than half invested in US government and agency bonds, does matter for the US and hence for the rest of the world. Finally, 'over 25 million Chinese employees now work for overseas companies inside China.' This makes it important for China that FDI flows do not dry up (Zhibin Gu 2009).

Going by an opposite view offered in December 2008, 'China ... is in a very unique position in that it has US$1.9 trillion in foreign currency reserves. China can now ... divert the focus away from an export driven economy to one that begins to focus on domestic demand.' Moreover, '... while every other country is desperately trying to formulate a rescue plan fuelled with an increase in the national debt, China does not have this worry and this will form its primary advantage' (Hughes 2008).

China over the last few years has been on a path of capital account opening which has drawn larger inflows of capital from abroad, both FDI and portfolio types. Of late, a surge in these inflows has introduced problems for the monetary authorities in continuing with an autonomous monetary policy in China, especially with large additions to official reserves. Monetary policy has aimed at avoiding further appreciation of the national domestic currency. Liberalization of capital flows has also changed its composition, with volatile flows of portfolio capital having a much larger share. This development is discussed later in this chapter.

Summing up, China today seems to be closely integrated with the outside world, not only with its huge exports and foreign direct investment (FDI) inflows but also in terms of short-term capital flows. The first two contribute to output and employment, while generating foreign exchange, adding nearly US$ 2 trillion to the country's official reserve stocks. This chapter analyses China's deep integration with the world economy and the systemic risks associated with such integration. In Section 2, I discuss briefly China's trade patterns, which I follow up with a more lengthy discussion of China's financial integration (in Section 3). As I show later, FDI also has been instrumental in providing a major share of exports and gross domestic capital formation, apart from providing employment.

THE CHANGING PATTERN OF TRADE INTEGRATION

To assess the implications of the evolving pattern of China's trade we look at the changing mix of its trade partners, identifying the countries/regions, which of late have been important in China's trade. Tracing back the changes in the shares of different regions, it is revealing that the relative share of the advanced capitalist country exports in China's trade has been changing dramatically over 1990–2007 (Table 8.1). While the developing region absorbed nearly two-thirds of China's exports in 1990, which was more than 50 per cent in 2007, fell to less than half by 2007. The opposite was the case with the advanced capitalist countries, with their current share dropping to less than half by 2007. Incidentally, continuing the earlier pattern, the US has continued to absorb nearly one-fifth or a little less of China's exports and Hong Kong also has remained a major trade partner. Asia today stands out as a major export destination for China, catering to more than one-third of exports on an average during 2002–7. However, the share of South Asia in China's total exports has been consistently low, reaching only 2.08 per cent over 2002–7 (IMF, International Financial Statistics, various issues).

China's trade links with the rest of world also rely on its growing imports, with Asia staging a comeback as a major source of imports

Table 8.1   Exports from China (percentages)

	1990–5	1996–2001	2002–7
Industrial countries	43.31	55.06	53.04
US	13.32	19.85	20.88
Developing countries	55.62	44.61	46.70
Asia	47.13	35.12	33.11
China, Hong Kong	34.46	20.17	16.64
South Asia	1.47	1.47	2.08

Source: IMF, International Financial Statistics.

(Table 8.2). Incidentally, unlike the case with exports, Hong Kong was never a major source of imports for China. As for industrial countries, their share has fallen behind those of developing countries since 2000. The US, as can be expected from its large trade deficits with China is not a major import source. This may reflect China's low-end manufacturing exports and the US high-end manufactures. Both the pattern of exports and imports are reflected in the statistics on China's trade balances (Table 8.3).

Table 8.2   Imports of China (percentages)

	1990–5	1996–2001	2002–7
US	11.74	11.28	7.94
Industrial countries	51.76	50.29	40.40
Developing countries	46.91	47.07	52.05
Asia	37.43	36.34	37.39
Hong Kong	17.51	4.58	2.16

Source: IMF, International Financial Statistics.

Table 8.3   China's Trade Balance (US$ million)

	1990–5	1996–2001	2002–7
World	5,415.6	28,816.8	105,041.0
US	3,169.3	21,413.8	100,666.3
Industrial countries	2,246.3	7,402.9	4,374.7
Developing countries	10,047.2	7,689.6	18,595.5
Asia	10,528.3	7,407.8	8,781.5

Source: IMF, Direction of International Trade.

China's exports grew at an annual average rate of nearly 22 per cent over 2005–7. Of late the slump in the world economy has affected China's exports, especially with its close links to the US, which had been absorbing more than 20 per cent on an average since 2000. During 2009 the value of goods exported was US$1.2 trillion, down 16 per cent year-on-year, while the value of goods imported was US$1.01 trillion, decreasing by 11.2 per cent from the previous year (*China Daily* 2010a). As for the impact of the recent global economic crisis and the recession on China's trade, a clear picture of the effects is likely to emerge over time.

Consequences of the recent turmoil in global markets can be partly assessed by observing the available 2008 monthly figures for aggregate exports and imports (Figure 8.1). The trade data indicate moderate to sharp declines in both exports and imports by the last quarter of 2008 when the worldwide slump had begun. The country's aggregate exports started faltering since the last quarter of 2008, sliding down further in the first quarter of 2009. A large part of it was related to the recession in the rest of world, especially in the US and other advanced capitalist countries. These tendencies were reinforced by the ongoing protectionist moves by these very same countries.

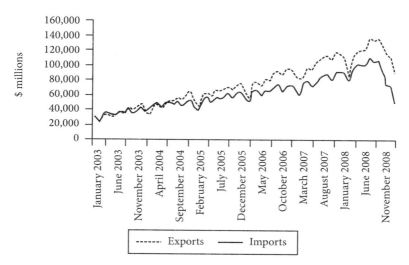

Figure 8.1   China's Monthly Trade (US$ million)

Source: IMF, *International Financial Statistics.*

The changing shares of the different regions and countries in China's exports and imports are reflected in the trade balance across the same groups (Table 8.3). However, it continues to be the case that the US contributes the most to China's trade surplus and even finances its deficits with other regions, including industrial countries and developing countries from Asia. Hence, it is natural that a recession in advanced economies, especially the US, which is a major destination for China's exports, impinges heavily on China's exports and thus on the level of accumulation of official reserves. We may recall here that exports from China dropped by 40 per cent during 2008–9. Chinese exports plummeted 21.8 per cent through the January–June period in 2009, which was the sharpest decrease in a decade after the global financial crisis. The declining exports drove down the trade surplus to US$96.94 billion in the first half of 2009, down 1.3 per cent year-on-year. Nevertheless, China's foreign exchange reserves topped US$2.13 trillion by the end of June 2009, up 17.84 per cent year-on-year (*China Daily* 2010b) (Figure 8.2).

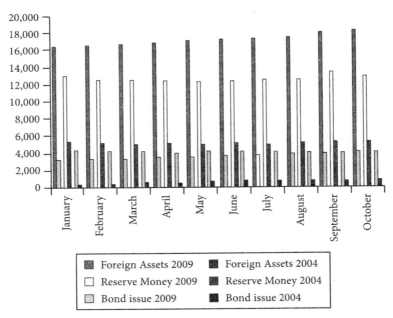

Figure 8.2 Foreign Assets, Reserve Money, and Bond Sales (millions RMB)
Source: People's Bank of China, www.pbc.gov.cn/english.

FINANCIAL INTEGRATION OF CHINA WITH THE REST OF THE WORLD

The extent to which an individual country relies on the rest of the world economy also depends on the extent of deregulation of the financial sector, which affects the magnitude as well as the composition of capital flows. It can be observed that deregulated finance encourages capital flows of a short-term nature, which can impact the functioning of the country's stock market, the level of official reserves and even the exchange rate. This also happened in China with the deregulation of the financial sector after 2005.

China's entry to the global financial market seems to have gone through *two* distinct phases. The first until 2005 had strict state controls over the financial sector. While some concessions for the capital account were made with China's membership to the WTO in 2003, controls continued to remain over capital flight, following a strategy of 'easy in and difficult out' capital flows. The 1997 Asian financial crisis influenced such a strategy. The second phase, starting from 2005, signalled considerable relaxation of earlier controls and regulation over inflows of overseas finance and over the exchange rate of RMB, which was until then under a fixed dollar peg. Consequently, FDI as well as portfolio capital inflows have gone up since then, at a pace which has continued until the onset of the global economic crisis in the fall of 2008. The exchange rate of the RMB also has gone through upward adjustments, recording a 20 per cent appreciation during 2005–8. However, by July 2008, the US dollar started appreciating, recording a 20 per cent hike against the euro.

In the meantime, the Chinese monetary authorities had stopped monitoring the RMB peg with the dollar, which also slowed down inflows of hot money to China, relieving the upward pressure on RMB and the constraints on credit so far faced by monetary authorities in China. Easier bank credit followed which helped growth in China during 2008–9. However, the near zero interest rate policy in the US, largely in response to the ongoing crisis, along with the moderate drop in the dollar rate in 2010, has again revived the stream of hot money flows to China, largely with expectations of further rise in the RMB rate. Consequently, China again faces export constraints, compelling China to reactivate a constrained credit policy, largely with higher reserve ratios and open market policies in the bond market

(McKinnon 2010). This development can be viewed as one where China's monetary policy is no longer influenced by its own dictates, rather it is affected by cheap credit policy in the US, forcing accommodative actions by China. However, overall China has been able to withstand the near 40 per cent drop in export earnings by means of credit expansion, almost 30 per cent in 2009 and with fiscal expansions in 2010. The looming currency war between China and the US is possibly not that imminent, with the US Treasury stalling a bill which was about to name China as a currency manipulator (McKinnon 2010, Yong 2010).

China, in the earlier years of financial opening (until about 2005), provides a unique example of liberalizing its financial sector with close state monitoring, which has been described elsewhere as a situation of 'guided finance' (Sen 2007). Banks in China have continued as the main conduit of financial intermediation within the country, handling until recently 80 per cent or more of financial flows in the country. Four major state-owned banks (SOBs) oversee 70 per cent of deposits and advances in the Chinese banking industry. Thus, the security market in China until recently remained at a nascent stage and no Chinese bank was permitted to invest in securities.

Again, despite having access to the market for securities, the state-owned enterprises (SOEs) relied on banks rather than the stock market for finance. For example, in 2001 the SOEs raised only US$14 billion by floating shares and borrowed more than US$157 billion from banks (Green 2003). Banks in China were closely guided by the State Council, not only in terms of handling the balance sheet, but also in terms of the direction in the allocation of credit. Credit advanced by banks was subject to monitoring, if not control, by the state, in terms of the 'guide book' provided by the State Committee, which specified the desired directions (not volume) of credit. Reforms of China's financial institutions even accommodated state guidance with initiatives by the latter in the handling and cancellation of doubtful assets held by the SOBs.

The security market in China thus maintained a rather low profile as an alternate source of finance in China, a fact, which was reflected in the hesitant flows of portfolio finance until about 2004–5. Stock market capitalization in China, net of non-tradable shares, had been rather low, at 17 per cent of GDP during 2000–5, as compared to such ratios in other Asian countries such as South Korea (52 per cent), Malaysia (136 per cent), and Singapore (136 per cent) around the same time (Green 2003).

'Guided finance' in China even separated shares sold in the stock market by currency denomination based on whether these were RMB or dollar denominated stocks. The government also restrained the tradability of nearly two-thirds of shares in the market, thus leaving only one-third of shares to be exchanged. Stock exchanges, initiated in Shanghai and Shengen in December 1990 had a bifurcated structure in terms of distinct share categories, with A shares denominated in RMBs and B shares in US dollars. Qualified Foreign Institutional Investors (QFIIs) were approved by the China Security Regulatory Commission (CSRC) to deal only in B shares. The stock market thus had few takers despite the industrial boom in the country, which was largely driven by domestic banks and FDI.

Regarding capital inflows and China's global integration, we can observe the spectacular rise in FDI to China over the last two decades (Table 8.4). State directives to banks in the disbursement of credit and the incentives offered by the state for industry in China attracted foreign investors. Clearly, a large share of FDI inflows is likely to be related to the success of China in having a 'guided financial market'. Benefits of these inflows, in the process, were reaped by both industry and finance, as opposed to a situation of finance-led growth alone in other deregulated financial markets, where speculation dominates the financial flows.

In China the regulatory institutions in the area of banking, securities and insurance were given wide-ranging powers, keeping a close vigil on the functioning of both finance and industry. Banks, a few of which could float equities in the market, were also forbidden to enter as buyers of stocks, a practice which reminds us of the norms of segregated banking and the Glass-Stegall Act of the US. As we have pointed out elsewhere, universal banking, the much acclaimed practice of financial markets in the era of global finance, while creating opportunities for profitable speculation, can ignore the real sphere of the economy at the expense of production and employment (see for the conceptual arguments, Sen 2003, 2004).

China, however, has also been a significant investor abroad since 2004. The flow tapered off slightly in 2007. As noted by *The Washington Post*:

Table 8.4 Foreign Investments from and to China (US$ million)

	2000	2001	2002	2003	2004	2005	2006	2007
Direct Investment Abroad	−916	−6,884	−2,518	152	−1,805	−11,305	−21,160	−16,994
FDI in China	38,399	44,241	49,308	47,076	54,936	79,126	78,094	138,413

Source: IMF, International Financial Statistics.

... Even as global financial flows have slowed sharply overall, China has dramatically stepped up its outbound investment. In 2008, its overseas mergers and acquisitions were worth US$52.1 billion—a record, according to the research firm Dealogic. In January and February (of 2009) Chinese companies invested US$16.3 billion abroad, meaning that if the pace holds, the total for 2009 could be nearly double last year's. (Cha 2009, p. A01)

Recent news reports also indicate that China has stepped up its purchases of raw materials from other developing countries, possibly to take advantage of the low prices in the downswing and keep up with increasing demand at home. *The Washington Post* further reports that '... Chinese companies have been on a shopping spree in the past month, snapping up tens of billions of dollars' worth of key assets in Iran, Brazil, Russia, Venezuela, Australia and France in a global fire sale set off by the financial crisis' (Cha 2009, p. A01). These developments illustrate how China is inextricably linked to the world economy.

It is important to recognize that exports from China and FDI inflows bear a high export/FDI ratio, of 8.75 on an average between 2000 and 2007 (Table 8.5). A large proportion of China's exports might have been FDI-driven. Using panel data for six leading exporting and FDI receiving manufacturing sectors over the period from 1995 to 2004, a recent paper suggests that FDI inflow to China has a statistically significant positive effect on exports as a whole, but its specific impacts vary by sector. Also FDI in non-labour-intensive sectors are more efficient in stimulating exports than those in labour-intensive ones (Awokuse and Gu 2007). Thus, exports are likely to face a second-round shock if FDI flows to China falter as a consequence of the crisis. FDI also seems to have been important for China's gross domestic capital formation. Thus, the annual average ratio of the gross domestic capital formation to FDI has been 10:1 or greater between 2000 and 2007. Much of the capital formation resulted from FDI inflows. China's links with the crisis-ridden advanced economies through exports and FDI thus remain important in determining the impact of a crisis originating in those economies on the domestic economy of China.

As we have mentioned above, China has gone through a rapid pace of financial liberalization since 2005. By June 2005, foreign investors were allowed to have stakes in the publicly listed firms and buy their tradable *A* shares. As reported by the domestic media, this was part of

Table 8.5   FDI/GDP, Exports/FDI, Exports/GDP, and GFCF/FDI

	2000	2001	2002	2003	2004	2005	2006	2007
FDI/GDP	0.032	0.033	0.029	0.028	0.028	0.033	0.027	0.04
Exports/FDI	6.4	6.01	6.6	9.3	10.8	9.6	12.4	8.8
Exports/GDP	0.2	0.2	0.22	0.26	0.3	0.3	0.3	0.3
GFCF/FDI	10.6	10.3	10.6	13.7	14.3	11.9	14.4	9.9

Source: IMF, International Financial Statistics.

an ongoing plan to do away with non-tradable state shares. However, foreign investors taking strategic stakes through their purchases of A-share were subject to 'lockup' periods up to a specified time, before they could sell them.[1] The year 2005 also marks the de-linking of RMB to the dollar peg, followed by the appreciation of the nominal RMB rate by 20 per cent between 2005 and 2008. Controls over foreign finance were further relaxed by 2007 as Chinese investors were permitted to buy H-shares in the Hong Kong stock exchange. Until then such investments were only permissible on the part of the Qualified Domestic Institutional Investors (QDIIs) which included banks and other domestic financial institutions. This reflects attempts on the part of the monetary authority to offset some of the capital inflows pouring into the country through FDI-led corporate investments and the soaring trade surplus (Bradsher 2007). By July 2007 the inflation rate within the country had soared to 5.7 per cent, largely because of high domestic demand (*The Financial Express* 2009).

Capital inflows by way of speculative portfolio capital became substantial by 2008, with FDI and trade surplus accounting for only 52 per cent of net accumulations to reserves (Ma and McCauley 2007). These portfolio flows were often motivated by the expected appreciation of the RMB rate until July 2008 when the currency peg of RMB was fixed at 6.83 per dollar. Apprehending the consequences of an overheated financial sector, the Chinese State Administration of Foreign Exchange (SAFE) sought to tighten its control to stop over-invoicing of exports, remittances, and FDI, especially the latter two, which were linked to Hong Kong (*Economist* 2008). Restraints on credit expansion were relaxed for some time after July 2008 as inflows of hot money tapered off due to the relative stability of the dollar–RMB rate. However, the low interest rate in the US dampened the dollar rate by September 2009, prompting speculators to expect RMB appreciation (McKinnon 2010). This has brought back credit restraints in China, with higher reserve ratios as well as bond sales. However, interest rates were not used as a tool of monetary management.

The steady dismantling of controls that has taken place in China's financial sector generated a qualitative change in the composition of financial inflows, with portfolio investments shooting up by 2006 (Table 8.6). The measures also impacted China's stock markets, which faced an unprecedented boom in turnover as well as in share prices

Table 8.6 Portfolio and Direct Investments (US$ million)

	2000	2001	2002	2003	2004	2005	2006	2007
Portfolio Investment Liabilities, n.i.e.	7,316	1,249	1,752	8,443	13,203	21,224	42,861	20,996
Direct Investments in Rep. Econ. n.i.e.	38,399	44,241	49,308	47,076	54,936	79,126	78,094	138,413

Source: IMF, International Financial Statistics.

since 2006. Figure 8.3 provides an approximate indicator of volatility for the Shanghai stock index (http://www.theglobalguru.com/).

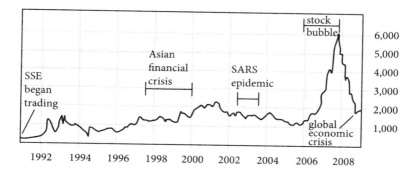

Figure 8.3 Shanghai (SSE) Composite Index Chart

Source: http://en.wikipedia.org/wiki/Shanghai_Stock_Exchange - 98k -.

As one commentator observes:

> ... With the Chinese index up sevenfold during the past five years, and valuations stretching into P/Es of 60 or more, the Chinese stock market has little to do with fundamentals. Although many liken it to a casino, a better analogy is a game of musical chairs. The object is to make sure you get a seat before the music stops.

Again, as for the impact, the same commentator notes:

> ... the collapse of China's stock market could be a lot worse than previously thought. Merrill Lynch estimates that Chinese retail investors—up to 150 million people—have sunk 22% of their capital into the stock market. Say the stock market drops by half (it's already down about 20%) and Chinese urban households will lose about 20% of their overall net worth. Pundits estimate that a 50% decline in the stock market might lop 1–1.5% off China's double-digit percentage GDP-growth rate.[2]

.   Recently, foreign institutional investors have been active in pumping money in and out of China's stock markets. Thus, the Shanghai stock market had been subject to volatility, including a 6.7 per cent tumble on Monday, 31 August 2009, which was the biggest single-day fall in 15 months (Asia Markets 2009).

All told, China's recent financial developments paint a rather awkward picture when one views the country's integration to the world economy, especially after the global economic crisis. One witnesses declines in both portfolio and FDI flows to the country since the onset of the global crisis in the fall of 2008. As for FDI, there has been change in recent times with advanced industrialized countries—which have been China's major investors through Hong Kong—are now staying away. According to some sources, 'China's main FDI sources viz. the US, Europe and Japan, are languishing and there is no sign that their economies are bottoming out. This has blurred the prospects for FDI into China' (Qingfen 2009). However, China is still seen as the most favourable destination for investment by foreigners (Qingfen 2009).

That foreign investments in China have been hit by the global economic crisis is clearly evident. FDI flows more than halved between the Q1 2008 and Q1 2009. Portfolio investments, as pointed out above, have also plummeted occasionally, causing sharp declines in stock indices.

Recently, China's economy, like other emerging markets, is facing a renewed surge of portfolio capital inflows, with a large part directed by speculation. As it was pointed out above, a large part of this is related to the US having a near-zero rate of interest and the related downslide in the dollar rate. With the surge in these capital inflows causing upward pressure on the RMB rate and the domestic interest rate failing to provide an 'uncovered parity' in terms of the two exchange rates, it was natural that expectations of an RMB appreciation surfaced in the market, providing an impetus to currency speculation.

Analysing further, China, like some other developing countries, today faces the 'impossible trilemma' (Krugman 1999, Palley 2009) of managing the exchange rate with near complete capital mobility and national autonomy in their monetary policy. However, while China is able to sustain the current spread between its prime lending rate at around 5.36 per cent in contrast to the US rate at 0.25 per cent (Reuters 2010), it does not signify China's success in avoiding the hazards of a typical trilemma as arises with open capital flows, managed exchange rates, and an autonomous monetary policy.[3] China has been steadily sterilizing a significant part of the rising capital inflows by selling government bonds and using higher rates of cash reserves, which partly reduced the related expansion of high-powered reserve money and money supply. However, selling government bonds is bound to face its own limits, especially in terms of the related fiscal burden of the rising interest costs.[4] These developments indubitably indicate the seriousness of the trilemma currently faced as well as handled by China: keeping its capital flows free and managing both monetary policy and the exchange rate in the interest of the national economy.

As for the role of China as a growth propeller, integrated with the rest of world, the high-growth Chinese economy has been still propelling growth elsewhere. Concerns expressed by the rest of world on the trade-displacing effects of the cheap exports alone, however, appear exaggerated if we remember that China is also a large importer, especially of intermediate goods. Its exports are import-intensive, much of which is generated by operations of the subsidiaries of foreign firms in China. While it is too early to have a total picture, the growing alliances within Asia between China and other Asian countries in terms of trade integration signifies a decoupling tendency between the industrialized and the developing countries. However, this may also go with further changes in the composition of trade within Asia, with Chinese manufactures displacing those from other Asian countries. The new pattern of Asian economic integration may also dampen the impact of further deceleration in the West on Asian economies, at least via the trade route if not via capital flows. We also need to remind ourselves that growth in China is not just a case of a typical export-led process as happened in some other countries in Asia. It is an instance of a state-led industrialization as in Japan earlier and more recently in South Korea, along with the opening up of large domestic as well as external markets. Also, industrialization in China has not remained confined to an export enclave, especially with its vast territory and the swarming population providing the base for economic expansion from within. As pointed out by a recent study, domestic demand generates much of the domestic activities as well as exports (Pairault 2009). Recently, the second generation of FDI inflows from the EU, Japan, and the US has been directed to a niche within the home market, which, unlike the first generation flows, catered more to export markets (Ali and Guo 2005).

We also need to recall the role of the 'three legs' (exports, property market, and government spending), which are considered to support the Chinese economy. Of these, government spending seems to be functioning better. One needs to focus on the changes in the rising value as well as the composition of such spending in China since the

onset of the global economic crisis. In devising and sustaining autonomy in monetary policy, China has been using expansionary fiscal
policy to tackle the impact of shrinking export demand. The recent
drive on the part of the Chinese authorities to boost real demand in the
countryside and to revamp the domestic market shows an approach
much different from the rescue packages for the financial sector in
advanced capitalist countries. Recently, China has announced a 4
trillion RMB (US$586 billion) package of fiscal expenditure, which
represents about 16 per cent of China's economic output last year, and
is roughly equal to the total of all central and local government spending in 2006. New spending of even half that amount would be next
to China's 6 trillion RMB annual budget for 2010. Strategies such as
these aim to bolster domestic demand and help avert a global recession by spending on housing, infrastructure, agriculture, health care,
and social welfare, along with tax deduction for capital spending by
companies.[5] Concerns, however, have been raised on the inadequacy
of those measures on employment and poverty in the countryside,
goals which may not be achieved by the priorities set through infrastructural development. Overall, it is probably too early to identify the
possible impact of this expansionary spending on China's economy.
Data from China's National Bureau of Statistics project a year-on-year
11.9 per cent output growth rate in the first quarter of 2010 while
predictions by the Chinese Academy of Social Sciences (CASS) and
the Asian Development Bank (ADB) respectively put the 2010 GDP
growth at 9.9 per cent and 9.6 per cent (*China Daily* 2010c, Sin and
Rabinovitch 2010). However, questions remain as to whether the
overall growth rates will satisfy the needs of the society, given the
phenomenon of 'jobless recovery' and the serious vulnerability faced
by migrant workers (*The Economist* 2010).

* * *

Based on the analysis of China's integration with the rest of the world,
presented in this chapter, three observations are in order. First, China's
trade integration has of late been more with Asia rather than with
the advanced capitalist countries. Even the integration of Hong Kong,
which was a conduit for China's trade with the industrialized countries, has diminished in recent years. Given the pattern of growing
instability in advanced economies, this may work out to be a favourable factor for China in terms of being able to withstand the potential

hazards of a sudden collapse in the export markets in the advanced capitalist countries.

Second, China's financial relations with the world economy are very different when it comes to capital flows. Today, China is closely integrated with the financial markets of advanced capitalist economies, both with long-term FDI and short-term portfolio capital flows. While FDI forges links between China's real sector and the rest of the world, particularly with China's exports, capital formation, and employment, portfolio flows open up the possible dangers of a sudden flight of capital. The latter makes the country's economy vulnerable to shocks from outside and can affect the domestic financial structure including exchange rates as well as future monetary management.

Third, on balance, the new pattern of China's integration with the rest of the world is beset by both positive and negative signals for the Chinese economy. Given that China's growth and stability have assumed a degree of importance for the rest of world, which was never as significant as it is now, the future of the Chinese economy remains an important issue for the well-being of the world as a whole.

NOTES

1. 'A Shares to be Open to Non-Chinese Investors', www.chinaview.cn. Also, www.nytimes.com/2007/8/20/business.

2. http://www.nicholasvardy.com/global-guru/articles/the-china-stock-bubble/, accessed 11 August 2012. See also Cesar Bacani/Hong Kong, Wednesday, 1 July 2009, 'Is a China Stock Bubble Forming?', http://www.time.com/time/world/article/0,8599,1908032,00.html. Global FDI flows halved in first quarter of 2009 primarily from rich nations, http://www.mysinchew.com/node/26403.

3. According to one view, the fact that China's interest rates do not follow changes in US interest rates is indicative of an autonomy in China's monetary policy. The view, however, can be contested, as shown in the text above.

4. At the same time, a higher interest rate is what makes possible the sale of bonds by making those attractive to the public and simultaneously dampens the rate of inflation. But the higher rate may also encourage further inflows of capital, both with interest rate differentials (from overseas) which adds to currency speculation, betting against the managed exchange rate which is expected to appreciate. Finally, the higher rates also go against the interests of the real economy.

5. Comparing notes, the US pushed through a US$168 billion stimulus package in 2009, equal to about 1 per cent of GDP, and the Federal Reserve has aggressively cut interest rates, complementing the Treasury's US$700 billion for troubled financial institutions. Japan has a US$51.5 billion package that largely consists of payouts to families and tax relief for businesses, and Germany is moving

on tax breaks and loans that will cost the government around US$29.9 billion over four years. 'China Sets Big Stimulus Plan in Bid to Jump-Start Growth', *Wall Street Journal*, 8 October 2008, http://online.wsj.com/article/SB122623724868611327.html.

REFERENCES

Ali, S. and W. Guo. 2005. 'Determinants of FDI in China', www.gbata.com/docs/jgbat/v1n2/v1n2p3.pdf.

Asia Markets. 2009. 'China's Stock Gyrations Not the Work of Small Investors', 2 September, http://www.marketwatch.com/story/.

Awokuse, T.O. and W. Gu. 2007. 'The Contribution of Foreign Direct Investment to China's Export Performance: Evidence from Disaggregated Sectors', mimeo.

Bradsher, K. 2007. 'China Further Loosens Its Capital Controls', *The New York Times*, Monday, 20 August.

Cha, A.E. 2009. 'China Gains Key Assets in Spate of Purchases Oil, Minerals are among Acquisitions Worldwide', http://www.washingtonpost.com/wp-dyn/content/article/2009/03/16/AR2009031603293.html, (accessed 11 August 2012).

China Daily. 2010a. 'China's Foreign Trade Value Down 13.9% in 2009', 28 April, http://www.chinadaily.com.cn/china/2010-02/25/content_9506001.htm (accessed 11 June 2012).

———. 2010b. 'CASS Predicts Chinese Economy to Grow 9.9% in 2010', *China Daily*, 27 April.

———. 2009. 'China's Forex Reserves Top $2.13t by End of June', *China Daily*, 15 July.

The Economist. 2010. 'Surplus ca Change', *The Economist*, 22 April.

———. 2008. 'Capital Inflows to China: Hot and Bothered', *The Economist*, 26 June.

The Financial Express. 2009. 'China Sees Threat from Abnormal Capital Flows', *The Financial Express*, 3 December.

Glick, R. and M. Hutchison. 2008. 'Navigating the Trilemma: Capital Flows and Monetary Policy in China', Working Paper no. 2008-32, Federal Reserve Bank of San Francisco.

Green, S. 2003. *China's Stock Market: Eight Myths and Some Reasons to Be Optimistic*. A report from the China project, London: The Royal Institute of International Affairs Asia Programme, February.

Gu, G.Z. 2009. 'China vs Global Financial Crisis', 1 May 2009, www.financialsense.com.

Hughes, A. 2008. 'China and the Financial Crisis', 17 December 2008, www.global research.com.

IMF (International Monetary Fund). 2010. International Reserves by Reporting Country, http://www.imf.org/external/np/sta/ir/IRProcessWeb/colist.aspx (accessed 11 April 2010).

Krugman, P. 1999. 'O Canada: A Neglected Nation Gets Its Nobel', *State*, 19 October.

Ma, G. and R. McCauley. 2007. 'Do China's Capital Controls still Bind?', BIS Working paper no. 233, Basel: Bank for International Settlements.

McKinnon, R. 2010. 'A Stable Yuan-dollar Exchange Rate Forever?', East Asia Forum, http://www.eastasiaforum.org/2010/03/17/a-stable-yuandollar-exchange-rate-forever/ (accessed 17 March 2010).

Ng, E. 2008. 'Global Financial Crisis Will Hurt China Much More than the US', posted in China Economy, http://cnreviews.com/china_economy/china_financial_crisis_20081125.html.

Pairault, T. 2009. 'Foreign Investment in China', mimeo.

Palley, T. 2009. 'Rethinking the Economics of Capital Mobility and Capital Control', *Revistia de Economia Politica*, São Paulo, 29 (3, July/Sept).

Qingfen, D. 2009. 'China Still Top Destination for FDI', *China Daily*, http://www.chinadaily.com.cn/bizchina/2009-06/09/content_8262095.htm.

Reuters. 2010. 'FactBox-Global Interest Rates in 2010', London, Tuesday, 6 April, 3:50 a.m. EDT.

Sen, S. 2003. *Global Finance at Risk: On Stagnation and Instability in the Real Economy*. London: Palgrave-Macmillan.

—————. 2004. *Global Finance at Risk: On Stagnation and Instability in the Real Economy*. New Delhi: Oxford University Press.

—————. 2007. 'China in the Bull Shop: Dealing with Finance after WTO', in A.K. Bagchi and Gary Dymski (eds), *Capture and Exclude*. Delhi: Tulika. (An earlier version as 'China's Finance after WTO', *Economic and Political Weekly*, 2007 and 'Finance in China' in China Model or Beijing Consensus for Development, Social Science Academic Press, 2006 [in Chinese].)

Zhou, and X.S. Rabinovitch. 2010. 'China's Economy Roars into 2010', http://www.reuters.com/article/2010/04/15/us-china-economy-idUSTRE63EOCB20100415?feedType=RSS&feedName=everything&virtualBrandChannel=11563 (accessed 10 August 2012).

Yong, W. 2010. 'Avoiding a US-China Currency War: Need for Rational Calculation', East Asia Forum, http://www.eastasiaforum.org/2010/04/11/avoiding-a-us-china-currecny-war-need-for-rational-calculation/ (accessed 10 April 2010).

9

Outward FDI from China and India

An Exploratory Note

R. NAGARAJ*

China and India are the world's most populous and, lately, fast-growing nations, with limited natural resource. By any yardstick, they together account for a sizable share of world output, though their output per capita is as yet modest. According to the International Monetary Fund (IMF) estimates, in 2008, in current US dollars, per capita income for China and India is US$3,259 and US$1,017 respectively. Lately, these as yet poor countries are exporting (non-financial) capital—the speed and spread of which appears to have caught the world by surprise.

The outward foreign direct investment (OFDI) raises many questions: Why are they, still poor countries, exporting capital on such a large scale, with what implications for themselves? What are the similarities and differences in the outward flows from China and

* An earlier version of the paper was presented at the conference on 'International Competitiveness, Globalization and Multinational Firms: A Comparison of China and India', in Tokyo in November 2009. I am grateful to the participants of the conferences in Kolkata and Tokyo for their comments and suggestions on my presentation. I am most grateful to Anthony P. D'Costa and Amiya Kumar Bagchi for their detailed comments on my draft paper, though I am not sure if I have adequately responded to all their queries and suggestions. Needless to add, all the remaining errors in the paper are mine.

India? Considering that international investments are inherently riskier (especially cross-border mergers and acquisitions), firms from which of the two countries seem better placed to face the challenges of international competition, and why?

Historically, countries have run large trade and current account deficits in the early stages of economic development, as they use a growing share of their domestic output for capital formation. However, as countries accumulate resources and grow richer, they, in turn, look overseas for profitable investment opportunities. One of the distinguishing features of economic development of the twentieth century is the emergence of multinational corporations (MNCs), seeking to leverage their firm-specific advantages across many countries and markets, or trying to secure raw materials to sustain their domestic growth. In the early post-war period, American firms came to dominate the world investment outflows; European and Japanese firms followed them with some lag.

While the mainstream economic theory largely ignored the emergence of MNCs' growing power and visibility, Stephen Hymer's classic study highlighted their significance to suggest that they represent a new phase of capitalist development wherein such firms seek to leverage their firm-specific advantages in many countries and markets and they seek raw materials for sustaining their domestic growth. Hymer's conceptualization of the institutional differences of MNCs opened floodgates of fresh research, culminating in John Dunning's 'eclectic paradigm' of the theory of international firms, which has been analytically rich enough to illuminate a variety of empirical realities.[1]

In the early 1980s, Louis T. Wells Jr. (1983) and Sanjaya Lall (1982) independently detected the nascent tendency of firms from developing countries to set up factories and firms abroad, mainly in manufacturing industries, requiring relatively standardized technologies with modest fixed capital, for instance textile mills in East Africa by Indian entrepreneurs. It is worth recalling the words of late Sanjaya Lall, who in 1982, described Tata Engineering and Locomotive Company (TELCO) [now Tata Motors] as '... (the) first real automotive multinational to emerge from the Third World with its own trademark and technology ...' (Lall 1982, p. 41).

Now, after a gap of over a quarter century, in a much more open and integrated world economy, outward investments from industrializing countries has apparently grown into a much bigger force, with capital flowing across many more countries and regions, industries and sectors, in a greater variety of institutional forms—joint ventures, majority-owned subsidiaries, branch plants, and so on.

However, to place these trends in perspective, outward foreign direct investment (OFDI) from developing countries is as yet a modest fraction of the global capital flows; and, within the developing countries, the outflows from China and India are not the largest, though their sharp surge recently seems to warrant a closer look. According to the *World Investment Report*, 2009, global OFDI in 2008 was US$1,856 billion; the majority of it was within the developed world. For China and India OFDI was US$52 billion and US$18 billion respectively.

This chapter briefly describes the broad dimensions of the OFDI from these two economies and seeks to understand their motivations and their implications for the respective economies. The structure of the chapter is as follows: the initial section describes the main trends in OFDI from China and India, the following section interprets the trends in terms of their development strategies and national economic performance. Discerning the similarities and differences in the pattern of the outward flows, the last section summarizes and concludes the main findings of the study.

CHARACTERISTICS OF OFDI FROM CHINA AND INDIA

The Initial Conditions

India has somewhat extended experience with OFDI: starting in the 1960s, private corporate firms began setting up textile and engineering plants in less developed economies to take advantage of their experience in running firms in similar economic and technological conditions where competition from the advanced economies was limited (Morris 1987). The 1970s witnessed a surge in Indian joint ventures abroad, mostly to less developed countries (LDCs) as a conscious policy, in which Indian partners usually held a minority shareholding, supplying machinery and equipment as their share of equity capital. Conceivably, policy-induced domestic restrictions on private corporate investment also perhaps contributed to the search for overseas investment opportunities.[2] After a gap of nearly two decades, OFDI boomed in the 2000s, with the gradual loosening of investment controls (see Appendix 9A.1 for an account of the recent evolution of the policy). But the direction of investment this time around is mostly to developed economies—representing what Ravi Ramamurti (2009) has classified as 'up market FDI'.

Pre-reform China had, understandably, severe restrictions on capital outflows, conserving the scarce capital for domestic growth. After the reforms, especially in the 1980s, China aggressively sought to invite FDI as a means to acquire technology and managerial expertise to promote labour-intensive manufactures for exports. However, since the early 1990s China has also gradually opened doors for capital outflows. In the initial years of reforms, one suspects, the outflow represented China's bilateral external assistance to developing economies routed through its enterprises. However, since 2004, just as in India around the same time, foreign investment decisions were freed from the nation's balance of payment considerations, as China's foreign exchange reserves began to swell (see Appendix 9A.2 for a documentation of changes in China's OFDI policy).

Aggregate Trends

Using the *World Investment Report* data, Figure 9.1 describes the yearly outflows of direct investments from China and India from 1995 to 2008. Evidently, reflecting the loosening of the investment rules mentioned above, both the countries witnessed a steep rise after 2000, though it is much faster for China than India. The figures for 2008 were US$51.2 billion and US$17.7 billion for the two countries respectively. The same is evident in the cumulative figures, reported in Figure 9.2, for the years since 2000. China's investment outflow data, however, presents some puzzles. While the cumulative total between 1980 and 2007 is US$117 billion as per Chinese official statistics, it is US$150 billion as per the *World Investment Report*, and is US$100 billion as per the Economist Intelligence Unit (EIU) estimates.

Distribution of OFDI by Sectors and Regions

For India, as per the *World Investment Report*, the cumulative OFDI between 1980 and 2008 is US$61.7 billion. Indian official records indicate that the cumulative figure from 2001 to 2008 is US$41.9 billion (Table 9.1). Manufacturing accounts for a little over one-third

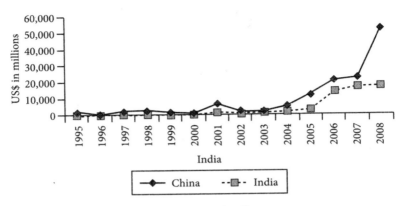

Figure 9.1 OFDI Outflows from China and India

Source: *World Investment Report*, various issues.

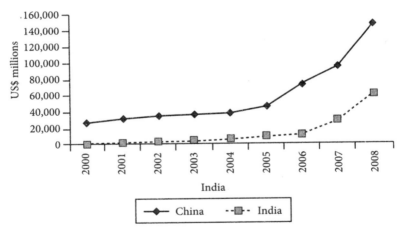

Figure 9.2 OFDI Stock from China and India

Source: *World Investment Report*, various issues.

of the total, followed by non-financial services (28 per cent). Within manufacturing, prominent industries are pharmaceuticals, consumer goods, metals, automotive components, fertilizers, and chemicals; and in services it is mainly software and business process outsourcing. In terms of their destination, a quarter of the outflows is to the US, followed by Europe; one-third of it has flown to offshore financial

Table 9.1 OFDI from India and Its Industry-wise Distribution, 2001–8 (US$ million)

Sector	2000–1	2001–2	2002–3	2003–4	2004–5	2005–6	2006–7	2007–8
Manufacturing	169	528	1,271	893	1,068	1,538	4,185	5,409
Financial services	6	4	3	1	7	156	28	88
Non-financial services	470	350	404	456	283	531	7,527	1,748
Trading	52	79	82	113	181	215	659	1,050
Other	12	20	38	31	108	239	1,499	10,435
Total	709	981	1,798	1,494	1,647	2,679	13,898	18,730

Source: Nayyar (2008); Reserve Bank of India, *Annual Report* (2009).

centres (tax havens), namely Mauritius, Virgin Islands, and Bermuda (Nayyar 2008).

Sixty-seven per cent of China's OFDI is to Asia, followed by 21 per cent to Latin America (Table 9.2). A more disaggregated data (not reported here) shows that, 73 per cent of all the investments have gone to tax havens, mostly Hong Kong (*Chinese Statistical Year Book 2009*). Four-fifths of the Chinese cumulative outward investments fall under: (*a*) leasing and business services (26 per cent), (*b*) wholesale and retail trade (17 per cent), (*c*) financial intermediation (14 per cent), (*d*) mining (13 per cent), and (*e*) transport and storage (10 per cent) (Table 9.3).

Table 9.2   Chinese Cumulative OFDI by Regions, between 1980 and 2007 (in US$ 10,000)

Regions	OFDI	Percentage share
Asia	7,921,793	67.2
Africa	446,183	3.8
Europe	445,854	3.8
Latin America	2,470,091	20.9
North America	324,089	2.7
Oceania	183,040	1.6
Total	11,791,050	100

Source: *China Statistical Yearbook*, hpps://www. stats.gov.cn.

As the majority of China's OFDI has gone to tax havens—which, for the obvious reasons, do not represent its final destination—they are mere conduits for investments elsewhere, via sovereign wealth funds. We, therefore, know little about the final destinations of such investments, or end-use of the investment of such outflows from China. Scholars have speculated that a part of the OFDI perhaps represents Chinese domestic savings that return home via Hong Kong—by means of what is widely known as 'round tripping' of capital.[3]

Much of China's overseas investments are shown under 'leasing and business services'—the largest category by industry of use. Though by many accounts most of these investments are for acquiring mines, natural resources, and manufacturing, they are not disaggregated in the official classification. So, much of the public discussion, therefore, is based on some of the widely known cases of large investments and

Table 9.3   Chinese Cumulative OFDI by Sector, between 1980 and 2007 (in US$ 10,000)

Sector	OFDI	Percentage share
Agriculture	120,605	1.0
Mining	1,501,381	12.7
Manufacturing	954,425	8.1
Electricity, gas, and water	59,539	0.5
Construction	163,434	1.4
Transport, storage, and post	1,205,904	10.2
Information transmission, computer services, and software	190,089	1.6
Wholesale and retail trade	2,023,288	17.2
Hotel and catering services	12,067	0.1
Financial intermediation	1,671,991	14.2
Real estate	451,386	3.8
Leasing and business services	3,051,503	25.9
Scientific research, technical services, and geologic prospecting	152,103	1.3
Management of water conservancy, environment, and public facilities	92,121	0.8
Services to households and other services	129,885	1.1
Education	1,740	0.0
Health, social security, and social welfare	369	0.0
Culture, sports, and entertainment	9,220	0.1
Public management and social organization		
Total	11,791,050	

Source: China Statistical Yearbook, official website: hpps://www. ststs.gov.cn.

acquisitions. Table 9.4 provides an illustrative list of the prominent acquisitions since 2004.

Comparing OFDI Trends

As noted earlier, the outward investments have surged in both the countries in 2000s, though much more steeply in China than in India. As in 2007, OFDI from China, at US$100 billion (as per EIU estimates), is about 2.5 times of the outflow from India.

Table 9.4 Major Chinese Foreign Acquisitions since 2004

	Acquirer	Target	Sector	Year	Value (US$ million)
1.	CNOOC	South Atlantic Petroleum	Oil and Gas	2006	2,268
2.	CNPC	PetroKazakhstan	Oil and Gas	2005	4,180
3.	CNPC	Canadian Energy	Oil and Gas	2005	1,420
4.	Nanjing Automobile, Shanghai	MG Rover	Automobile	2005	205
5.	Lenovo Group Ltd.	IBM PC Business	IT	2004	1,760
6.	Shanghai Automobile	Ssangyong Motors	Automobile	2004	509
7.	CNPC	Pluspetrol Norte	Oil and Gas	2004	200
8.	Ningbo Qingchun Clothing Factory.	Younghwa Weaving and Dyeing	Textile	2004	84
9.	Cosco (China Ocean Shipping Co.).	Peninsular and Oriental Steam Navigation Co.	Shipping	2004	181
10.	China Merchants Group	Ming Wah Universal Transportation	Infrastructure	2004	168
11.	Sinopec	First International Oil	Oil and gas	2004	160

Source: Rui and Yip (2008).

Table 9.5 shows OFDI flow from China and India as proportions of gross fixed capital formation (GFCF) from 1995 to 2008. The ratio is rising in both the countries, though at a faster rate in India in recent years. In other words, OFDI (relative to their economy) is quantitatively much more significant for India than for China.

Table 9.5   OFDI Flow as Proportion of GFCF, 1995–2008

Year	China	India
1995	0.8	–
1996	0.8	0.3
1997	0.8	0.1
1998	0.8	0.1
1999	0.5	0.1
2000	0.2	0.5
2001	1.5	1.3
2002	0.5	1.0
2003	0.4	1.0
2004	0.7	1.2
2005	1.3	1.2
2006	1.9	4.8
2007	1.6	4.5
2008	2.9	4.1

Source: *World Investment Report*, various issues.

Table 9.6 reports OFDI stock from China and India as a proportion of GDP for 1990, and from 2000 to 2008. While the ratio has risen gradually for China, it has increased steeply for India, from 0.4 per cent in 2000, to 5.0 per cent in 2008.

Further, the mode of the outward investment from China and India seems different. India has registered a much larger number of cross-border mergers and acquisitions than China (Table 9.7). However, the average value of acquisition is higher for China than India (Table 9.8).

Thus, though following a similar trend, China's outward investment is much larger than India's; China makes more in green field investment, and its average size of acquisition is also higher than India's, though the composition is different.

Table 9.6   OFDI Stock as Proportion of GDP, 1990–2008

Year	China	India
1990	1.1	–
2000	2.3	0.4
2001	2.7	0.5
2002	2.8	0.5
2003	2.6	0.9
2004	2.4	1.0
2005	2.1	1.2
2006	2.8	1.5
2007	3.0	2.6
2008	3.4	5.0

Source: World Investment Report, various issues.

Table 9.7   Number of Cross-border M&A Deals—Net Purchases, 2006–8

Year	China	India
2003	73	57
2004	59	64
2005	102	122
2006	36	134
2007	57	171
2008	65	161

Source: World Investment Report, 2009.

UNDERSTANDING THE INVESTMENT OUTFLOWS

Motives

At a macro level, a common motivation for the outward investments from China and India is that both the countries are (relative to their size) natural resource poor, given their industrial requirement and national ambitions. Both the countries have a mature industrial base, fostered over five decades of rapid industrialization (China much faster than India). As these countries strive to expand their industrial capabilities, they are constrained by lack of access to advanced

Table 9.8   Value of Cross-border M&A Deals—Net Purchases
(US$ million)

Year	China	India
1988	17	22
1989	202	11
1990	60	–
1991	3	1
1992	573	3
1993	485	219
1994	307	109
1995	249	29
1996	451	80
1997	799	1,287
1998	1,276	11
1999	101	126
2000	476	910
2001	452	2,195
2002	1,047	270
2003	1,647	1,362
2004	1,125	863
2005	9,546	4,958
2006	12,053	6,715
2007	2,388	29,076
2008	36,861	11,662

Source: World Investment Report, various issues.
Note: Net purchase is defined as: 'Net cross-border M&A purchase by a home economy = Purchase of companies abroad by home based TNCs (–) sale of foreign affiliates of home based TNCs. The data covers only those deals that involve an acquisition of an equity stake of more than 10%' (*World Investment Report*, 2008, p. 269).

technology markets, which tend to be imperfect, concentrated in the hands of a few firms in the advanced economies. Moreover, in an increasingly tighter intellectual property regime, China and India probably find it hard to acquire technology though the normal trade and investment route (without yielding managerial control to technology providers, or to political pressure).

Markets: As industrial capabilities in these economies mature, and their domestic markets saturate, China and India seem to be eager to find external markets for their goods and services; just as many industrialized countries sought to penetrate less-developed countries about a century ago. The compulsion to do so is perhaps more for China as it has invested heavily in export-oriented manufacturing capacity, and where economic growth is widely perceived to be a political imperative.

Geopolitical reasons: Considering their size and history, it is but natural to expect China and India to harbour political ambitions as they acquire economic heft. Commensurate with its ambition and the need to sustain domestic growth, China has invested heavily in securing natural resources right from 1978 (Rui and Yip 2008). In contrast, India seems to have taken its eyes off the national and strategic considerations, as the liberal economic reforms since the 1990s have concentrated more on promoting market forces and re-drawing the boundaries of the state.

While the foregoing macroeconomic and strategic considerations could determine the national urge for overseas investments, could there be, as Rugman (2009) asked, country-specific advantages (CSAs) that propel outward investments? Further, what, if any, could be the microeconomic factors that propel firms from China and India to make these investments abroad? Multinational firms from the advanced countries usually have accumulated firm-specific advantages (FSAs) by way of proprietary technology, managerial strengths, organizational practices, or marketing skills which they seek leverage across many countries and markets. As the eclectic paradigm in the theory of MNCs suggests, there are FSAs that an international firm seeks to leverage across the world. If so, what are the possible FSAs that Chinese and Indian firms are seeking to leverage? We try to understand these factors by looking at the recent evolution of these economies, especially their industrial sectors.

India

In response to the industry and trade policy reforms initiated since 1991, the Indian manufacturing sector underwent considerable restructuring—layoffs and retrenchments, domestic mergers and acquisitions, plant closures and relocations, hike in promoters' equity holdings to ward off threats of hostile takeovers, and so on. Faced with increased external competition and in the expectation of a surge in demand after the reforms, incumbent firms made large-scale investments to expand manufacturing capacity and distribution networks (to fortify their market strength).

Industrial output boomed for four years after the economic reforms since 1992–3, but it went bust in 1995–6, leaving behind huge excess capacity (Nagaraj 2003). The experience has apparently taught Indian businesses the perils of excessive dependence on the domestic market in an increasingly open economy. In response, bigger and more successful firms have gradually sought to diversify overseas. In the gloomy scenario of the late 1990s, the international success of Indian software firms demonstrated the advantages of low-cost skilled workforce, and their managerial strength.

To mitigate the problem of inadequate domestic investment (from the mid-1990s until 2002–3), policy changes allowed Indian firms to invest overseas up to twice their domestic net worth, enabling them to acquire productive assets in advanced countries where industrial assets were on sale at a discount due to the global economic downturn in the early 2000s (Nagaraj 2006).

In principle, such acquisitions allowed firms to combine their low production costs at home with low interest rates in international capital markets to emerge as low-cost producers accessing the world market. By acquiring existing businesses, Indian firms seem to have gotten access to customers and markets, securing a toehold into closely-knit supply chain networks, and earned consumers' brand loyalty.

Such investments seem to have enabled the firms to produce labour-intensive parts/sub-assemblies/processes in India and use the facilities in advanced countries to undertake capital or technology-intensive parts of the production. Such a business strategy is perhaps best exemplified by Tata Steel's acquisition of the European steel giant, Corus. In this deal, Tata Steel, one of the most efficient producers of the basic metal, proposes to use its low-cost base metal to make finer steel using Corus facilities in locations closer to its consumers thus also saving on transport costs.[4] Moreover, the speed with which many Indian firms spread overseas was perhaps also driven by the desire to get access in a variety of markets divided into trading blocs, and the complex bilateral free trade agreements across the world—the spaghetti bowl—as Jagdish Bhagwati picturesquely described the emerging framework of world trade.

However, it needs to be reiterated that the foundation for the overseas expansion was laid much earlier under the regime of import substituting industrialization (Lall 1982). It is well worth remembering that given the large size of the domestic market, India had acquired international competitiveness in many industries using standardized and mature technologies, mainly based on the low cost of a skilled workforce.

China

As is widely known, economic reforms in China began in 1978 in agriculture, boosting its land productivity, giving rise to a large and growing market for light manufactures or for consumer goods, which was met by town and village enterprises (TVEs) employing the surplus labour from rural areas. Building on their success, China opened its doors to inward FDI in 1984 by building Special Economic Zones (SEZs) to encourage foreign capital (especially from Hong Kong) to take advantage of its cheap labour, and in turn enabling domestic firms to acquire technical skills, and managerial capability to tap the external markets. While such a strategy, over two decades, turned China into the 'world's factory floor', domestic value addition (and perhaps profit margins too) in such activities perhaps remained low since intermediate inputs were mostly imported from the other East Asian neighbours (Branstetter and Lardy 2008). As is widely known, China runs a trade deficit with Japan, Korea, and Taiwan as it imports intermediate inputs (mostly components and sub-assemblies). Further, the unprecedented pace of industrialization and urban infrastructure increased domestic demand for natural resources.

In response, China gradually relaxed rules for its firms to invest overseas, initially in neighbouring Asia to get access to raw materials and to export light manufactures (Frost 2004). For instance, China imports food and primary resources from Thailand, Indonesia, and so on. Perhaps the most recent and significant policy change occurred in 2004 when Chinese firms were permitted to invest abroad entirely based on private profitability considerations, regardless of its implications for balance of payments (Murukawa 2010).

Advantages of Chinese and Indian Firms

In the aggregate, the advantages of China and India in the world market seem somewhat similar: cheap labour, comparative advantage in many lines of mature manufacturing industries and a few services. Unlike in advanced economies, state support for domestic firms is higher both in China and India, perhaps much more in China since most large firms are state-owned enterprises (SOEs) or indirectly supported by the state; moreover, in China the dividing line between state-supported firm and the so-called private firm can be ambiguous. On the other hand, Indian firms have the experience of working under the rule of law, in an increasingly competitive domestic market, having access to a deep financial sector and other market-based institutions.

If the foregoing reasoning is well founded, then most of these advantages are CSAs, and the firms probably possess little by way of FSAs like proprietary technology or unique managerial practice. In contrast to the MNCs from the advanced economies, Chinese firms are perhaps venturing overseas *precisely to acquire firm specific capabilities*, by taking advantage of their CSAs. The case of Indian firms is perhaps slightly different and might be somewhat better, as they have developed proprietary knowledge in low-cost manufacture of generic drugs (through years of reverse engineering under a looser intellectual property rights [IPR] regime) (Athreye and Godley 2009) and have apparently mastered the delivery model of IT services across the globe to increasingly compete with leading technology consultancy firms like IBM and Accenture.

So, it seems reasonable to infer that Chinese and Indian firms are mainly seeking to exploit external markets on the basis of their CSAs; and in turn, use these resources and the experience of working in international environments to acquire FSAs, mainly technology and managerial skills. Overseas investments in energy sources and industrial raw materials by SOEs are intended to sustain domestic development, which is expected to enhance CSAs.

However, the process seems unlikely to be a smooth one, given the potential challenges.

Potential Pitfalls

China is likely to succeed in its objective of securing raw materials and strategic geopolitical goals better than India, given the undivided focus of its policy-makers. This is evident from China's growing role in Africa and Latin America. Though 'India, too, has lately stepped up its economic assistance to Africa to facilitate private investment, the scale and scope of it seems modest compared to China's, despite India's long-standing political closeness (as India championed the cause of de-colonization in the third world).

But in acquiring technology from foreign operations, and assimilating it productively to exploit its synergies with domestic capabilities, Indian private firms are perhaps better placed given their long established traditions of domestic market-based institutions, managerial capability, and wider use of English language in India (Huang and Khanna 2003).

In contrast, as most large industrial and commercial firms in China are directly or indirectly state-controlled, they are likely to face increasing political resistance in host countries; Rio Tinto is a case in point. China seems to still suffer from a lack of clarity of property rights, lack of well-defined institutions governing the private sector, and poor corporate governance. Therefore, private sector firms in China may perhaps be less capable of exploiting the opportunities offered by outward FDI.

Lenovo's acquisition of IBM's PC business is perhaps a case in point. Lenovo is a complex legal entity owned by many organs of the state, including the Chinese Academy of Sciences. Given its complex governance structure and lack of clarity on property rights, the Lenovo–IBM joint venture is registered in Hong Kong to give assurance to the foreign partner, via a shell company, though it operates from China. One suspects that such legal and organizational hurdles could be problematic for foreign partners in Chinese OFDI entities, where they could face difficulty in securing their commercial interests in case of a dispute.

In contrast, well-defined property rights as guaranteed by the national constitution, reasonably well-functioning courts (despite long delays), well-functioning domestic institutions of capital markets and the rule of law could prove advantageous for Indian firms. Success of its firms abroad—be it in IT or in manufacturing—in a seemingly wider range of businesses is perhaps a testimony to India's long experience in dealing with institutions of a market economy.

* * *

China and India are both large labour-surplus and natural-resource-scarce economies with strong and growing domestic capabilities, especially in manufacturing, built over the last five decades of industrialization. In recent years, if China is hailed as the 'factory of the world', India is perceived as its back office. Though clichéd, such a characterization probably contains a kernel of truth.

According to one estimate, between 1991 and 2007, the capital outflow from China was about two and half times that from India; both economies have seen gradual loosening of the restrictions since the early 1990s. Of course, China's per capita income, domestic savings rate and the pace of industrial growth is ahead of India—sustained over a longer period. China has followed its strategic economic and political interest consistently by providing foreign aid to developing countries to perhaps facilitate its commercial interests to follow.[5]

In contrast, up to 1991, India promoted joint ventures in developing countries as a means of exporting capital goods, but did not pursue its strategic economic and political interests by capital export, as China did—certainly not to the same extent. As part of the economic reforms, regulations on capital outflows by Indian firms were also made easier leading to a boom in the recent years—to developed countries, to secure technology and access the markets.

Both the countries are seeking external markets, natural resources to sustain domestic growth, and to access technology and management expertise to move up the value chain. So, China and India are competitors in the world market in these respects. Therefore the pattern of evolution of OFDI policy in these countries seems quite similar—perhaps China is ahead, given its more secure macroeconomic and financial position.

China is a far bigger economy; hence it has far greater resources to support OFDI. The majority of the capital flows out to tax havens (principally to Hong Kong) where China operates sovereign wealth funds (SWFs) to support its firms.[6] India, on the other hand, has refused to set up SWFs so far (perhaps because of its commitment to neo-liberal orthodoxy); however, about one-third of OFDI from India goes to tax havens, from where Indian business groups operate investment firms. China remains a state-led economy, while India is much more market driven with a strong base of domestic entrepreneurs. So, China's large SOEs have been at the forefront of the FDI outflows to acquire natural resources, which often get political support. In contrast, the Indian state's support to its firms is probably modest and tacit, though its attempts to acquire natural resources via SOEs.

If state support is China's strength, India's advantages probably lie in its institutions—rule of law, depth of domestic capital market, the capabilities to operate under the rules and norms of a market-based economy. India's comparative advantage currently seems more in services and skill-intensive manufacturing, while China's is mostly in labour-intensive manufacturing. India's advantage in services largely comes from widespread use of English language and technical education. A greater share of India's OFDI is used for acquisition of existing firms and factories, whereas China seems to spend more in greenfield investments. The majority of India's OFDI is to developed economies, or 'up-market FDI', whereas the bulk of China's investments seems to go to other developing countries or resource-rich nations.

Sanjaya Lall's pioneering paper, referred to earlier, ended with following words:

> A final note on a new form of overseas investment by some NICs [newly industrializing countries] which is also expected to grow in the future: the taking of equity shares in some high technology firms in developed countries in order to obtain direct access to their technology.... [I]n principle there is no reason why small, specialized producers ... in the developed countries should resist the offer of equity participation from the NICs. Even large firms, facing financial difficulties..., may look to the new giant corporations in the NICs for cooperation. But there is, ... little known about this particular mode of technology transfer, ...
> (Lall 1983, p. 626)

A quarter century later, Lall's prognosis seems prescient. Firms from these economies have not only taken equity shares in prominent firms in the developed countries, but have also acquired managerial control in some of them—representing a significant stride in their industrial maturity.

Yet, so far, the OFDI from these two giants seems to be mostly leveraging their country-specific advantages—of cheap and skilled labour, and comparative advantage in using standardized technologies—seeking to acquire firm-specific advantages. This is perhaps more true of firms from China, which have prospered in a different economic and political environment at home. Relatively speaking, Indian firms are perhaps leveraging their firm-specific advantages like the capabilities in low-cost drug manufacture acquired over years of reverse engineering, or, their unique business models of IT service delivery across the world.

NOTES

1. Theories of FDI and MNC behaviour are voluminous and rich in details. Even a modest summary of the literature would be too large for a short paper like this one. So, we restrict the references of that literature only to the studies on FDI from developing countries.

2. There are, however, cases of Indian entrepreneurs who effectively emigrated from India: for instance, Swaraj Paul in the 1960s, and the Mittals in the 1980s, and Vedanta (Steralite Industries) more recently. Such cases may perhaps have extra economic reasons for moving out, since, in principle, capital yields higher returns in capital-scarce countries that are politically stable and growing steadily. Our focus in this study is on firms and business houses owned and managed by Indian nationals and firms registered in India.

3. From 1993 onwards, many Chinese enterprises have been successfully listed on the Hong Kong Stock Exchange, and have often been many times over-subscribed. However, as many Chinese SOEs do not meet the requirements of the Hong Kong stock exchange listing, especially with respect to international accounting and reporting standards, some of them have acquired Hong Kong companies that are already listed in the exchange, or have acquired non-listed Hong Kong companies that satisfy the requirements and subsequently listed them, or have established holding companies by themselves in Hong Kong that meet the requirements. Some of the funds raised are used to support investment projects in China, establishing a direct link between outward and inward FDI. OFDI, in these cases, is a means for Chinese TNCs to overcome domestic capital scarcity (Cai 1999, p. 870).

4. Kumar and Chadha (2008, pp. 256–7) said:
Steel production is based on process know-how and requires large investments. Although the basic technology of steel making is matured and may be available off-the-shelf, some application technologies such as for special steels alloys for special applications are more closely held. The second characteristic of the steel industry is its scale intensity. The third characteristic is its highly raw-material-dependent nature. Steel production requires abundant access to iron ore, coal, and energy. These factors namely increasing consumption in the emerging markets, technological maturity, scale economies, and raw material intensity are leading to some consolidation of the industry. The Arcelor-Mittal merger followed by the Tata-Corus mergers are part of the trend of consolidation of the industry. Steel companies are acquiring upstream companies to utilize cheap resources of raw materials or downstream producers to get access to customers across borders.

5. While the Chinese investments surely signal a change in the world pecking order, it is perhaps premature to talk of emerging 'imperialism'.

6. As is widely known, Hong Kong forms an independent territory with separate legal and political systems, as part of China's 'one country, two systems' policy.

REFERENCES

Athreye, S. and A. Godley. 2009. 'Internationalisation and Technological Leapfrogging in Pharmaceutical Industry', *Industrial and Corporate Change*, 18 (2): 295–323.

Branstetter, L. and N. Lardy. 2008. 'China's Embrace of Globalisation', in B. Loren and G.R. Thomas (eds), *China's Great Economic Transformation*, pp. 633–82. New York: Cambridge University Press.

Cai, K.G. 1999. 'Outward Foreign Direct Investment: A Novel Dimension of China's Integration into the Regional and Global Economy', *The China Quarterly*, 160 (December): 856–80.

Frost, S. 2004. 'Chinese Outward Direct Investment in Southeast Asia: How Big are the Flows and What Does it Mean for the Region?', *The Pacific Review*, 17 (3): 323–40.

Huang, Y. and T. Khanna. 2003. 'Can India Overtake China', *Foreign Policy*, July/August, 74–81.

Kumar, N. and A. Chadha. 2009. 'India's Outward Direct Investments in Steel Industry in a Chinese Comparative Perspective', *Industrial and Corporate Change*, 18 (2): 249–67.

Lall, S. 1982. *Developing Countries as Exporters of Technology*. London: Macmillan.

————. 1983. 'The Rise of Multinationals from the Third World', *Third World Quarterly*, 5 (3): 618–26.

Morris, S. 1987. 'Trends in Foreign Direct Investment from India (1950–1982)', *Economic and Political Weekly*, 22 (46 and 47): 1963–9 and 1909–18.

Murukawa, T. 2010. 'On the Motives of Chinese Firms' Multinationalisation', in H. Esho and P. Xu (eds), *International Competitiveness, Globalisation, and Multinational Firms: A Comparison of China and India: Proceedings*, pp. 54–65. Tokyo: Institute of Comparative Economic Studies, Hosei University.

Nagaraj, R. 2003.' Industrial Policy and Performance: Which Way Now?', *Economic and Political Weekly*, 38 (35): 3707–15.

————. 2006. 'Indian Investments Abroad: What Explains the Boom?' *Economic and Political Weekly*, 41 (46): 4716–18.

Nayyar, D. 2008. 'Internationalisation of Firms from India: Investments, Mergers and Acquisitions', *Oxford Economic Studies*, 30 (1): 111–31.

Ramamurti, R. 2009. 'What Have We Learnt about the Emerging Market MNEs?', in R. Ramamurti and J.V. Singh (eds), *Emerging Multinationals in Emerging Economies*, pp. 399–426. New York: Cambridge University Press.

Rugman, A.M. 2009. 'Theoretical Aspects of MNEs from Emerging Economies', in R. Ramamurti and J.V. Singh (eds), *Emerging Multinationals in Emerging Economies*, pp. 42–63. New York: Cambridge University Press.

Rui, H. and G.S. Yip. 2008. 'Foreign Acquisitions by Chinese Firms: A Strategic Intent Perspective', *Journal of World Business*, 43: 213–26.

Wells, L.T., Jr. 1983. *Third World Multinationals: The Rise of Foreign Investment from Developing Countries*. Cambridge, MA: MIT Press.

Yeung, H.W.-Chung and W. Liu. 2008. 'Globalizing China: The Rise of Mainland Firms in the Global Economy', *Eurasian Geography and Economics*, 49 (1): 57–86.

UNCTAD. 2009: *World Investment Report*. New York: United Nations.

Appendix 9A.1

INDIA'S OVERSEAS INVESTMENT—MAJOR LIBERALIZATION MEASURES SINCE 2000*

The introduction of FEMA [Foreign Exchange Management Act] in 2000 brought about significant policy liberalization. The limit for investment up to US$ 50 million, which was earlier available in a block of three years, was made available annually without any profitability condition. Companies were allowed to invest 100 per cent of the proceeds of their ADR/GDR issues for acquisitions of foreign companies and direct investments in JVs and WOSs [joint ventures/ wholly owned subsidiaries].

Automatic route was further liberalised in March 2002 wherein Indian parties investing in JVs/WOSs outside India were permitted to invest an amount not exceeding US$ 100 million as against the earlier limit of US$ 50 million in a financial year. Also, the investments under the automatic route could be funded by withdrawal of foreign exchange from an authorised dealer (AD) not exceeding 50 per cent of the net worth of the Indian party.

With a view to enabling Indian corporates [corporate firms] to become global players by facilitating their overseas direct investment, permitted end-use for ECB was enlarged to include overseas direct investment in JVs/WOSs in February 2004. This was designed to facilitate corporates to undertake fresh investment or expansion of

* This has been reproduced from 'Indian Investment Abroad in Joint Ventures and Wholly Owned Subsidiaries: 2009–10 (April–June)', *Reserve Bank of India Monthly Bulletin*, October 2009: 1786–7.

existing JV/WOS including mergers and acquisitions abroad by harnessing resources at globally competitive rates.

In order to promote Indian investment abroad and to enable Indian companies to reap the benefits of globalisation, the ceiling of investment by Indian entities was revised from 100 per cent of the net worth to 200 per cent of the net worth of the investing company under the automatic route for overseas investment. The limit of 200 per cent of the net worth of the Indian party was enhanced to 300 per cent of the net worth in June 2007 under automatic route (200 per cent in case of registered partnership firms). In September 2007, this was further enhanced to 400 per cent of the net worth of the Indian party.

As a simplification of the procedure, share certificates or any other document as an evidence of investment in the foreign entity by an Indian party which has acquired foreign security should not be submitted to the Reserve Bank. The share certificates or any other document as evidence of investment where share certificates are not issued would be required to be submitted to and retained by the designated AD category–I bank, which would be required to monitor the receipt of such documents to ensure bona fides of the documents so received.

The Indian venture capital funds (VCFs), registered with the SEBI, are permitted to invest in equity and equity-linked instruments of off-shore venture capital undertakings, subject to an overall limit of US$ 500 million and compliance with the SEBI regulations issued in this regard.

The Liberalised Remittance Scheme (LRS) for Resident Individuals was further liberalized by enhancing the existing limit of US$ 100,000 per financial year to US$ 200,000 per financial year (April–March) in September 2007.

The limit for portfolio investment by listed Indian companies in the equity of listed foreign companies was raised in September 2007 from 35 per cent to 50 per cent of the net worth of the investing company as on the date of its last audited balance sheet. Furthermore, the requirement of reciprocal 10 per cent shareholding in Indian companies has been dispensed with.

The aggregate ceiling for overseas investment by mutual funds, registered with SEBI, was enhanced from US$ 4 billion to US$ 5 billion in September 2007. This was further raised to US$ 7 billion in April 2008. The existing facility to allow a limited number of qualified

Indian mutual funds to invest cumulatively up to US$ 1 billion in overseas Exchange Traded Funds, as may be permitted by the SEBI, would continue. The investments would be subject to the terms and conditions and operational guidelines as issued by SEBI.

Registered Trusts and Societies engaged in manufacturing/educational sector have been allowed in June 2008 to make investment in the same sector(s) in a Joint Venture or Wholly Owned Subsidiary outside India, with the prior approval of the Reserve Bank.

Registered Trusts and Societies which have set up hospital(s) in India have been allowed in August 2008 to make investment in the same sector(s) in a JV/WOS outside India, with the prior approval of the Reserve Bank.

Appendix 9A.2

EVOLUTION OF CHINA'S POLICY ON OUTWARD FDI, 1979–2007

STAGE ONE (1979–83): Case-by-Case Approval

Only state-owned trading corporations and provincial or municipal-based international economic and technology cooperation enterprises were permitted to invest overseas on a case-by-case basis. The State Council was the sole authority responsible for examining and approving overseas investment. Outward FDI was in effect prohibited unless specifically approved by the State Council, and there were no regulations on outward FDI as such.

STAGE TWO (1984–92): Standardization of Approval Procedures

Prohibitions against outward FDI were liberalized during this period as the government allowed a wider range of enterprises to invest overseas. Non-state firms, for example, were permitted to establish subsidiaries in other countries. Prior approval was still required from the central authorities, but the approval process moved gradually from a case-by-case approach to more standardized procedures.

STAGE THREE (1993–98): Greater Scrutiny of Overseas Investment Projects

A surge in outward FDI in the previous period, encouraged both by the relaxation of rules and by an overvalued exchange rate, led to a number of debacles by Chinese entities speculating on the Hong Kong real estate and stock markets. Consequently, the central government introduced a more rigorous process for screening and monitoring of outward FDI projects to ensure that these investments were for 'genuinely productive purposes'.

STAGE FOUR (1999–2002): Overseas Investment in Processing Trade Activities

The period straddling China's entry into the World Trade Organization was a turning point in Chinese policy toward outward FDI. Recognizing the increasingly important role of Chinese enterprises in global trade and production networks, the government put in place new policies to encourage firms to engage in overseas activities that augmented China's export drive, also known as 'processing trade' projects. The light industrial goods sector (e.g., textiles, machinery, and electrical equipment) was encouraged to establish manufacturing facilities overseas that would use Chinese raw materials or intermediate goods. The government offered a variety of incentives including export tax rebates, foreign exchange assistance, and direct financial support.

STAGE FIVE (2002–Present): The 'Stepping Out' Strategy

At the Chinese Communist Party's Sixteenth Congress in 2002, the leadership announced a new strategy of encouraging Chinese companies to 'Step Out' into the global economy not only through exports, but also by investing overseas. This policy shift was seen as a necessary concomitant to the successful inward investment and export policies of the 1980s and 1990s, and as part of the ongoing reform and liberalization of the Chinese economy. It also reflects a desire on the part of the Chinese government to create world-class companies and brands, whereby Chinese firms are seen as more than secondary nodes in production networks that are ultimately controlled by TNCs based in industrialized developed countries. Recent changes in outward FDI policy have focused on five areas: creating incentives for outward investment; streamlining administrative procedures, including greater transparency of rules and decentralization of authority to local levels of government; easing capital controls; providing information and guidance on investment opportunities; and reducing investment risks.

Source: Yeung and Liu (2008).

10

Science and Technology for Governance in China

PARTHASARATHI BANERJEE*

China has been making rapid progress in all areas of science and technology (S&T) (Parayil and D'Costa 2009). Interested observers noticed that growth pervaded all aspects of high and pure sciences, the designing and manufacturing of goods, and the widespread diffusion of the S&T system from the large cities to the small towns. Rise in S&T has been the most spectacular since the adoption of the 15-year Plan (Serger and Breidne 2007, Cao et al. 2009). Scientific output necessarily helped transformation of the economy. The economy grew by leaps and bounds. The question is: Did S&T support economic and political governance of this transformation? Was S&T the preferred instrument of governance in China? Putting it differently, how was growth and governance held together? Was it through S&T?

To address these questions I argue that S&T investment economically and politically bound different Chinese regions in a system of governance. Funds needed for S&T and for innovation had to be provided through the fiscal mechanism of and through developmental

* I thank Professor Amiya Kumar Bagchi for giving me the opportunity to present a draft version of this chapter at the Institute of Development Studies, Kolkata conference on India and China in December of 2010 and gratefully acknowledge Professor Anthony D'Costa's detailed editorial comments on the chapter.

projects involving land reuse by the state. In turn, innovation transformed the previously existing relations of powers between the central and provincial governments to appropriate and distribute funds.
How S&T served as a mechanism for national governance in China is
discussed below.

Previous research on how S&T in China is coupled with economic
and political governance is scant. Most observers have analysed
Chinese S&T as an autonomous system (Hu and Jefferson 2004,
Li 2009, Xue 1997); a few have looked into the economic and
innovation linkages of the S&T (Shulin 2001, Hu 2007) and even
fewer have analysed S&T in relation to issues of political governance
(Montinola et al. 1995, Parayil and D'Costa 2009). The autonomous
perspective leads to a linear analysis of the growth of S&T as if it were
derived essentially from within S&T or at best from within a broader
system of S&T and knowledge professionals. Such analysis of
autonomous or near-autonomous systems yields important results
but also hides causal engines of the dynamics of autonomous systems.
I argue that this convergence of systems of S&T and governance was
made possible by the political power by way of allocating funds,
monitoring the dynamics post-allocation, and exercising control
over both outcomes and expectations. In adopting this approach
we find that S&T acts as an engine of growth linking the different
mechanisms of governance. Governance here is understood as guided
transformation.

There is of course no prior reason to disbelieve that the radical
changes in fiscal and economic structures had enjoyed a close and
possibly causal link to the system of S&T and innovation. However,
my reading suggests how investments in S&T, secured through fiscal
changes and land conversion, transformed asset ownership and economic power structures and how such powers generated inter-regional
competition as a driver of economic growth. The key to governance
in China, I argue, remains in controlling and directing competition
between regions. The central–local antagonism has been replaced by
local–local competitive relations.

The rest of the chapter is divided as follows. In the next section,
I investigate the interplay of S&T development and economic and
political governance in theory. In the third section, I present selected
investments in S&T and its output to indicate the federalized powers and the functioning of the S&T establishment. The fourth section

presents changes over the last two decades in the fiscal structure with particular attention to the various dimensions of federalized governance. The final section concludes, linking fiscal federalism and S&T to demonstrate the interrelated dynamics of transformation of S&T and the economic system. The chapter concludes by reiterating the interrelationships between S&T governance, economic transformation, and the fiscal system.

S&T AND ECONOMIC AND POLITICAL GOVERNANCE FOR TRANSFORMATION

Science for development and for economic growth is a well-researched topic. But how science causes structural transformation including radical shifts in property rights and in institutions of the economy and society and how governance over this radical change process makes use of science is not so well understood. Prior research indicates the importance of the following in the transformation: (*a*) dynamics within and growth of science leading sometimes to the growth of a market on property rights from science, (*b*) distribution of science as a resource to competing entities, especially regions, (*c*) entrepreneurial organization of novel resources such as science causing structural transformation, and (*d*) fiscal powers as redistributing incentives to access funds.

In reviewing the above four issues surrounding transformation it is evident that over the last two decades radical changes in the fiscal system in China accompanied the steady high growth of the economy. Several scholars studied what has been variously described as the fiscal decentralization and the rise of the extra budgetary component (Wong 1991). However, the typical economist's approach to governance rested on the theoretical construct of fiscal decentralization, captured in terms of devolution of powers or differentially shared between the central and local governments. Bardhan (2002) and Rodden (2004), for example, embrace the sharing of fiscal power between the dipole of central and state government while bypassing first, the inter-local government competition and second, how S&T financing by the local governments can cause or engender a shift in the dynamics of fiscal power. A large literature on 'decentralization' and on fiscal power (Jian et al. 1996, Kanbur and Zhang 2005, Lyons 1991) while dealing with various facets of shifts in and the location of fiscal power in relation to politics of governance do not discuss the role of investment in and the outputs of S&T in this shift and therefore in political governance. S&T in extant views stands sanitized, distant, and devoid of power politics. Investigating China reveals that the centre–local relationship is constituted over local–local differences, inequalities, and competitions over which the centre enjoys jurisdiction. Such inter-governmental dynamics are beyond the descriptive power of the theory behind decentralization. I propose to use the term 'federalized structure' to capture this specific mode of constitution of governance.

It appears that a very large part of the funds of local governments deployed for S&T is derived from undertaking projects by way of readjustment and/or sale of agricultural/rural land. The resulting space where all local governments undertake projects, innovations, and land-sales simultaneously with multiple forms of bond issuances has contributed to the monetization of previously locked assets. Consequently, the central government shifts the control from budgeting to financial control or directional control over S&T. The central control over the formation of modes of extra-budgetary sources happens partially through fiscal instruments and partially through projects and innovation investments and thus through S&T investments. At local levels therefore, S&T investments and sales/conversion of land and undertaking of projects go together. This can be seen as a mode of governance through the application of S&T instrumentality over and above the use of fiscal instruments.

The typical description of central–local dichotomies and decentralization, as captured by Rodden (2004), differs significantly from what is observed in China. For example: (*a*) inter-local conflicts and competition including inter-local inequalities appear to be dominant, perhaps shadowing the centre–local tension, (*b*) inter-local commerce has remained low in China and local governments are more autonomous than what prevails in most other governance set ups, (*c*) the central government now enjoys higher punitive authority and greater command over directed local spending. The fiscal system can now vigorously enforce central policies since the mode of funding has become fairly large. Thus the centre can directly mandate a 'town' government at the bottom, bypassing as it were the provincial government, (*d*) the fiscal and the expenditure system evolved through political negotiations since the constitution does not define the sharing formula; and (e) local governments and the business enterprises share similar interests and the putative boundary of a business 'firm' melts into the local governance set up.

Moreover most analyses of Chinese S&T or fiscal dynamics (Pei 2002) have been unilinear and closed. For example, discussions on fiscal issues in China scarcely touched upon related significant projects of governance, such as the project of urbanization, the inter-regional competition, and non-fiscal domains where the local governments could increase their powers. A straight power relation between central and local government informs us less on inter-regional inequality in the command over resources. Further, sharing of domains of power between multiple tiers of local governments is a crucial issue, often involving considerable conflict between cities, towns, and regions of China. S&T can be seen as an important gun in the local armoury. S&T, I argue, mediates between multiple aspects of governance such as between different local governments. Further, governance often amounts to directed transformational power, hence understanding S&T development in China is likely to provide an important clue to the contemporary role of S&T–based transformative governance (Bagchi 1980).

In another view, transformative power has been vested with entrepreneurs (Blanchard and Schleifer 2001). Advocates of entrepreneurial agency have discovered immense growth of entrepreneurial capitalism in China and rising expenditure on R&D by business has been cited as the evidence of growing markets (Qian and Weingast 1997) founded upon entrepreneurial feat, albeit still enmeshed with party bureaucracy (Wank 1999). However, very intimate relations between fiscal revenues which is partially dependent upon local value addition, the presence of local business that are promoted by the local government, and the structure of fiscal expropriations for S&T–based developmental projects suggest that inter-regional relations bordering on adversity such as competition for S&T–based development drive China's demand for S&T–based innovation (Changbiao 2002). Further, entrepreneurial business demands a prior presence of transactable rights that can be traded in pecuniary terms and an adjudication system for settlement of disputes. However, property rights emergent from new or future innovative S&T cannot be currently transacted in pecuniary terms and markets cannot be currently cleared unless a force external to economic rights intervenes to set a price and the terms of exchange.

In case political power dictates the pecuniary terms of transaction in rights, the agency of entrepreneurship as the creator of novel values would appear mythical. This leads us to reject the thesis of entrepreneurship as the driver of transformative growth.

The basic definition of innovation in a Schumpeterian system deals with the emergence of novel rights, which cannot be cleared off through current market transactions and whose pecuniary worth cannot be determined beforehand. Thus, S&T or R&D would engender such future unclear rights as cannot be squared off currently in pecuniary terms. In contrast, a business enterprise might even, when property rights are not clearly established (North 1981), turn to minimizing transaction costs. This cost would depend upon the milieu of the prevailing institutions of rules and unwritten norms. For North, the fundamental rules of competition and cooperation provide the structure of property rights that maximize the gains to the current power-holders. Only within such maximizing structures are the transaction costs reduced most to achieve maximum social output and high fiscal income for the state. This institution of fundamental rules therefore stands upon specific negotiated rules of competition and cooperation.

The power presiding over institutional changes resides in specific organizations such as enterprises, the cities, R&D organizations, S&T parks, the export processing zones, and so on. Shultz (1953) had emphasized urban–industrial organizations as the key to S&T governance structure. The capacity of urban–industrial structure, according to Shultz, was to draw and process very large human, financial and knowledge resources into transactable products and services in high volumes. Bagchi (2005) argued that evolution of political and organizational structures, and more importantly the transactional relations between these organizations and institutions, are indicative of the existence of manipulative economic interests behind the evolution of organizations and institutions. Thus the political structure behind the organization of rights is crucial to understanding the structure of governance.

Jain (2010) captured this manipulative power by critically examining the formulation of Coase (1960) related to rights and argued that when non-pecuniary considerations remain important the Coasian formulation does not hold true; in other words, only with neglect of non-pecuniary considerations does the Coasian theorem hold true.

The Coasian formulation means that under conditions of zero transactions cost any well-defined law will be equally good and an individualized court decision will be efficient. Extending Jain (2010), we could argue that not all states can translate property rights exhaustively such that non-pecuniary transactions can be neglected and transactions can be efficiently undertaken. The existence of a set of rules or laws (and thus a court) does not provide enough institutional support to economic legal logic to situations with relative lack of clarity in property rights as prevails in environmental disputes or knowledge claims arising from new scientific technological advancement. Such rules or laws can be strategically manipulated, Jain argues, to serve the interests of one party in a dispute. Limitations on translatability of knowledge claims then open up a vast domain where agents in power converge for negotiations on what S&T be undertaken by whom and in which organizations and for what kind of transactable goods.

This power is derived from two modes: the first mode is secured through agglomeration of an otherwise dispersed geography as a regional entity; and the second mode differentiates one region from other regions. The local–central tension is thus underplayed while governance over local–local competition acts as a source of power (Peng 2001). Based on Jain (2010) we infer that there exists a large set of economic goods where property rights cannot be exhaustively described, delineated, and established within the logic of economics, where pecuniary market-clearing fails to happen and adjudication of disputes cannot be accomplished. Thus Coase's 'lighthouse in economics' metaphor (Coase 1988), which proposes substitutability of state functions with that of a market can be interrogated. The experience of China as will be shown has a governing state that is un-substitutable. Governance of regional innovation systems cannot thus be constituted by the infrastructure of governance and the superstructure of business, as claimed by Cooke et al. (2004) and as based upon an extension of Coase's lighthouse argument. Innovations in a region, if constituted over rights that are yet to emerge, cannot be undertaken by the proverbial entrepreneurs, and in contrast, we argue, local regional governing powers enjoy incentives and jurisdiction over creation of rights and over expropriation of such rights.

The great transformation in post-Mao China opened up huge resources that were to be organized and directed towards higher growth. The question is if the S&T-based innovative entrepreneurs failed to organize and direct this upsurge in resources, what other organizational structures and their powers prevailed. Powers resident in social and economic organizations that are broader than entrepreneurial firms had to therefore step in and it is this locus of residence of power that experienced great shifts. I argue that local governments, in particular the provincial governments, attempted to seize the most power by reducing the powers of other local governments especially village governments and the power of entrepreneurial organizations. Structure of local governments has changed considerably and so have negotiating powers of emergent groups of new entrepreneurs, workers, highly skilled migrants, professionals, local service providers, the People's Liberation Army (PLA) and the village level non-farm occupation holders, and above all the farmers. Stakeholders behind economic transactions have wielded structural power and have cleverly manoeuvred alliances to control S&T resources and reinforce these powers. Such active engagement of S&T by the powers resident in the shifting structures thus provided ample scope for strategic negotiations and temporary truces (Peilin 2002a, Shulian 2000, Wanli 2002). The most important shift possibly happened in the area of 'land'. The peasant perspective on land has been possibly completely given up because of complete changes in the nature of assets, intergenerational distributive issues and in the modes of revenue generation now disfavouring the peasant mode of sustained accumulation. What is clear is that China's transformation of historic proportions has been brought out, post-reform, by urbanization, which has been argued to be tightly related to competition for S&T resources.

CHANGING STRUCTURE OF S&T INVESTMENTS AND OUTPUTS IN CHINA

Descriptions of S&T in China are replete with statistics on the sharply increasing factor resources and equally growing outputs from the sciences. Analysing the distribution of inputs and outputs over two time periods is likely to provide insights into structural changes of S&T (Shulin 2001, see Table 10.1). A broad picture of investments in macro-terms indicates that local governments in China undertake very significant investment in S&T and education. Also, these governments undertake significant investment in innovation and in S&T projects (Xue 1997, Li 2009). China has been investing significantly under the budget head of innovation and most such investments are under the jurisdiction of local governments. Directly related to investment in innovation are developmental projects often with significant S&T inputs and R&D inputs under the central government. The S&T expenditure, which includes a small component related to education, is also largely under the local government. The significant voice that a local government in China enjoys can be shown to be structurally related to governance.

Table 10.1   S&T Resources and Output in China

	2001	2002	2003	2004
Personnel engaged in S&T activities (in 10,000)	314.1	322.2	328.4	348.1
Full-time equivalent R&D personnel (10,000 man year)	95.7	103.5	109.5	115.3
Expenditure on R&D (100 million yuan)	1,042.5	1,287.6	1,539.6	1,966.3
Number of major achievements in S&T	28,448	26,697	30,486	31,720
Inventions patent certified	16,296	21,473	37,154	49,360
Utility patent models applications certified	54,359	57,484	68,906	70,623
Designs patent applications certified	43,596	53,442	76,166	70,255
Transactions value in technical market (100 million yuan)	783	884	1,085	1,334 (1,551 in year 2005)

Source: Statistical Yearbook of China (2005).

The incomplete evolution of the market for S&T rights leads us to look into the non-pecuniary dimension of the evolving property rights. In post-Mao China property rights in S&T outcomes have evolved under two modes and the growth in property claims, however unformed and un-amenable to pecuniary transactions has been phenomenally spectacular. The first mode has been the intellectual property rights (IPR) to inventions, designs and utilities (see Table 10.1). The second mode has been the authorship rights to research papers. In IPR, China has provided for short-life utility claims and rights along with the more conventional invention patents of longer life and enlarged claims. Further a growing proportion of inventions and utilities belong to the class of design. Growth in utility and design-type has been most spectacular while the growth in invention-type has been relatively modest rising significantly only in the last few years.[1] Authored research papers and rights to such papers have grown very significantly only in recent years. Most ownership in utility-types of IPR remains with individuals, small enterprises, and local communities including prefectures and provinces.

The ownership of invention-type IPR rests mostly with large and medium enterprises (LME) and large R&D organizations under the central government. The domestic market in technology transaction has grown significantly.[2] Growth in technology transactions was also facilitated by associated changes in corporate tax policies that favoured domestic and inter-corporate transactions over transactions with foreign entities (Pan 2008) to facilitate the formation of large businesses. Since 1999, R&D organizations were transformed (known as 'system conversion') so as to make market-friendly the R&D institutes subordinate to the central government. Distance from market caused by public administrative control was thus removed and the development of S&T rights-based market was assisted by bringing R&D organizations under market control. Through the 'system conversion' by 2001 a total of 1,232 R&D institutes were transformed into industrial enterprise groups, large S&T business, S&T business, S&T intermediary firms, and merged with major universities such as the Tsinghua University, and the Beijing University or otherwise closed (China 2002). Table 10.1 provides a summary picture of S&T in China.

The evolution of property rights market in China has been led by non-pecuniary forces. Even if separate values of utility, design, and invention-type transactions are not known, a design property right to an individual inventor or to a small enterprise has little strategic worth of 'exclusionary' rights. A large number of invention types are valued more for their 'exclusionary' monopoly rights than for their pecuniary values in market transactions. Authorship rights are not amenable to pecuniary transactions directly. Most research publications have multiple authors who benefit from better career prospects and hence in potential pecuniary payoffs in the future under the aegis of the administrative-rule framework of an S&T organization. More importantly, research paper outputs help the organization in building its reputation. Authorship has grown fast in organizations under the central and provincial governments and in S&T areas that are more theoretical and farthest from the immediately implementable innovation cases. Central R&D organizations take care of comparatively long-term research and innovation goals while the local government-owned engineering-driven innovation organizations take care of implementation and marketing of innovative products. Based on rights, it is clear that the market for S&T in China rests on non-pecuniary factors.

China has witnessed large growth in S&T organizations, often under the corporate umbrella of the Chinese Academy of Science (CAS). Local S&T organizations have remained, however, under the non-national governance. The strategic manoeuvring power of organizations, fiscal power of local governments, and the local S&T system have acted together in multiple forms for value creation. Several features of these modes are: (*a*) increasing number of S&T organizations and intra-regional organizational division of labour, (*b*) expenditure of specific type of funds by different groups of organizations including the bypass mechanism to short-circuit markets, (*c*) central government controlled research programme-led grouping and funding, and (*d*) use of S&T projects towards local developmental projects, such as real estate.

In the first nationwide survey on S&T establishments in 1985 (Shulin 2001), it was found that apart from the CAS with its 122 research organizations and 32,000 scientists and engineers, under several central ministries there were 622 organizations with 93,000 scientists and engineers, while the local governments together had 3,946 affiliated organizations with 106,000 scientists and engineers. In 1999 the total number of research organizations was 5,573 and subsequent to restructuring and conversion the number by 2002 was 4,347. Of these, 744 (including 98 organizations under CAS) were under the central government. The smaller number of central institutes, however, commanded over half of the S&T funding (Hu and Jefferson 2004). Beyond these organizations, the higher education sector including universities has their own R&D units, which mostly fall under the provincial system of governance. Business enterprises have also increased their R&D spend considerably. As per tax laws, provincial factories of a corporate holding company with a distant headquarter, report to the local government and as a result, R&D of the LME is reported under the provinces (Table 10.2) allowing local governments to compete with each other for enhanced control.

Table 10.2 Government S&T Appropriation and Other Expenditure (in 100 million yuan)

	2000	2001	2002	2003	2004	2005
Special project funds for S&T	277.2	359.6	398.6	416.6	484.0	609.7
Operating funds	189.0	223.1	269.9	300.8	335.9	389.1
Capital funds	61.5	63.4	70.0	80.2	95.9	112.5
Others	47.9	57.2	77.8	147.0	179.5	223.6
Government S&T appropriation	575.6	703.3	816.2	944.6	1,095.3	1,334.9
—Of that, by central	350	444	511	609	692	808
—Of that, by local	226	259	305	336	403	527
S&T appropriation as % of total govt expenditure	3.6	3.7	3.7	3.8	3.8	3.9

Source: www.most.gov.cn.

S&T organizations reporting to the provincial or lower-level governments had from the beginning set up targeted objectives of providing engineering solutions to development. In fact, since 1985 the year S&T system was drawn into the reform processes, policies related to rural and urban reforms, the registration system and the contract system of household production, and the state-owned enterprises (SOEs) reform, all coherently targeted close interaction among R&D organizations, business enterprises, local development projects, and local and provincial governments (Peilin 2002b). The local registration system, which was never perfect, was now virtually given up and the farmers were allowed to give up land rights. The entire policy set therefore took upon the task of reorganizing labour with S&T-based production system, re-appropriating land for non-farm S&T-based operations and engendering a new regime of accumulation based upon S&T-based innovations (Xueyi 2002). The goal was that R&D organizations would directly relate to business enterprises without being mediated by the local government. A new law on Patent and Technological Contracts was adopted (subsequently China adapted to the TRIPS on joining the WTO) with the specific objective of developing a large market for technology (see Table 10.1).

Three related aspects of structural transformation of S&T deserve attention. The first is about the emergence of putatively called market-based transactions in technology. The second aspect refers to the role that special programmes played (see Table 10.2). The third aspect draws attention to the emergence of real estate as among the most important form of investments for S&T development. Technology transactions at the rural or town levels were between enterprises (Jianzhong 2002), thus facilitating the flows of technology to the immediate region and into the R&D organization belonging to the same geographic entity (Jianzhong 2002). Effectively therefore a set of locally transacting business, R&D and political developmental units came together for competitive bargaining with other regions who too had very similarly organized their enterprises. For all practical purposes these units acted as units of a holding company of that region. These transacting units represent the interests of that geography (Che and Qian 1998, Peng 2001, Wank 1999) and thus the interests of the local political establishment. No wonder several regions developed S&T and industrial specialization along similar lines. Changbiao (2002) analysed closely the coefficient of inter-provincial industrial specialization and found that the provinces had similar industries. Montinola et al. (1995) show how land readjustment by way of changing property rights after land is taken for developmental project and feeds into real estate development for S&T-based innovation projects. This mechanism along with the emergence of Town and Village Enterprises (TVEs) could not thus possibly be ascribed to evolving markets and entrepreneurship as claimed by a number of China scholars (Nee and Young 1991).

In examining the funding patterns of S&T we observe large variations in investment across multiple regional governments. The GERD by region in 2006 and in 100 million yuan varied from the high of 433.0 for Beijing, 346.1 for Jiangsu, 258.8 for Shanghai or 313.0 for Guangdong to the low of only 2.1 for Hainan, 3.3 for Qinghai, 0.5 for Tibet, and 5.0 for Ningxia. Similarly, S&T expenditure as a percentage of total local government expenditure (which again varies widely as per fiscal entitlement) for 2006 varied from 0.45 for Tibet or 0.94 for Anhui or 1.01 for Ningxia to the high of 4.66 for Beijing, 2.79 for Tianjin, 5.23 for Shanghai, or 4.29 for Zhejiang. The local governments, as I argued above, are keen to advance innovations, and local production based on value-adding S&T inputs. The regions therefore, I argue, are under increasing pressure to secure funding from sources other than budgetary appropriations from the central pool (see Table 10.2). This in turn has forced local governments to obtain funding from land based or other forms of bank sourced borrowings; as a result the expenditure on S&T drawn from appropriation remained very low at less than 4 per cent of the total (see Table 10.2). The structure of the R&D fund for the year 2004 reveals that of total 154 billion yuan R&D fund, 39.9 billion yuan was spent by government organizations, 96.0 billion by Chinese business, 16.2 billion by higher education and 1.8 billion by others. The business sector provided 2.1 billion fund to the government R&D agencies and 5.8 billion to the higher education agencies. The government provided 4.8 billion to the business, 32.0 billion to R&D organizations and 8.8 billion to higher education. From this it is clear that cross flows of R&D funds across different sectors are indicative of strong coupling between multiple local organizations.

Funds for S&T are secured first through the mechanism of appropriation and additionally through competition for funds under special projects (see Table 10.2). The appropriation mechanism has remained under pressure since the beginning of reforms. Funds of both business and local development were secured through transactions in real estate and from various kinds of debts incurred by the local governments. They therefore developed sources of funding locally. This is the reason why and how regions differed in investments in S&T and innovations. I argue later that a significant part of this local investment pool was determined through centrally designed fiscal measures.

The post-Mao period saw the emergence of several special programmes for S&T designed and directed by the central government. The Torch Programme of S&T (initiated in 1988) had the objective of setting up S&T parks and commercialization of new technologies and products meeting global standards. Another programme, the Spark (initiated in 1986), was aimed at the rural economy by setting up 100,000 demonstration projects by 2004 in 85 per cent of rural areas. The 'Key Technologies' Programme, initiated in 1982, also targeted rural economic development. As a result the pooling of resources led to incubation and nurturing and promotion of S&T-based local business enterprises. The provincial and prefectural governments, and the R&D organizations participated in two other high technology programmes, the '863 Program' initiated in 1986 and the '973 Program' initiated in 1992. In this entire programme mode of funding the central government defined the framework of growth and investment and the allowable share of programme fund. Local governments therefore competed for larger shares in these funds. Such programmes were to be implemented locally. Hence local capacity, capability and above all inter-local competitiveness were raised through the intervention of centrally designed and directed programmes.

The central government intensified directed mode of intervention, as in 2006 the State Council initiated the first batch of consolidated rules for implementing '99 Supporting Policies' under the national medium- and long-range plans of S&T (Serger and Breidne 2007). Table 10.3 (and Table 10.2) provide a breakdown of spending power between the two divisions of the executive—between the centre and the local or provincial governments.

To recall: (a) S&T deepened the inter-regional differences in investment and competition for similar mode of scientific specialization and innovation, and (b) S&T provided for the instruments of securing larger funds. Both these resulted from the emergence of regional power as the undertaker of innovation. Entrepreneurial or rights-based

Table 10.3 Budgetary Expenditure Example Items in 2005 for Central and Local Governments (in 100 million yuan)

	Total Expenditure	By Central Government	By Local Government
Capital construction	4,031.34	1,365.56	2,675.78
Innovation funds for S&T promotion funds	1,494.59	337.89	1,156.70
—of that, enterprises innovation funds	884.90	15.67	869.33
—of that, S&T promotion	609.69	322.32	287.37
Additional expenses for circulating capital	18.17	17.10	1.07
Geological prospecting	132.70	39.95	92.75
Operating expenses for Department of industry	444.15	91.38	352.77
For supporting rural production	1,792.40	147.53	1,644.87
For culture, education, science & health care	6,104.18	587.67	5,516.51

Source: Statistical Yearbook of China 2006.

market mechanisms could not play a significant role. Inter-regional competition for S&T-based innovation furthered the governance of regions and the transformation of fiscal system. In short, S&T and fiscal systems together undertook transformational governance.

CHANGES IN FISCAL STRUCTURE

In the post-reform period and especially since 1994 when the Tax Sharing System was introduced, local governments continued to lose sources of revenue while the responsibility of spending continued to remain high on the local government (Park *et al.* 1996, Wong 1991, Zhang 1999). The pressure thus created forced local governments to resort to undertaking multiple forms of projects and incur debts. S&T now found a new role, which perhaps was not an intended outcome, to not only contribute to economic and technological transformation of China but also to act as a mechanism for governance. Thus the common understanding of the conflict as between the centre and the local (Shen *et al.* 2006) must be interpreted as principally due to inter-regional conflicts.

These conflicts correspond to the central government and four other tiers of government in China, namely provincial, prefectural or city-based, county, and town. In the pre-reform period the local tiers of governments depended for revenue earnings on negotiated share of profits from the SOE. With the decline in SOE performance the revenue earnings of both central and local governments dwindled. The central government, especially in the pre-reform period, used to plan for the local government, approved the local budget, and set the priorities. With serious erosion of the role of budgetary revenue and the emergence of local powers during the post-reform period, governance took new forms. The central government wrested the control of defining fiscal power as one not being between the centre and the local, rather several tiers of local governments sought powers within other instruments, such as in education, health, social security and above all in S&T and innovation.

Wong (1991) describes this in the context of rapidly declining share of government budget revenues in the total national income, for example, from a high of 46.9 per cent in 1960 through 35.3 per cent in 1980 to 24.7 per cent in 1989. The most important source of revenue, the SOEs and the control over industry, have been virtually given up to the local entrants who were now capturing most of the industrial revenues, spawning inter-local government competition or 'trade wars' and fomenting regional tensions within China. I argue that this latter aspect of inter-regional or inter-geography competition has remained crucial to governance. In parallel fashion the dependence on extra-budgetary (*yusuanwai*) funds has gone up sharply (see Table 10.4). By 1989 these funds totalled 20 per cent of national income. Nearly 80 per cent of such funds belong to non-state actors; however, the local governments continue to wield significant degree of control over their use.

This fiscal contracting system of 1988 could not arrest the erosion in revenue earnings. Local governments enjoyed powers to define several areas of taxability and these governments had incentives to collect less tax that were to be transferred to the centre. There was no income or corporate tax. Tax revenues were collected by the local governments and the fiscal contracting system was aligned with SOE ownership. The ownership was revised several times during the 1980s and new levies were introduced by the centre especially for generating funds, such as the Energy and Transport Key Construction Fund. In

Table 10.4 Extra-budgetary Revenues and Expenditures (in 100 million yuan)

	Total Revenue	Central	Local	Total Expenditure	Central	Local
1986	1,737.31	41.2%	58.8%	1,578.37	40.6%	59.4%
1995	2,406.50	13.2%	86.8%	2,321.26	15.1%	84.9%
2000	3,826.43	6.5%	93.5%	3,529.01	6.0%	94.0%
2004	4,699.18	7.5%	92.5%	4,351.73	9.0%	91.0%

Source: China Statistical Yearbook (2005).

a parallel fashion the local responsibility for expenditure continued to grow. For example, from 45 per cent of total expenditure in 1981 the share of local resources grew to about 72 per cent in 1993. The tension around the fiscal contracting system, which introduced six types of central–local revenue sharing methods such as 'contracted sharing rate with fixed yearly growth rate of revenue or fixed local shared rate in total revenue', among others, continued and the system was extended to 1993. The 1994 Tax Assignment System specified the whole sharing of taxes between the central and provincial governments. This Tax Reform introduced VAT, replacing the turnover-based system, while corporate income tax was smoothened along with other taxes such as the consumption tax. The central government launched its own tax collection administration; the local tax collectors continued but with vastly curbed powers. With a new assignment system the centre immediately gained its share in the total revenue (from 22 per cent in 1993 to 56 per cent in 1994; Shen et al. 2006). The decline in revenue to GDP ratio too was arrested. The 1994 assignment system divided the total revenue in three components: for central, for the divisible pool and for the local. The local government receives 27 per cent of VAT, 97 per cent of business tax, 40 per cent of individual income tax and 100 per cent of a set of taxes such as land use tax, property tax, land appreciation tax, stamp tax, contract tax, and so on, while the central government retains 73 per cent of VAT, 60 per cent of enterprise income tax, and 100 per cent of excise tax and of the tariffs.

Unlike the central government, local governments do not enjoy the power of taxation, define the scope of taxation, revenue-sharing ratios, and so on, on their own. They are not allowed to run deficits or enjoy credit financing of deficits. They therefore promoted the tax base by making direct investments in industry. The growth of TVEs resulted largely from this revenue-generating urge of the local governments. Since the 1994 reform, local governments have relied on business tax, share of the VAT, enterprise income tax, personal income tax, etc. These taxes constitute about 70 per cent of the local revenue. Overall, the provinces spent about a quarter of the revenue on S&T, culture and education, and health and another 15 per cent on construction. The expenditure system, however, is strongly tilted towards the local government, which remains responsible for about 70 per cent of the total public expenditure (Table 10.4). A large portion of expenditure is shared between the central and the local governments for supporting R&D, higher education, heavy industry, large infrastructure projects, and social security. The local system remains exclusively responsible for most hospitals, school education, local infrastructure, housing, and large areas under social security.

Furthermore, the provinces or prefectures with large businesses necessarily receive proportionately large central transfers. For example, 90 per cent of revenue for Beijing was from the transfer pool, and 60 per cent of Chongqing revenue was from the transfer pool while for provinces with nearly no business such as Shaanxi this share was negligible (with business category at near zero). Also, VAT alone constitutes for the poor regions the transferred share. This disparity gets aggravated further. For example, while Shanghai could spend 2,355 yuan per capita on education in 2003, Chongqing 3,064 yuan and Beijing 679 yuan, the poor province Hainan could spend only 19 and Tibet only 15 yuan per capita on education. Similarly, rich regions, especially because land prices are astronomically high, earn more by furthering urbanization and innovation projects. The fiscal system post-1994 has thereby generated intense inter-geography inequality based competition. The picture gets worse when transfers down the hierarchy and below the provincial level are considered (Shen et al. 2006).

Local governments thus resorted to borrowing based on local state enterprises and multiple forms of trust companies or investment companies (one mode has been described in the previous section). The project mode of securing finances has been very popular. The local governments could approve investment projects under 50 million yuan and S&T or innovation projects under 30 million yuan. This policy resulted in very large numbers of small projects, such as in local power generation. While local governments do not have the power of setting tax rates, they can set the effective rates of taxation on profits by defining contracts, or the size of the taxable income, or by waiving indirect taxes, and also part of the revenue from sale of land. Since 1993 with the demise of the fiscal contracting system and the substitution of the 1994 revenue-sharing system with a tax-sharing system, the earnings by SOEs and revenues captured by government departments were no longer treated as part of the fiscal revenue. In 1992 the total extra-budgetary revenue was equivalent to about 98 per cent of the budgetary revenue. Out of the three sources of local government financing—budgetary revenue, extra-budgetary revenue and the off-budget revenue—the last has grown explosively. This off-budget gets extracted from various local sources—in some cases the off-budget is about three times the budgetary revenue. This includes users' fees, tax surcharges, bond issues, income from sale of state assets, a variety of local levies, and profit remittances of local enterprises (Zhang 1999).

In short, the fiscal system went through multiple transitions where in each step the regional governments progressively reduced dependence on budgetary transfer while necessarily increasing entitlements from other fiscal sources. Most such fiscal mechanisms drew upon S&T and innovation-based projects involving often re-appropriation of land. Regional growth path thus drew close the fiscal and science instruments.

S&T FOR ECONOMIC AND POLITICAL GOVERNANCE: CONCLUDING REMARKS

As new resource constraints emerge, local governments especially at the lower tiers are forced to take care of the increasing gap between receipts and expenditure by aligning with entrepreneurs and by undertaking new innovation and developmental projects. Such alignment removes effectively the boundary of a firm. The oversight of innovation and developmental projects that the government is expected to undertake, however, requires separation between government and business. Consequently, in the Chinese context the oversight gets replaced by a joint product of economic interests of business and governance functions of local government. Since governance considerations are non-pecuniary in nature they cannot translate claims into transactable property rights. In short China's institutions could not exhaustively codify property rights in pecuniary terms. Such failures in writing and in translating property rights were perhaps inevitable because rapid growth called for resources such as land, materials and knowledge, and China has been a new entrant in the capitalist path with little experience in developing markets and enterprises based on well-defined property relations. Necessarily transactions could be enforced by those who enjoyed power and the terms of transactions were settled in favour of the strategic manoeuvres of those in power. S&T and innovations as well as the developmental projects proved to be most beneficial for the non-pecuniary domain. Most rights in these domains are yet to emerge. Expectations become crucial determinant of expansion of economic activities and therefore of growth. This expectation in search of new resources found the most opportunity in S&T, innovation and developmental projects.

In China the government and business thus became virtually one. Inter-enterprise competition thus was rendered into inter-geography competition. Fiscal transfers progressively over the years made inter-geography states of affairs more iniquitous and forced regional governments to align with enterprises. Entrepreneurship in China thus cannot be interpreted as Schumpeterian since the visible hand of the state is pervasively present.

In conclusion, I argue that a reading of post-Mao reforms in China suggests a strong dependence of governance on dynamics of S&T and innovation. On the face of it this role appears to be statist. Indeed the strong influence of S&T and innovation on the governance of Chinese provinces and governments under the provinces has gone through ups and downs but the linkage in the post-reform period is unambiguously clear. S&T achieved this role not through creation of a market of rights instead, defining and leading local governmental land-based innovative science projects brought science and fiscal power together to shape the local government. Reading S&T as an autonomous system or merely as an input into innovation and the economic system enjoys certain dominance. However, little was known on the role of S&T for governance. This chapter has made an attempt to advance our understanding on this particular role of S&T.

The mechanism through which S&T undertakes a governance role is laid through a complex interdependent system of fiscal dynamics, economic reforms, and business enterprises. The much talked about role of a market in property rights defined unambiguously and completely in pecuniary terms I argued, could not exist in China because much of the emergent rights had non-pecuniary aspects. No wonder the entrepreneurship and the business enterprises that arose from transactions in such rights had to negotiate with and leverage the dominant political powers in their favour. This opened up a slow but definite convergence of entrepreneurial interests and business organization on one side with the powers in government on the other side. The result was a form of business and a form of governance that operated through myriad forms of resource generating, organizing, and accumulating functions.

Further, my approach to analysing China's S&T system led to setting up regions and cities competing for more political power to generate and organize resources and accumulate more. Inter-regional competition and not inter-enterprise competition is the defining bedrock of governance in China. The very intimate relationship between innovation and local government in China is a strong pointer to convergence of local governance with locally undertaken business and innovations. Consequently regions competing with each other suggest a departure from the decentralized governance thesis. Our examination into post-Reform China shows this new form of S&T-based innovation in league with local government as the arbiter. The central government repositioned several times the fiscal powers of the local governments who armed with varying powers over resources made significant use of S&T and innovation. Both theoretically and empirically my analysis showed how inconsequential a free entrepreneur is in China and how difficult it is for a proverbial firm to organize, generate, and accumulate resources.

This inquiry has now opened up a new frontier of research. It would be rewarding to look into the governance functions of S&T and innovation. An examination of this dimension in the context of many other countries is likely to generate a storehouse of empirical understanding from which a robust theory based upon such facts could be developed. Two important and related dimensions that were not examined were: (*a*) how does governance function affect and possibly even transform the research agenda, the S&T contents and the S&T organization, and (*b*) what are the modes of governance within S&T especially when S&T is poised to undertake political governance function. Both these questions are important for future research. Finally, we have for long been fed the utopian science for development ideal. This inquiry has revealed a dystopian shock where S&T as a party to the governance of a system is not one that could be described as ideal.

NOTES

1. Research paper publications (in English language) as covered by the SCOPUS database indicate that the number of papers from China was 7,012 in year 1989, was 15,339 in year 1995, 44,586 in year 2000, 152,423 in year 2005, and 232,887 in year 2008. Research papers published in Chinese language, when added to the above, and when papers not covered in this database are also considered, the growth appears to be remarkable. Papers from China in the top 2,000 most cited category were during 1995–8 for biology 4, for chemistry 21, for engineering 25 and for mathematics 35; these numbers grew to during 2005–8 respectively 34, 213, 175, and 252. I am indebted to Avinash Kshitij for the data on publications. For patents, see Appendix 10A.1.

2. Transactions in technical markets grew from 43,582.28 million yuan in 1998 to 88,417.13 million yuan in 2002 which further grew to 155,136.94 million yuan in 2005. Region-wise Shanghai grew from 3,141 million in 1998 to 17,170 million yuan in 2004, Beijing grew from 8,156 million to 42,500 million while Guizhou, for example, failed to grow with 141 in 1998 to 135 in 2004.

REFERENCES

Bagchi, A.K. 1980. 'Formulating a Science and Technology Policy: What Do We Know about Third World Countries?', *Economic and Political Weekly*, 15 (5–7): 303–10.

————. 2005. *Perilous Passage: Mankind and the Global Ascendancy of Capital.* Oxford: Rowman & Littlefield Publishers, Inc.

Bardhan, P. 2002. 'Decentralization of Governance and Development', *Journal of Economic Perspectives*, 16 (4): 185–205.

Blanchard, O. and A. Schleifer. 2001. 'Federalism With and Without Political Centralisation: China versus Russia', IMF Staff Papers, 48, 'Transition Economics: How Much Progress?': 171–9.

Cao, C., R.P. Stuttmeier, and D.F. Simon. 2006. 'China's 15-year Science and Technology Plan', *Physics Today*, December, pp. 38–43.

Changbiao, Z. 2002. 'Domestic Inter-regional Division of Labor and Trade, and Interregional Competitiveness', *Social Sciences in China*, 23 (3): 52–8.

Che, J. and Y. Qian. 1998. 'Institutional Environment, Community Government, and Corporate Governance: Understanding China's Township-village Enterprises', *Journal of Law, Economics, and Organization*, 14 (1): 1–23.

China. 2002. 'Science and Technology Indicators 2002', *The Yellow Book on Science and Technology*, Vol. 6, Ministry of Science and Technology, The People's Republic of China, Beijing.

Coase, R. 1960. 'The Problem of Social Cost', *Journal of Law and Economics*, 3: 1–44.

—————. 1988. *The Firm, the Market and the Law*. Chicago: Chicago University Press.

Cooke, P.N., M. Heidenreich, and H.J. Braczyk. 2004. *Regional Innovation Systems: The Role of Governance in a Globalized World*. London: Routledge.

Gu, S. 2001. 'Science and Technology Policy for Development: China's Experience in the Second Half of the Twentieth Century', *Science, Technology and Society*, 6 (1): 203–34.

Hu, A.G.Z. 2007. 'Technology Parks and Regional Economic Growth', *Research Policy*, 36 (1): 76–87.

Hu, A.G.Z. and G.H. Jefferson. 2004. 'Science and Technology in China', in L. Brandt and T.G. Rawski (eds), *China's Great Economic Transformation*. Cambridge: Cambridge University Press.

Jain, S. 2010. 'The Coasian Analysis of Externalities: Some Conceptual Difficulties', http://papers.ssrn.com/sol3/papers.cfm?abstract_id=1627622 (accessed 11 June 2012).

Jian, T., J. Sachs, and A.M. Warner. 1996. 'Trends in Regional Inequality in China', Working Paper 5412, National Bureau of Economic Research.

Jianzhong, D. 2002. 'Newly Born Private Enterprise Owners in China', *Social Sciences in China*, 23 (1): 124–34.

Kanbur, R. and X. Zhang. 2005. 'Fifty Years of Regional Inequality in China: A Journey through Central Planning, Reform, and Openness', *Review of Development Economics*, 9 (1): 87–106.

Li, Xibao. 2009. 'China's Regional Innovation Capacity in Transition: An Empirical Approach', *Research Policy*, 36 (2): 338–57.

Lyons, T.P. 1991. 'Interprovincial Disparities in China: Output and Consumption, 1952–87', *Economic Development and Cultural Change*, 39: 471–506.

Montinola, G., Y. Qian, B.R. Weingast. 1995.' Federalism, Chinese Style: The Political Basis for Economic Success in China', *World Politics*, 48 (1): 50–81.

Nee, V. and F.W. Young. 1991. 'Peasant Entrepreneurs in China's 'Second Economy': An Institutional Analysis', *Economic Development and Cultural Change*, 39 (2): 293–310.

North, D.C. 1981. *Structure and Change in Economic History*. New York: Norton.

Pan, A. 2008. 'China's Tax Reform and its Impact on U.S. Investments in China', *Corporate Business Taxation Monthly*, 9 (9): 9–45.

Parayil, G. and A.P. D'Costa. (eds). 2009. *The New Asian Innovation Dynamics: China and India in Perspective*. Houndmills: Palgrave Macmillan.

Park, A., S. Rozelle, C. Wong, and C. Ren. 1996. 'Distributional Consequences of Reforming Local Public Finance in China', *The China Quarterly*, 147 (September): 751–78.

Pei, M. 2002. 'China's Governance Crisis', *Foreign Affairs*, 81 (5): 96–109.

Peilin, L. 2002a. 'Introduction: Changes in Social Stratification in China since the Reform', *Social Sciences in China*, 23 (1): 42–47.

—————. 2002b. 'Great Transformation: End of Villages—A Study of the Villages Located in Southern Urban China', *Social Sciences in China*, 23 (3): 3–10.

Peng, Y. 2001. 'Chinese Villages and Townships as Industrial Corporations: Ownership, Governance, and Market Discipline', *American Journal of Sociology*, 106 (5): 1338–70.

Qian, Y. and B.R. Weingast. 1997. 'Federalism as a Commitment to Preserving Market Incentives', *Journal of Economic Perspectives*, 11 (4): 83–92.

Rodden, J. 2004. 'Comparative Federalism and Decentralisation: On Meaning and Measurement', *Comparative Politics*, 36 (4): 481–500.

Serger, S.S. and M. Breidne. 2007. 'China's Fifteen-Year Plan for Science and Technology: An Assessment', *Asia Policy*, (4): 135–64.

Shen, C., J. Jin, and H. Zou. 2006. 'Fiscal Decentralization in China: History, Impact, Challenges and Next Steps', http://siteresources.worldbank.org/ INTPUBSERV/Resources/477250-1164926394169/Zou.Chen.Jing.China.Fisc aldecentralizat:on.28nov2006.processed.pdf (accessed 24 May 2012).

Shulian, Z. 2000. 'A Review of the Reform in Chinese State-owned Enterprises over the Last Twenty Years', *Social Sciences in China*, 21 (1): 14–28.

Shultz, T.W. 1953. *The Economic Organization of Agriculture*. New York: McGraw Hill.

Wank, D.L. 1999. *Commodifying Communism: Business, Trust, and Politics in a Chinese City*. Cambridge: Cambridge University Press.

Wanli, Z. 2002. 'Twenty Years of Research on Stratified Social Structure in Contemporary China', *Social Sciences in China*, 23 (1): 48–58.

Wong, C.P.W. 1991. 'Central-local Relations in an Era of Fiscal Decline: The Paradox of Fiscal Decentralization in Post-Mao China', *The China Quarterly*, 128: 691–715.

Xue, L. 1997. 'A Historical Perspective of China's Innovation System Reform: A Case Study', *Journal of Engineering and Technology Management*, 14 (1): 67–81.

Xueyi, L. 2002. 'China's Modernization Process: Urbanization of Rural Areas', *Social Sciences in China*, 23 (1): 109–15.

Zhang, Le-Yin. 1999. 'Chinese Central-provincial Fiscal Relationships, Budgetary Decline and the Impact of the 1994 Fiscal Reform: An Evaluation', *The China Quarterly*, 157: 115–41.

Appendix 10A.1

Table 10A.1 Patent Development in China

	1990	2000	2005
Total	41,469	170,682	476,264
Invention type	10,137	51,747	173,327
Utility type	27,615	68,815	139,566
Design type	3,717	50,120	163,371

Source: *China Statistical Yearbook* (2006).

11

Have China and India Become More Innovative Since the Onset of Reforms in the Two Countries?

SUNIL MANI*

China and India are two of the fastest growing economies of the world. Their continued surge in economic growth both before and after the recent (2008) global financial crisis has further lent credence to the hypothesis that the economic growth registered by the two countries is sustainable as it is based more on technological improvements rather than by using more factor inputs such as labour and capital. Recent estimates of total factor productivity growth lend some empirical support to this hypothesis. Both the countries have also been receiving sizeable chunks of foreign direct investment (FDI) in R&D by multinational corporations (MNCs). There are also press reports of a number of innovations emanating from the two countries although systematic empirical evidence on this issue is found wanting in the literature.[1] One of the avowed objectives of economic reforms in both the countries (embracing of market socialism in China since

* This is the revised version of a paper that I presented at China–India conferences at the University of Edinburgh on 31 October 2009 and at the Institute of Development Studies Kolkata in December 2009. I am grateful to the participants at these seminars for their comments and suggestions. I also thank V.S. Sreekanth for research assistance. The usual disclaimer holds good.

1979 and economic liberalization in India since 1991) was to promote competition between firms. Along with the possibility of increased competition, one also sees that both the countries have become increasingly integrated with rest of the world although on these counts China has a higher degree of integration and better record than that of India's. All these factors may pave the way for both the economies to invest in innovative activities as the firms in both the countries are no longer concerned with competition in their respective domestic economies, but internationally as well. In the context, the purpose of the present chapter is to compare the two economies with respect to their innovation record since the onset of the reforms in the two countries which, as argued, earlier should have facilitated this process to flourish.

The chapter is structured into five sections. The next section maps out the larger context in which this study is conducted. The third section marshals a fair amount of quantitative evidence on whether the two economies are becoming innovative. The fourth section identifies some disquieting features that may act as an impediment to the process in the two countries. The final section concludes the arguments presented in the chapter.

THE CONTEXT

In this section I present the larger context against which one may analyse the nature and extent of innovative activities in these two fast growing economies in the world. The context has four components: (a) China and India are the fastest growing economies in terms of efficiency of resource use, (b) There has been considerable improvement in China and India's rank summary measures of global innovation, (c) There has been a perceptible increase in the knowledge-intensity of China and India's manufactured and service exports, and (d) Both the countries have achieved international competitiveness in high technology areas such as space technology. I now elaborate on these four areas.

Fastest Growing Economies in Terms of Efficiency of Resource Use

Productivity growth is well recognized as a measure of an economy's health. This is because an economy may show rapid growth by increasing the level of investments in the key factor inputs of capital and labour. But what is more important is the efficiency with which these factor inputs are combined to produce an increasing level of output. Economists usually measure this efficiency of resource by computing a summary measure such as total factor productivity growth (TFPG) although the empirical measures of TFPG is subject to the quirks of methodology and the type of data used.

Among the various empirical exercises comparing TFPG in China and India, one of the recent and more systematic studies is by Bosworth and Collins (2008), examining the sources of economic growth in the two countries over the 25 year period 1978–2004 using a simple growth accounting framework that produces estimates of the contribution of labour, capital, education, and total factor productivity for the three sectors of agriculture, industry, and services as well as for the aggregate economy. Their analysis incorporates recent data revisions in both countries and includes extensive discussion of the underlying data series. The growth accounts, derived by the authors, show a roughly equal division in each country between the contributions of capital accumulation and TFP to growth in output per worker over the period of analysis, and an acceleration of growth when the period is divided at 1993. However, the magnitude of output growth in China is roughly double that of India at the aggregate level, and also higher in each of the three sectors in both sub-periods. In China the post-1993 acceleration was concentrated mostly in industry, which contributed nearly 60 per cent of China's aggregate productivity growth. In contrast, 45 per cent of the growth in India in the second sub-period came in from services.

A second study is by Cates cited in *The Economist* (2009) who computed the TFPG in emerging economies over the period 1990–2008 for the results of this study. According to this study, China had the fastest annual rate of TFPG at around 4 per cent per annum closely followed by India at around 2.5 per cent per annum during this period. Now the important question is to explain the determinants of this fast productivity growth. The three determinants that Cates identifies are: (*a*) rate of adoption of existing and new technologies, (*b*) the pace of domestic scientific innovations, and (*c*) changes in the organization of production. Using a composite index of technology diffusion and innovation, Cates finds a strong correlation between the rate of increase in an economy's technological progress and its productivity growth. In other words the study also points to an increase in the rate of innovations (defined in terms of conventional input and output indicators such as R&D expenditure and patents) in the two countries although this is not exactly probed into in detail in the study.

Improvements in Global Innovation Ranking

A number of composite indices of global innovation are available these days. One such index is the 'EIU Innovation Index' by the Economist Intelligence Unit.[2] Between 2002–6 and 2004–8, China rose from 59th to 54th in this index. This is most impressive as the prediction was that this sort of a moving up in the ranking will occur only within five years. One reason for the jump is that China is making a concerted effort to build a more innovative economy by investing heavily in R&D and education. India, on the contrary, is advancing at a steady pace up the innovation ranks as the number of patents granted increases and both innovation-specific and broad environmental factors improve. From 58th in 2002–6 it advanced to 56th in 2004–8. In 2009–13, it is forecast to reach 54th.

Increasing Technological Intensity of Exports

By applying the UNIDO (2009) definition of high-technology products to the UN Comtrade data (according to the SITC, Rev. 3 classification system) on manufactured exports from China and India during the period 1988–2008, I derived the manufactured exports from China and India. This is presented in Table 11.1. It shows that the high-tech export intensity of both the countries has doubled during the period under consideration. If one undertakes a detailed decomposition of the components of these high-technology exports then it can be seen that China is specializing in electronics and telecommunications equipment, while in the case of India the most important high-technology manufactured products are pharmaceutical products.

China has in fact become the largest exporter of telecommunications equipment in the world: its share of the world market has actually increased from 2.36 per cent in 1992 to about 23 per cent in 2008. The above focus on manufactured products may actually underestimate the technological content of exports as far as India is concerned as the country is now increasingly diversifying into exports

Table 11.1 High-technology Intensity of Manufactured Exports from
China and India, 1988–2008
(high-technology exports as a per cent of manufactured exports)

Year	China	India
1988	–	7.32
1989	–	10.12
1990	–	9.17
1991	–	9.16
1992	20.09	6.86
1993	22.76	7.21
1994	23.91	7.50
1995	25.77	8.95
1996	30.59	10.16
1997	32.44	10.23
1998	36.19	9.15
1999	38.68	9.28
2000	39.59	9.59
2001	40.92	12.34
2002	43.71	12.17
2003	47.33	12.04
2004	48.16	11.90
2005	48.42	11.12
2006	47.65	13.41
2007	46.72	14.54
2008	44.59	16.94

Source: Computed from UN Comtrade.

of services. Approximately 40 per cent of India's exports is in the form
of services. Within the service exports, I denote the following four
as knowledge-intensive services, namely: (a) IT services, (b) R&D
services, (c) architectural, engineering, and technical services, and (d)
communications services. The combined share of these four in India's
services exports have increased from about 55 per cent in 1999–2000
to about 80 per cent in 2007–8 (Reserve Bank of India 2010).

A mere increase in the technology content of exports and especially manufacturing does not necessarily mean that the country is
becoming innovative if this increased exports are merely based on

imported components and if the country in question does not have a clear record with respect to objective definitions of innovative activity in these products. It may well be the case that the country is merely importing components and parts, assembling them and exporting the finished product with very little local value addition (D'Costa 2004).

International Competitiveness in Certain High Technology Areas such as Astronautic Technology

Both China and India have an active space research programme, spend considerable amount of public funds on space research, and have increasingly demonstrated technological capability in designing satellites and satellite launch vehicles and even undertaking commercial launches of satellites on behalf of other countries. In order to measure the external competitiveness of the astronautic sector of China and India among other space-faring nations, I rely on the space competitiveness index (SCI) computed by Futron Corporation (2009). The SCI evaluates the spacefaring nations across 40 individual metrics that represent the underlying economic determinants of space competitiveness. These metrics assess national space competitiveness in three major dimensions: government, human capital, and industry. The ranks obtained by the ten major spacefaring nations are presented in Table 11.2.

Table 11.2   India's Rank in the Space Competitiveness Index in 2008 and 2009

Rank	Country	Govern-ment	Human Capital	Industry	2009 Score	2008 Score (rank)
1	US	38.42	13.96	37.94	90.33	91.43(1)
2	Europe	19.32	9.03	18.46	46.80	48.07(2)
3	Russia	18.57	3.04	10.83	32.44	34.06(3)
4	Japan	15.80	1.72	3.65	21.16	14.46(7)
5	China	12.42	2.98	4.06	19.46	17.88(4)
6	Canada	12.89	3.42	1.82	18.13	16.94(6)
7	India	12.24	1.71	1.39	15.34	17.51(5)
8	South Korea	8.39	1.34	2.31	12.03	8.88(8)
9	Israel	6.72	0.56	1.42	8.70	8.37(9)
10	Brazil	6.10	0.49	0.50	7.08	4.96(10)

Source: Futron Corporation (2009).

India was ranked fifth in 2008. Its rank has since slipped to 7 out of 10, although its score is better than Brazil, a country that is very strong in the aeronautical sector.

Thus on all these four broad indicators of innovation outcomes, both China and India show considerable improvements over time. However these indicators although suggestive, do not really prove that the two countries are becoming innovative. In order to measure the innovative activity, following Mani (2009), I rely on two of the conventional indicators that economists continue to employ to measure a country's record with respect to innovations. This exercise is the theme of the next section.

EVIDENCE ON INNOVATIVE ACTIVITY IN CHINA AND INDIA

Of the two indicators that economists usually employ to measure innovation, one is an input indicator, namely R&D expenditures and the second is an output indicator, namely the number of patents granted. Notwithstanding the limitations of these indicators, these are the only ones that are available for both the countries for sufficiently long periods of time. Further the definitions of both the indicators are standard across the two countries.

R&D Expenditure

In order to compare the Gross Expenditure on R&D (GERD) of the two countries, I have converted the GERD in national currencies to US dollars. Apart from the absolute levels of GERD, I also present the GERD intensities. These are presented in Table 11.3.

In both absolute and relative terms China's GERD has increased tremendously during the period under consideration. For instance, it has increased at an annual average rate of 22 per cent during the period compared to India's growth rate of 11 per cent. Second, China's research intensity has virtually trebled during this period, while India's has more or less remained constant. Finally China used to spend two times that of India towards the beginning of the period but this has increased to almost six times now. This better performance of China in terms of R&D investments may be attributable to the country having a more clearly articulated innovation policy with clear targets on

Table 11.3   Investments in Overall R&D in China and India, 1995–2006 (absolute values of GERD are in billions of US$ and relative values are GERD to GDP ratios in percentages)

Year	GERD China	GERD India	Ratio of China to India	GERD/GDP China	GERD/GDP India
1995	4.22	2.04	2.07	0.57	0.72
1996	4.89	2.11	2.31	0.57	0.69
1997	6.15	2.45	2.51	0.64	0.71
1998	6.66	2.57	2.59	0.65	0.76
1999	8.21	2.90	2.83	0.76	0.77
2000	10.83	3.20	3.38	0.90	0.81
2001	12.60	3.43	3.67	0.95	0.84
2002	15.57	3.51	4.44	1.07	0.81
2003	18.62	3.86	4.82	1.13	0.80
2004	23.77	4.35	5.46	1.23	0.78
2005	29.63	4.91	6.04	1.33	0.75
2006	37.03	6.35	5.83	1.42	0.88

Source: Chinese data are from OECD (2008); and Indian data are from Department of Science and Technology (2009).

R&D investments coupled with institutional changes and instruments to achieve those set targets within the stipulated time horizon. For instance, the Chinese government has set as a goal to increase R&D intensity to 2 per cent of GDP by 2010 and 2.5 per cent by 2020 (OECD 2008, 111). India too had a target of research intensity reaching 2 per cent by 2006–7,[3] but in actuality it is woefully short of this target. Care has to be exercised while interpreting these figures to mean that the overall relative investments in R&D in India have actually declined. This is because of certain peculiarities with respect to India's R&D performance. See Table 11.4 for a sector-wide distribution of R&D in the two countries. Even now, in India the government accounts for over 63 per cent of the total R&D performed within the country although the share of government has tended to come down over time. This has been accompanied by an increase in R&D investments by business enterprises which now account for about 30 per cent—a significant increase from just 14 per cent in 1991. For China the similar percentage is about 71 per cent by business enterprises and research institutes (read government) account for only 19 per cent: China has actually gone through an elaborate process of paring down the role of governmental research institutes in the performance of R&D by converting a large number of these institutes into business enterprises. As a result the number of government research institutes (GRIs) in China reduced significantly from 5,867 in 1991 to about 1,149 GRIs in 2004.[4] Increase in the share of R&D performed by business enterprises is generally considered to be a desirable trend as business enterprises tend to implement or productionize the results of their research more quickly than the government sector where much of the research does not fructify into products and processes for the country as a whole.[5]

Table 11.4   Evolution of the Chinese and Indian National Systems of Innovation, 1991–2007
(sector-wide performances of GERD, figures are percentage share of each sector in total GERD)

Year	Government		Business Enterprises		Higher Education	
	China	India	China	India	China	India
1991	51.6	86.16	39.8	13.84	8.6	–
1996	44.9	78.26	43.2	21.74	11.8	–
2000	31.2	77.21	60.3	18.46	8.6	4.33
2007	19.2	67.91	72.3	27.71	8.5	4.38

Source: OECD (2008) and Department of Science and Technology (2009).

The business enterprise sector in both the countries is now emerging as the core of the NSI (National System of Innovation) in both the countries although it is much more pronounced in the case of China than in India. In China, the business sector has become the largest R&D performer in terms of S&T inputs and outputs. According to these indicators, the business sector plays a dominant role in the S&T development of China. However, due to various historical and structural reasons, the efficiency and the innovation capacity of the business sector are still insufficient, despite a large and rapid increase in scale and scope. While S&T activities in government research institutes and the higher education sector have some similarities, the business sector is different from the previous two sectors in several aspects.

The R&D expenditure of the business enterprise sector of both the countries has risen, once again the Chinese annual growth rate at 31 per cent is much higher than that recorded for India and as a result the R&D expenditure of Chinese enterprises is almost 16 times its counterparts in India (Table 11.5). It must however be noted that both Chinese and Indian firms spent only less than a per cent of their sales turnover on R&D.

It looks as if the business enterprises in both China and India are becoming the core of both country's NSI. However OECD (2008) remarks that 'it would be wrong to conclude that firms already form the backbone of the Chinese NSI'. To a significant extent, the rapid increase in business sector R&D has resulted mechanically from the conversion of some public research institutes into business entities often without creating the conditions for them to become innovation-oriented firms.

Table 11.5 Business Enterprise R&D Expenditures in Both China and India, 1999–2006 (US$ billion)

Year	China	Growth rate (%)	India	Growth rate (%)	Ratio of China to India
1999	4.07		0.61		6.64
2000	6.49	59	0.59	–3.59	10.98
2001	7.62	17	0.62	4.75	12.30
2002	9.53	25	0.68	9.36	14.06
2003	11.61	22	0.75	10.85	15.46
2004	15.89	37	0.99	31.38	16.10
2005	20.24	27	1.37	38.79	14.78
2006	26.33	30	1.64	19.92	16.03

Source: OECD (2008) and Department of Science and Technology (2009).

If both Chinese and Indian business enterprises have increased their investments in intramural R&D, it will also be interesting to see the relationship between these investments and the costs incurred in importing technology from abroad. Combining the two aspects, I define a ratio called the average propensity to adapt. This is defined as the ratio of intramural R&D in business enterprises to cost incurred in technology purchases from abroad (Figure 11.1). If this ratio is greater than unity, it could be argued that under *cetris paribus* conditions, firms are developing local technological capabilities.

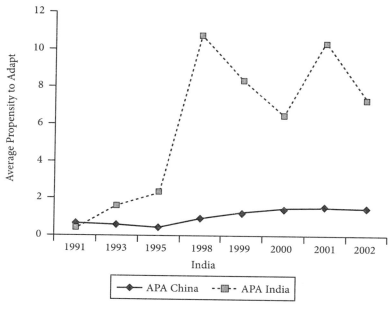

Figure 11.1 Average Propensity to Adapt in Chinese and Indian Business Enterprises, 1991–2002

Source: Computed from OECD (2008) and Department of Science and Technology (2009).

From the above, it could be seen that Indian business enterprises despite their lower levels of investments in R&D have a better propensity to adapt and thereby develop local capabilities compared to their Chinese counterparts. Although it must be said that both Chinese and Indian companies are increasingly improving their propensity to adapt. The exercise is admittedly very limited in terms of its scope. Further studies of a case study nature are very much required before one can draw strong conclusions or inferences of this type.

R&D Outsourcing

Another interesting aspect of R&D in business enterprises is the fact that both China and India have become important recipients of R&D outsourcing deals. R&D off-shoring started in India way back in 1984 with Texas Instruments setting up its first R&D centre in

Bangalore. China's R&D off-shoring trend began in the early 1990s with Motorola being the first company to take advantage of the local talent and low cost in China. No precise estimates of the size of this sector in both the countries exist. According to some private estimates[6] that are available, there exist 920 MNCs having 1,100 R&D centres in China. The number till December 2008 for India was about 671 MNCs with 781 R&D centres. Data on receipts under R&D services are lacking in the case of China, and in the case of India it has increased from US$ 221 million in 2004–5 to US$ 1,385 million in 2008–9 (Reserve Bank of India 2010, p. 580). Availability of high quality scientists and engineers and the lower costs of performing R&D are identified as the main reasons for the growth of this R&D outsourcing. Most of this R&D outsourcing is actually confined to certain high technology industries such as telecommunications equipment, information technology, pharmaceuticals, and biotech industries. Available studies in the case of China (Lan and Liang 2006) has shown that foreign R&D centres are hardly connected with the national system of innovation of China as their linkages are often enough with their own parent firms abroad. This is likely to be the same for India as well.

Industry-wide Distribution

In both the countries, R&D by business enterprises is concentrated in about 10 industries (Table 11.6), although the degree of concentration is slightly higher in India. Another interesting issue brought out by the table is the fact that China appears to specialize in the creation of electronics and telecommunications technologies while in the case of India it is the pharmaceutical technologies. In fact both the countries have become very important world players in these two industries. In other words, based on this data, it may not be incorrect to state that the NSI of the two countries are to a certain extent dominated and shaped by the Sectoral System of Innovation (SSI) of the two industries, electronics and telecommunications in the case of China and pharmaceuticals in the case of India. However, there is one manufacturing industry where both the countries are concentrating on, namely the transport equipment industry. This is also an industry where a number of high profile new product launches by domestic manufacturers have occurred.[7]

Table 11.6 Industry-wide Distribution of Business-wide R&D Expenditures in China and India

China (RMB 100 million)	2000	2003	2004
Electronics and telecommunication equipment	79.82	163.54	226.21
Transport equipment	42.27	95.65	127.47
Electrical machinery	29.49	74.49	93.43
Share of top 5 (%)	55.53	61.76	63.23
Share of top 10 (%)	74.95	80.27	80.51

India (INR million)	1999–2000	2000–1	2001–2	2002–3	2003–4	2004–5	2005–6
Drugs and Pharmaceuticals	478.98	554.15	739.63	1,026.79	1,441.43	2,237.12	2,826.86
Transportation	431.37	451.96	528.61	434.27	546.50	862.80	1,047.20
Electricals and Electronics Equipment	186.34	178.63	227.30	170.54	197.68	290.42	375.40
Information and Technology	110.36	156.10	173.60	110.02	194.28	221.24	306.63
Chemicals (Other than Fertilizers)	273.64	308.06	218.08	194.75	213.18	238.62	300.87
Total for top 5	1,480.69	1,648.90	1,887.22	1,936.38	2,593.08	3,850.20	4,856.96
Share of top 5 (%)	67.98	68.44	67.70	69.54	71.19	75.85	77.48
Biotechnology	54.97	50.32	53.78	108.72	136.84	187.51	277.74
Metallurgical Industries	83.89	80.11	42.29	82.61	104.43	131.83	142.87
Misc. Mechnical Engineering Industries	36.46	41.96	35.12	74.89	86.67	110.86	137.31
Soaps, Cosmetics Toilet Preparations	56.45	44.52	112.12	142.64	155.40	173.88	137.22
Telecommunications	30.51	69.13	76.57	55.04	92.18	81.81	98.67
Total for top 10	1,810.95	2,003.38	2,274.80	2,469.81	3,239.78	4,611.94	5,728.26
Share of top 10 (%)	83.14	83.15	81.61	88.69	88.94	90.86	91.38

Source: OECD (2008, p. 117) and Department of Science and Technology (2009).

Productivity of R&D

It is seen that China invests far greater amounts on R&D compared to that of India. So it will be instructive to analyse the productivity differential in R&D investments in the two countries. Admittedly this is a complex issue to be tackled. Nevertheless, a first attempt is made in terms of relating R&D investments in the two countries to their respective output in terms of patents granted. However, there are different types of patents, national, foreign and triadic.[8] Further there are utility and design patents. Utility patents are for new inventions where design patents are for ornamental changes in existing products. Given the fact that both national and triadic patents are very specific and depend on the norms adopted by individual patents, following the usual practice in the literature, I analyse the US utility patenting behaviour of Chinese and Indian inventors. These are then related to the GERD in both the countries to arrive at the amount of GERD per US utility patent (Table 11.7). The resulting exercise points to two important results: first, China's productivity has virtually remained constant over the years while India's productivity shows a definite increase over time and second, the productivity differential between the two countries has actually increased over time with India's productivity being more than the Chinese one. However, given the rudimentary nature of this exercise, one has to be careful in drawing strong conclusions about the productivity differential between the two giants, especially when the earlier results on TFP presents a better picture for China. This is an important issue that needs a further empirical probe at much disaggregated levels.

So based on this analysis of R&D expenditures it is somewhat clear that Chinese electronics and telecommunications sectors and the Indian pharmaceutical sectors have become more innovative since the onset of reforms. I propose to follow this argument through with an analysis of the patenting behaviour of the two countries.

Patenting Behaviour

R&D investment is an input measure of innovation while patents are an output measure. There are three different types of patents, namely patenting by Chinese and Indian inventors in the US, triadic patents and national patents in both China and India. I examine the record

Table 11.7 Productivity of R&D Investments: China vs India, 1995–2006
(GERD is in US$ billion, Patents granted are in numbers; productivity is US$ billion per patent granted)

Year	GERD China	GERD India	Patents China	Patents India	China Productivity	India Productivity	Ratio of China to India
1995	4.22	2.04	62	37	0.07	0.06	1.233
1996	4.89	2.11	46	35	0.11	0.06	1.760
1997	6.15	2.45	62	47	0.10	0.05	1.901
1998	6.66	2.57	72	85	0.09	0.03	3.059
1999	8.21	2.90	90	112	0.09	0.03	3.527
2000	10.83	3.20	119	131	0.09	0.02	3.723
2001	12.60	3.43	195	178	0.06	0.02	3.350
2002	15.57	3.51	289	249	0.05	0.01	3.828
2003	18.62	3.86	297	342	0.06	0.01	5.549
2004	23.77	4.35	404	363	0.06	0.01	4.907
2005	29.63	4.91	402	384	0.07	0.01	5.767
2006	37.03	6.35	661	481	0.06	0.01	4.245

Source: Table 11.3 and USPTO.

of the two countries in each of these. I begin with the US patenting record of the two countries, which for reasons seen above are one of the most important indicators about innovative activity. Both the countries have improved their US patenting record since the onset of reforms (Table 11.8), again China having more patents than India. In fact the difference between the two countries' record with respect to patenting has increased over time. But there is an important difference between the two countries. India has, relatively speaking, more utility patents (defined as those for new inventions). Increasingly, most of the Chinese patents are design patents accounting for as much as one-third of the total patents. Finally, both China and India together account for much of the patents that inventors from the BRICS have secured in the USA.

Technology-wide distribution of these patents also shows some important differences between the two countries although at the very same time it supports the finding that the analysis of R&D expenditure had indicated (in Table 11.6). Two important differences are discernible. First, Chinese inventors have focused more on developing electrical, electronic and telecommunications technologies while Indian inventors have been focusing much more on pharmaceutical and chemical technologies. Second, Indian inventors are, relatively speaking, more specialized (as the country has a much higher concentration in fewer technologies) than their Chinese counter parts. Finally, of the top fifteen classes of technologies emphasized by Chinese and Indian inventors there are only three classes in which both the countries have common interest. These are in pharmaceuticals (Class 424), telecommunications (Class 370) and software (Class 707). Of these three, India has a lead in the first while in the latter two classes both the countries have the same level of patents.

Another important issue is of the ownership of these patents, (See Table 11.9). Although there are some differences between the two countries, there are some important common points. In both countries many of the US patents are held by foreign companies, their level being much higher in China due essentially to the larger number of foreign companies in the two countries. However, over the last two years (namely in 2009 and 2010), the share of foreign enterprises in Chinese patenting in the US has tended to come down quite dramatically. For instance, the domestic business enterprises like the telecom

Table 11.8 Trends in US Patenting by Chinese and Indian Inventors (number of patents granted by the USPTO)

Year	Utility Patents			Design Patents			Total Patents			Ratio of Utility to Total Patents		
	Total world	China	India	Total world	China	India	Total world	China	India	Total world	China	India
1979	48,854	0	14	3,119	0	0	51,973	0	14	0.94	–	1
1991	96,511	50	22	9,569	2	1	106,080	52	23	0.91	0.96	0.96
2000	157,494	119	131	17,413	42	0	174,907	161	131	0.90	0.74	1.00
2001	166,035	195	178	16,871	70	1	182,906	265	179	0.91	0.74	0.99
2002	167,331	289	249	15,451	101	6	182,782	390	255	0.92	0.74	0.98
2003	169,023	297	342	16,574	127	7	185,597	424	349	0.91	0.70	0.98
2004	164,290	404	363	15,695	192	9	179,985	596	372	0.91	0.68	0.98
2005	143,806	402	384	12,951	163	16	156,757	565	400	0.92	0.71	0.96
2006	173,772	661	481	20,965	309	19	194,737	970	500	0.89	0.68	0.96
2007	157,282	772	546	24,062	462	24	181,344	1,234	570	0.87	0.63	0.96
2008	157,772	1,225	634	25,565	647	37	183,337	1,872	671	0.86	0.65	0.94
2009	167,349	1,655	679	23,116	613	38	190,465	2,268	717	0.88	0.73	0.95
2010	219,614	2,567	1,098	22,799	645	37	222,271	3,302	1,135	0.99	0.80	0.97

Source: Computed from USPTO.

equipment manufacturer, Huawei and universities such as Tsinghua have vastly improved their patenting record at the USPTO in 2009 and 2010. Domestic enterprises in both the countries have thus somewhat dissimilar levels of patenting. There are, however, two important differences: first, Indian Government Research Institutes (GRIs) and universities (actually almost entirely GRIs) have a higher share than their Chinese counterparts and second, Chinese individuals have a higher patenting record than Indian individuals.

Table 11.9   Ownership of US Patents, Cumulative 1963–2008 (percentage shares)

Patent ownership	China	India
Foreign	53.56	40.26
Individually owned patents	27.96	9.95
Domestic business enterprises	13.21	14.14
GRIs and universities	5.28	35.67
Total	100	100

Source: Computed from USPTO.

The higher share of Indian GRI's is due to two reasons. First, the CSIR network of laboratories had an explicit strategy of increasing their patent portfolio and this strategy was set into motion since the late 1990s although this does appear to be tapering off since 2003 (Mani 2009). Second, I had noted earlier that Chinese NSI had gone through a massive reorganization all through the 1990s wherein a number of hitherto GRIs were converted to business enterprises. The exercise thus shows that increasingly the surge in US patenting by both China and India is largely contributed by foreign R&D centres which are operating from the two countries and as such the surge in patents need not necessarily imply that the two countries are becoming more innovative. Rather the more correct inference may be that the two countries have indeed become important locations for innovative activities. The business press is replete with a large number of innovations that MNCs were able to carry out from the countries.

I continue the analysis with triadic patents from China and India. These patents being taken for the same family of technologies from three different patent offices (namely, the US, European, and Japanese) signify a very high level of quality as it is more difficult and costly not just to secure these patents but also to maintain them. Consequently firms and research institutes will in all probability self-select their best inventions to patent. So an increase in the number of triadic patents secured indicates not just your ability to innovate but also the quality of innovation (See Table 11.10).

Table 11.10 Triadic Patents Granted to Chinese and Indian Inventors, 1990–2006 (number of triadic patents)

Year	Brazil	Russian Federation	China	India	South Africa	World
1990	10	21	12	12	13	32,417
1991	6	36	12	8	18	29,786
1992	13	45	17	7	33	29,922
1993	22	34	16	8	32	30,794
1994	12	51	17	6	21	32,414
1995	17	60	21	11	25	35,731
1996	18	58	23	14	29	39,098
1997	29	69	43	22	34	41,515
1998	29	94	47	34	35	42,878
1999	31	60	62	40	31	45,507
2000	33	69	84	45	35	47,162
2001	47	56	114	85	24	45,565
2002	44	48	178	106	28	46,120
2003	51	51	252	120	30	48,093
2004	51	55	290	122	33	50,727
2005	56	64	384	133	31	50,569
2006	65	63	484	136	30	51,579
Growth rate (%)	18.77	10.38	27.86	20.98	8.39	3.04

Source: OECD (2009).

China and India have the highest growth rate and also accounts for the largest share among the BRICS.

National Patents

In both countries, there has been a tremendous surge in national patents. See Table 11.11. But in both the countries, most of the national patenting is still dominated by foreign inventors although the share of domestic inventors has been showing some fluctuations. Of the two, the share of domestic inventors is higher in China and in the case of India although the share of domestic inventors kept on rising (with some fluctuations) until 2005, it has started declining since that year. My hypothesis is that with the TRIPS compliance of Indian patent regime since 1 January 2005, MNCs have rushed to patenting in India so that Indian companies and especially the pharmaceutical ones may find it difficult to do incremental innovations.

DISQUIETING FEATURES

Although Chinese and Indian business enterprises have increased their investments in R&D, the surge in patenting that has occurred since the initiation of reforms is largely attributable to foreign enterprises that are located in the two countries. Domestic enterprises in the two countries, barring notable exceptions, are not innovative. Based on our review of the relevant literature and discussions with industry associations, there are two disquieting features or constraints that the NSI of the two countries suffer from, although it may be argued that the intensity of these two as constraints may vary across the two countries. The two constraints are: (*a*) availability and quality of scientists and engineers of the type that can innovate, and (*b*) financing of innovative activity. Of the two, there is now some evidence of the former issue as a constraint in both the countries, while the latter one is a typical constraint more in the case of India.

Availability and Quality of Scientists and Engineers

Although it is generally held that both China and India have a copious supply of scientists and engineers, the fact is that the real supply of scientists and engineers engaged in R&D and innovative activities is not large. For instance, in the case of China, OECD (2008) estimates that even if the current high levels of growth in the number of researchers is maintained there will be a large gap between the demand for and supply of scientific manpower. The OECD (2008, p. 329) argument runs as follows:

> [T]he Chinese government aims to raise R&D intensity from 1.34% of GDP (2005) to 2% in 2010 and 2.5% in 2020. Despite the rapid

Table 11.11 Trends in Patenting within China and India: Domestic vs Foreign Inventors (number of patents granted by SIPO and Controller General of Patents, Trade Marks, Designs, and Geographical Indications)

China	Domestic	Foreign	Ratio of Domestic to Foreign	India	Domestic	Foreign	Ratio of Domestic to Foreign
1995	1,530	1,863	0.82	1994–5	476	1,283	0.37
1996	1,395	1,581	0.88	1995–6	415	1,118	0.37
1997	1,532	1,962	0.78	1996–7	293	614	0.48
1998	1,655	3,078	0.54	1997–8	619	1,225	0.51
1999	3,097	4,540	0.68	1998–9	645	1,155	0.56
2000	6,177	6,506	0.95	1999–00	557	1,324	0.42
2001	5,395	10,901	0.49	2000–1	399	919	0.43
2002	5,868	15,605	0.38	2001–2	654	937	0.70
2003	11,404	25,750	0.44	2002–3	494	885	0.56
2004	18,241	31,119	0.59	2003–4	945	1,524	0.62
2005	20,705	32,600	0.64	2004–5	764	1,147	0.67
2006	25,077	32,709	0.77	2005–6	1,396	2,924	0.48
2007	31,945	36,003	–	2006–7	1,907	5,632	0.34
2008	46,590	47,116	–	2007–8	3,173	12,088	0.26
				2008–9	2,541	13,520	0.19
				2009–10	1,725	4,443	0.39

Source: Ministry of Science and Technology (2007), State Intellectual Property office of the PRC (2008), Controller General of Patents, Designs and Trade Marks (various issues).

growth of researchers in recent years and the expansion of the tertiary education sector, future needs may not be met. To project the future need for researchers, a simple estimate was made, based on the following assumptions: GDP growth at 8% on average until 2020, ratio of R&D intensity to GDP of 2.5% in 2020, and the wage level and the proportion of labour costs in total R&D expenditure equal to that of Korea in 2005. The result of the simple estimation suggests that raising China's R&D intensity to 2.5% of GDP may imply that the need for 3.7 million researchers by 2020, *i.e.* an additional 2.6 million researchers from the number in 2005. To meet this demand means an additional 170 000 researchers each year, or average annual growth of 8.3%. From 1998 to 2005 the average annual increase in researchers was 90 457. Therefore, even if the current level of growth in the absolute number of researchers is maintained, there will be a large gap. The average growth rate of researchers was 12.7% a year from 1998 to 2005; this is likely to be difficult to sustain in the future, as the number of researchers increases. However, for this reason, the gap in the supply of additional researchers is expected to be more accurate from 2010.

Similar is the case in India. The recent growth performance of knowledge-intensive industries in India is prompting many commentators to feel that India is transforming itself into a knowledge-based economy. The copious supply of technically trained human resources is considered to be one of the most important reasons for this growth performance. However, of late, the industry has been complaining of serious shortages in technically trained manpower. For instance, a study conducted by the Federation of Indian Chambers of Commerce and Industry (FICCI 2007) has revealed that the rapid growth in the globally integrated Indian economy has led to a huge demand for skilled human resources. However, lack of quality in the higher education sector has become a hindrance in filling the gap. The survey, based on a study conducted in 25 sectors, also showed that currently there is a shortage of about 25 per cent skilled manpower in the engineering sector.

In order to see the present supply of scientists and engineers for R&D, I introduce three categories of human resources in science and engineering:[9] human resource in science and technology (HRST), R&D personnel, and researchers. These are then estimated for both China and India. I estimate both the total and density as well (Table 11.12).

Table 11.12 Stock of Scientists and Engineers Engaged in R&D in China and India (full time equivalent basis as of 2005)

		HRST	R&D Personnel	Researchers
China	Total (million numbers)	70.34	1.36	1.18
	Density (per 10,000 labour force)	914.98	17.69	15.35
India	Total (million numbers)	40.20	0.39	0.15
	Density (per 10,000 labour force)	933.49	9.06	3.48

Source: Computed from OECD (2008), Department of Science and Technology (2009), and National Council of Applied Economic Research (2005).

On both the total number and on density as well, the numbers are far less than what one finds for other developed countries including that of Korea, an erstwhile developing country now having joined the club of developed countries.

Two issues have an impact on the potential supply of scientists and engineers, especially for domestic business enterprises. The first is an issue that has been in existence for a long time, namely the migration of high-skilled personnel from China and India to the west. There is every indication that this flow has increased in recent times. The second one is the growing FDI in R&D in both the countries. Foreign R&D centres are able to offer better incentives, both pecuniary and otherwise to domestic researchers and R&D personnel than domestic business enterprises. As a result the small stock of scientists and engineers may get attracted to the foreign R&D centres and a 'crowding out' of sorts may take place. Lan and Liang (2006) have already noted this for China and my own discussions (although not based on a statistically random sample) with domestic research-oriented firms have indicated this possibility.

Apart from this supply, doubts also have been expressed about the quality of the science and engineering workforce in both the countries although the quality is often difficult to measure in an objective manner.

Fortunately the governments in both China and India are very much aware of this constraint and over the last few years have instituted a large number of programmes to increase both the supply of science and technology personnel in the two countries and to improve its quality as well. China, especially has put in place many schemes to even reverse the 'brain drain' from the country although India is depending much more on market means to reverse high-skilled migration from the country.

Financing of Innovation

Studies done across the world and especially the innovation surveys have time and again brought to the fore the importance of financing innovations as this is an area which is characterized by severe market failures. I discuss this constraint in the context of the two countries.

According to OECD (2007) some important constraints on China's financial system affect innovative activity in the business enterprise sector:

- China's financial system does not meet the funding needs of private firms, notably SMEs. The capital market is underdeveloped and SMEs find it difficult to secure loans since banks favour large companies, particularly SOEs. Smaller, privately owned firms thus largely depend on self-funding. Recent initiatives to address this issue propose funding mechanisms to support science and technology and innovation activities; and
- There is a severe lack of capital for financing new ventures, which are one important source of innovation. China lacks both the expertise and the necessary legal and regulatory conditions for an adequately functioning venture capital system. Domestic venture capital firms have been set up by the government, at national or provincial level, and are run by government officials who do not always have adequate technical, commercial, or managerial skills.

India has two types of financial schemes for financing innovations: first, research grants and loans at concessional rates of interest and second, tax incentives for committing resources to R&D. First, recent analysis by Mani (2010a) showed that much if not all of the small number of research grants and loans available for financing innovations (such as those by the Technology Development Board) are directed largely at the public sector although, as we have just demonstrated many of the innovations actually emanate from private sector enterprises. In short, there is a mismatch in the financing of innovations in the sense that research grants and concessional loans are not directed towards those sectors which are active in innovations. Second, the country has a tax incentive scheme for encouraging more investments in R&D. These incentives have been correctly fine-tuned to encourage innovations in ten high and medium technology-based industries which are at the same time active in innovative activity.

Mani (2010a) attempted to estimate the coefficient of elasticity of R&D with respect to tax foregone as a result of this incentive scheme. The elasticity of R&D expenditure with respect to tax foregone as a result of the operation of the R&D tax incentive is less than unity for all the relevant industries, although it is significant only in the case of the chemicals industry. In two of the industries, namely in automotive and electronic industries, the elasticity is even negative, although not significant. From this the reasonable interpretation that is possible is that tax incentives do not have any influence on R&D, except possibly in the chemicals industry where they have some influence although even in this case the change in R&D as a result of tax incentives is less than the amount of tax foregone. This lack of significant relationship between R&D and tax foregone can be rationalized by the fact that the tax subsidy covers only a very small percentage share (on an average 6 per cent) of R&D undertaken by the enterprises in the four broad industry groups. So our conclusion is that for a tax incentive to be effective in raising R&D expenditures it must form a significant portion of R&D investments by an enterprise. It is not thus a determinant of R&D investments by enterprises for the present.

* * *

China and India are definitely on a higher economic growth path, although the contribution of technology to economic growth is still not very clearly estimated. There is evidence to show that innovative activities in the industrial sector in both the countries have shown some significant increases during the post-reform process. Knowledge content of both domestic output and exports is increasing in both the countries. The Chinese NSI is dominated by the SSI of the electronics and telecommunications industries and in the case of India it is led by the SSI of the pharmaceutical industry. In both the countries, increasingly much of the innovative activities are contributed by MNCs. In other words, both China and India have become important locations for innovative activities. There is even some macro-evidence to show that the productivity of R&D investments in India is higher than in China, although this proposition requires careful empirical scrutiny before firm conclusions can be reached. However, a continued rise in innovative activity is limited by the availability of finance and of good quality scientists and engineers. Although the available supply appears to be very productive, it is important that to sustain this on a long-term basis and also to spread the innovation culture to other areas of the industrial establishment, concerted efforts will have to be made to increase both the quantity and quality of scientific manpower. Fortunately, the governments are aware of this problem and have started initiating a number of steps towards easing the supply of technically trained personnel. The governments still have to rethink financial support schemes by reducing as much as possible the distortions that are currently in this area.

NOTES

1. For a detailed count of these see, *Business Week*, http://www.businessweek.com/magazine/toc/05_34/B3948chinaindia.htm (accessed 5 April 2010).

2. The Economist Intelligence Unit's Innovation Index analyses the innovation performance of 82 economies. It is based on countries' innovation output, as measured by the number of patents granted by the patent offices of the US, European Union, and Japan, and innovation inputs, based on the Economist Intelligence Unit's Business Environment Ranking (BER) model. The Index measures the following direct innovation inputs: R&D as a percentage of GDP, the quality of local research infrastructure, the education of the workforce, technical skills, the quality of information, and communications technology infrastructure and broadband penetration. The innovation environment includes political conditions, market opportunities, policy towards free enterprise, policy towards foreign investment, foreign trade and exchange controls, taxes, financing, the labour market, and infrastructure.

3. See Government of India, 2003, http://www.india.gov.in/outerwin.php?id=http://dst.gov.in (accessed 9 April 2010).

4. For detailed account of this see Gu and Lundavall (2006) and Schaaper (2009).

5. Governmental R&D in India is expended by atomic energy, defence, space, health, and agricultural sectors. The spillover of government research to civilian use is very much limited in the Indian context although in more recent times conscious efforts have been made by the government and it is slowly beginning to

produce results. This especially so in the area of astronautic research. For details see Mani (2010b).

6. http://zinnov.com/blog/?p=160 (accessed 6 April 2010).

7. For instance, the launch of the small car, Tata Nano in the case of India.

8. Triadic patent families are defined by the OECD as a set of patents taken at the European Patent Office (EPO), the Japan Patent Office (JPO), and granted by the US Patent and Trademark Office (USPTO), to protect the same invention. In terms of statistical analysis, indicators on triadic patent families improve the international comparability of patent-based statistics (no home advantage). Furthermore, patents that belong to the family are typically of higher value (as regards additional costs and delays involved in extending protection to other countries).

9. The definition of HRST is broad and covers 'people actually or potentially employed in occupations requiring at least a first university degree' in S&T, which includes all fields of science, technology, and engineering. R&D personnel, as defined by the OECD *Frascati Manual* (2002), are 'all persons employed directly on R&D', which includes those providing direct services such as R&D managers, administrators and clerical staff. The *Frascati Manual* defines researchers as 'professionals engaged in the conception or creation of new knowledge, products, processes, methods and systems and in the management of the projects concerned'.

REFERENCES

Bosworth, B. and S.M. Collins. 2008. 'Accounting for Growth: Comparing China and India', *Journal of Economic Perspectives*, 22 (1): 45–66.

Cates, A. cited in *The Economist*. 2009. 'Secret Sauce', *The Economist*, 12 November, http://www.econ.jku.at/members/winterebmer/files/teaching/managerial/total-factor-productivity.pdf (accessed 8 April 2010).

Controller General of Patents, Designs and Trade Marks, *Annual Report*, various issues.

Department of Science and Technology. 2009. *R&D Statistics*. New Delhi: Government of India.

D'Costa, A.P. 2004. 'Export Growth and Path-Dependence: The Locking-in of Innovations in the Software Industry', in A.P. D'Costa and E. Sridharan (eds), *India in the Global Software Industry: Innovation, Firm Strategies and Development*, pp. 51–82. Basingtoke: Palgrave Macmillan.

————. 2008. 'The International Mobility of Technical Talent: Trends and Development Implications,' in A. Solimano (ed.), *International Mobility of Talent and Development Impact*, pp. 44–83. Oxford: Oxford University Press.

FICCI (Federation of Indian Chamber of Commerce and Industry). 2007. *FICCI Survey on Emerging Skill Shortages in the Indian Industry*, http://www.ficcihen.com/Skill_Shortage_Survey_Final_1_.pdf (accessed 8 April 2010).

Futron Corporation. 2009. *Futron's 2009 Space Competitiveness Index, A Comparative Analysis of How Nations Invest in and Benefit from Space Industry,* http://www.futron.com/resource_center/store/Space_Competitiveness_Index/FSCI-2008.htm (accessed 5 March 2010).

Government of India. 2003. *Science and Technology Policy*. New Delhi: Department of Science and Technology.

Gu, S. and B.A. Lundvall. 2006. 'China's innovation system and the move towards harmonious growth and endogenous innovation', *Innovation: Management, Policy Practice*, 8 (1–2): 1–26.

Lan, X. and Z. Liang. 2006. 'Multinational R&D in China: Myth and Realities', School of Public Policy and Management, Tshingua University, Beijing (Unpublished).

Mani, S. 2010a. 2009. 'Is India Becoming More Innovative since 1991? Some Disquieting Features', *Economic and Political Weekly*, 44 (46): 41–51.

―――――. 'Financing of Industrial Innovations in India: How Effective are Tax Incentives for R&D', *International Journal of Technological Learning, Innovation and Development*, 3 (2).

―――――. 2010b. 'The Flight from Defence to Civilian Space: Evolution of the Sectoral System of Innovation of India's Aerospace Industry', Working Paper Series, No: 428, Trivandrum: Centre for Development Studies.

Ministry of Science and Technology. 2007. *China Science & Technology Statistics Data Book*, http://www.most.gov.cn/eng/statistics/2007/200801/P020080109573867344872.pdf (accessed 5 April 2010).

National Council of Applied Economic Research. 2005. *India Science Report, Science Education, Human Resources, and Public Attitude towards Science and Technology*. New Delhi: NCAER.

OECD. 2008. *Reviews of Innovation Policy: China*. Paris: OECD.

―――――. 2009. *OECD Factbook 2009: Economic, Environmental and Social Statistics*, http://titania.sourceoecd.org/vl=4169706/cl=23/nw=1/rpsv/factbook2009/07/01/04/index.htm (accessed 8 April 2010).

Reserve Bank of India. 2010. 'Invisibles in India's Balance of Payments: An Analysis of Trade in Services, Remittances and Income', *Reserve Bank of India Bulletin*, 44 (3): 555–93.

Schaaper, Martin. 2009. 'Measuring China's Innovation System National Specificities and International Comparisons', STI Working Paper 2009/1, Statistical Analysis of Science, Technology and Industry, DSTI/DOC (2009)1, Paris: OECD.

State Intellectual Property of the PRC. 2008. *Annual Report*, August, http://www.sipo.gov.cn/sipo_English/laws/annualreports/AnnualReport2008/ (accessed 18 August 2011).

12

Increasing Industrialization of R&D in China

Empirical Observations of the Role of the State

Bikramjit Sinha

Over the last few decades China's growth rates have been spectacular. This unprecedented growth has been possible due to the series of fundamental and ongoing reforms of the economic system initiated since the late 1970s. China's consistent economic growth by almost 10 per cent during 1979 to 2009 was possible partly by an increased research and development (R&D) investment (leading to development of advanced technologies) owing to the restructuring of the R&D system through several science and technology (S&T) policy interventions (Romer 1994, Naughton 2007a, Kim and Mah 2009). Expenditures on R&D reflect the scale of a nation's S&T input and the R&D intensity (ratio of R&D expenditure to GDP) indicates the emphasis on S&T. The scale and intensity of R&D are widely used internationally to reflect the strength of S&T and the core competitiveness of a country.

That China is employing technology-driven economic growth is reflected in increasing investment on R&D. During the period 2001–7, the annual average economic growth was 10.2 per cent while corresponding R&D expenditure growth was 22.5 per cent, and this rate of growth is much higher as compared to all the developed countries. Prior to this (more precisely during 1990–2000), the lag between R&D

spending and growth was comparatively less. Based on R&D expenditure, when normalized in terms of purchasing power parity, China has significantly improved its position to occupy the third position, next only to USA and Japan. China's transformation to a market economy and its integration with the global economy is shifting the status of the Chinese economy from a mere developing nation towards more of the Organisation of Economic Co-operation and Development (OECD) countries.

However, the most popular interpretation of China's extraordinary economic growth is more or less like this. China is gradually transforming from a socialistic economy to a capitalist economy, has liberalized the domestic market, and is growing on imported technologies because of the opening up of international trade. Most industrial and service enterprises are privately owned, and now produce the bulk of GDP, due mainly to their superior efficiency with respect to state-owned enterprises (SOEs) (Gabriele 2009). The bulk of the production today takes place in private firms and most prices in China today are driven by the market (Lindbeck 2008). The R&D activity by the private sector is sharply increasing thereby reducing the government R&D activities (Yuan 2005). The view is that private enterprises are rising sharply and are increasingly playing an important role in the economic development of China (Ye 2009). The innovation system is dominated by the industrial sector, which is often equalled with the business sector or private sector accounting for as high as 70 per cent of the gross domestic expenditure on R&D (GERD). This is similar to some of the most economically developed countries. In a nutshell, the role of the state in innovations in the Chinese economy in general is severely underestimated and the unplanned, market-based regulatory mechanisms are believed to play a dominant role. Admittedly, the structure of reporting innovation parameters such as R&D investment has some inherent drawbacks; the state's investment is shown independent of the huge amount invested by relatively few but exceptionally large SOEs and state-holding enterprises. The present argument leads to the assumption that the role of the state will wither away by the time a fully capitalist economy takes over the traditional centrally planned system.

Although, it is assumed that the business sector would drive the innovation process, the state, through adoption of effective R&D measures, allocation of resources, identification of R&D subjects, and its influence on the general framework of innovation, is going to play a central role in China's technological and economic development (Gradziuk 2008, Varum *et al.* 2008). It is rather a conscious strategic planning by the state to promote industrial development while retaining substantial regulatory power, which constitutes a unique characteristic of market socialism (Gabriele 2009),[1] quite distinct from either a pure capitalist or a pure socialist nation. In fact, China exerts its role in the economy through the state enterprises, even at the cost of the private sector as evident during the recent global recession (Naughton 2009).[2]

This chapter focuses on the growth of R&D expenditure in China—a major indicator of innovation, and the role of the state or the public sector. In order to refute the popular understanding of the diminishing role of the state both quantitative as well as qualitative evidence is used to show that the government is indeed outsourcing the R&D activities to different players, mainly enterprises. In the next section, growth of R&D expenditure in China is discussed with an overview of its implications in the international context. Using select indicators of innovation and industrial output of the large and medium enterprises (LMEs), the third section shows that the share of public sector in total GERD is more than the private sector. In the fourth section, I will elaborate how the government provides direct and indirect support to private R&D and innovation. The fifth section discusses the long-term guidance and strategic visioning provided by the government in R&D in particular and S&T development in general. The final section concludes.

OVERVIEW OF GROSS DOMESTIC EXPENDITURE ON R&D IN CHINA

An immediate outcome of the S&T reform policies initiated during 1978 could be seen in appropriation of about 1.5 per cent of the GDP for R&D in 1980. China's R&D expenditure grew substantially over the years and reached 457 billion yuan in 2008 (Figure 12.1). The figures include the R&D projects self-financed by firms as well as those supported by the government and foreign investors. In terms of purchasing power parity (PPP), China's R&D expenditure ranked third in the world, next only to USA and Japan. The R&D intensity has also increased gradually and reached 1.52 per cent in 2008. It is evident that both total R&D expenditure as well as R&D intensity have grown

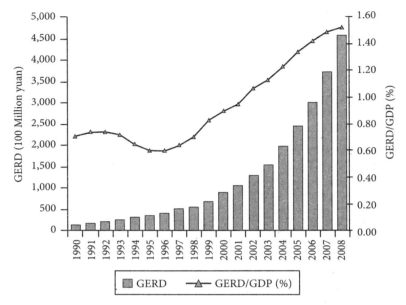

Figure 12.1   Trends in Gross Expenditure on R&D (GERD) in China
Source: China Science and Technology Indicators, Ministry of Science and Technology.

almost exponentially since 1991 except the relative slowing down during 1995 and 1996. During these two years, R&D expenditures reached the lowest level amounting to only 0.6 per cent of China's GDP. This was believed to be due to the rapid expansion of GDP in these two years (Kim and Mah 2009). Now, China aims to invest 2.5 per cent of GDP in R&D by 2020. R&D intensity reflects the core S&T competitiveness of country, and in the case of China it is clearly reflected in the country's progression in the global S&T competitiveness ranking from 21st position in 1998 to 15th position in 2007.[3] Thus, growing emphasis on R&D can be seen as an indicator of transforming into a knowledge-intensive economy (National Science Foundation 2008).

GERD by Sectors of Performance

In 1991, China spent about 12.6 billion yuan in R&D. Of this, more than half of the expenditure was done by the government. If the amount spent by the higher education sector is included under the government expenditure, then government R&D expenditure becomes about 60 per cent of GERD and industry performed the rest. The share of R&D performed by the government sector, mostly carried out by research institutes such as the Chinese Academy of Sciences (CAS) decreased substantially from 51.6 per cent in 1991 to 19.2 per cent in 2007 (Table 12.1), whereas industry's share has increased dramatically from 39.8 per cent in 1991 to 72.3 per cent in 2007. This trend is due to the government's decision to change the nation's R&D system, once heavily dependent on public research institutes, into a more market-orientated one (Kim and Mah 2009). It is also due to the government's intention to lighten its burden of R&D expenditure, easing its worry about the economic returns of public, large-scale investment in R&D projects (Baark 2001). The R&D performed by

Table 12.1   Chinese Gross Domestic Expenditure on R&D by Sector (per cent)

Year	Government	Industry	Higher Education
1991	51.6	39.8	8.6
1992	48.5	41.8	9.7
1993	47.1	41.7	11.2
1994	44.2	43.1	12.6
1995	44.2	43.7	12.1
1996	44.9	43.2	11.8
1997	44.9	42.9	12.1
1998	44.8	44.8	10.4
1999	41.1	49.6	9.3
2000	31.2	60.3	8.6
2001	29.7	60.4	9.8
2002	28.7	61.2	10.1
2003	27.1	62.4	10.5
2004	23.0	66.8	10.2
2005	21.8	68.3	9.9
2006	19.7	71.1	9.2
2007	19.2	72.3	8.5

Source: China Science and Technology Indicators, Ministry of Science and Technology.

the higher education sector in China shows a fluctuating trend, but it was continuously declining since 2005, and in 2007 it accounted for 8.5 per cent of the total R&D performed in the country.

GERD by Areas of Activity

The pattern of R&D investment in different types of R&D gives an indication of the national priorities and economic policies. Basic research generally has low short-term returns but builds intellectual capital and lays the groundwork for future advances in S&T (National Science Foundation 2008). Despite its growing R&D investment, China has one of the lowest basic research/GDP ratios (0.07 per cent) in the world, though it has increased slightly from the 0.03 per cent share in 1991. This indicates the lower emphasis on building up domestic intellectual capacity in the country. However, China has maintained the share of basic research[4] to total R&D at 5 per cent (Table 12.2) over the last decade or so which appears to be done consciously to ensure a basic minimum theoretical base; and the trade-offs

Table 12.2   Gross Domestic Expenditure on R&D by Area of Activity (per cent)

Year	GERD (100 million yuan)	Basic Research (%)	Applied Research (%)	Experimental Development (%)
1995	349	5.2	26.4	68.4
1996	404	5.0	24.5	70.5
1997	481	5.7	27.1	67.2
1998	551	5.2	22.6	72.1
1999	679	5.0	22.3	72.7
2000	896	5.2	17.0	77.8
2001	1,042	5.0	16.9	78.1
2002	1,288	5.7	19.2	75.1
2003	1,540	5.7	20.2	74.1
2004	1,966	6.0	20.4	73.7
2005	2,450	5.4	17.7	77.0
2006	3,003	5.2	16.3	78.5
2007	3,710	4.7	13.3	82.0

Source: China Science and Technology Indicators, Ministry of Science and Technology.

being made between applied research and experimental development. The share of applied research[5] has slowed down gradually while that of experimental development[6] has increased steadily from 68 per cent in 1995 to 82 per cent in 2007 which clearly indicates China's desire to attain technological capability.

GERD by Sources of R&D Funds

Details of R&D funding prior to the year 2000 was not provided in the commonly available sources such as the Science and Technology Indicators compiled by the Ministry of Science and Technology and China Statistical Yearbooks. However, according to an earlier report by the National Science Foundation, USA (National Science Foundation 1993), of the 12.6 billion yuan spent on overall R&D in China during 1991, the government financed around 60 per cent and the enterprises or industry financed the rest. Bulk of the direct government funding (about 86 per cent in 2006) goes to research institutes and institutes of higher education. As per the available information, share of industry-funded R&D has increased from 58 per cent in 2000 to 70 per cent in 2007 while the share of government funding has decreased from 33 per cent in 2000 to 25 per cent in 2007 (Figure 12.2). The increased financing of R&D by the industries is attributed to the market-oriented reforms of the R&D systems since 1985. Decreasing direct government funding is an indication that the research institutes have to manage a large part of their R&D funds through collaboration with other stakeholders such as industries. Only a small share of gross domestic expenditure on R&D is funded from abroad (foreign direct investment [FDI] and multinational corporations [MNCs]), that too showed a declining trend.

It is obvious that R&D is being increasingly industrialized in China. However, the argument that the government share of R&D funding has sharply declined is totally unjustified and this chapter argues that the state is playing and will keep on playing a proactive role in R&D or promoting it. The perceived low share of the R&D funding, in fact has more to do with the inherent problem of reporting R&D expenditure. In the subsequent sections it will be shown that direct government R&D funding is in fact much more than the reported share of about 25 per cent. The state is stimulating R&D by the private sector through various mechanisms such tax incentives. The state is

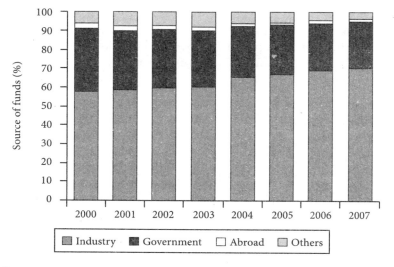

Figure 12.2   Gross Expenditure on R&D by Source of Funds (per cent)

Source: China Science and Technology Indicators, Ministry of Science and Technology.

also guiding the entire innovation system and R&D through long-term planning.

SHARE OF THE STATE IN CHINA'S GERD

From the above it is apparent that the share of government R&D, both in terms of activity undertaken as well as the source of funds has been declining over time. The decrease in undertaking of R&D by the government affiliates can be interpreted as a deliberate attempt on the part of government to lessen the burden of R&D expenditure and to concentrate on other strategies. However, there are apprehensions about the projected alarming low share of government in R&D funding. Although the enterprise sector's share of total R&D expenditure is reported to have risen from one-third to more than two-thirds over the last decade, the change appears to result in large part from the conversion of government research institutes into SOEs. Moreover, most enterprise R&D is conducted by SOEs; of the 50 Chinese companies with the largest R&D expenditures in 2006, more than 80 per cent were state owned. Thus, Chinese statistics appear to understate the role of government in the direction and financing of R&D.[7]

This chapter will not go in to the debate whether this is a purposeful endeavour to show to the outside world or an oversight by the National Bureau of Statistics of China. However, it is argued here that the government is outsourcing the R&D activity by creating conducive policy environment mechanisms while contributing substantially in the financing of R&D through various direct subsidies and tax incentives. In fact, almost all state R&D is being operated thorough different agencies, largely enterprises in contrast to the common notion of viewing enterprise R&D as different from state R&D. This fact is being analysed in the context of large and medium enterprises (LMEs), which share a major part of the GERD. The LMEs accounting for only about 11 per cent of the above-designated (> 5 million yuan annual sales turnover) enterprises, contributed about 65 per cent of the gross industrial output of above designated enterprises (Table 12.3). Furthermore, the R&D expenditure of LMEs accounted for 79 per cent of the industrial R&D expenditure, 57 per cent of the GERD, and 49 per cent of the national R&D personnel.

As the LMEs constitute a major part of the industries in China these LMEs may be considered as the representative of Chinese industry and their ownership would indicate the scale of government contribution in industrial R&D expenditure. Within the LMEs, state-owned and state-holding enterprises contributed around 48 per cent of the R&D expenditure by LMEs while private enterprises (including those funded from Hong Kong, Macao and Taiwan and also foreign-funded enterprises) accounted for 52 per cent of the expenditure (Table 12.4). Further in China, many of the most advanced formally private industrial enterprises are in fact related to the public domain by a web of state ownership, financial ties, and other linkages, to an extent that is qualitatively different and deeper than that of their counterparts in capitalist countries (Gabriele 2009); thus extending the role of the state beyond the public enterprises. As per a report by Jain and Khrabanda (1999), in 1994 China's R&D expenditure was financed by government and industry in the ratio of 70:30, and interestingly all the industries were public-owned, highlighting the total absence of private enterprises in China until that time. Though

Table 12.3 R&D Expenditure and Industrial Output of Large and Medium Enterprises

Year	1998	1999	2000	2001	2002	2003	2004	2005	2006	2007
No. of LMEs/above designated (%)	14	14	13	13	13	12	10	11	11	11
LMEs gross output/above designated output (%)	55	57	57	60	59	67	66	67	66	65
R&D expenditure by LMEs (100 million yuan)	197	250	353	442	560	721	954	1,250	1,630	2,112
R&D/sales revenue LMEs (%)	0.5	0.6	0.7	0.8	0.8	0.7	0.7	0.7	0.8	0.8
LMEs R&D expenditure/GERD (%)	36	37	39	42	44	47	49	51	54	57
LMEs R&D expenditure/industrial R&D (%)	80	74	65	70	71	75	73	75	76	79
Full-time equivalent of R&D personnel (10,000 man-year) in LMEs	n.a.	n.a.	34	38	42	48	44	61	70	86
R&D personnel in LMEs/national R&D personnel (%)	n.a.	n.a.	37	40	41	44	38	44	46	49

Source: China Statistical Yearbooks, National Bureau of Statistics, China.

Note: Above designated enterprises are those with revenue from principal business > 5 million yuan.

China's majority funding appears to be from industry, much of these might be government-held industries and the actual share of government is not clear due to insufficient data.[8]

Table 12.4   Ownership of LMEs and Their R&D Activities in 2007

Ownership	R&D Expenditure (10,000 yuan)	Share of LMEs (%)	Full-time Equivalent of R&D Personnel (man-year)	Share of LMEs (%)
State-owned Enterprises	1,820,905	8.62	101,793	11.9
State-owned and State-holding Enterprises	10,055,351	47.60	426,523.83	49.7
Private Enterprises[a]	11,069,210	52.40	431,125.91	50.3

Source: China Statistical Yearbooks, National Bureau of Statistics, China.
Note: [a] Includes enterprises with funds from Hong Kong, Macao and Taiwan, and foreign funded enterprises.

The proportion of the government as a source of funds would be even greater if research support by public industries could be disaggregated from enterprises and counted as government spending (National Science Foundation 1993). Thus, if government's direct R&D funding, research support by public enterprises (as depicted in Table 12.4) and the amount incurred by the state because of tax incentives to private enterprises are clubbed together (discussed in the next section), then the proportion of government as a source of funds would certainly be higher than the one usually reported. This indicates a far greater role of the state in R&D activities. In fact, Chinese innovation and R&D activities are heavily dependent on public funding as evident from observation made by an OECD review of innovation policy in China.[9]

STATE SUPPORT FOR ENTERPRISE R&D

The main instrument through which the government supports R&D by enterprises is tax incentives. The state usually spends substantial amounts for its R&D tax incentives to private enterprises including MNCs. For instance, the Canadian federal government spent about US$3 billion on its R&D tax incentives programme in 2006 (Baghana and Mohnen 2009). Tax incentives and tax credits have been, and continue to be, an important government policy instrument for encouraging more and more R&D among enterprises (Mcfetridge and Warda 1983). Tax incentives may be direct or indirect such as tax credits, to business fixed investment and others. Observations are that a dollar in tax credit for R&D stimulates a dollar or more of additional R&D expenditure by enterprises, particularly private enterprises. However, much of these substantiations are based on experience of Western countries, mainly the US and European nations. Some of the studies pertaining to effectiveness of tax incentives on industrial expenditures in developed countries were those of Mansfield and Switzer (1985), Bernstein (1986), Lach (2002), Duguet (2004), Kaiser (2006), and Gonzalez and Pazo (2008). Similarly, the U.S. Bureau of Labor Statistics estimates that every dollar of tax benefit has spurred an additional dollar in private R&D (National Science Foundation 2008). Literature in this aspect of R&D is piling up which also resulted in some excellent reviews (Hall and Van Reenen 2000). However, studies on the effectiveness of tax incentives in developing countries and/or emerging economies appear to have just picked up recently (Ozcelik and Taymaz 2008). They found a significant and positive effect, termed as 'acceleration effect', of public support on private R&D investment particularly in Turkey.

Studies on the effectiveness of tax incentives on industrial R&D spending in China are very rare. However, a recent study by Zhu *et al.* (2006) of the impact of government's direct funding and tax incentives on R&D investments in industrial sectors in Shanghai reported some contrasting evidence. They observed that direct government funding has positive effects on industrial R&D investment while the effect of the tax incentives is mild. Industries tended to switch to more general and less costly science and technology activities which can be seen as an undesirable effect of the tax incentives. This observation finds support from the argument that R&D tax credit is not necessary because it rewards companies for doing what they would have done anyway (National Science Foundation 2008). However, it is also true that some companies will continue to perform R&D regardless of the status of credit. But R&D is dependent on the location and magnitude of resources involved, which in turn depend on credit in place. Thus, market incentives alone are insufficient to stimulate private R&D spending (OECD 2008).

Tax Incentives to Foreign Invested Enterprises (FIEs): Promoting FDI

In China, qualified FIEs, R&D centres are entitled to the following tax incentives:

- Exemptions totalling 17 per cent on VAT and related import duties on equipment used for R&D activities.
- Exemptions totalling 5 per cent on business tax imposed on income from technology transfers, development, related consulting, and technical support services.
- Current year income tax deductions of up to 150 per cent on certain qualified R&D expenditures provided that the firm's R&D spending has increased by 10 per cent from the prior year.
- Five-year graduated tax holidays if the R&D centre also qualifies as a manufacturer.
- Additional tax holidays and reduced tax rates if the R&D centre qualifies as a 'new- and high-tech enterprise' (exporting more than 70 per cent of their products) or as a 'technologically advanced enterprise'.

China offers both sector-wide and location-oriented tax incentives to FIEs giving importance to development of high technology as well as to ensure regional balance. Sector-wide incentives are offered primarily to FIEs engaged in manufacturing. Location-oriented incentives, including reduced tax rates and financial support programmes, are aimed at encouraging foreign investment in certain areas such as Beijing/Zhongguancun, and Shanghai/Pudong Lujiazui (Quinn *et al.* 2007). The PRC government has also provided specific tax incentives to enterprises based in the western, central, and Northeastern China in its efforts to 'balance' China's economic growth.

Recent Developments: Protection to Domestic Enterprises and Indigenization

Now that China has reached a level of technological maturity, it is promoting domestic enterprises by reducing incentives for foreign-funded enterprises. This could be a response to counter the opening of the domestic market to foreign-funded enterprises due to its obligation under World Trade Organization (WTO) which China signed in 2001. The new Corporate Income Tax (CIT) and regulations that became effective from 1 January 2008 removed various tax incentives provided to foreign enterprises earlier. Now, both domestic and foreign-funded enterprises will be taxed at the uniform rate of 25 per cent, in contrast to the earlier effective rate of 15 per cent for FIEs and 33 per cent for domestic enterprises (DEs). The new law no longer provides for a tax refund to foreign investors for reinvestment in China.

The new tax law, however, expanded certain tax incentives to high and new technology enterprises (HNTE) such as an additional 50 per cent bonus tax deduction for R&D expenditures incurred in connection with certain R&D activities such as development of new technology, new products or new craftsmanship (CIT Article 30-1). However, the products (services) of the NHTE should satisfy certain operation ratio requirements as specified in the detailed implementation regulation (DIR) Article 93-2, such as:

- R&D expenditures to sales expenses;
- income from high-/new-tech products/services to total income;
- number of technicians to total number of employees; and
- other conditions as prescribed in the administrative measures for the assessment of HNTE.

These latest developments have created both challenges and opportunities for major foreign investors like the United States and Japan (Pan 2008). A more recent attempt to promote domestic enterprises and indigenous development of technology is a proposed new law under which government accreditation will be provided to only those companies that are capable of 'indigenous innovation' instead of relying entirely on imported technology (Dasgupta 2009).

Financial Support through Nationalized Banks

In addition to direct and indirect tax incentives to enterprises for R&D, the state provides financial support through the nationalized banks. While the China Exim Bank provides financial assistance for exporting high-tech products, the China Development Bank provides financial assistance for technological upgrading. The mission of China Development Bank is to strengthen the competitiveness of the economy by supporting technological innovation. The bank is providing financial support to major R&D projects in the communication equipment manufacturing enterprises and in the automobile sector.[10] The new Medium- and Long-term S&T Plan (2006) also issued guidelines for more financial support to R&D-based enterprises through nationalized and commercial banks. These are:

1. Policy banks to provide loans to R&D-focused enterprises, finance imports and exports, and support agricultural technology application and industrialization.
2. Commercial banks encouraged to provide loans based on government guarantees and provide discounted interest rates.
3. Encourage venture capital investment with government funding, policy bank, and commercial loans. Further, industrial R&D is supported through the mechanism of preferential insurance services for taking up technological innovation especially in the high-tech business sector.

GOVERNMENT R&D PROGRAMMES AND POLICIES: GUIDANCE AND MENTORING

With the sudden withdrawal of Soviet support in the late 1960s the Chinese government began to reorient the economy towards more of a market-driven one. Hectic deliberations resulted in initial economic reforms in 1978. Simultaneously, the state realized that if China has to progress and catch up with the developed nations, the S&T system needs to be strengthened, thus the S&T system was also restructured with special emphasis on R&D. Today, China has a well-established national R&D programme to promote scientific research and innovation. The central government implements two distinct types of programmes supporting basic research and commercialization of technologies. Through these programmes the government remains directly engaged with R&D activities as well as promotes overall technological development. Some of the important programmes are briefly discussed here highlighting the major objectives and activities.

National Key Technologies Research and Development Programme

Launched in 1982 with a focus on promoting basic research and implemented through four Five-year Plans, the programme has made remarkable contributions to the technical renovation and upgrading of traditional industries and the formation of new industries. The programme concentrates on the R&D of key and common technologies that drive technical upgrading and restructuring of industries that promote sustainable social development.

National Hi-tech Research and Development Programme (The 863 Programme)

Launched in 1986 to meet the global challenges of the new technology revolution and competition, the programme led to the improvement of China's overall high-tech development, R&D capacity, socio-economic development, and national security. In line with national objectives and market demands, the programme addressed a number of cutting-edge high-tech issues of strategic importance and foresight during the Tenth Five-year Plan period, such as:

1. Develop key technologies for the construction of China's information infrastructure.
2. Develop key biological, agricultural, and pharmaceutical technologies to improve the welfare of the Chinese people.
3. Master key new materials and advanced manufacturing technologies to boost industrial competitiveness.
4. Achieve breakthroughs in key technologies for environmental protection, resources and energy development to serve the sustainable development of our society.

Spark Programme

This programme was launched in 1986 with the prime objective of revitalizing the rural economy through S&T upgradation and support for technology transfer to rural areas.

Torch Programmes

Launched in August 1988, the programme focused on broadening the sources of funds available to non-governmental enterprises and establishing science parks, economic and technological development zones (ETDZs), and high-tech industrial development zones (HTDZ) throughout the country. The programme helped in commercialization of high-tech and new technologies resulting from the '863' programme and 'National Key Technologies Programme'.

National Basic Research Programme (The 973 Programme)

Launched in 1998, the programme focuses on development of basic scientific research. It mainly involves multi-disciplinary, comprehensive research on important scientific issues in such fields as agriculture, energy, information, resources, population, health, and materials, providing theoretical basis and scientific foundations for solving problems.

National Science and Technology Infrastructure Programme

In the 10th Five-year Plan period, the 'R&D Infrastructure and Facility Development Programme' constitutes a major component of the national S&T planning system. The endeavour aims to adjust, enrich, and strengthen the S&T capacity of national S&T research bases of different kinds. Programme contents include: State Key Laboratories Development Programme, National Key Science Projects Programme, National Engineering Technology Research Centers Development Programme, R&D Infrastructure and Facility Development Programme, S&T Basic Work Programme, Programme on Research for Public Good, and Programme on Key International S&T Cooperative Projects.

These national R&D programmes are designed and implemented by centralized apex S&T body, the Ministry of Science and Technology in collaboration with the implementing and coordinating agencies such as the Chinese Academy of Sciences. While the state directly funds a major part of these programmes such as 90 per cent in the 973 programme and 44 per cent in the 863 programme, the rest is mobilized through indirect funding using various incentive mechanisms.

Policy Initiatives

Besides designing and implementing different ambitious national R&D programmes, the government also provides long term guidance and mentoring of the overall R&D activities of China. The state plays a central role in China's technological development through adoption of favourable policy measures, defining the R&D subjects and monitoring the general framework of innovation in the country. The 'S&T Progress Law, 1993' vows to restructure and improve the S&T system to develop high-tech industries for economic construction and social development, and recommended preferential treatments to enterprises which apply new techniques to develop and produce new products. The government stepped up its efforts to promote technology-intensive industries, issuing two important documents regarding its R&D policy: the 1995 Decision on Accelerating Scientific and Technology Progress and the 1999 Decision on Strengthening Technological Innovation and Developing High-Technology and Realizing Industrialization.

The government placed more emphasis on tax incentives, establishment of science parks, and increasing its financial support for R&D activities (Baark 2001). During the Ninth Plan, the government regarded science and technology as a major driving force for economic development (Kim and Mah 2009) such as a partial tax deduction for R&D expenditures; a tax exemption for all income earned from the transfer or development of new technologies; a preferential 6 per cent value-added tax rate for software products developed and produced in China; complete VAT exemption and subsidized credit for high-tech exports. During the 10th Five-Year Plan (2001–5) and the 11th Five-Year Plan (2006–10), more emphasis was laid on strengthening R&D capabilities and the development of its indigenous technology, which successfully contributed to upgrading its industrial structure (Kim and Mah 2009). The Medium- and Long-Term National Science and Technology Programme (2006–20) issued in January 2006 also reflects the involvement of the state as the decision-maker of the national R&D strategy and overall technological progress in China. The S&T Plan further mandates particular areas for R&D including 11 key fields, 68 priority subjects, and 17 large-scale or mega-projects. The main objectives of the government's current R&D policy are building an innovation-based economy by nurturing indigenous innovation capability; developing an enterprise-centred innovation system and promoting the innovation capabilities of Chinese firms; and making a great leap forward in targeted strategic areas of technological development and basic research (OECD 2007).

* * *

China has recorded rapid economic growth since its economic reform started in 1978. Compelled by the circumstances and growing realization of S&T as a key element in societal and economic development, and to be self-sufficient avoiding dependence on developed countries, China has transformed its S&T system by emphasizing R&D. This is reflected in the rapid increase in the scale and intensity of R&D which is much higher than the growth of GDP during the same period. A growing industrialization of the R&D is also evident.

However, this chapter showed that the share of the state is not only much higher than portrayed but qualitatively it also plays a much bigger role of monitoring and regulating the national R&D system. As shown, the government as a source of R&D funds would be higher if the amount invested by SOEs and various direct and indirect tax subsidies to non-state-enterprises (NSOEs) are counted as public R&D. State enterprises which are usually large play an important role in the Chinese economy even today (Naughton 2007a). The contributions of the SOEs are so crucial that the present day reformed SOEs are often described as the dynamic dynamo of the future Chinese economy (Ralston *et al.* 2006). Gabriele (2009) in assessing the role of the state in China's industrial development has rightly pointed out that,

> The role of the public sector, moreover, goes beyond that of those enterprises which are owned or controlled by the State. In the specific Chinese context, many of the most advanced formally private industrial enterprises are in fact related to the public domain by a web of ownership, financial, and other linkages, to an extent that is qualitatively different and deeper than that of their counterparts in capitalist countries.
>
> The public sector is paramount in engineering an extraordinary boom in S&T and R&D activities. (Gabriele 2009, p. 1)

Thus, the state appears to be outsourcing its R&D activities to different players, largely enterprises, using different mechanisms. More importantly, the government is stimulating enhanced R&D by the enterprises by providing support in the form of various direct and indirect tax incentives on R&D expenditure, financial support through the nationalized banks and through the mechanism of preferential insurance. Further, the state controls the overall growth of the national R&D system while providing long-term guidance and oversight to different stakeholders (Naughton 2007b).

NOTES

1. In a 'market socialist' system, the capitalists are not strong enough to constitute a hegemonic and dominant social class, as it happens in 'normal' capitalist countries (Gabriele and Schettino 2007).

2. China pulled its economy through the financial crisis by recourse to a massive fiscal and monetary stimulus. Because it was channelled through state banks to state firms, the stimulus strengthened the relative position of state firms and extended the state's reach into the economy.

3. See *World Competitiveness Yearbook 2008*, International Institute for Management Development, Switzerland.

4. Basic research refers to empirical or theoretical research aiming at obtaining new knowledge on the fundamental principles regarding phenomena or observable facts to reveal the intrinsic nature and underlying laws and to acquire new discoveries or new theories.

5. Applied research refers to creative research aiming at obtaining new knowledge on a specific objective or target. The purpose of applied research is to identify the possible uses of results from basic research, or to explore new (fundamental) methods or new approaches.

6. Experiments and development refer to systematic activities aiming at using the knowledge from basic and applied researches or from practical experience to develop new products, materials and equipment, to establish new production process, systems and services, or to make substantial improvement on the existing products, process or services.

7. See Lv (2007) and Serger and Breidne (2007).

8. See Duga *et al.* (2008).

9. The government will need to move away from a top-down approach, reduce over-reliance on public R&D funding programmes and adopt a view of innovation that goes beyond high technology sectors (OECD 2007, p. 168).

10. See Gradziuk (2008).

REFERENCES

Baark, E. 2001. 'Technology and Enterprises in China: Commercialization Reforms in the Science and Technology', *Policy Studies Review*, 18 (1): 112–29.

Baghana, R. and P. Mohnen. 2009. 'Effectiveness of R&D Tax Incentives in Small and Large Enterprises in Québec', UNU-MERIT Working paper, 2009–10.

Bernstein, J.I. 1986. 'The Effect of Direct and Indirect Tax Incentives on Canadian Industrial Expenditures', *Canadian Public Policy*, 12 (3): 438–48.

Dasgupta, S. 2009. 'China Curbs Foreign Tech Flows', *Times of India*, 12 December, p. 11.

Duga, J., M. Grueber, and T. Studt. 2008. '2009 Global R&D Funding Forecast: Change Becomes Watchword for 2009's World of R&D', *R&D Magazine* (online), December, pp. 3–34, http://www.rdmag com//2009GlobalFundingForecast. pdf (accessed 22 October 2009).

Duguet, E. 2004. 'Are R&D Subsidies a Substitute Or a Compliment To Privately Funded R&D? Evidence from French Using Propensity Score Methods for Non-Experimental Data', *Revue d'Economie Politique*, 114 (2): 263–92.

Gabriele, A. 2009. 'The Role of the State in China's Industrial Development: A Reassessment', MPRA Paper No. 14551, http://mpra.ub.uni-muenchen.de/14551/ (accessed 23 October 2009).

Gabriele, A. and F. Schettino. 2007. 'Market Socialism as a Distinct Socioeconomic Formation Internal to the Modern Mode of Production', MPRA paper No. 7942, http://mpra.ub.uni-muenchen.de/7942/ (accessed 23 October 2009).

Gonzalez, X. and C. Pazo. 2008. 'Do Public Subsidies Stimulate R&D Spending?', *Research Policy*, 37 (3): 371–89.

Gradziuk, A. 2008. 'The Role of the State in China's Economic Development', ECAN Annual Conference, Brussels, 4–5 December 2008.

Hall, B.H. and J. Van Reenen. 2000. 'How Effective are Fiscal Incentives for R&D? A Review of the Evidence', *Research Policy*, 29 (4–5): 449–69.

Jain, A. and V.P. Kharbanda. 1999. 'Science and Technology Strategies and their Implementation during Various Plan Periods since Independence in India and China—a Comparative Study', in V.P. Kharbanda and A. Jain (eds), *Science and Technology Strategies for Development in India and China—A Comparative Study*. New Delhi, India: Har-Anand Publications.

Kaiser, U. 2006. 'Private R&D and Public Subsidies: Macroeconomic Evidence from Denmark', *Danish Journal of Economics*, 144 (1): 1–17.

Kim, M.J. and J.S. Mah. 2009. 'China's R&D Policies and Technology-intensive Industries', *Journal of Contemporary Asia*, 39 (2): 262–78.

Lach, S. 2002. 'Do R&D Subsidies Stimulate or Displace Private R&D? Evidence from Israel', *Journal of Industrial Economics*, 50 (4): 369–90.

Lindbeck, A. 2008. 'Economic-Social Interaction in China', *Economics of Transition*, 16 (1): 113–39.

Lv, W. 2007. 'An Analysis of the Characteristics of China's Innovation System', *China Development Review* (online), 9 (1). Available at: http://www.drc.gov.cn/english/ (accessed 22 October 2011).

Mansfield, E. and L. Switzer. 1985. 'How Effective are Canada's Direct Tax Incentives for R&D', *Canadian Public Policy*, 11 (2): 241–6.

Mcfetridge, D.G. and J.P. Warda. 1983. *Canadian R&D Incentives: Their Adequacy and Impact*. Toronto, Canada: Canadian Tax Foundation.

National Science Foundation. 1993. *Human Resources for Science and Technology: The Asian Region*. Arlington, VA: NSF 93-303.

Naughton, B. 2007a. *The Chinese Economy: Transitions and Growth*. Cambridge: The Massachusetts Institute of Technology Press.

————. 2007b. 'Strengthening the Center, and Premier Wen Jiabao', *China Leadership Monitor* (online), 21. Available from http://media.hoover.org/ (accessed 23 November 2009).

————. 2009. 'Loans, Firms, and Steel: Is the State Advancing at the Expense of the Private Sector?', *China Leadership Monitor* (online), 30. Available from: http://media.hoover.org/sites/default/files/documents/CLM30BN.pdf (accessed 23 November 2009).

OECD. 2007. *OECD Reviews of Innovation Policy: China*, www.oecd.org/dataoecd/54/20/39177453.pdf (accessed 22 October 2009).

————. 2008. OECD *Science Technology and Industry Outlook 2008*, www.oecd.org/ff/?404;http://www.oecd.org:80/sti/outlook (accessed 20 November 2009).

Ozcelik, E. and E. Taymaz. 2008. 'R&D Support Programmes in Developing Countries: The Turkish experience', *Research Policy*, 37 (2): 258–75.

Pan, A. 2008. 'China's Tax Reform and Its Impact on U.S. Investments in China', *Corporate Business Taxation Monthly*, 9 (9): 9–18.

Quinn, T., M. Ho, and A. Pan. 2007. 'Aligning Tax and Operational Strategies', *China Business Review* (online), January–February 2007, pp. 34–7, http://www.chinabusinessreview.com (accessed 20 October 2009).

Ralston, D.A., J. Terpstra-Tong, R.H. Terpstra, X. Wang, and C. Egri. 2006. 'Today's State-owned Enterprises of China: Are They Dying Dinosaurs or Dynamic Dynamos', *Strategic Management Journal*, 27 (9): 825–43.

Romer, P. 1994. 'The Origins of Endogenous Growth', *Journal of Economic Perspectives*, 8 (1): 3–22.

Serger, S.S. and M. Breidne. 2007. 'China's Fifteen-Year Plan for Science & Technology: An Assessment', *Asia Policy*, http://asiapolicy.nbr.org (accessed 31 November 2009).

————. 2008. 'Science and Engineering Indicators, 2008', http://www.nsf.gov/statistics/seind08.htm (accessed 11 June 2012).

Varum, C.A., C. Huang, and J.J.B. Gouveia. 2008. *China: Building an Innovative Economy*. Oxford, England: Chandos Publishing.

Ye, C. 2009. 'Private Enterprises and China's Economic Development', *Transnational Corporations Review*, 1 (4): 10–14.

Yuan, W. 2005. 'China's Government R&D Institutes: Changes and Associated Issues', *Science Technology and Society*, 10 (1): 11–29.

Zhu, P., W. Xu, and N. Lundin. 2006. 'The Impact of Government's Fundings and Tax Incentives on Industrial R&D Investments—Empirical Evidences From Industrial Sectors in Shanghai', *China Economic Review*, 17 (1): 51–69.

Contributors

Amiya Kumar Bagchi is Professor, Economics, and Director, Institute of Development Studies Kolkata. He is also the Chancellor of Tripura University and Honorary Adjunct Professor of Monash University, Australia. He currently serves on the Editorial and Editorial Advisory Boards of *Bangladesh Development Studies*, *Cambridge Journal of Economics*, *International Journal of Institutions and Economics* and *the Social Scientist*. His books include *Private Investment in India 1900–1939* (1972), *The Political Economy of Underdevelopment* (1982), a four-volume history of the State Bank of India (1987–97) starting with the *Evolution of the State Bank of India* (1987), *Public Intervention and Industrial Restructuring in China, India and the Republic of Korea* (1987), *Capital and Labour Redefined: India and the Third World* (2002), *The Development State in History and in the Twentieth Century* (2004), *Perilous Passage: Mankind and the Global Ascendancy of Capital* (2005/2006), and *Colonialism and Indian Economy* (2010). His edited or co-edited books include *Change and Choice in Indian Industry* (1981); *New Technology and the Worker's Response: Microelectronics, Labour and Society* (1995); *Democracy and Development* (1995); *Economy and Organization: Indian Institutions under the Neoliberal Regime* (1999); *Webs of History: Information, Communication and Technology from Early to Post-colonial India* (2005); *Maladies, Preventives and Curatives* (2005); *Capture and Exclude: Developing Economies and the Poor in Global Finance* (2007).

Lopamudra Banerjee is Assistant Professor of Economics at the New School for Social Research, New York, USA. Her work broadly encompasses two fields of study—distributional aspects of development and disaster studies. Her earlier research has explored the interconnections between poverty and disaster vulnerability, particularly in the case of Bangladesh. She has also worked on issues of economic distribution in China and India. Her co-edited volume *Development, Equity and Poverty: Essays in Honor of Azizur Rahman Khan* (with A. Dasgupta and R. Islam) was published in 2010 jointly by the United Nations Development Programme (UNDP, New York), and Macmillan Publishers India Limited (New Delhi). Currently, she is working on economic analyses of catastrophic risks and uncertainty, and on economic theories of power, as part of a research programme that examines disasters and discontinuities in the natural physical system, and disorders and disequilibria in the social system.

Parthasarathi Banerjee, Director, National Institute of Science Technology & Development Studies (NISTADS), New Delhi, India, is a researcher with interest in S&T policies and governance, innovation, business policies, and technological change. His forthcoming book jointly with two other authors is about business strategies and business organization; his last two books from Palgrave/Macmillan and Har-Anand are on Indian software and biomedical innovations respectively. Banerjee has published several papers in refereed journals and has written several research reports.

Nirmal Kumar Chandra, now retired, taught at the Indian Institute of Management Calcutta for many years. Apart from journal articles, he has published two books: *The Retarded Economies: Foreign Domination and Class Relations in India and Other Emerging Nations* (1988) and *Political Economy of India in the South Asian Context* (1994). His areas of interest include economic development in India, the process of globalization and economic transformation in Russia, Eastern Europe, and China.

Anthony P. D'Costa is Professor, Indian Studies, and Research Director, Asia Research Centre, Department of International Economics and Management, Copenhagen Business School, Copenhagen, Denmark. Prior to this appointment in 2008 he was with the University of Washington for 18 years. As a political economist working with steel, auto, and IT sectors he has written extensively on globalization, development, innovation, and industrial restructuring in India and other Asian countries. Of his seven books, his most recent ones are: *Globalization and Economic Nationalism in Asia* (edited, 2012), *A New India? Critical Reflections in the Long Twentieth Century* (edited, 2010) and *The New Asian Innovation Dynamics: China and India in Perspective* (co-edited, 2009). He is currently working on his next book, *Global Capitalism and the Mobility of Technical Talent*. He has been a fellow of the Abe Program, Japan Foundation, American Institute of Indian Studies, Fulbright-Hays, Korea Foundation, Social Science Research Council, NY, and UN University's World Institute of Development Economics Research (WIDER) in Helsinki and has conducted commissioned projects for the ILO, World Bank, and WIDER. He served on the Board of Trustees of the American Institute of Indian Studies and currently serves on the International Advisory Board of India–US World Affairs Institute, Washington DC, and the Nordic Centre in India.

Ashwini Deshpande is Professor of Economics at the Delhi School of Economics, University of Delhi, India. Her research interests include the international debt crisis of the 1980s, economics of discrimination with a focus on caste and gender in India, and aspects of the Chinese economy. She is the editor of *Globalization and Development: A Handbook of New Perspectives*, 2007; *Capital without Borders: Challenges to Development*, 2010; and *Global Economic Crisis and the Developing World* (with Keith Nurse), Routledge, 2012. Her forthcoming book is *The Grammar of Caste: Economic Discrimination in Contemporary India*, (Oxford University Press, New Delhi). She received the EXIM Bank award for outstanding dissertation in 1994 and the VKRV Rao Award for Indian economists under 45 for the year 2007.

Shailaja Fennell is a University Lecturer in Development Studies attached to the Department of Land Economy, and a Fellow of Jesus College, University of Cambridge. She was awarded BA, MA, and MPhil in Economics from the University of Delhi, and her MPhil and PhD at the Faculty of Economics and Politics, University of Cambridge. Her doctoral research work has examined the long-term trends in cereal production in China and India and she has a long-standing interest in institutional reform. She has recently completed a five-year research project on public–private partnerships in education as part of a DFID, funded research consortium on educational outcomes and poverty (RECOUP). Shailaja's research focuses on examining the sub-fields of institutional reform, agricultural transformation, gender and ethnicity, and comparative economic development. Her recent publications include *Rules, Rubrics and Riches: The Relationship between Legal Reform, Institutional Change and International Development* (2009) Routledge, *Gender Education and Development: Conceptual Frameworks, Engagements and Agendas* (2007) Routledge.

Ho-Fung Hung is an Associate Professor of Sociology at Johns Hopkins University. Prior to this appointment he was the Director of the Research Center on Chinese Business and Politics and a faculty member of the Sociology department at Indiana University, Bloomington. He researches on Chinese political economy and state–society interaction in historical and global perspectives. Hung is the author of *Protest with Chinese Characteristics* (Columbia University Press, 2011; winner of President's Book Award, Social Science History Association) and editor of *China and the Transformation of Global Capitalism* (Johns Hopkins University Press, 2009). His articles have appeared in *American Journal of Sociology, American Sociological Review, Swiss Journal of Sociology*, and *Review of International Political Economy*, among others. His paper on China and the global crisis won the 2010 first prize research paper award of the World Society Foundation in Zurich, Switzerland. His other papers won awards in four different sections of the American Sociological Association, including the sections on Comparative and Historical Sociology, Political Sociology, Political Economy of the World System, and Asia and Asian Americans.

Sunil Mani is Professor, Planning Commission Chair at the Centre for Development Studies, Trivandrum, Kerala, India. He is also a visiting faculty at the Indian Institute of Management, Calcutta and at the annual Globelics Academy (organized during alternative years at Lisbon Technical University, Portugal and at the University of Tampere, Finland). His current research interests include three aspects of innovations in India, namely the TRIPS compliance of the IPR regime and its effects on national innovation capacity, growth of knowledge-intensive entrepreneurship, and understanding the sectoral systems of innovations of high-technology industries such as aerospace and telecommunications.

Yan Ming is Professor of Sociology at the Institute of Sociology, Chinese Academy of Social Sciences. Her current research focuses on poverty and social exclusion in Chinese urban communities. She is the author of *A Discipline and a Time: Sociology in Modern China* (2004, 2010, in Chinese).

R. Nagaraj is Professor at the Indira Gandhi Institute of Development Research in Mumbai. His research interests include industrialization, economic growth and distribution, and policy reforms. A selection of his research papers is now available in a book entitled, *Aspects of Economic Growth and Reforms in India*, New Delhi, 2006. Among many, his most recent research papers include, 'Industrial Performance, 1991–2008', in *India Development Report*, 2011, 'Is Services Sector Output Overestimated? An Inquiry', *Economic and Political Weekly*, 31 January 2009; 'India's Recent Economic Growth: A Close Look', *Economic and Political Weekly*, 12 April 2008; 'Disinvestment and Privatisation in India: Assessment and Options', in *Trade Policy, Industrial Performance and Private Sector Development in India*, 2008 for Asian Development Bank; and 'Labour Markets in India' (co-authored with T.C.A. Anant *et al.*), in J. Filipe and R. Hasan edited, *Labour Markets in Asia: Issues and Perspectives* 2006.

Carl Riskin is Distinguished Professor of Economics at Queens College, City University of New York, and Senior Research Scholar at Columbia University. He is the author of *China's Political Economy: The Quest for Development Since 1949; Inequality and Poverty in China in the Age of Globalization* (with A.R. Khan); co-editor of *China's Retreat from Equality,* and author of many articles dealing with poverty reduction, income inequality and other aspects of human development in China. He worked with UNDP to produce the first two *China Human Development Reports* as well as on many other projects. His current research involves China's effort to rebalance its economy and the end of the 'dual economy' model there.

Sanjay Ruparelia is Assistant Professor of Politics at the New School for Social Research, New York, USA. His areas of research encompass comparative politics, political economy and democratic theory with a focus on modern India. He is the co-editor of *Understanding*

India's New Political Economy: A Great Transformation? (2011) and has published articles on Hindu nationalism, the politics of recognition, and national coalition governments in India in various journals, including *Comparative Politics, Economic & Political Weekly,* and *International Journal of Culture, Politics and Society.* He is currently finishing a book on the origins, dynamics and consequences of India's coalition politics, provisionally titled, *Divided We Govern.*

Ashwani Saith is Professor of Rural Economics at the International Institute of Social Studies, The Hague. He has researched and published extensively in the fields of colonial economic history; comparative contemporary development; on processes of peasant differentiation, agrarian change, and rural development; poverty, vulnerability, and inequality; labour, employment, and migration; and ICT and development. The regional focus of his work has been principally on India and China, drawing on extensive fieldwork in rural India since the 1960s, and in rural China since 1979. His recent publications offer critiques of official methodologies of poverty recognition and of the millennium development goals; the instrumental and intrinsic salience of inequalities; and comparative assessments of the Indian and Chinese development trajectories. He has served on the editorial boards of several leading development journals, including *Journal of Development Studies, Journal of Peasant Studies, Journal of Agrarian Change, Indian Journal of Labour Studies,* and *Indian Journal of Human Development*; he has been an editor of *Development and Change* since 1983, and chairs its editorial board.

Sunanda Sen is a national fellow of the Indian Council of Social Science Research and a visiting professor at the Institute for Studies in Industrial Development, Delhi; Jamia Millia Islamia University, Delhi; and the Institute of Development Studies, Kolkata, among other institutions in India and overseas. She previously taught for nearly three decades at the Centre for Economic Studies and Planning, Jawaharlal Nehru University, Delhi. In 1994, she held the Joan Robinson Memorial Lectureship at Cambridge University, and she is a life fellow of Clare Hall, Cambridge. Sen's current research relates to global finance, money, development, labor, economic history, and gender studies. In addition to contributing articles to academic journals, she has published, most recently, *Unfreedom and Waged Work: Labour in*

India's Manufacturing Industry (with B. Dasgupta), 2009; *Globalisation and Development*, (2007); *Global Finance at Risk: On Real Stagnation and Instability*, (2003, 2004); and *Trade and Dependence: Essays on the Indian Economy*, 2000.

Bikramjit Sinha holds a PhD in an interdisciplinary area encompassing both social sciences and biological sciences, from Gauhati University, Guwahati. His doctorate thesis was on understanding sociological issues associated with and scientific validation of ITKs on pest management in the upland farming areas of North East India. He also has a master's degree in ecology. Sinha is currently a Scientist with the National Institute of Science Technology and Development Studies, New Delhi, an institute of the Council of Scientific and Industrial Research, India. He has several publications in national and international journals in the areas of science and technology. He also has an interest in measurement of S&T output. He is currently working on innovation and R&D management in government and the private sector, and renewable and sustainable energy, particularly bio-energy and solar energy.

Vamsicharan Vakulabharanam is Associate Professor of Economics at the University of Hyderabad in India, researches inequality in contemporary India and China. He has specifically worked on globalization and agrarian change in India, and consumption and wealth inequality during the period of economic reforms in India and China. One of his major arguments is that both countries have tended to neglect their agricultural sectors during this period thereby causing agrarian distress to millions of farmers and a sharp increase in rural–urban divide during the past few decades. He has also argued that the sharp class divide that has emerged since the 1990s is the strongest contributor to the rise in inequality in these economies. Vamsi has published his work in academic journals, including *World Development, Journal of Development Studies, Economic and Political Weekly, Review of Radical Political Economics,* and *Ethique Economique*, and has chapters in edited books.

Wei Zhong is Professor of Economics and the Director of the Institute of Economics, Chinese Academy of Social Sciences. He has spent the last 10 years studying income distribution at the Chinese Academy of Social Sciences (CASS), a prestigious 'think tank' in China. As a professor and director of the Institute of Economics at CASS, his work has included policy research for international organizations, governments and NGOs, published reports in Chinese media and academic journals, research in macroeconomics and a term as editor of the *Economic Research Journal* in China.

Index